JavaScript™

in 10 Simple Steps or Less

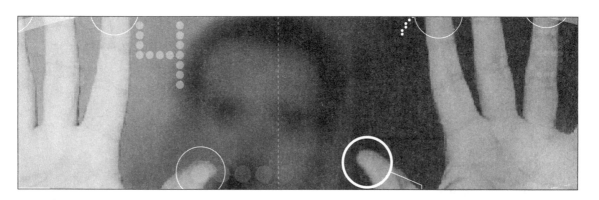

JavaScript™
in 10 Simple Steps or Less

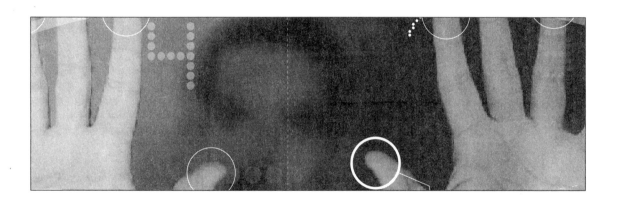

Arman Danesh

WILEY

Wiley Publishing, Inc.

JavaScript™ in 10 Simple Steps or Less

Published by
Wiley Publishing, Inc.
10475 Crosspoint Boulevard
Indianapolis, IN 46256
www.wiley.com

Copyright © 2004 by Wiley Publishing, Inc., Indianapolis, Indiana

Published simultaneously in Canada

Library of Congress Control Number: 2003114066

ISBN: 0-7645-4241-9

Manufactured in the United States of America

10 9 8 7 6 5 4 3 2 1

1Q/QZ/RS/QT/IN

To my beloved Tahirih for her support and encouragement.

Credits

Acquisitions Editor
Jim Minatel

Development Editor
Sharon Nash

Production Editor
Felicia Robinson

Technical Editor
Will Kelly

Copy Editor
Joanne Slike

Editorial Manager
Kathryn Malm

Vice President & Executive Group Publisher
Richard Swadley

Vice President and Executive Publisher
Robert Ipsen

Vice President and Publisher
Joseph B. Wikert

Project Coordinator
Courtney MacIntyre

Graphics and Production Specialists
Elizabeth Brooks, Joyce Haughey, Jennifer Heleine,
LeAndra Hosier, Heather Pope, Mary Gillot Virgin

Quality Control Technician
John Tyler Connoley, John Greenough,
Charles Spencer

Proofreading and Indexing
Sossity R. Smith, Johnna VanHoose

About the Author

Arman Danesh is the Internet Coordinator for the Bahá'í International Community's Office of Public Information. In that capacity, he manages the development of numerous Web sites, including The Bahá'í World (www.bahai.org), the official Web site of the Bahá'í Faith, and the Bahá'í World News Services (www.bahaiworldnews.org), an online news service, both of which use JavaScript. Additionally, he is the Technical Director for Juxta Publishing Limited (www.juxta.com). He has been working with JavaScript since the mid-1990s and is the author of some of the earliest books on the subject, including *Teach Yourself JavaScript in a Week* and *JavaScript Developer's Guide*. Arman has authored more than 20 books on technology subjects, including *ColdFusion MX Developer's Handbook* (Sybex), *Mastering ColdFusion MX* (Sybex), *SAIR Linux & Gnu Certified Administrator All-in-One Exam Guide* (Osborne/McGraw-Hill), and *Safe and Secure: Secure Your Home Network and Protect Your Privacy Online* (Sams). He is pursuing an advanced degree in computer science at Simon Fraser University outside Vancouver, British Columbia.

Acknowledgments

The task of writing these long computer books is a daunting one, and it is a process that requires significant contributions from many people who help these projects see their way to completion. For this project, I need to thank the entire team, including Sharon Nash and Jim Minatel at Wiley, as well as all the myriad others involved in preparing, designing, and producing the books there.

I also need to thank my family for their patience during the writing of the book. In particular, my wife, Tahirih, and son, Ethan, deserve credit for tolerating the time I had to devote to the preparation of this book.

Contents

Introduction

Since the mid-1990s when Netscape introduced version 2 of its flagship Netscape Navigator browser, JavaScript has been part of the Web development landscape. Providing a mechanism to implement dynamic interactivity in the browser, without connecting to the server, JavaScript is at the core of the Dynamic HTML model, which allows today's modern browsers to host sophisticated applications and user interfaces.

This book is a recipe book that provides you with quick, digestible examples of how to perform specific tasks using JavaScript. These tasks range from simple tasks such as displaying dynamic output in the browser window to complex tasks such as creating a dynamic, interactive menu system.

This book isn't a tutorial in JavaScript. It is designed to be a useful reference when you are actively engaged in building your Web applications and need quick answers to the question "How do I do this in JavaScript?" For most tasks of low and medium complexity, you will likely find an example in this book. Completing complex tasks can often be achieved by combining more than one sample tasks from the book.

tip

If you don't have any experience with JavaScript, you will probably want to supplement this book with a tutorial introduction to programming in JavaScript. For instance, you might consider *JavaScript for Dummies* by Emily A. Vander Veer (John Wiley & Sons, 0-7645-0633-1).

About the Book

This book is divided into 11 parts:

Part 1: JavaScript Basics

This part provides tasks that illustrate some fundamental JavaScript techniques and skills. If you have never used JavaScript before, this part is for you. It provides examples that illustrate the basics of creating scripts and using JavaScript.

Part 2: Outputting to the Browser

This part covers some core techniques for using JavaScript to generate dynamic output to the browser window, including outputting dynamic values such as dates.

Part 3: Images and Rollovers

Using JavaScript, you can manipulate images, producing effects such as rollover effects and random slide shows. The tasks in this part illustrate techniques for working with images from JavaScript.

Part 4: Working with Forms

Forms involve more than just submitting data to the server. This part illustrates how to create dynamic client-side forms in the browser and to build forms that work with the user without contacting the server.

Part 5: Manipulating Browser Windows

This part provides tasks that illustrate the creation and closing of windows, how to manage the attributes of those windows, and how to work with frames. All these features are key to developing sophisticated user interfaces with JavaScript.

Part 6: Manipulating Cookies

Normally, cookies are created by your server and sent to the browser for storage. The browser then sends them back to the server when the user connects to that server. Now with JavaScript, you can create cookies and access them later without any interaction with the server.

Part 7: DHTML and Style Sheets

JavaScript is part of a threesome that forms Dynamic HTML. The other parts are the Domain Object Model and cascading style sheets. The tasks in this part show you how to work with the DOM and style sheets.

Part 8: Dynamic User Interaction

This part provides tasks that illustrate some of the most popular uses of JavaScript for dynamic user interaction—from creating pull-down menus to producing floating windows and handling drag-and-drop user interaction.

Part 9: Handling Events

JavaScript is an event-driven scripting language. This means you don't create linear programs but instead can write your programs to respond to events. Events might be the user clicking on a button or the completion of a task by the browser, such as completing loading of the current document.

Part 10: Bookmarklets

Bookmarklets are an interesting application of JavaScript that combines JavaScript with the bookmarks or favorites feature of browser. Bookmarklets are short, self-contained JavaScript scripts that perform some useful task that you can add to your favorites or bookmarks and then run at any time by selecting the relevant favorite or bookmark.

Part 11: Cross-Browser Compatibility and Issues

As JavaScript has become more advanced and its features have expanded, browser compatibility has become an issue. As would be expected, different browser vendors have different ideas about the right way to do things in their implementations of JavaScript. The result is a plethora of browsers with subtle differences in the way JavaScript works. The tasks in this part provide you with some techniques for handling these browser differences in your applications.

The appendices provide you quick references to JavaScript and cascading style sheets you can consult in developing your applications when you need reminders of the correct property, method, or style attribute name.

Finally, the complete source code for each task can be found on the companion Web site at www.wiley. com/10stepsorless. This makes it easy for you to try the code illustrated in the task or adapt the code for your own purposes.

Conventions Used in this Book

As you go through this book, you will find a few unique elements. We'll describe those elements here so that you'll understand them when you see them.

Code

If a single line of code is too long to appear as one line in the printed book, we'll add the following symbol to indicate that the line continues: ⊃

Text You Type and Text on the Screen

Whenever you are asked to type in text, the text you are to type appears in bold, like this:

Type in this address: **111 River Street**.

When we are referring to URLs or other text you'll see on the screen, we'll use a monospace font, like this:

Check out `www.wiley.com`.

Icons

A number of special icons appear in the margins of each task to provide additional information you might find helpful.

note	*tip*	*caution*	*cross-reference*
The Note icon is used to provide additional information or help in working in JavaScript.	The Tip icon is used to point out an interesting idea or technique that will save you time, effort, money, or all three.	The Caution icon is used to alert you to potential problems that you might run into when working in JavaScript.	Although this book is divided into tasks to make it easy to find exactly what you're looking for, few tasks really stand completely alone. The Cross-Reference icon provides us the opportunity to point out other tasks in the book you might want to look at if you're interested in this task.

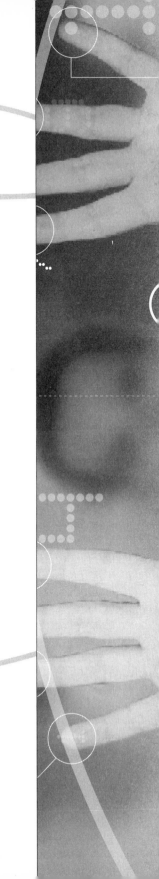

Part 1: JavaScript Basics

Creating a `script` **Block**

J avaScript is a dynamic scripting language that allows you to build interactivity into otherwise static HTML pages. This is done by embedding blocks of JavaScript code almost anywhere in your Web page.

To make this work, blocks of JavaScript code are delineated by opening and closing `script` tags:

```
<script ...>
   JavaScript code goes here
</script>
```

The `script` tag takes one important attribute: `language`. This attribute specifies what scripting language you are using. Typically, its value will be either `JavaScript` or `JavaScript1.0`, `JavaScript1.1`, `JavaScript1.2`, and so on. By specifying a specific JavaScript version number, you indicate to the browser this script can only run on a browser that supports the specified version of JavaScript. Without that, every JavaScript-capable browser will assume the script is one it should try to run.

For instance, the following is an example of a complete `script` tag:

```
<script language="JavaScript">
   JavaScript code goes here
</script>
```

The following steps outline how to create a simple HTML document with a single embedded script block. The script is responsible for outputting the word "Hello" to the user's browser:

1. Open a new HTML document in your preferred HTML or text editor.

2. Create the body of the document with opening and closing `body` tags:

   ```
   <body>

   </body>
   ```

3. Insert a script block in the body of the document:

   ```
   <body>
      <script>

      </script>
   </body>
   ```

notes

- For the purposes of simplicity, you will use JavaScript as the value of the language attribute in all `script` tags in this book.

- The current version of JavaScript in the newest browsers in JavaScript 1.5.

4. Specify `JavaScript` as the language for the `script` tag:

```
<body>
   <script language="JavaScript">

   </script>
</body>
```

5. Place any JavaScript code in the script block so that the final code looks like Listing 1-1.

```
<body>
   <script language="JavaScript">

      document.write("Hello");

   </script>
</body>
```

Listing 1-1: Creating a script block.

6. Save the file.

7. Open the file in your browser. You should see the word "Hello" in your browser, as in Figure 1-1.

Figure 1-1: Script code can be placed anywhere in your document, including in the body of the document.

cross-reference

- The JavaScript code here uses `document.write` to output text to the browser window. `document.write` is covered in a little more depth in Task 9 and in greater depth in Task 45.

Hiding Your JavaScript Code

Task 1 showed how to embed JavaScript code in your document. For instance, the following embeds one line of JavaScript code in the body of an HTML document:

```
<body>
    <script language="JavaScript">

        document.write("Hello");

    </script>
</body>
```

However, there is a fundamental problem with this code: If this page is opened in a browser that doesn't support JavaScript or if the user has disabled JavaScript in his or her browser, the user may see the code itself, depending on the specific browser he or she is using.

To address this issue, you need to use HTML comments inside the script block to hide the code from these browsers.

HTML comments work like this:

```
<!-- One or more lines of comments go here -->
```

Used in the context of a JavaScript script, you would see the following:

```
<body>
    <script language="JavaScript">
    <!--

        document.write("Hello");

    // -->
    </script>
</body>
```

The following steps show how to create a script block in the body of a document that includes these comments:

1. Open a new HTML document in your preferred HTML or text editor.

2. Create the body of the document with opening and closing body tags:

    ```
    <body>

    </body>
    ```

3. Insert a script block in the body of the document:

    ```
    <script>

    </script>
    ```

notes

- Luckily, JavaScript uses different comment syntax than HTML, so you can use HTML comments to hide JavaScript code without preventing execution of that code in browsers that support JavaScript.

- In the closing - - > of the introductory source code (discussed in Step 5), you see it is preceded by two slashes. These indicate a JavaScript comment. What's happening here is that once the first line of JavaScript appears in the script block, all subsequent lines are assumed to be JavaScript code. The double slash is a JavaScript comment that hides the closing HTML comment from being processed as JavaScript; otherwise, a JavaScript error would occur, since the browser would treat the closing HTML comment as JavaScript. JavaScript comments are discussed in Task 5.

4. Specify JavaScript as the language for the script tag:

```
<script language="JavaScript">
```

5. Place opening and closing HTML comments in the script block:

```
<!--

// -->
```

6. Place any JavaScript code in the script block so that the final code looks like Listing 2-1.

```
<body>
   <script language="JavaScript">
   <!--

       document.write("Hello");

   // -->
   </script>
</body>
```

Listing 2-1: Creating a script block.

7. Save the file.

8. Open the file in a browser that supports JavaScript. You should see the word "Hello" in your browser. Open it in a browser that doesn't support JavaScript, and you should see nothing, as in Figure 2-1.

Figure 2-1: Script code is hidden from non-JavaScript-capable browsers and is hidden from display.

Providing Alternatives to Your JavaScript Code

In Task 2 you saw how to hide JavaScript code from non-JavaScript browsers by using HTML comments. The result is that browsers that don't support JavaScript see nothing at all where the script block normally would be. However, there are cases where the purpose of the JavaScript code is essential to the page and users of non-JavaScript capable browsers need to be told that they are missing this vital part of the page.

Luckily, there is a solution to this: the noscript tag. The noscript tag allows you to specify HTML to display to the browser only for browsers that don't support JavaScript. If a browser supports JavaScript, it will ignore the text in the noscript block.

To use this, you simply place any HTML for non-JavaScript browsers between opening and closing noscript tags. The following steps show how to embed a script in the body of a document and provide alternative HTML to display for non-JavaScript browsers:

1. Open a new HTML document in your preferred HTML or text editor.

2. Create the body of the document with opening and closing body tags:

   ```
   <body>

   </body>
   ```

3. Insert a script block in the body of the document:

   ```
   <script>

   </script>
   ```

4. Specify JavaScript as the language for the script tag:

   ```
   <script language="JavaScript">
   ```

5. Place opening and closing HTML comments in the script block:

   ```
   <!--

   // -->
   ```

note

- The noscript tag works on a simple principle: JavaScript-aware browsers will recognize the tag and will honor it by not displaying the text inside the block. Older, non-JavaScript browsers, on the other hand, will not recognize the tag as valid HTML. As browsers are supposed to do, they will just ignore the tag they don't recognize, but all the content between the opening and closing tags will not be ignored and, therefore, will be displayed in the browser.

caution

- It is important to consider carefully if you want to restrict use of your pages to users with JavaScript-capable browsers. However small the percentage of users with these older browsers may be, you will be excluding part of your audience if you do this.

6. Place any JavaScript code in the script block:

```
document.write("Hello");
```

7. Add a `noscript` block immediately after the script block:

```
<noscript>

</noscript>
```

8. In the `noscript` block, place any text to display to the non-JavaScript-capable browser:

```
<noscript>

    Hello to the non-JavaScript browser.

</noscript>
```

9. Save the file.

10. Open the file in a browser that supports JavaScript. You should see the word "Hello" in your browser. Open it in a browser that doesn't support JavaScript, and you should see the alternate message, as in Figure 3-1.

Figure 3-1: Other browsers display the text in the `noscript` block.

Including Outside Source Code

As you begin to work more extensively with JavaScript, you will likely find that there are cases where you are reusing identical JavaScript code on multiple pages of a site. For instance, you might be creating a dynamic menu common to all pages in JavaScript.

In these cases, you don't want to be maintaining identical code in multiple HTML files. Luckily, the `script` tag provides a mechanism to allow you to store JavaScript in an external file and include it into your HTML files. In this way you can build and maintain one JavaScript file containing the common code and simply include it into multiple HTML files.

This is achieved using the `src` attribute of the `script` tag, which allows you to specify a relative or absolute URL for a JavaScript file, as in the following:

```
<script language="JavaScript" src="filename.js"></script>
```

The following example uses this technique to include an external JavaScript file in an HTML document:

1. In your editor, create a new file that will contain the JavaScript file's code.

2. In this file, enter any JavaScript code you want included in the external JavaScript file:

```
// JavaScript Document

document.write("Hello");
```

3. Save the file as `4a.js` and close the file.

4. In your editor, create a new file that will contain the HTML file.

5. Create the body of the document with opening and closing `body` tags:

```
<body>

</body>
```

6. In the body of the document, create a script block:

```
<body>
    <script></script>
</body>
```

notes

▪ Even when there is no JavaScript code in the script block, you still need to close the `script` tag. Otherwise, all HTML code following the `script` tag will be seen by browsers as JavaScript and not HTML. This can cause errors in the browser and will definitely mean your pages will not look the way you expect.

▪ Notice that this file has no `script` tags. This will be an external JavaScript and not an HTML file. The `script` tag is an HTML file that marks the location of JavaScript code. In a JavaScript file, no such markers are needed.

7. Specify `JavaScript` in the `language` attribute of the `script` tag:

```
<body>
    <script language="JavaScript"></script>
</body>
```

8. Use the `src` attribute of the `script` tag to include the JavaScript file created earlier in Steps 1 to 3:

```
<body>
    <script language="JavaScript" src="4a.js"></script>
</body>
```

9. Save the file and close it.

10. Open the HTML in your browser. The word "Hello" should appear in the browser window, as illustrated in Figure 4-1.

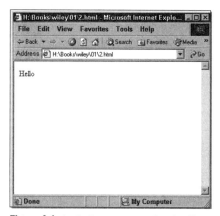

Figure 4-1: Including an external script file.

tip

 The convention is to use the `.js` extension for JavaScript files.

Commenting Your Scripts

All the script examples seen in the previous tasks have been short. At most they have been a couple of lines long. However, as your skills advance, you will likely build long, complicated scripts. To ensure that your scripts can be understood by other developers and also to help remind you of your own thinking when you return to your code after a period of time, you should insert comments into the code that explain why the code is designed the way it is.

JavaScript provides two types of comments:

- Single-line comments that start anywhere in the line and continue to the end of the line. Therefore, both of the following are valid single-line comments:

```
// This is a comment
document.write("Hello"); // This is a comment
```

- Multiline comments that start with `/*` and end with `*/`. The following is an example of a multiline comment:

```
/*
All of this
is a comment
*/
```

You can include as many or as few comments as you like in your JavaScript code. The following example builds a simple HTML page with a JavaScript script containing two comments:

1. Open a new HTML document in your preferred HTML or text editor.

2. Create the body of the document with opening and closing `body` tags:

```
<body>

</body>
```

3. Insert a script block in the body of the document:

```
<script>

</script>
```

4. Specify `JavaScript` as the language for the `script` tag:

```
<script language="JavaScript">
```

5. Place any JavaScript code in the script block:

```
document.write("Hello");
```

6. Add a single-line comment before the `document.write` command:

```
// This is a one-line comment

document.write("Hello");
```

7. Add a multiline comment after the `document.write` command so that the final script looks like Listing 5-1.

```
<body>
   <script language="JavaScript">

      // This is a one-line comment

      document.write("Hello");

      /*
         This is a multiline
         comment
      */

   </script>
</body>
```

Listing 5-1: Using comments.

8. Save the file.

9. Open the file in your browser. You should see the word "Hello" in your browser, as in Figure 5-1.

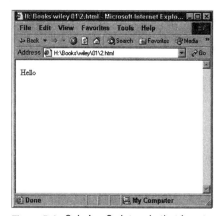

Figure 5-1: Only JavaScript code that is not part of a comment is executed.

tip

▪ Commenting your code is considered good programming practice regardless of the language you are programming in. Writing clear, concise, meaningful comments to describe your code allows other developers you might work with to understand your code. Plus, they can help you as well: If you come back to your code after a long absence they remind you of the logic you used in building your programs or scripts.

Writing a JavaScript Command

In the previous tasks you have seen examples of JavaScript commands. All JavaScript scripts are made up of a series of commands. In its most basic form, a command is some set of JavaScript code ending with a semicolon. For instance, all the following could be considered commands:

```
var a = "Yes";
document.write("Hello");
result = window.confirm(a);
```

You can string these commands together in pretty much any way:

- Line-by-line:

```
var a = "Yes";
document.write("Hello");
result = window.confirm(a);
```

- On the same line:

```
var a = "Yes"; document.write("Hello"); result = ↵
window.confirm(a);
```

- Any combination:

```
var a = "Yes"; document.write("Hello");
result = window.confirm(a);
```

The following task illustrates a script with three commands:

1. Open a new HTML document in your preferred HTML or text editor.

2. Create the body of the document with opening and closing body tags:

```
<body>

</body>
```

3. Insert a script block in the body of the document:

```
<script>

</script>
```

4. Specify JavaScript as the language for the script tag:

```
<script language="JavaScript">
```

5. Place opening and closing HTML comments in the script block:

```
<!--

// -->
```

notes

- A JavaScript program, or a script, is essentially a series of commands executed in sequence or following some specified order.

- There is no particular format to the commands. They might assign a value as in the first example, they might simply call a method as in the second example, or they might call a method in order to assign a value as in the third example. Still, they are all JavaScript commands.

6. Create the first command in the script block. Make sure the command ends with a semicolon:

```
document.write("Hello");
```

7. Create the second command, ending with a semicolon:

```
document.write("Hello");
document.write(" there");
```

8. Finally, add the third command to the script so that the final page looks like Listing 6-1.

```
<body>
    <script language="JavaScript">
    <!--

        document.write("Hello");
        document.write(" there");
        document.write(".");

    // -->
    </script>
</body>
```

Listing 6-1: Placing three commands in a script.

9. Save the file.

10. Open the file in a browser that supports JavaScript. You should see the phrase "Hello there." in your browser, as in Figure 6-1.

Figure 6-1: The three commands ran in sequence.

Temporarily Removing a Command from a Script

notes

- Debugging is the act of finding and eliminating problems in your code; these problems are known as bugs and can range from simple typographical errors to obscure problems in the logic of your scripts.

- Commenting out lines of code is not the only debugging technique. There are numerous other approaches to debugging, including using tools designed to help you debug. These are advanced subjects not covered in this book.

Sometimes when you are working on some particularly complicated JavaScript code or are facing a bug that you just can't locate, you need to remove lines of code one at a time until you identify the line of code that is causing you grief.

However, you don't want to really delete the line, because once you've identified and fixed the problem, you will need to re-create any lines you deleted. That's where comments come in.

By way of example, in the following code, the second line will not be executed because the document.write command is after the double slash:

```
var myVariable = "Hello";
//document.write("Hello");
```

In fact, if this code alone were executed by the browser, nothing would be displayed, since the only command for outputting anything to the browser is commented out.

The following task starts with an existing script and shows the effects of commenting out portions of the script. This task starts with the script from Task 6.

1. Open the script from Task 6.

2. Comment out the second command by placing a double slash in front of it:

    ```
        document.write("Hello");
    //    document.write(" there");
        document.write(".");
    ```

3. Save the file and open it in a browser. You should see just the word "Hello ." as in Figure 7-1. Because of the comment, the second command will not execute.

4. Continue editing the file, and comment out the first command as well:

    ```
    //    document.write("Hello");
    //    document.write(" there");
        document.write(".");
    ```

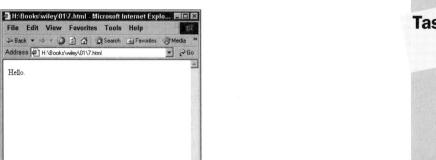

Figure 7-1: The second command is commented out.

5. Save the file and open it in a browser. You should see just a dot, as in Figure 7-2.

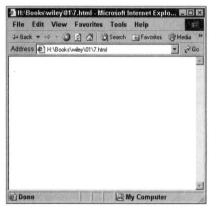

Figure 7-2: Two commands commented out.

6. Continue editing the file, and remove the two double slashes. Place /* before the first command and */ after the last command:

```
/*      document.write("Hello");
       document.write(" there");
       document.write(".");*/
```

7. Save the file and open it in a browser. You should see an empty window, because all the commands are now contained in a multiline comment.

cross-reference

- Comments were introduced in Task 5. They allow you to hide parts of your script so that they are not executed as JavaScript.

Using Curly Brackets

In addition to simple commands that end with a semicolon, such as those you saw in Task 7, JavaScript supports the notion of a compound command. A *compound command* is a group of commands that together are treated as a single command and can be used wherever JavaScript calls for a single command.

As an example, consider a condition in JavaScript. You build a conditional operation in JavaScript as follows:

```
if (condition) command
```

The basic logic of this statement is this: If the condition is true, then execute the command.

For the command, you have two choices: Use a single command ending in a semicolon or use multiple commands bundled together as one.

With a single command, you might have the following:

```
if (condition) document.write("Hello");
```

Here, if the condition is true, then `document.write` is executed.

Similarly, the following example groups together three `document.write` commands as a single compound command:

```
if (condition) {
    document.write("Hello");
    document.write(" there");
    document.write(".");
}
```

The following example shows how to build a compound command using curly brackets:

1. Open a new HTML document in your preferred HTML or text editor.

2. Create the body of the document with opening and closing `body` tags:

   ```
   <body>

   </body>
   ```

3. Insert a script block in the body of the document:

   ```
   <script>

   </script>
   ```

note

- The compound command in the introductory source code starts with a curly bracket and ends with a curly bracket. The entire package from the opening to the closing bracket is considered a single command for the purposes of such things as the `if` statement.

4. Specify `JavaScript` as the language for the `script` tag:

   ```
   <script language="JavaScript">
   ```

5. Place opening and closing HTML comments in the script block:

   ```
   <!--

   // -->
   ```

6. Create the first command in the script block. Make sure the command ends with a semicolon:

   ```
   document.write("Hello");
   ```

7. Create the second command, ending a semicolon:

   ```
   document.write("Hello");
   document.write(" there");
   ```

8. Finally, place opening and closing curly brackets before and after the two commands so that the final script looks like Listing 8-1:

   ```
   <body>
      <script language="JavaScript">
      <!--

      {
         document.write("Hello");
         document.write(" there");
      }

      // -->
      </script>
   </body>
   ```

   Listing 8-1: A compound command built out of two commands.

9. Save the file.

10. Open the file in a browser that supports JavaScript. You should see the phrase "Hello there" in your browser.

cross-reference

* Conditions and `if` statements are introduced in Task 34. We won't look at specific conditions here.

Task 9

Writing Output to the Browser

One of the most practical aspects of JavaScript is the ability to output text and HTML into the browser output stream from within your scripts so that the text and HTML appears in the browser as if it were part of the actual HTML of the document.

The key to this is the `document.write` method. The `document.write` method outputs any text or HTML contained in its argument to the browser. For instance, if you issue the following `document.write` command:

```
document.write("<strong>Hello</strong>");
```

the browser receives the following HTML and renders it:

```
<strong>Hello</strong>
```

An important point to remember is that `document.write` does not output any end-of-line-type characters after the text it displays. This means that if you have two `document.write` commands in a row, the output from those two commands is right next to each other. To illustrate this, consider the following pair of commands:

```
document.write("Hello");
document.write("Good-bye");
```

You might be inclined to think this will result in the following being sent to the browser:

```
Hello
Good-bye
```

In reality, though, this is not the case. The following is sent:

```
HelloGood-bye
```

To solve this problem, the document object also includes the `writeln` method. This method outputs the text followed by a new-line character. Consider the following JavaScript code:

```
document.writeln("a");
document.write("b");
```

This would be sent to the browser as:

```
a
b
```

notes

- An *argument* is any value passed to a method. A *method* is a function associated with an object; when you use it, it performs some specified function based on the arguments you provide. The `document` object is an object associated with the current document being rendered into the browser window.

- It doesn't matter that the `document.write` commands are on separate lines. All that gets sent is the text in the arguments, and `document.write` does nothing to create line separations after the text it outputs.

- If you look at the end of the introductory material, you'll see that the key is that `document.writeln` is used to output the a.

The following task illustrates the use of the `document.write` and `document.writeln` methods:

Task **9**

1. Open a new HTML document in your preferred HTML or text editor.

2. Create the body of the document with opening and closing `body` tags, and inside it specify `pre` tags:

```
<body><pre>

</pre></body>
```

3. Insert a script block in the body of the document:

```
<script>

</script>
```

4. Specify `JavaScript` as the language for the `script` tag:

```
<script language="JavaScript">
```

5. Place opening and closing HTML comments in the script block:

```
<!--

// -->
```

6. Create a series of `document.write` and `document.writeln` commands in the script block. The final page should look like Listing 9-1.

```
<body><pre>
   <script language="JavaScript">
   <!--

       document.write("He");
       document.writeln("llo");
       document.write("there");

   // -->
   </script>
</pre></body>
```

Listing 9-1: Using `document.write` and `document.writeln`.

7. Save the file.

8. Open the file in a browser that supports JavaScript. You should see the phrase "Hello there" in your browser.

Task 10

Creating a Variable

A key programming concept is the notion of a *variable*. Like many other programming languages, JavaScript has variables. Variables can be thought of as named containers. You can place data into these containers and then refer to the data simply by naming the container. You create a variable by a simple assignment operation:

```
variable name = some data;
```

For instance, you might create a variable named day and assign the value Tuesday to it:

```
day = "Tuesday";
```

As a matter of good programming practice, you will also want to declare your variables the first time you use them. Declaring a variable helps the browser efficiently and accurately process and manage your variables. To declare a variable, simply use the JavaScript statement var:

```
var myVariable;
```

This declares a variable named myVariable but doesn't assign any values to it. You can proceed to assign a value to it in a subsequent JavaScript command:

```
var myVariable;
...
myVariable = "some value";
```

If you want to declare a variable and assign a value to it right away, you can use a shortcut to do this in one step:

```
var myVariable = "some value";
```

You can also assign values to variables multiple times and each time the value of the variable is replaced with the new value. For instance, consider the following:

```
var day = "Tuesday";
day = "Thursday";
day = "Monday";
```

At the end of this code, the value of the day variable is Monday.

The following steps show the creation of an actual variable in the header of an HTML document:

1. Create a new HTML document in your editor.

2. In the header of the document, create a script block:

```
<head>
    <script language="JavaScript">

    </script>
</head>
```

3. In the script block, create the variable named myVariable and assign a value to it:

```
var myVariable = "Hello";
```

4. Create a body for the document to display any HTML you want to present in the browser. The final page looks like Listing 10-1.

```
<head>
    <script language="JavaScript">

        var myVariable = "Hello";

    </script>
</head>

<body>
    We created a variable in the header.
</body>
```

Listing 10-1: Creating variables.

5. Save the file and close it.

6. Open the file in a browser. You should only see the body of the document, as illustrated in Figure 10-1.

Figure 10-1: Creating a variable in JavaScript does not cause any output to be directed to the browser.

tip

▪ Although you can get away without declaring variables, it doesn't hurt to do it and it is good programming practice (see introductory paragraphs).

Task

Outputting a Variable

Variables, introduced in Task 10, are containers that hold values. You can use them wherever you would normally use the same values. A perfect example of this is text strings.

You can use the `document.write` method to output strings of text to the browser, for instance. There is no reason why a string of text could not be assigned to a variable and then the variable be used to output that text. You just use the variable in place of the string of text as the argument to the `document.write` method:

```
document.write(myVariable);
```

This will output the contents of the variable `myVariable`.

The following example shows how to set a variable and the output it in a script:

1. Open a new HTML document in your preferred HTML or text editor.

2. Create the body of the document with opening and closing `body` tags:

```
<body>

</body>
```

3. Insert a script block in the body of the document:

```
<body>
    <script>

    </script>
</body>
```

4. Specify `JavaScript` as the language for the `script` tag:

```
<body>
    <script language="JavaScript">

    </script>
</body>
```

5. Place opening and closing HTML comments in the script block:

```
<body>
    <script language="JavaScript">
    <!--

    // -->
    </script>
</body>
```

note
- Variables are named containers in which you can store data. You can then refer to that data in your script by the name of the container.

6. Create a variable named `myVariable` and assign a text string to it:

```
<body>
    <script language="JavaScript">
    <!--

        var myVariable = "Hello";

    // -->
    </script>
</body>
```

7. Use `document.write` to output the content of the variable so that the final code looks like Listing 11-1.

```
<body>
    <script language="JavaScript">
    <!--

        var myVariable = "Hello";
        document.write(myVariable);

    // -->
    </script>
</body>
```

Listing 11-1: Outputting a variable.

8. Save the file.

9. Open the file in a browser that supports JavaScript. You should see the word "Hello" in your browser, as in Figure 11-1.

Figure 11-1: The contents of the variable, not its name, are output.

cross-reference

▪ You will notice that there are no quotation marks around `myVariable` (see introductory paragraphs). As noted in Task 12, quotation marks denote a string of text; when outputting the content of a variable, you don't use quotation marks. Otherwise, the name of the variable will be output instead of the content.

Creating a String

When working with data and variables in JavaScript, you need to be aware of the data types you are using. Different data types are managed in different ways, and it is important to understand a few fundamental data types.

One such data type is a string. A *string* refers to any sequence of text that can contain letters, numbers, and punctuation. When specifying a text string in JavaScript, you need to enclose the string in single or double quotes. For instance, the following are valid strings:

```
"Hello there"
'My Phone number is 123-456-7890'
```

But the following are not valid text strings:

```
"Hello'
What is your name?
```

In the first case, the opening quote is a double quote, but the closing one is a single quote; you can use either single or double quotes, but the opening and closing ones must match.

You use these strings in different contexts—for instance, as arguments to a function or method:

```
document.write("This is a string");
```

You also use them as values assigned to variables:

```
var aVar = "This is a string";
```

In both these cases, failure to enclose the string in quotes will actually cause the browser to display an error, because it will treat the string as JavaScript code and the text in the string is not valid JavaScript code.

The following task shows the creation of a variable containing a string value in a script:

1. Open a new HTML document in your preferred HTML or text editor.

2. Create the body of the document with opening and closing body tags:

   ```
   <body>

   </body>
   ```

note

- There are a number of different data types in JavaScript. The most basic types are numbers (numeric values), strings (text), and boolean (binary, either-or, values typically represented as true/false or 1/0).

3. Insert a script block in the body of the document:

```
<body>
    <script>

    </script>
</body>
```

4. Specify JavaScript as the language for the script tag:

```
<body>
    <script language="JavaScript">

    </script>
</body>
```

5. Place opening and closing HTML comments in the script block:

```
<body>
    <script language="JavaScript">
    <!--

    // -->
    </script>
</body>
```

6. Create a variable named myVariable and assign a text string to it:

```
<body>
    <script language="JavaScript">
    <!--

        var myVariable = "Hello";

    // -->
    </script>
</body>
```

7. Save the file and close it.

cross-reference

▪ Task 10 introduces the creation of variables.

Creating a Numeric Variable

When working with data and variables in JavaScript, you need to be aware of the data types you are using. Different data types are managed in different ways, and it is important to understand a few fundamental data types.

One such data type is a number. A *number* refers to any number, positive or negative, that contains only numbers, minus signs, and decimal points. When specifying a number in JavaScript, you should not enclose the string in single or double quotes; if you do, it will be treated as a text string and not a number. For instance, the following are valid numbers:

```
100
-152.56
```

But the following are not valid text strings:

```
"250.3"
ab32
```

In the first case, the quotes make the value a text string, and in the second, the letters mean this is not a valid numeric value.

You use these numbers in different contexts—for instance, as arguments to a function or method:

```
document.write(375);
```

You also use them as values assigned to variables:

```
var aVar = 375;
```

The following task shows how to create a variable containing a numeric value in a script:

1. Open a new HTML document in your preferred HTML or text editor.

2. Create the body of the document with opening and closing body tags:

   ```
   <body>

   </body>
   ```

note

- There are a number of different data types in JavaScript. The most basic types are numbers (numeric values), strings (text), and boolean (binary, either-or, values typically represented as true/false or 1/0).

3. Insert a script block in the body of the document:

```
<body>
   <script>

   </script>
</body>
```

4. Specify `JavaScript` as the language for the `script` tag:

```
<body>
   <script language="JavaScript">

   </script>
</body>
```

5. Place opening and closing HTML comments in the script block:

```
<body>
   <script language="JavaScript">
   <!--

   // -->
   </script>
</body>
```

6. Create a variable named `myVariable` and assign a number to it:

```
<body>
   <script language="JavaScript">
   <!--

      var myVariable = 100;

   // -->
   </script>
</body>
```

7. Save the file and close it.

Performing Math

When working with numeric values in JavaScript, you can perform mathematics with the numbers. Not only can you add, subtract, multiply, and divide numbers, but you can also perform other advanced mathematical calculations.

The four basic mathematical operations are as follows:

- **Addition:** For instance, 10 + 20
- **Subtraction:** For instance, 20 – 10
- **Multiplication:** For instance, 10 * 20
- **Division:** For instance, 20 / 10

In addition, you can build complex mathematical expressions using combinations of these operations. For instance, the following expression subtracts 10 from the result of 100 divided by 5:

```
100 / 5 - 10
```

You can override the order of operation with parentheses. Consider the following mathematical expression:

```
100 / (5 - 10)
```

This will calculate the value of 100 divided by the result of subtracting 10 from 5.

There are two important points to note about these sorts of mathematical expressions:

- You can use them wherever JavaScript expects a single numeric value. For instance, you can assign the results of an expression to a variable:

  ```
  var myVariable = 100 / 5;
  ```

- You can use variables containing numeric values anywhere in your mathematical expressions in place of actual numbers. For instance, if thisVar is a variable with the value 5, then the results of the following JavaScript code are the same as the preceding example:

  ```
  var myVariable = 100 / thisVar;
  ```

The following task calculates and displays the result of adding 100 and 200 through the use of variables and mathematical operations:

1. Open a new HTML document in your preferred HTML or text editor.

2. Create the body of the document with opening and closing body tags:

   ```
   <body>

   </body>
   ```

3. Insert a script block in the body of the document:

```
<script language="JavaScript">
<!--

// -->
</script>
```

4. Create a variable named myVariable and assign the value 100 to it:

```
var myVariable = 100;
```

5. Create a second variable named anotherVariable and assign the value 200 to it:

```
var anotherVariable = 200;
```

6. Add the values of myVariable and anotherVariable and assign the results to a third variable named anotherVariable:

```
var finalResults = myVariable + anotherVariable;
```

7. Display the results so that the final page looks like Listing 14-1:

```
<body>
   <script language="JavaScript">
   <!--

      var myVariable = 100;
      var anotherVariable = 200;
      var finalResults = myVariable + anotherVariable;
      document.write(finalResults);

   // -->
   </script>
</body>
```

Listing 14-1: Performing mathematical operations.

8. Save the file and close it.

9. Open the file in a browser. You should see the number 300 displayed in the browser.

tip

▪ Expressions are a powerful programming concept available in many languages, including JavaScript. They can be mathematical, as in this task, or they can involve any other data types such as strings. At the core, though, they are simple: Expressions are specifications of one or more operations to perform on one or more values; the complete set of operations in the expressions must ultimately evaluate down to a single value. This means expressions can be used anywhere a discrete value would be used.

cross-reference

▪ For examples of other types of expressions that are not mathematical, see Task 15, which provides an example of a string-based expression.

Task 15

Concatenating Strings

note

* When you are working with strings, keep in mind that the plus sign no longer has its mathematical meaning; instead, it indicates that concatenation should be performed.

With text strings you cannot perform mathematical operations like those described for numbers in Task 14. The most common operation performed with text strings is concatenation. *Concatenation* refers to the act of combining two text strings into one longer text string. For instance, the following combines the strings "ab" and "cd" into the combined string "abcd":

```
"ab" + "cd"
```

As with numeric mathematical operations, there are two points to note about concatenation:

* You can use concatenation wherever JavaScript expects a single string value. For instance, you can assign the results of a concatenation to a variable:

  ```
  var myVariable = "ab" + "cd";
  ```

* You can use variables containing string values anywhere in your concatenation in place of actual strings. For instance, if thisVar is a variable with the value "cd" then the results of the following JavaScript code are the same as the preceding example:

  ```
  var myVariable = "ab" + thisVar;
  ```

The following task concatenates two strings stored in variables and displays the results:

1. Open a new HTML document in your preferred HTML or text editor.

2. Create the body of the document with opening and closing body tags:

   ```
   <body>

   </body>
   ```

3. Insert a script block in the body of the document:

   ```
   <script language="JavaScript">
   <!--

   // -->
   </script>
   ```

4. Create a variable named myVariable and assign the value "Hello" to it:

   ```
   var myVariable = "Hello";
   ```

5. Create a second variable named `anotherVariable` and assign the value `"there"` to it:

```
var anotherVariable = "there";
```

6. Concatenate the values of `myVariable` and `anotherVariable`, along with a space between them, and assign the results to a third variable named `finalResults`:

```
var finalResults = myVariable + " " + ⊃
anotherVariable;
```

7. Display the results so that the final page looks like Listing 15-1.

```
<body>
   <script language="JavaScript">
   <!--

      var myVariable = "Hello";
      var anotherVariable = "there";
      var finalResults = myVariable + " " + anotherVariable;
      document.write(finalResults);

   // -->
   </script>
</body>
```

Listing 15-1: Using concatenation.

8. Save the file and close it.

9. Open the file in a browser. You should see the string "Hello there" displayed in the browser as in Figure 15-1.

Figure 15-1: Displaying the results of concatenation.

tip

- These concatenation examples are expressions. Expressions are a powerful programming concept available in many languages, including JavaScript. They can be mathematical, as in this task, or they can involve any other data types, such as strings. At the core, though, they are simple: Expressions are specifications of one or more operations to perform on one or more values; the complete set of operations in the expressions must ultimately evaluate down to a single value. This means expressions can be used anywhere a discrete value would be used.

cross-reference

- Anywhere you can use a string, you can use a concatenation expression like the examples in this task. For instance, you can use a concatenation expression as an argument to the `document.write` method, which was introduced in Task 9.

Searching for Text in Strings

When working with text strings, sometimes you need to determine if a string contains some specific substring, and if it does, you need to determine where in the string that substring occurs.

For instance, if you have the string `what is happening here` and you search for the substring `is`, you want to know that the string contains "is" but also where "is" occurs. You can perform this type of search with the `search` method of the `string` object.

To perform this search is simple. If `what is happening here` is stored in the variable `testVariable`, you would search for "is" with the following:

```
testVariable.search("is");
```

This method returns a numeric value indicating the position in the string where it found "is". In this case, that position is 5.

The following task searches for a substring in another string stored in a variable and displays the position where that substring is found:

1. Open a new HTML document in your preferred HTML or text editor.

2. Create the body of the document with opening and closing `body` tags:

```
<body>

</body>
```

3. Insert a script block in the body of the document:

```
<script language="JavaScript">
<!--

// -->
</script>
```

4. Create a variable named `myVariable` and assign the value `Hello there` to it:

```
var myVariable = "Hello there";
```

5. Create a second variable named `therePlace` and assign the results of searching for `there` to it:

```
var therePlace = myVariable.search("there");
```

notes

- When you create a string value, an object with properties and methods associated with the string is created and you can access these properties and methods. Assuming you have assigned the string to a variable, you access these as `variableName.propertyName` and `variableName.methodName`

- If you count, you will see that "is" starts at the sixth character in the string. But JavaScript, like many programming languages, starts counting at zero, so the first character is in position 0, the second in position 1, and so on. Therefore, the sixth character is in position 5, and this is the number returned by the `search` method.

- If the substring is not found, then the `search` method returns -1 as the position.

- The number 6 is displayed (see Step 8), since "there" starts at the seventh character.

6. Display the results of the search so that the final page looks like Listing 16-1.

```
<body>
    <script language="JavaScript">
    <!--

        var myVariable = "Hello there";
        var therePlace = myVariable.search("there");
        document.write(therePlace);

    // -->
    </script>
</body>
```

Listing 16-1: Searching for a substring.

7. Save the file and close it.

8. Open the file in a browser. You should see the number 6 displayed in the browser as in Figure 16-1.

Figure 16-1: Displaying the results of searching for a substring.

Task

Replacing Text in Strings

In Task 16 you saw that it is possible to search for text in strings. Sometimes, though, you will want to search for, find, and replace text in a string. The string object provides the replace method for just such purposes.

Consider a variable named thisVar containing the string "Today is Monday". You could search and replace "Monday" with "Friday" with the following:

```
thisVar.replace("Monday","Friday");
```

When you use the replace method, the method returns a new string containing the results of performing the replacement. The original string is not altered. For instance, consider assigning the results of the replacement above to a new variable:

```
var newVar = thisVar.replace("Monday","Friday");
```

In this case, thisVar will continue to contain "Today is Monday" but newVar will contain "Today is Friday".

The following task creates a variable and assigns text to it, replaces that text with new text, and then displays the results in a browser:

1. Open a new HTML document in your preferred HTML or text editor.

2. Create the body of the document with opening and closing body tags:

   ```
   <body>

   </body>
   ```

3. Insert a script block in the body of the document:

   ```
   <script language="JavaScript">
   <!--

   // -->
   </script>
   ```

4. Create a variable named myVariable and assign the value "Hello there" to it:

   ```
   var myVariable = "Hello there";
   ```

note

▪ The replace method works in pretty much the same way as the search method, except that you must provide two strings as arguments: The first is the substring to search for, while the second is the substring to replace it with, assuming the first substring is found.

5. Create a second variable named `newVariable` and assign the results of replacing "there" with "Arman" to it:

```
    var newVariable = ⊃
myVariable.replace("there","Arman");
```

6. Display the results of the search and replace so the final page looks like Listing 17-1.

```
<body>
   <script language="JavaScript">
   <!--

      var myVariable = "Hello there";
      var newVariable = ⊃
myVariable.replace("there","Arman");
      document.write(newVariable);

   // -->
   </script>
</body>
```

Listing 17-1: Search and replace in a string.

7. Save the file and close it.

8. Open the file in a browser. You should see the text "Hello Arman" displayed in the browser as in Figure 17-1.

Figure 17-1: Displaying the results of searching for a substring and replacing it.

Formatting Strings

When you create a text string in JavaScript, a `string` object is associated with that string. The `string` object provides a series of methods you can use to adjust the format of the string. This can be useful when you want to display a string and quickly apply some formatting to it. The methods are as follows:

- `big`: Returns the string in `big` tags
- `blink`: Returns the string in `blink` tags
- `bold`: Returns the string in `b` tags
- `fixed`: Returns the string in `tt` tags (for fixed-width display)
- `fontcolor`: Returns the string in `font` tags with the `color` attribute set to the color you specify as an argument
- `fontsize`: Returns the string in `font` tags with the `size` attribute set to the size you specify as an argument
- `italics`: Returns the string in `i` tags
- `small`: Returns the string in `small` tags
- `strike`: Returns the string in `strike` tags (for a strikethrough effect)
- `sub`: Returns the string in `sub` tags (for a subscript effect)
- `sup`: Returns the string in `sup` tags (for a superscript effect)
- `toLowerCase`: Returns the string with all lowercase characters
- `toUpperCase`: Returns the string with all upper case characters

Assuming you have assigned a string to a variable, you call these methods as follows:

```
variableName.big();
variableName.fontcolor("red");
variableName.toLowerCase();
etc.
```

The following task displays the same string using each of these methods:

1. Open a new HTML document in your preferred HTML or text editor.

2. Create the body of the document with opening and closing `body` tags:

```
<body>

</body>
```

note

- Notice that each `document.write` method in the introductory source code outputs the string adjusted by one of the formatting functions and then displays a `br` tag so that the browser will display each instance on separate lines. Without this, all the instances would appear on one continuous line.

3. Insert a script block in the body of the document:

```
<script language="JavaScript">
<!--

// -->
</script>
```

4. Create a variable named `myVariable` and assign the value "Hello there" to it:

```
var myVariable = "Hello there";
```

5. Use the `document.write` method to display the value of the variable as altered by each of the formatting methods, as shown in Listing 18-1.

```
<body>
    <script language="JavaScript">
    <!--

        var myVariable = "Hello there";
        document.write(myVariable.big() + "<br>");
        document.write(myVariable.blink() + "<br>");
        document.write(myVariable.bold() + "<br>");
        document.write(myVariable.fixed() + "<br>");
        document.write(myVariable.fontcolor("red") + "<br>");
        document.write(myVariable.fontsize("18pt") + "<br>");
        document.write(myVariable.italics() + "<br>");
        document.write(myVariable.small() + "<br>");
        document.write(myVariable.strike() + "<br>");
        document.write(myVariable.sub() + "<br>");
        document.write(myVariable.sup() + "<br>");
        document.write(myVariable.toLowerCase() + "<br>");
        document.write(myVariable.toUpperCase() + "<br>");

    // -->
    </script>
</body>
```

Listing 18-1: Using string formatting functions.

6. Open the file in a browser. You should see the text "Hello there" displayed once for each of the formatting methods.

Applying Multiple Formatting Functions to a String

In Task 18, you saw how to apply formatting functions to a string manually. However, you can apply multiple formatting if you want. An obvious way to do this is by assigning the new string to a variable at each step of the way:

```
var firstString = "My String";
var secondString = firstString.bold();
var thirdString = secondString.toLowerCase();
etc.
```

You can shortcut this by relying on the fact that each of these formatting methods returns a string that is an object that, in turn, has its own set of formatting methods that can be called. This allows you to string together the functions like this:

```
var firstString = "My String";
var finalString = firstString.bold().toLowerCase().fontcolor("red");
```

The end result of this is the following HTML stored in `finalString`:

```
<font color="red"><b>my string</b></font>
```

In the following task you take a string and apply bolding, italicization, coloring, and sizing to it before displaying it:

1. Open a new HTML document in your preferred HTML or text editor.

2. Create the body of the document with opening and closing body tags:

   ```
   <body>

   </body>
   ```

3. Insert a script block in the body of the document:

   ```
   <script language="JavaScript">
   <!--

   // -->
   </script>
   ```

4. Create a variable named `myVariable` and assign the value "Hello there" to it:

   ```
   var myVariable = "Hello there";
   ```

note

▪ Assigning the new string to a variable at each step works, but it is cumbersome and creates far more variables than are needed.

5. Apply bolding, italicization, coloring, and sizing to the string and assign the results to `newVariable`:

```
     var newVariable = ⤵
myVariable.bold().italics().fontcolor("blue").fontsize⤵
("24pt");
```

6. Use the `document.write` method to display the final string so that the final page looks like Listing 19-1.

```
<body>
    <script language="JavaScript">
    <!--

        var myVariable = "Hello there";
        var newVariable = ⤵
myVariable.bold().italics().fontcolor("blue").fontsize⤵
("24pt");
        document.write(newVariable);

    // -->
    </script>
</body>
```

Listing 19-1: Applying multiple styles.

7. Open the file in a browser. You should see the text "Hello there" displayed with the formatting applied as in Figure 19-1.

Figure 19-1: Displaying a string with multiple formats applied.

Creating Arrays

In addition to simple data types such as text strings and numbers, JavaScript supports a more complicated data type known as an array. An *array* is a collection of individual values grouped together. An array essentially contains a series of numbered containers into which you can place values. Each container can contain a string, a number, or any other data type.

You refer to containers in the array as `arrayName[0]`, `arrayName[1]`, `arrayName[2]`, and so on. Each of these individual containers can be manipulated and used just like a regular variable. You can imagine an array as illustrated in Figure 20-1; here you see a set of boxes where each box is numbered and each box has something inside it. The box numbers are the indexes for each box, and the value inside is the value of each array entry.

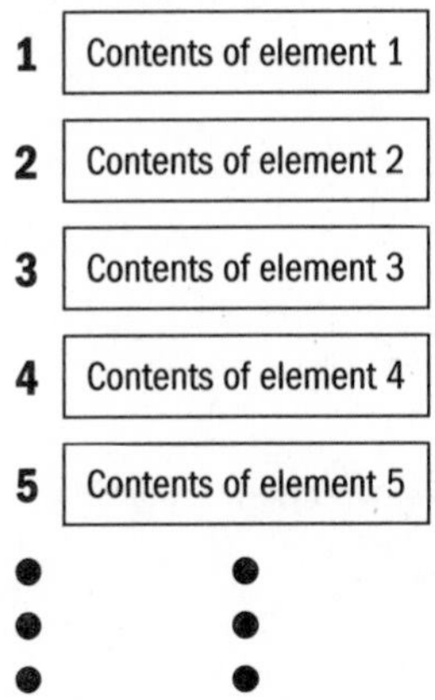

notes

* You probably noticed that the first container is numbered 0. Like many programming languages, JavaScript starts counting at zero, so the first container in an array is numbered 0.

* The number representing each container in an array (such as 0, 1, or 2) is known as the *index*.

* If you create an array with 5 elements, then the indexes of the elements are 0, 1, 2, 3, and 4.

1	Contents of element 1
2	Contents of element 2
3	Contents of element 3
4	Contents of element 4
5	Contents of element 5

Figure 20-1: Visualizing an array.

To create a new array, you create a new instance of the `Array` object:

```
var arrayName = new Array(number of elements);
```

The number of elements is just the initial number of elements in the array; you can add more on the fly as you work with the array, but it is a good idea to initialize the array with the likely number of elements you will use. The array is then accessed through `arrayName`.

The following task creates an array in a script in the header of a document:

1. Open a new HTML document in your preferred HTML or text editor.

2. Create the head of the document with opening and closing `head` tags:

   ```
   <head>

   </head>
   ```

3. Insert a script block in the head of the document:

   ```
   <head>
       <script language="JavaScript">
       <!--

       // -->
       </script>
   </head>
   ```

4. Create a variable named `myArray` and initialize it as a new array with five elements:

   ```
   <body>
       <script language="JavaScript">
       <!--

           var myArray = new Array(5);

       // -->
       </script>
   </body>
   ```

5. Save the file and close it.

Populating an Array

Task 21 showed you how to create an array. An array isn't very useful, however, unless you can populate its elements with values. You populate the elements of an array by assigning values to the elements just as you assign values to normal variables:

```
arrayName[0] = value 1;
arrayName[1] = value 2;
etc.
```

In addition, you can actually populate the array at the time you create it; instead of specifying the number of elements to create in the array when you create it, you can specify a comma-separated list of values for the elements of the array:

```
var arrayName = new Array(value 1, value 2, value 3, etc.)
```

The following task illustrates the creation of two arrays that will contain an identical set of five elements. The two arrays are created and populated using these two different techniques.

1. Open a new HTML document in your preferred HTML or text editor.

2. Create the head of the document with opening and closing `head` tags:

   ```
   <head>

   </head>
   ```

3. Insert a script block in the head of the document:

   ```
   <head>
      <script language="JavaScript">
      <!--

      // -->
      </script>
   </head>
   ```

4. Create a variable named `myArray` and initialize it as a new array with five elements:

   ```
   var myArray = new Array(5);
   ```

note

- The numeric value for each container in an array is known as the *index*.

5. Assign values to the five elements:

```
myArray[0] = "First Entry";
myArray[1] = "Second Entry";
myArray[2] = "Third Entry";
myArray[3] = "Fourth Entry";
myArray[4] = "Fifth Entry";
```

6. Create a second array named `anotherArray` and assign five values to it at the time it is created. The final script should look like Listing 21-1.

```
<head>
    <script language="JavaScript">
    <!--

        var myArray = new Array(5);
        myArray[0] = "First Entry";
        myArray[1] = "Second Entry";
        myArray[2] = "Third Entry";
        myArray[3] = "Fourth Entry";
        myArray[4] = "Fifth Entry";

        var anotherArray = new Array("First Entry","Second ⤷
Entry","Third Entry","Fourth Entry","Fifth Entry");

    // -->
    </script>
</head>
```

Listing 21-1: Two methods for creating arrays.

7. Save the file and close it.

tips

- You don't need to populate the elements in order and can leave elements empty. For instance, you might populate the fifth, first, and second elements in an array in that order and leave the third and fourth elements empty. That's just fine.

- You can also assign other types of values to array elements other than strings. We just happen to use strings in this example. If you want, you could assign numbers or even other arrays as values of an array's elements.

Sorting an Array

Once you have populated an array as outlined in Task 21, you might find it useful to sort the elements in the array. Sometimes you will want to output the elements of the array in the order in which they were created and added to the array, but at others times you will want them sorted.

The array object provides a `sort` method that does just this: It returns a comma-separated list of the elements in sorted order. Sorting is performed in ascending order alphabetically or numerically as appropriate.

To use the method, simply call it:

```
arrayName.sort();
```

The following task creates an array with five elements and then displays the elements in sorted order:

1. Open a new HTML document in your preferred HTML or text editor.

2. Create the body of the document with opening and closing `body` tags:

   ```
   <body>

   </body>
   ```

3. Insert a script block in the body of the document:

   ```
   <script language="JavaScript">
   <!--

   // -->
   </script>
   ```

4. Create a variable named `myArray`, and initialize it as a new array with five elements:

   ```
   var myArray = new Array(5);
   ```

5. Assign values to the five elements:

   ```
   myArray[0] = "z";
   myArray[1] = "c";
   myArray[2] = "d";
   myArray[3] = "a";
   myArray[4] = "q";
   ```

note

■ Notice that in Step 6 the `myArray.sort` method is used as the argument for the `document.write` method. The latter expects a string value as an argument, and the former returns just that: a string containing a sorted list of elements.

6. Use the `document.write` method and the `sort` method to output the sorted list of elements so that the final script looks like Listing 22-1.

Task **22**

```
<body>
    <script language="JavaScript">
    <!--

        var myArray = new Array(5);
        myArray[0] = "z";
        myArray[1] = "c";
        myArray[2] = "d";
        myArray[3] = "a";
        myArray[4] = "q";

        document.write(myArray.sort());

    // -->
    </script>
</body>
```

Listing 22-1: Displaying a sorted array.

7. Save the file and close it.

8. Open the file in a browser, and you should see a comma-separated list of elements sorted in alphabetical order, as in Figure 22-1.

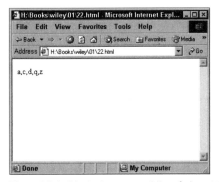

Figure 22-1: Displaying a sorted list of elements from the array.

cross-reference

▪ The techniques for creating an array are discussed in Task 20. Creating an array is the first step toward populating an array with values, which is the subject of Task 21.

Splitting a String at a Delimiter

In programming, it is not uncommon to deal with data represented in delimited lists. A *delimited list* is typically a string that contains a number of substrings separated by a specific character; each of the substrings is an element in the list.

For instance, the following string has three elements separated by commas:

```
"First element,Second element,Third element"
```

The `string` object provides the `split` method, which you can use to split a string into elements at a specified delimiter. These elements are then placed in an array, and that array is returned by the method.

For instance, consider the following:

```
var thisVar = "First element,Second element,Third element";
var anotherVar = thisVar.split(",");
```

`anotherVar` is now an array containing three elements.

The following task illustrates this by splitting a string containing a list into its component elements and then outputting those elements from the resulting array:

1. Open a new HTML document in your preferred HTML or text editor.

2. Create the body of the document with opening and closing `body` tags:

   ```
   <body>

   </body>
   ```

3. Insert a script block in the body of the document:

   ```
   <script language="JavaScript">
   <!--

   // -->
   </script>
   ```

4. Create a variable named `myVariable` and assign a comma-separated text string to it:

   ```
   var myVariable = "a,b,c,d";
   ```

note

- Notice in Step 8 that the letters have no spaces or other separators between them. This is because the `document.write` method does not insert any type of separator after the text it outputs, and you have not added any HTML to create the separation.

5. Use the split method to split the string at the commas and assign the resulting array to the variable `stringArray`:

```
var stringArray = myVariable.split(",");
```

6. Use the `document.write` method to output the elements of the array so that the final script looks like Listing 23-1.

```
<body>
    <script language="JavaScript">
    <!--

        var myVariable = "a,b,c,d";
        var stringArray = myVariable.split(",");

        document.write(stringArray[0]);
        document.write(stringArray[1]);
        document.write(stringArray[2]);
        document.write(stringArray[3]);

    // -->
    </script>
</body>
```

Listing 23-1: Splitting a list into an array.

7. Save the file and close it.

8. Open the file in a browser, and you should see the text "abcd", as in Figure 23-1.

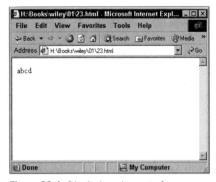

Figure 23-1: Displaying elements from an array built from a comma-separated list.

cross-reference

▪ The creation and population of arrays is discussed in Task 20 and 21.

Calling Functions

I n many tasks throughout the book, you will see examples of calling functions or methods. A *function* is a self-contained procedure or operation that you can invoke by name. In invoking it, you can provide data to the function (known as arguments), and then the function, in turn, can return a result based on its operations.

To call a function, you simply use the following form:

```
functionName(argument 1, argument 2, etc.);
```

If a function expects no arguments, you still need the parentheses:

```
functionName();
```

Also, if a function returns a value, you can use that function call wherever you would use any other text or numeric value. For instance, you can assign the value to a variable:

```
var variableName = functionName();
```

Similarly, you could use the results of one function as an argument to another function:

```
function1Name(function2Name());
```

The following task calls the JavaScript Escape function and then displays the results that are retuned in the browser:

1. Open a new HTML document in your preferred HTML or text editor.

2. Create the body of the document with opening and closing body tags:

   ```
   <body>

   </body>
   ```

3. Insert a script block in the body of the document:

   ```
   <body>
      <script language="JavaScript">
      <!--

      // -->
      </script>
   </body>
   ```

notes

- Methods are the same as functions except that they are associated with specific objects. Calling them and using them is technically the same.

- When embedding functions as the arguments to other functions, take care with the parentheses to make sure each opening parenthesis is closed by a closing one. A common mistake is to omit a closing parenthesis, which will cause errors in the browser and, at times, can be hard to identify when you try to debug you code.

- The Escape function takes a text string as an argument and returns it in URL-encoded format. In URL-encoded format, special characters that are invalid in URLs (such as spaces and some punctuation) are converted into special code.

4. Call the `Escape` function and pass a text string as an argument. Assign the string that is returned to the `myVariable` variable:

```
<head>
    <script language="JavaScript">
    <!--

        var myVariable = Escape("This is a test.");

    // -->
    </script>
</head>
```

5. Use the `document.write` method to output the value of `myVariable` so that the final script looks like Listing 24-1.

```
<body>
    <script language="JavaScript">
    <!--

        var myVariable = Escape("This is a test.");
        document.write(myVariable);

    // -->
    </script>
</body>
```

Listing 24-1: Escaping a text string.

6. Save the file and close it.

7. Open the file in a browser, and you should see the text string in its URL-encoded representation as in Figure 24-1.

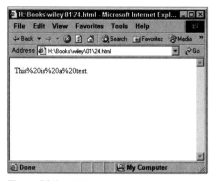

Figure 24-1: A URL-encoded text string.

Alerting the User

The `window` object provides the `alert` method, which allows you to display a simple dialog box containing a text message followed by a single button the user can use to acknowledge the message and close the dialog box.

Figure 25-1 illustrates an alert dialog box in Microsoft Internet Explorer; Figure 25-2 shows the same dialog box in Netscape.

notes

- The dialog boxes created by the `window.alert` method are quite generic and have clear indications that they come from the current Web page (Internet Explorer places its name in the title bar, and Netscape clearly says "JavaScript Application"). This is done for security: You can't pop up a dialog box with this method that represents itself as anything but the result of a JavaScript script running in the current page.

- When the alert dialog box displays (see Step 4), inter-action with the browser window is blocked until the user closes the dialog box by clicking the button in the dialog box.

Figure 25-1: An alert dialog box in Internet Explorer.

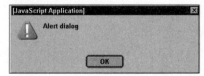

Figure 25-2: An alert dialog box in Netscape.

The following steps show how to display an alert dialog box:

1. Open a new HTML document in your preferred HTML or text editor.

2. Create the header of the document with opening and closing `header` tags:

   ```
   <head>

   </head>
   ```

3. Insert a script block in the header of the document:

```
<head>
   <script language="JavaScript">
   <!--

   // -->
   </script>
</head>
```

4. Call the `window.alert` method to display a message in a dialog box:

```
<head>
   <script language="JavaScript">
   <!--

      window.alert("Hello");

   // -->
   </script>
</head>
```

5. Save the file and close it.

6. Open the file in a browser, and you should see a dialog box like the one in Figure 25-3.

Figure 25-3: Displaying an alert dialog box.

cross-reference

- Alert dialog boxes are the simplest you can create with JavaScript. There is no real user interaction; there is just text and a single button for closing the dialog box. This makes them good for displaying messages to the user. The next task illustrates how to create a slightly more complicated dialog box with two buttons: one to accept and one to cancel.

Confirming with the User

notes

- The dialog boxes created by the window.confirm method are quite generic and have clear indications that they come from the current Web page (Internet Explorer places its name in the title bar and Netscape clearly says "JavaScript Application"). This is done for security: You can't pop up a dialog box with this method that represents itself as anything but the result of a JavaScript script running in the current page.

- The window.confirm method returns a value: true if the user clicks on OK or false if the user clicks on Cancel (see Step 4).

In addition to the alert method discussed in Task 25, the window object also provides the confirm method, which allows you to display a dialog box containing a text message followed by two buttons the user can use to acknowledge or reject the message and close the dialog box. Typically these buttons are labeled OK and Cancel.

Figure 26-1 illustrates a confirmation dialog box in Microsoft Internet Explorer; Figure 26-2 shows the same dialog box in Netscape.

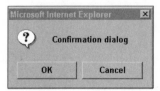

Figure 26-1: A confirmation dialog box in Internet Explorer.

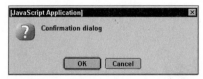

Figure 26-2: A confirmation dialog box in Netscape.

The following steps show how to display a confirmation dialog box and then display the user's selection in the browser:

1. Open a new HTML document in your preferred HTML or text editor.

2. Create the body of the document with opening and closing body tags:

```
<body>

</body>
```

3. Insert a script block in the body of the document:

```
<body>
    <script language="JavaScript">
    <!--

    // -->
    </script>
</body>
```

4. Call the `window.confirm` method to display a message in a dialog box; assign the selection of the user, which is returned by the method, to the `result` variable:

```
<body>
    <script language="JavaScript">
    <!--

        var result = window.confirm("Click OK to continue");

    // -->
    </script>
</body>
```

5. Save the file and close it.

6. Open the file in a browser, and you should see a dialog box like the one in Figure 26-3.

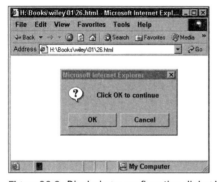

Figure 26-3: Displaying a confirmation dialog box.

7. If you click on OK, you should see "true" in the browser window as in Figure 26-4.

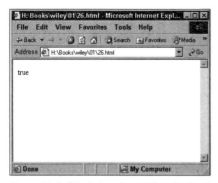

Figure 26-4: Displaying the user's selection in the browser window.

cross-reference

- Confirmation dialog boxes only provide primitive user interaction; they don't let users enter any data. Task 117 illustrates how to create a slightly more complicated dialog box with a text entry field for the user to enter data.

Creating Your Own Functions

Not only does JavaScript have a large body of built-in functions and methods, it also allows you to create your own functions. Creating a function is fairly straightforward:

```
function functionName() {
    Your function code goes here
}
```

The code in the function can be any valid JavaScript code that you would use elsewhere in your scripts.

The following task creates a function that outputs "Hello" to the browser and the proceeds to call that function in order to display the text:

1. Open a new HTML document in your preferred HTML or text editor.

2. Create the header of the document with opening and closing `head` tags:

   ```
   <head>

   </head>
   ```

3. Insert a script block in the header of the document:

   ```
   <script language="JavaScript">
   <!--

   // -->
   </script>
   ```

4. Create a function named `hello` that takes no arguments:

   ```
   function head() {

   }
   ```

5. In the function, use `document.write` to output "Hello" to the browser:

   ```
   document.write("Hello");
   ```

6. Create the body of the document with opening and closing `body` tags:

   ```
   <body>

   </body>
   ```

7. Insert a script block in the body of the document:

```
<script language="JavaScript">
<!--

// -->
</script>
```

8. In the script block, call the `hello` function so that the final page looks like Listing 27-1.

```
<head>
    <script language="JavaScript">
    <!--

        function head() {
            document.write("Hello");
        }

    // -->
    </script>
</head>

<body>
    <script language="JavaScript">
    <!--

        hello();

    // -->
    </script>
</body>
```

Listing 27-1: Creating and calling your own function.

9. Save the file.

10. Open the file in a browser, and you should see "Hello" in the browser.

cross-reference

▪ Functions perform operations on data and return the results of those operations. That means you will want to pass data to your functions (this is outlined in Task 28) and return the results of the function's processing (this is outlined in Task 29).

28 Passing an Argument to Your Functions

Task 27 showed you how to create a function, but the function created in that task did not accept any arguments. To create a function that accepts arguments, you must specify names for each argument in the argument definition:

```
function functionName(argumentName1,argumentName2,etc.) {
   Your function code goes here
}
```

The following task creates a function that accepts a single numeric argument, squares that number, and outputs the result:

1. Open a new HTML document in your preferred HTML or text editor.

2. Create the header of the document with opening and closing head tags:

   ```
   <head>

   </head>
   ```

3. Insert a script block in the header of the document:

   ```
   <script language="JavaScript">
   <!--

   // -->
   </script>
   ```

4. Create a function named `square` that takes one argument named number:

   ```
   function square(number) {

   }
   ```

5. In the function, square the number and assign the results to a variable, and then use `document.write` to output that result:

   ```
   var result = number * number;
   document.write(result);
   ```

6. Create the body of the document with opening and closing body tags:

   ```
   <body>

   </body>
   ```

7. Insert a script block in the body of the document:

```
<script language="JavaScript">
<!--

// -->
</script>
```

8. In the script block, call the `square` function and pass in a value of 100 so that the final page looks like Listing 28-1.

```
<head>
    <script language="JavaScript">
    <!--

        function square(number) {

            var result = number * number;
            document.write(result);

        }

    // -->
    </script>
</head>

<body>
    <script language="JavaScript">
    <!--

        square(100);

    // -->
    </script>
</body>
```

Listing 28-1: Creating and calling your own function with a single argument.

9. Save the file.

10. Open the file in a browser, and you should see 10000 in the browser.

tips

- The argument names in the introductory paragraph should appear in the order in which the arguments will be provided when the function is being called. The list of names essentially creates variables accessible only inside the function, and it is through these variables that you can access and work with the argument data provided when the function is called.

- To make effective use of functions, you need to be sensitive to the logic of your application. Functions are useful for encapsulating program logic that you will repeat multiple times. For instance, if you will be squaring numbers at several points in your script, you might want to consider a function for squaring numbers. If you do this in only one place, a function is not necessary.

Returning Values from Your Functions

In Task 28, you created a function that squares numbers and then outputs the result.

The problem with this function is that it isn't very practical. Instead of outputting the result of the operation, what you really want to do is return the result so that the result can be assigned to a variable or used in a mathematical expression.

To do this, you use the `return` command as the last command in a function:

```
function functionName() {
    some code
    return value;
}
```

To illustrate this, the following task creates a function for squaring numbers that returns the result instead of outputting it. The function is then called, the result is stored in a variable, and then that variable is used to output the results:

1. Open a new HTML document in your preferred HTML or text editor.

2. Create the header of the document with opening and closing `head` tags:

   ```
   <head>

   </head>
   ```

3. Insert a script block in the header of the document:

   ```
   <script language="JavaScript">
   <!--

   // -->
   </script>
   ```

4. Create a function named `square` that takes one argument named

   ```
   function square(number) {

   }
   ```

5. In the function, square the number and assign the results to a variable; then use `return` to return that result:

   ```
   var result = number * number;
   return result;
   ```

6. Create the body of the document with opening and closing body tags:

```
<body>

</body>
```

7. Insert a script block in the body of the document:

```
<script language="JavaScript">
<!--

// -->
</script>
```

8. In the script block, call the square function, pass in a value of 10, and assign the results to the variable mySquare. Next, output that with document.write so that the final page looks like Listing 29-1.

```
<head>
   <script language="JavaScript">
   <!--

      function square(number) {

         var result = number * number;
         return result;

      }

   // -->
   </script>
</head>

<body>
   <script language="JavaScript">
   <!--

      var mySquare = square(10);
      document.write(mySquare);

   // -->
   </script>
</body>
```

Listing 29-1: Creating and calling your own function, which returns a result.

9. Save the file.

10. Open the file in a browser, and you should see 100 in the browser.

tip

▪ To make effective use of functions, you need to be sensitive to the logic of your application. Functions are useful for encapsulating program logic that you will repeat multiple times. For instance, if you will be squaring numbers at several points in your script, you might want to consider a function for squaring numbers. If you do this in only one place, a function is not necessary.

Passing Multiple Parameters to Your Functions

In Tasks 28 and 29, you created functions that took single arguments. You also can create functions that take multiple arguments. To do so, you must specify names for each argument in the argument definition:

```
function functionName(argumentName1,argumentName2,etc.) {
   Your function code goes here
}
```

The following task creates a function that accepts two numeric arguments, multiplies them, and returns the result:

1. Open a new HTML document in your preferred HTML or text editor.

2. Create the header of the document with opening and closing head tags:

    ```
    <head>

    </head>
    ```

3. Insert a script block in the header of the document:

    ```
    <script language="JavaScript">
    <!--

    // -->
    </script>
    ```

4. Create a function named multiple that takes two arguments named number1 and number2:

    ```
    function multiple(number1,number2) {

    }
    ```

5. In the function, multiply the numbers and assign the results to a variable; then use return to output that result:

    ```
    var result = number1 * number2;
    return result;
    ```

note
- These names should be in the order in which the arguments will be provided when the function is being called. The list of names essentially creates variables accessible only inside the function, and it is through these variables that you can access and work with the argument data provided when the function is called.

6. Create the body of the document with opening and closing body tags.

7. Insert a script block in the body of the document.

8. In the script block, call the multiply function and pass in the values 10 and 20; assign the result that is returned to a variable, and then output that variable so that the final page looks like Listing 30-1.

```
<head>
    <script language="JavaScript">
    <!--

        function multiple(number1,number2) {

            var result = number1 * number2;
            return result;

        }

    // -->
    </script>
</head>

<body>
    <script language="JavaScript">
    <!--

        var result = multiply(10,20);
        document.write(result);

    // -->
    </script>
</body>
```

Listing 30-1: Creating and calling your own function with multiple arguments.

9. Save the file.

10. Open the file in a browser, and you should see 200 in the browser.

Calling Functions from Tags

One of the benefits of JavaScript is to be able to tie interactivity to elements of the HTML page. One way you can do this is to set up links in HTML that actually trigger calls to JavaScript functions when the link is clicked.

There are two ways to do this:

1. Use the `onClick` attribute of the a tag to call the function:

```
<a href="#" onClick="functionName()">Link text</a>
```

2. Use a `javascript:` URL in the `href` attribute of the a tag to call the function:

```
<a href="javascript:functionName()">Link text</a>
```

The following task illustrates these two methods of calling a function from a link by creating a function that displays an alert dialog box to the user and then providing two separate links for the user to use to call the function:

1. Open a new HTML document in your preferred HTML or text editor.

2. Create the header of the document with opening and closing head tags:

```
<head>

</head>
```

3. Insert a script block in the header of the document:

```
<script language="JavaScript">
<!--

// -->
</script>
```

4. Create a function named `hello` that takes no arguments:

```
function hello() {

}
```

5. In the function, use the `window.alert` method to display an alert dialog box:

```
window.alert("Hello");
```

notes

- `onClick` is an event handler; this means it specified JavaScript code to execute when an event occurs. In this case, the event that must occur is the click event: The user must click on the link.

- The question of which technique to use really depends on your circumstance and needs. For instance, with `onClick` you can also specify a URL to follow when the link is clicked so the JavaScript can be executed and then the link will be followed. You can't do that with the `javascript:` URL approach.

6. Create the body of the document with opening and closing body tags.

7. In the final page create two links that call the hello function using onClick and the javascript: URL techniques so that the final page looks like Listing 31-1.

```
<head>
    <script language="JavaScript">
    <!--

        function hello() {

            window.alert("Hello");

        }

    // -->
    </script>
</head>

<body>

    <a href="#" onClick="hello();">Call hello() from ⤷
onClick.</a>⤷
    <br>⤷
    <a href="javascript:hello();">Cal hello() from href.</a>

</body>
```

Listing 31-1: Calling a function from a link.

8. Save the file.

9. Open the file in a browser, and you should see two links in the browser.

10. Click on either link and you should see a dialog box.

cross-reference

• The process of creating functions is discussed in Tasks 27 to 30.

Calling Your JavaScript Code after the Page Has Loaded

Sometimes you will want to execute JavaScript code only once the HTML page has fully loaded.

Doing this requires two steps:

1. Place the code you want to execute after the page has completed loading into a function.

2. Use the `onLoad` attribute of the `body` tag to call the function.

This results in code like the following:

```
<head>
   <script language="JavaScript">
      function functionName() {
         Code to execute when the page finishes loading
      }
   </script>
</head>

<body onLoad="functionName();">
   Body of the page
</body>
```

The following task creates a function that displays a welcome message in a dialog box and then only invokes that function once the page has completed loading:

1. Open a new HTML document in your preferred HTML or text editor.

2. Create the header of the document with opening and closing head tags.

3. Insert a script block in the header of the document:

```
<head>
   <script language="JavaScript">
   <!--

   // -->
   </script>
</head>
```

note

- In Step 7 `onLoad` is an event handler; this means it specified JavaScript code to execute when an event occurs. In this case, the event that must occur is the completion of loading of the document.

4. Create a function named `hello` that takes no arguments:

```
function hello() {

}
```

5. In the function, use the `window.alert` method to display an alert dialog box:

```
window.alert("Hello");
```

6. Create the body of the document with opening and closing body tags.

7. In the `body` tag, use the `onLoad` attribute to call the `hello` function:

```
<body onLoad="hello();">
```

8. In the body of the page, place any HTML or text that you want in the page so that the final page looks like Listing 32-1.

```
<head>
    <script language="JavaScript">
    <!--

        function hello() {

            window.alert("Hello");

        }

    // -->
    </script>
</head>

<body onLoad="hello();">

    The page's content.

</body>
```

Listing 32-1: Using `onLoad` to call a function after the page loads.

9. Save the file.

10. Open the file in a browser, and you should see the page's content, as well as the alert dialog box.

tip

- You might want to wait for a page to load before executing your code, because your code relies on certain page elements being rendered or just because you don't want a certain effect to occur too early.

Using for **Loops**

Sometimes you will not want your code to proceed in a straight, linear fashion. In these situations you will want to make use of flow control techniques to adjust the way that the processing of your code proceeds. One such technique is *looping*, which allows you to specify that a section of code repeats one or more times before proceeding with the rest of your script.

Typically, loops are created with a for statement:

```
for (conditions controlling the loop) command
```

The command, of course, can be a single command or multiple commands combined with curly brackets:

```
for (conditions controlling the loop) {
   JavaScript command
   JavaScript command
   etc.
}
```

Typically, for loops use an index variable to count, and on each iteration of the loop, the index variable's value changes (usually incrementing) until the index variable reaches some limit value. For instance, the following loop counts from 1 to 10 using the variable i as the index variable:

```
for (i = 1; i <= 10; i ++) {
   Code to execute in the loop
}
```

Condition controlling the loop breaks down into three parts separated by semicolons:

1. The first part specifies the initial value of the index variable. This will be the value on the first iteration of the loop.

2. The second part specifies the condition that the index variable must meet for the next iteration of the loop to occur. Basically, this test occurs before each iteration of the loop, including the first.

3. The third part indicates how to change the value of the index variable at the end of each iteration of the loop. In this case, the index variable is incremented by one.

Inside the body of the loop, the index variable is available and will contain the appropriate value for the current iteration.

To illustrate this, the following steps use a `for` loop to count from 1 to 10 and display the numbers to the browser:

1. Create a new HTML document in your preferred editor.

2. In the body of the document, create a script block.

3. In the script block, create a `for` loop:

   ```
   for () {

   }
   ```

4. Use the appropriate conditions to count from 1 to 10 in the loop, using `i` as the index variable:

   ```
   for (i = 1; i <= 10; i++) {

   }
   ```

5. In the loop, display the current value of the index variable followed by a `br` tag so each number displays in a separate line in the browser. The final page should look like Listing 33-1.

   ```
   <body>
       <script>
       <!--

           for (i = 1; i <= 10; i++) {

               document.write(i + "<br>");

           }

       // -->
       </script>
   </body>
   ```

   Listing 33-1: Using a `for` loop.

6. Save the file and close it.

7. Open the file in a browser, and you should see the numbers 1 to 10 on separate lines.

cross-references

* Loop-based flow control, such as that created with a `for` loop, is not the only type of flow control. Another type of flow control is conditional branching, such as is illustrated in Task 34.

* The loops created with the `for` command are typically called *index-based loops*. Another form of looping is *condition-based looping*, which is discussed in Task 36.

Testing Conditions with `if`

As mentioned in the previous task, sometimes you will not want your code to proceed in a straight, linear fashion. In these situations you will want to make use of flow control techniques to adjust the way that processing of your code proceeds. One such technique is *conditional branching looping*, which allows you to specify that a certain section of code executes only when a certain condition exists.

Conditional branching is performed with the `if` statement:

```
if (condition) command
```

The command, of course, can be a single command or multiple commands combined with curly brackets:

```
if (condition) {
   JavaScript command
   JavaScript command
   etc.
}
```

To illustrate the effective use of `if` statements, the following presents a dialog box asking the user to click on OK or Cancel, and then tests the user's response and displays an appropriate message in the browser window:

1. Create a new HTML document in your preferred editor.

2. In the body of the document, create a script block.

3. In the script block, use the `window.confirm` method to ask the user to click on OK or Cancel and to store the result in a variable named `userChoice`.

    ```
    var userChoice = window.confirm("Choose OK or ⤶
    Cancel");
    ```

4. Create an `if` statement to test if the value of `userChoice` is `true`. If it is, the user has clicked on OK, and you need to display an appropriate message in the browser:

    ```
    if (userChoice == true) {
       document.write("OK");
    }
    ```

5. Create an `if` statement to test if the value of `userChoice` is `false`. If it is, the user has clicked on Cancel, and you need to display an

appropriate message in the browser. The final page should look like Listing 34-1.

```
<body>
   <script>
   <!--

       var userChoice = window.confirm("Choose OK or ⤶
Cancel");

       if (userChoice == true) {
          document.write("OK");
       }

       if (userChoice == false) {
          document.write("Cancel");
       }

   // -->
   </script>
</body>
```

Listing 34-1: Using `window.confirm`.

6. Save the file and close it.

7. Open the file in a browser. You should see a confirmation dialog box like the one in Figure 34-1.

Figure 34-1: Letting the user choose between OK and Cancel.

8. Click on OK or Cancel, and an appropriate message should display in the browser window.

cross-reference

- Refer to Task 26 for a discussion of the `window.confirm` method.

Using Short-Form Condition Testing

JavaScript provides a short-form method of testing a condition and then returning a value based on that condition. It is useful when you want to assign a value to a variable: If a condition is true, it gets one value; otherwise, it gets another value.

This type of short-cut evaluation and assignment looks like the following:

```
var myVar = (condition) ? value to assign if condition is true : ↵
value to assign if condition is false;
```

note

- The `window.confirm` method returns `true` if the user clicks on OK and `false` if the user clicks on Cancel.

The key syntactical components of this are as follows:

- The condition must evaluate to true or false just like for an `if` statement (as mentioned in Task 34).

- The question mark indicates this is short-form condition testing.

- The colon separates the value to return if the condition is true from the value to return in a false condition. The value for true is always on the left of the colon.

To illustrate effective use of short-form condition testing, the following presents a dialog box asking the user to click on OK or Cancel and stores the choice in a variable. Based on that a second variable is created with an output message dependant on the user's choice; this is done with short-form testing. Finally, the message is displayed to the user.

1. Create a new HTML document in your preferred editor.

2. In the body of the document, create a script block.

3. In the script block, use the `window.confirm` method to ask the user to click on OK or Cancel and store the result in a variable named `userChoice`:

   ```
   var userChoice = window.confirm("Choose OK or ↵
   Cancel");
   ```

4. Use short-form condition testing on the value of `userChoice` to assign either `"OK"` or `"Cancel"` to a new variable called `result`:

   ```
   var result = (userChoice == true) ? "OK" : "Cancel";
   ```

5. Display the value of result so that the final page looks like
    Listing 35-1.

```
<body>
   <script>
   <!--

      var userChoice = window.confirm("Choose OK or ↵
Cancel");

      var result = (userChoice == true) ? "OK" : "Cancel";

      document.write(result);

   // -->
   </script>
</body>
```

Listing 35-1: Using short-form conditional testing.

6. Save the file and close it.

7. Open the file in a browser. You should see a confirmation dialog box.

8. Click on OK or Cancel, and an appropriate message should display
    in the browser window. Figure 35-1 shows the message that appears
    when the user clicks on Cancel.

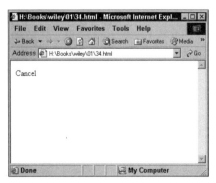

Figure 35-1: Clicking on Cancel.

cross-reference

▪ You could achieve results
identical to the introductory
source code with an if
statement (discussed in
Task 34). This is just a
more compact way to make
a decision when assigning
a value.

Looping on a Condition

In Task 33 you saw an example of a for loop; this loop was used for counting. Another useful type of loop is a conditional loop. The form of the loop is simple:

```
while (condition) command
```

The command, of course, can be a single command or multiple commands combined with curly brackets so that you get the following:

```
while (condition) {
   JavaScript command
   JavaScript command
   etc.
}
```

This task illustrates this by repeatedly presenting a dialog box asking the user to click OK or Cancel until such a time as the user clicks on OK:

1. Create a new HTML document in your preferred editor.

2. In the body of the document, create a script block.

3. In the script block, use the window.confirm method to ask the user to click on OK or Cancel, and store the result in a variable named result:

```
var result = window.confirm("Choose OK or Cancel");
```

4. Create a while loop:

```
while () {

}
```

5. As the condition for the loop, test if the user clicked on Cancel by comparing result to false:

```
while (result == false) {

}
```

6. Inside the loop, call window.confirm again, and save the user's selection in result:

```
while (result == false) {

   result = window.confirm("Choose OK or Cancel");

}
```

notes

- A conditional loop continues as long as a single condition is true; once the condition becomes false, the loop ends.

- The condition must evaluate to true or false. Before each iteration of the loop, the condition is tested; if it is true, another iteration of the loop happens. Otherwise, the looping stops.

7. After the loop, output a message indicating the user finally clicked on OK. The final page should look like Listing 36-1.

```
<body>
   <script>
   <!--

      var result = window.confirm("Choose OK or Cancel");

      while (result == false) {

         result = window.confirm("Choose OK or Cancel");

      }

      document.write("You finally chose OK!");

   // -->
   </script>
</body>
```

Listing 36-1: Using a conditional loop.

8. Save the file and close it.

9. Open the file in a browser. You should see a confirmation dialog box.

10. The dialog box will keep reappearing until the user clicks on OK, and then a message will be displayed in the browser as illustrated in Figure 36-1.

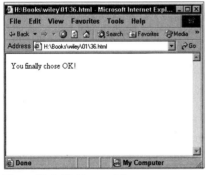

Figure 36-1: Clicking on OK.

Task

Task 37

Looping through an Array

Task 22 introduced the notion of an array: a set of numbered containers for storing values. Sometimes you will want to be able to loop through each element in the array. This can be done using a `for` loop so that the index variable of the loop matches one of the array indexes for each iteration through the loop. `for` loops were illustrated in Task 33.

To do this, you want to be able to dynamically determine the length of the array so that you can set the conditions for the `for` loop. You do this with the `length` property of the array object. The following loop, for instance, loops through each of the indexes from the `myArray` array:

```
for (i = 0; i < myArray.length; i++)
```

The following task creates an array and then loops through it to display each element of the array in the browser window:

1. Create a new HTML document in your preferred editor.

2. In the body of the document, create a script block:

```
<body>
    <script>
    <!--

    // -->
    </script>
</body>
```

3. In the script block, create a new three-element array named `myArray`:

```
var myArray = new Array(3);
```

4. Populate the elements of the array:

```
myArray[0] = "Item 0";
myArray[1] = "Item 1";
myArray[2] = "Item 2";
```

5. Create a `for` loop to loop through the array:

```
for (i = 0; i < myArray.length; i++) {

}
```

notes

- Notice that you start counting at 1. This is because the first index is 0 in any array. Similarly, you test for `i` being less than (not less than or equal to) the length of the array. This is because if the length of the array is 5, then the last index is 4. If you tested for being less than or equal to the length of the array, then the loop would count to 5 and not stop at 4 as it should.

- Notice in Step 6 the use of the variable `i` for the index of `myArray` in the loop. This works because `i` is being used to count through valid index values for the loop.

6. In the loop, display the current element of the array to the browser
    window with `document.write`. The final page should look like
    Listing 37-1.

```
<body>
   <script>
   <!--

      var myArray = new Array(3);
      myArray[0] = "Item 0";
      myArray[1] = "Item 1";
      myArray[2] = "Item 2";

      for (i = 0; i < myArray.length; i++) {
         document.write(myArray[i] + "<br>");
      }

   // -->
   </script>
</body>
```

Listing 37-1: Looping through an array.

7. Save the file and close it.

8. Open the file in a browser, and a list of the elements should be dis-
    played as in Figure 37-1.

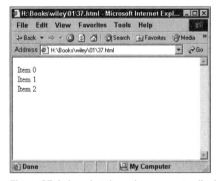

Figure 37-1: Looping through an array to display its elements.

cross-reference

▪ The `document.write`
method, which is used to
display output to the
browser, is covered in
Task 9.

Scheduling a Function for Future Execution

Sometimes you will want to execute a function in an automated, scheduled way. JavaScript provides the ability to schedule execution of a function at a specified time in the future. When the appointed time arrives, the function automatically executes without any user intervention.

Scheduling is done with the `window.setTimeout` method:

```
window.setTimeout("function to execute",schedule time);
```

The function to execute is specified as if you were calling the function normally but in a text string; the text string contains the actual text of the command to execute. The schedule time specifies the number of milliseconds to wait before executing the function. For instance, if you want to wait 10 seconds before executing the function, you need to specify 10000 milliseconds.

To illustrate this, the following script creates a function that displays an alert dialog box and then schedules it to execute five second later:

1. Create a new HTML document in your preferred editor.

2. In the header of the document, create a script block:

```
<head>
   <script>
   <!--

   // -->
   </script>
</head>
```

3. In the script block, create a function named `hello` that takes no arguments:

```
<head>
   <script>
   <!--

      function hello() {

      }

   // -->
   </script>
</head>
```

note

■ The argument specifying the function to execute should be specified as a text string, and the string should include the complete call to the function including any arguments being passed to the function.

4. In the function, use `window.alert` to display a dialog box:

```
<head>
   <script>
   <!--

      function hello() {
          window.alert("Hello");
      }

   // -->
   </script>
</head>
```

5. After the function, schedule the function to execute five seconds in the future:

```
<head>
   <script>
   <!--

      function hello() {
          window.alert("Hello");
      }

      window.setTimeout("hello()",5000);

   // -->
   </script>
</head>
```

6. Save the file and close it.

7. Open the file in a browser. Wait five seconds, and then an alert dialog box should appear, as in Figure 38-1.

Figure 38-1: Scheduling a function to execute.

cross-reference

▪ The process of creating functions is discussed in Tasks 27 to 30.

Scheduling a Function for Recurring Execution

Task 38 showed you how to schedule a function for a single automatic execution in the future. But what if you wanted to schedule the same function to execute repeatedly at set intervals?

To do this, you need to do two things:

- As the last command in the function, use `window.setTimeout` to reschedule the function execute again.
- Use `window.setTimeout` outside the function to schedule initial execution of the function.

The results look something like this:

```
function functionName() {
    some JavaScript code
    window.setTimeout("functionName()",schedule time);
}
window.setTimeout("functionName()",schedule time);
```

To illustrate this, the following script creates a function that displays an alert dialog box and then schedules it to execute every five seconds:

1. Create a new HTML document in your preferred editor.

2. In the header of the document, create a script block.

3. In the script block, create a function named `hello` that takes no arguments:

   ```
   function hello() {

   }
   ```

4. In the function use `window.alert` to display a dialog box:

   ```
   function hello() {
       window.alert("Hello");
   }
   ```

5. Complete the function by using `window.setTimeout` to schedule the function to run every five seconds:

   ```
   function hello() {
       window.alert("Hello");
       window.setTimeout("hello()",5000);
   }
   ```

note

- The alert dialog boxes will appear every five seconds indefinitely (see Step 8). To get out of this, simply close the browser window in one of the intervals between dialog boxes.

6. After the function, schedule the function to execute five seconds in the future. The final page should look like Listing 39-1.

```
<head>
   <script>
   <!--

      function hello() {
         window.alert("Hello");
         window.setTimeout("hello()",5000);
      }

      window.setTimeout("hello()",5000);

   // -->
   </script>
</head>
```

Listing 39-1: Scheduling a function to execute.

7. Save the file and close it.

8. Open the file in a browser. Wait five seconds, and then an alert dialog box should appear, as in Figure 39-1. After you close the dialog box, another should reappear after five seconds. This should continue indefinitely.

Figure 39-1: Scheduling a function to execute.

cross-reference

▪ Task 25 discusses the use of the `window.alert` method to display dialog boxes.

Canceling a Scheduled Function

In Task 38 you saw how to schedule a function for future execution using `window.setTimeout`. Using a related method, `window.clearTimeout`, you can cancel a scheduled execution event before it occurs.

When you create a scheduled event, the `window.setTimeout` method returns a pointer to that event. You can then use the pointer to cancel the scheduled event. You simply pass that pointer to `window.clearTimeout`:

```
var pointer = window.setTimeout(...);
window.clearTimeout(pointer);
```

The following task illustrates this by creating a function and scheduling it to execute five seconds after the page loads, but then immediately canceling that scheduled execution so that nothing happens:

1. Create a new HTML document in your preferred editor.

2. In the header of the document, create a script block:

   ```
   <head>
       <script>
       <!--

       // -->
       </script>
   </head>
   ```

3. In the script block, create a function named `hello` that takes no arguments:

   ```
   function hello() {

   }
   ```

4. In the function use `window.alert` to display a dialog box:

   ```
   window.alert("Hello");
   ```

5. After the function, schedule the function to execute five seconds in the future, and save the pointer in a variable:

   ```
   var myTimeout = window.setTimeout("hello()",5000);
   ```

Task **40**

6. Cancel the scheduled event so that the final page looks like Listing 40-1.

```
<head>
    <script>
    <!--

        function hello() {
            window.alert("Hello");
        }

        var myTimeout = window.setTimeout("hello()",5000);
        window.clearTimeout(myTimeout);

    // -->
    </script>
</head>
```

Listing 40-1: Canceling a scheduled event.

7. Save the file and close it.

8. Open the file in a browser. Nothing should appear except a blank browser window, as in Figure 40-1.

Figure 40-1: Scheduling a function to execute and then canceling it.

41 **Adding Multiple Scripts to a Page**

JavaScript integrates into your HTML documents in a flexible way. In fact, there is nothing preventing you from having multiple script blocks wherever you need them in the header and body of your document. The script blocks will be processed by the browser in order with the rest of the HTML in the page.

The following task illustrates two script blocks in a single document:

1. Create a new HTML document.

2. In the body of the document, create a script block:

```
<body>
   <script language="JavaScript">
   <!--

   // -->
   </script>
</body>
```

3. In the script block, output some text with `document.write`:

```
document.write("The first script");
```

4. After the script block, place some regular HTML code:

```
<hr>
```

5. Create another script block:

```
<script language="JavaScript">
<!--

// -->
</script>
```

6. In the second script block, output some more text so that the final page looks like Listing 41-1.

7. Save the file and close it.

```
<body>
   <script language="JavaScript">
   <!--

      document.write("The first script");

   // -->
   </script>

   <hr>

   <script language="JavaScript">
   <!--

      document.write("The second script");

   // -->
   </script>
</body>
```

Listing 41-1: Multiple scripts in a page.

8. Open the file in a browser. You should see the results of both scripts, as illustrated in Figure 41-1.

Figure 41-1: Using multiple script blocks.

tip

- You can actually include more than two script blocks in a page; there is no limit. The limits are practical more than anything else. Ideally, you want to group as much of your code together as possible in the header of your document in functions. Having lots of script blocks makes it harder to follow the logic of your application and debug and manage your code.

cross-reference

- All scripts need to be contained in a script block. Task 1 introduces the creation and use of a script block.

Calling Your JavaScript Code after the Page Has Loaded

Sometimes you will want to execute JavaScript code only when the user tries to leave your page. You might want to do this because you want to bid the user farewell or remind the user he or she is leaving your site.

note

• onUnload is an event handler; this means it specified JavaScript code to execute when an event occurs. In this case, the event that must occur is the user navigating to another page.

Doing this requires two steps:

• Place the code you want to execute after the page has completed loading into a function.

• Use the onUnload attribute of the body tag to call the function.

This results in code like the following:

```
<head>
   <script language="JavaScript">
      function functionName() {
         Code to execute when the page finishes loading
      }
   </script>
</head>

<body onUnload="functionName();">
   Body of the page
</body>
```

The following task creates a function that displays a goodbye message in a dialog box and then only invokes that function when the user leaves the page:

1. Open a new HTML document in your preferred HTML or text editor.

2. Create the header of the document with opening and closing head tags.

3. Insert a script block in the header of the document.

4. Create a function named bye that takes no arguments:

```
function bye() {

}
```

5. In the function, use the `window.alert` method to display an alert dialog box:

```
window.alert("Farewell");
```

6. Create the body of the document with opening and closing body tags.

7. In the body tag, use the `onUnload` attribute to call the bye function:

```
<body onUnload="bye();">
```

8. In the body of the page, place any HTML or text that you want in the page so that the final page looks like Listing 42-1.

```
<head>
    <script language="JavaScript">
    <!--

        function bye() {

            window.alert("Farewell");

        }

    // -->
    </script>
</head>

<body onUnload="bye();">

    The page's content.

</body>
```

Listing 42-1: Using `onUnload` to call a function after the user leaves a page.

9. Save the file.

10. Open the file in a browser, and you should see the page's content. Navigate to another site and you should see the farewell dialog box.

Check If Java Is Enabled with JavaScript

note

- Why might you want to test if Java is enabled in the browser? One reason would be if you plan to output HTML code to embed a Java applet in the browser: By testing first, you could output alternate HTML if the browser doesn't support Java.

Sometimes it is useful to know whether or not Java is enabled and to use that information in composing your pages. For instance, based on that information, you could dynamically adjust the content of your page to include or not include Java-based content.

Luckily, JavaScript provides a simple mechanism for determining this: the `navigator.javaEnabled` method. This method returns `true` if Java is enabled in the browser and `false` otherwise.

The following task displays a message in the browser window indicating whether or not Java is enabled:

1. Create a new HTML document.

2. In the body of the document, create a script block:

```
<body>
   <script language="JavaScript">
   <!--

   // -->
   </script>
</body>
```

3. In the script block, call `navigator.javaEnabled` and assign the results to a variable:

```
<body>
   <script language="JavaScript">
   <!--

      var haveJava = navigator.javaEnabled();

   // -->
   </script>
</body>
```

4. Use `document.write` to display a relevant message to the user:

```
<body>
    <script language="JavaScript">
    <!--

        var haveJava = navigator.javaEnabled();
        document.write("Java is enabled: " + haveJava);

    // -->
    </script>
</body>
```

5. Save the file and close it.

6. Open the file in a browser. You should see an appropriate message based on the Java status in your browser. In Figure 43-1, Java is enabled.

Figure 43-1: Testing if Java is enabled.

cross-reference

▪ As an example of a case where it might be useful to test if Java is enabled, see Task 243, which uses Java to obtain the IP address of the user's computer.

Part 2: Outputting to the Browser

Accessing the document Object

The document object is an extremely powerful and important object in JavaScript that allows you to output data to the browser's document stream, as well as to access elements in the current document rendered in the browser. Using this object, you can generate dynamic output in your document, and you can manipulate the state of the document once rendered. The document object provides a lot of information, methods, and access to objects reflecting the current document, including the following:

- Arrays containing anchors, applets, embedded objects, forms, layers, links, and plug-ins from the current document.

- Properties providing information about the current page, including link colors, page background color, associated cookies, the domain of the page, the modification date, the referring document, the title, and the URL of the current document.

- Methods to allow outputting text to the document stream, events to handle events, and an event to return text currently selected in the document.

The following example illustrates a simple use of the document object by displaying the domain of the current page in a dialog box:

1. Create a script block with opening and closing script tags:

```
<script language="JavaScript">

</script>
```

2. Assign the current URL to a temporary variable called myURL with the following command:

```
<script language="JavaScript">

   var myURL = document.URL;

</script>
```

note

- The window.alert method takes a single string as an argument; the string should be the message you want to be displayed in the dialog box. In this case, the URL of the current document is what you want to display, and this has been placed in the myURL variable so you can just pass that variable as an argument to the method.

3. Include the `window.alert` method to display a dialog box:

```
<script language="JavaScript">

   var myURL = document.URL;
   window.alert();

</script>
```

4. Pass the `myURL` variable to `window.alert` as its argument so that the final script looks like Listing 44-1.

```
<script language="JavaScript">

   var myURL = document.URL;
   window.alert(myURL);

</script>
```

Listing 44-1: A script to display the current URL.

5. Save the script in an HTML file, and open the HTML in your browser. You should see a dialog box like Figure 44-1.

Figure 44-1: Displaying the current URL in a dialog box.

cross-references

- The creation of variables, including the appropriate selection of variable names, is discussed in Task 10.

- The `window.alert` method displays a dialog box with a single text message and a single button to dismiss the dialog box. This method is discussed in Task 25.

Outputting Dynamic HTML

Whenever you need to output dynamic HTML content into your document stream, you can do this using the `document.write` method. This method allows you to specify any text to be included in the document stream rendered by the browser.

The concept is simple. Consider the following simple partial HTML document:

```
<p>The following value is dynamic output from JavaScript:</p>
<script language="JavaScript">
    document.write("<p><strong>Dynamic Content</strong></p>");
</script>
<p>Thus ends the dynamic output example.</p>
```

The result is that the browser will render output as if the following plain HTML source code had been sent to the browser:

```
<p>The following value is dynamic output from JavaScript:</p>
<p><strong>Dynamic Content</strong></p>
<p>Thus ends the dynamic output example.</p>
```

Using the `document.write` method, you can output any dynamic strings generated in HTML to the document stream. The following example outputs the referring page, the domain of the current document, and the URL of the current document using properties of the `document` object to obtain those values:

1. Start a script block with the `script` tag:

   ```
   <script language="JavaScript">
   ```

2. Display an introductory message using `document.write`:

   ```
   document.write("<p>Here's some information about this ⤵
   document:</p>");
   ```

3. Output a `ul` tag to start an unordered list:

   ```
   document.write("<ul>");
   ```

4. Output the referring document as a list entry:

   ```
   document.write("<li>Referring Document: " + ⤵
   document.referrer + "</li>");
   ```

notes

- In this task you see uses of concatenation. *Concatenation* is the act of combining one or more strings into one long string using the + operator.

- The `document.write` method takes a single argument. This argument must be a string. The concatenation operation used in Steps 4 and 5 evaluates down to a single string so the entire concatenation expression can be passed as an argument to `document.write`.

5. Output the domain of the current document as a list entry:

```
document.write("<li>Domain: " + document.domain + ⤵
"</li>");
```

6. Output the URL of the current document as a list entry:

```
document.write("<li>URL: " + document.URL + "</li>");
```

7. Close the script by outputting a closing ul tag; the resulting script should look like Listing 45-1.

```
<script language="JavaScript">
    document.write("<p>Here's some information about this ⤵
document:</p>");
    document.write("<ul>");
    document.write("<li>Referring Document: " + ⤵
document.referrer + "</li>");
    document.write("<li>Domain: " + document.domain + ⤵
"</li>");
    document.write("<li>URL: " + document.URL + "</li>");
    document.write("</ul>");
</script>
```

Listing 45-1: A script to dynamic information in the document stream.

8. Save the script in an HTML file, and open the file in a browser. The result should look like Figure 45-1.

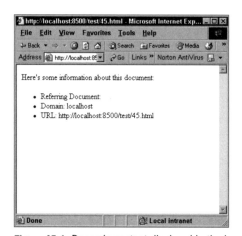

Figure 45-1: Dynamic content displayed in the browser.

cross-reference

▪ The document.write method is used to output content to the browser window from within your JavaScript script. The method is introduced in Task 9.

Including New Lines in Output

notes

■ Normally, the fact that document.write doesn't output a new-line character doesn't have much, if any, impact on your code. After all, new-line characters in standard HTML don't actually get rendered in the browser. Still, this doesn't mean that you can simply ignore the lack of new-line characters.

■ In preformatted blocks of code, new-line characters are actually rendered as new-line characters. This means that if you expect that placing two output lines in document. write commands on separate lines will cause them to render on separate lines, you will be surprised by the results.

The document.write method is useful, but on occasion, it has limitations. In particular, the document.write method doesn't output new-line characters at the end of each string it outputs.

Consider the following JavaScript extract:

```
document.write("<strong>a</strong>");
document.write("b");
```

In essence, this is the same as the following HTML code:

```
<strong>a</strong>b
```

Notice that the "b" is on the same line as the "a", although they are output in two document.write commands on separate lines of the JavaScript code. This means the output is displayed without a space between the letters, as in Figure 46-1.

Figure 46-1: document.write does not output new-line characters

Of course, this is a little different than if you had the HTML on two separate lines as:

```
<strong>a</strong>
b
```

In this case, the new line after the first line of code would be rendered as a space by the browser.

This problem becomes more acute in blocks of preformatted text (text inside pre tags).

To rectify the problem, the document object also offers the document .writeln method. This method is exactly the same as the document.write method, except that it outputs a new-line character to the browser at the end of the string. This means that the following code

```
document.writeln("<strong>a</strong>");
document.writeln("b");
```

is essentially the same as the following HTML code:

```
<strong>a</strong>
b
```

This is useful in situations where new lines are important and you want to ensure that a new line is output at the end of each line of text displayed through JavaScript.

To illustrate the use of `document.writeln`, the following example is a variation of the example in Task 45, except that the data is output as preformatted text using the `document.writeln` method:

1. Start a script block with the `script` tag:

   ```
   <script language="JavaScript">
   ```

2. Display an introductory message using `document.write`:

   ```
   document.writeln("<p>Here's some information about this ⊃
   document:</p>");
   ```

3. Output a `pre` tag to start a section of preformatted text:

   ```
   document.writeln("<pre>");
   ```

4. Output the referring document:

   ```
   document.writeln("   Referring Document: " + ⊃
   document.referrer);
   ```

5. Output the domain of the current document:

   ```
   document.writeln("   Domain: " + document.domain);
   ```

6. Output the URL of the current document:

   ```
   document.writeln("   URL: " + document.URL);
   ```

7. Close the script by outputting a closing `pre` tag followed by a closing `script` tag:

   ```
       document.writeln("</pre>");
   </script>
   ```

8. Save the script in an HTML file, and open the file in a browser. The result is as shown in Figure 46-2.

Figure 46-2: Dynamic content displayed in the browser in a preformatted text block.

tip

- You need to be careful using `document.write` and `document.writeln`. In particular, if the string passed as an argument is contained in double quotes, then you can't just include double quotes in the string. You would need to escape the double quote in the string as `\"`. If you don't do this, the double quote will end the string and everything after it will not be considered part of the argument, causing JavaScript to generate an error message. The same applies if you enclose the string in single quotes: You need to escape single quotes in the string as `\'`.

Outputting the Date to the Browser

Using `document.write` and `document.writeln` becomes useful when there is a genuine need to display dynamic content in the browser that cannot be pregenerated but must be generated at the time the document is to be displayed.

A good example of this is displaying the current date and time within a page. For instance, a site that delivers time-sensitive news probably wants people to know that the news on the site is up-to-date as of the current time and could do that by always displaying the current time in the page.

Luckily, JavaScript provides a `Date` object with which you can quickly and easily obtain the current date and then output that date to the browser. Basic use of the `Date` object for these purposes is straightforward, and the following script can be inserted in an HTML file wherever you want to display the current date and time:

1. Start a script block with the `script` tag:

   ```
   <script language="JavaScript">
   ```

2. Create a new `Date` object and assign it to the variable `thisDate`:

   ```
   <script language="JavaScript">
      var thisDate = new Date();
   ```

3. Display the date using the `toString` method of the `Date` object:

   ```
   <script language="JavaScript">
      var thisDate = new Date();
      document.write(thisDate.toString());
   ```

4. Close the script with a closing script tag; the final source code for this script should look like Listing 47-1.

   ```
   <script language="JavaScript">
      var thisDate = new Date();
      document.write(thisDate.toString());
   </script>
   ```

Listing 47-1: A script for displaying the current date.

notes

- The `Date` method used here is known as a *constructor method*. Most objects have a constructor method that creates a new instance of the object. Here, using the `Date` constructor method with no arguments results in a `Date` object with the date set to the current date and time.

- The `toString` method of the `Date` object returns the current date and time in a standard format as a string. You don't have any direct control of that formatting.

5. Include this script anywhere in an HTML document that you want to display the current date. For instance, Listing 47-2 is a simple HTML document that includes the script; when displayed in the browser, this page looks like Figure 47-1.

```html
<html>
    <body>
        <p>
            The current date is:
            <script language="JavaScript">
                var thisDate = new Date();
                document.write(thisDate.toString());
            </script>
        </p>
    </body>
</html>
```

Listing 47-2: Including the script in the body of a document.

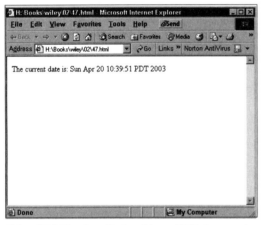

Figure 47-1: The date displayed in an HTML document.

Task **48**

Outputting the Date and Time in a Selected Time Zone

Using Greenwich Mean Time (also known as Universal Time Coordinate) as a common starting point, you can create a script that will always be able to display the time in your time zone regardless of the time zone of the user's computer. This is made possible because of two facts:

- The Date object can tell you the offset of the user's time zone from GMT time. So, if the user is five hours earlier than GMT, you can find this out.

- You know your offset from GMT when you write your script.

Combining these, you can always calculate the number of hours' difference between your time zone and the user's time zone and can adjust the time from the user's time zone to yours before manipulating that data or displaying it for the user.

Doing this requires the use of two methods of the Date object:

- getTimezoneOffset: This method returns the number of minutes' difference between the current browser's time zone and GMT time.

- setHours: This method is used to determine the hours part of the time in the current Date object. Using this you could reset the time to the time in your time zone.

The following script displays the current time in Central European Time (two hours later than Greenwich Mean Time). This will work regardless of the time zone of the user's computer.

1. Start a script block with the script tag:

   ```
   <script language="JavaScript">
   ```

2. Set the time zone offset from GMT in the myOffset variable. This value should be the number of hours' change needed to change the target time zone into GMT. For the case of Central European Time, which in the summer is two hours later than GMT, this means a value of -2 to indicate that it is necessary to move two hours back from CET to reach GMT:

   ```
   var myOffset = -2;
   ```

3. Create a new Date object with the current date and time, and assign it to the currentDate variable:

   ```
   var currentDate = new Date();
   ```

Task **48**

4. Use `getTimezoneOffset` to extract the offset for the user's time zone; since this will be in minutes and this script is going to work in hours, this value should be divided by 60. The final value is stored in the `userOffset` variable:

```
var userOffset = currentDate.getTimezoneOffset()/60;
```

5. Calculate the time zone difference between the target time zone and the user's time zone, and assign the number of hours' difference to the variable `timeZoneDifference.`:

```
var timeZoneDifference = userOffset - myOffset;
```

6. Reset the hours part of the time using the `setHours` method. The new time should be the current hours (using `getHours`) plus the time zone difference. Luckily, using `setHours` like this will accommodate cases where the time zone difference pushes the date into the previous or next day and will adjust the date accordingly.

```
currentDate.setHours(currentDate.getHours() + ⤴
timeZoneDifference);
```

7. Display the current date and time in the browser window with the `document.write` method:

```
document.write("The time and date in Central Europe is: ⤴
" + currentDate.toLocaleString());
```

8. Close the script block with a closing `script` tag. The final script looks like Listing 48-1.

```
<script language="JavaScript">
    var myOffset = -2;
    var currentDate = new Date();
    var userOffset = currentDate.getTimezoneOffset()/60;
    var timeZoneDifference = userOffset - myOffset;
    currentDate.setHours(currentDate.getHours() + ⤴
timeZoneDifference);
    document.write("The time and date in Central Europe is: ⤴
" + currentDate.toLocaleString());
</script>
```

Listing 48-1: A script for displaying the date in another time zone.

9. Save the script in an HTML file and open that file in a browser to see the date and time in Central Europe displayed, as in Figure 48-1.

Figure 48-1: Displaying the date and time in Central Europe.

tip

▪ To make this script in Listing 48-1 display the time and date in a time zone other than Central Europe, just change the value of `myOffset` appropriately.

Task **49**

Controlling the Format of Date Output

In addition to the toString method, the Date object also offers the following methods for quickly outputting the current date and time:

notes

- UTC stands for Coordinated Universal Time or Universal Time Coordinate. UTC is the same as Greenwich Mean Time but has become the preferred name for this default standard time zone.

- Using the JavaScript event model, you can run JavaScript code when a user clicks on an object. This is done using the onClick event handler. The onClick event handler is commonly used with form buttons and links, but you can apply it to other objects as well.

- toGMTString: Returns the time as a string converted to Greenwich Mean Time. The results look like this:

  ```
  Thu, 17 Apr 2003 17:47:44 UTC
  ```

- toLocaleString: Returns the time as a string using the date formatting conventions of the current locale. The results look like this in Canada:

  ```
  April 17, 2003 10:47:44 AM
  ```

- toUTCString: Returns the time as a string converted to Universal Time. The results look like this in North America:

  ```
  Thu, 17 Apr 2003 17:47:44 UTC
  ```

In addition, the Date object has a series of methods to return specific information about the current date that you can then combine into a fully customizable presentation of the date and time:

- getDate: Returns the current day of the month as a number

- getDay : Returns the current day of the week as a number between 0 (Sunday) and 6 (Saturday)

- getFullYear: Returns the four-digit year

- getHours: Returns the hour from the current time as a number between 0 and 23

- getMinutes: Returns the minutes from the current time as a number between 0 and 59

- getMonth: Returns the current month as a number between 0 (January) and 11 (December)

Using these methods, for instance, it is possible to output the current date in a custom form such as:

```
22:00 on 2003/4/15
```

The following code outputs the date in just this way:

1. Start a script block with the script tag:

   ```
   <script language="JavaScript">
   ```

2. Create a new Date object and assign it to the variable thisDate:

   ```
   var thisDate = new Date();
   ```

3. Build a string containing the time by using the `getHours` and `getMinutes` methods; this string is assigned to the variable `thisTimeString`:

```
var thisTimeString = thisDate.getHours() + ":" + ⤵
thisDate.getMinutes();
```

4. Build a string containing the date by using the `getFullYear`, `getMonth`, and `getDate` methods; this string is assigned to the variable `thisDateString`:

```
var thisDateString = thisDate.getFullYear() + "/" + ⤵
thisDate.getMonth() + "/" + thisDate.getDate();
```

5. Display the date and time to the browser using the `document.write` method:

```
document.write(thisTimeString + " on " + thisDateString);
```

6. Close the script with a closing script tag. The final source code looks like Listing 49-1.

```
<script language="JavaScript">
    var thisDate = new Date();
    var thisTimeString = thisDate.getHours() + ":" + ⤵
thisDate.getMinutes();
    var thisDateString = thisDate.getFullYear() + "/" + ⤵
thisDate.getMonth() + "/" + thisDate.getDate();
    document.write(thisTimeString + " on " + thisDateString);
</script>
```

Listing 49-1: A script for displaying the current date in a custom format.

7. Include the script in an HTML document where you want to display the date, and then open that document in a Web browser. The date displays as shown in Figure 49-1.

Figure 49-1: The custom formatted date displayed in a Web browser.

Customizing Output by the Time of Day

Rather than just presenting this time information to the user and trusting the user not to attempt to use the chat application during the time in question, you can customize the output of the relevant support page based on the time of day so that a link to the chat application only appears during the appropriate hours of the day.

The following example is a script that could be included in such an application. Between 9 A.M. and 5 P.M. on weekdays, a link to the chat application is displayed to the user, but outside those hours, a notice indicating that live Web support is closed is presented.

1. Start a script block with the `script` tag:

   ```
   <script language="JavaScript">
   ```

2. Create a new `Date` object and assign it to a variable named `thisDate`:

   ```
   var thisDate = new Date();
   ```

3. Test the current date to see if it represents a weekday and is in the correct time range using an `if` statement (refer to Task 34 for an introduction to the `if` statement):

   ```
   if ((thisDate.getDate() >= 1 && thisDate.getDate() <= 6)
   && (thisDate.getHours() >= 9 && thisDate.getHours() <=
   15)) {
   ```

4. Display the HTML for the case where the support desk is open:

   ```
   document.write("The support desk is open. Click <a
   href='http://my.url/'>here</a> for live Web support.");
   ```

5. Use the `else` statement to provide an alternative action:

   ```
   } else {
   ```

6. Display HTML for the case where the support desk is closed:

   ```
   document.write("The support desk is closed now. Come
   back between 9 a.m. and 5 p.m. Monday to Friday.");
   ```

7. Close the `if` block with a closing curly bracket:

   ```
   }
   ```

8. Close the script block with a closing `script` tag. The final code should look like the following:

   ```
   <script language="JavaScript">
      var thisDate = new Date();
   ```

```
     if ((thisDate.getDate() >= 1 && thisDate.getDate() <=
6) && (thisDate.getHours() >= 9 && thisDate.getHours()
<= 15)) {
        document.write("The support desk is open. Click <a
href='http://my.url/'>here</a> for live Web support.");
     } else {
        document.write("The support desk is closed now.
Come back between 9 a.m. and 5 p.m. Monday to Friday.");
     }
</script>
```

9. Include this script in an HTML document, and open the document in a browser. Between 9 A.M. and 5 P.M. on weekdays, you should see the message shown in Figure 50-1. At other times you will see the message shown in Figure 50-2.

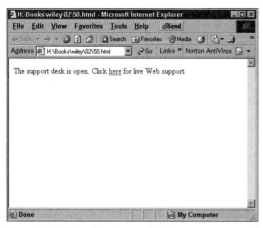

Figure 50-1: When the support desk is open, users can link to live Web support.

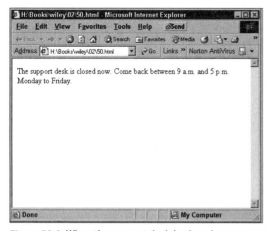

Figure 50-2: When the support desk is closed, users are told when to return.

51

Generating a Monthly Calendar

It is simple to leverage the Date object, using looping (as discussed in Task 33) and the output capabilities of the document.write method to generate a calendar for the current month.

Use the following steps to create a script to generate a calendar in a table in your documents:

1. In a script block, create an array containing the names of months:

```
var months = new Array();
months[0] = "January"; months[1] = "Feburary";
months[2] = "March"; months[3] = "April";
months[4] = "May"; months[5] = "June";
months[6] = "July"; months[7] = "August";
months[8] = "September"; months[9] = "October";
months[10] = "November"; months[11] = "December";
```

2. Create a new Date object for the current date, and store it in the currentDate variable. Take the month from the current date and store it in the currentMonth variable; then set the day of the month to the first day using the setDate method of the Date object:

```
var currentDate = new Date();
var currentMonth = currentDate.getMonth();
currentDate.setDate(1);
```

3. Output the top of the table plus the first row, which contains the day of the month. The second row of the table, after the month name, should be column headers indicating the days of the week:

```
document.write("<table border=1 cellpadding=3 ⤶
cellspacing=0>");
document.write("<tr>");
document.write("<td colspan=7 align='center'>" + ⤶
months[currentMonth] + "</td>");
document.write("<tr>");
document.write("<td align='center'>S</td>");
document.write("<td align='center'>M</td>");
document.write("<td align='center'>T</td>");
document.write("<td align='center'>W</td>");
document.write("<td align='center'>T</td>");
document.write("<td align='center'>F</td>");
document.write("<td align='center'>S</td>");
document.write("</tr>");
```

notes

- In many applications, you will want to display a monthly calendar. You might use this simply to display the current month so the user can type in the current date. You might choose to display event information inside the calendar. In any case, there is some basic JavaScript logic you can use to render a monthly calendar in a table without having to manually code the calendar for a specific month.

- The setDate method of the Date object is related to the getDate method. Where getDate returns the current day of the month as a number, the setDate method resets the day of the month; you provide the numeric value of the day of the month as an argument to the method.

- The day of the month is selected by using the value of the currentMonth variable as the index for the months array.

- If the first day of the month is not Sunday, then you need to display blank table cells for the days prior to the first day of the month in the first row of table dates in the table. To do this, make sure the current day is not a Sunday, and if it is not, loop from 0 to the day before the current day of the week and display an empty table cell for each day.

- The while loop should continue as long as the current date being processed is in the month being displayed (which is stored in the currentMonth variable).

4. The next step is to handle the case where the first day of the month is not a Sunday. The result, for instance, is a first row of the table dates like the one illustrated in Figure 51-1, when the first day of the month falls on a Tuesday:

```
if (currentDate.getDay() != 0) {
    document.write("<tr>");
    for (i = 0; i < currentDate.getDay(); i++) {
        document.write("<td> </td>");
    }
}
```

		1	2	3	4	5

Figure 51-1: Blank table cells may be needed to pad the first row of the month.

5. The next step is a `while` loop to display each day's individual cell:

```
while (currentDate.getMonth() == currentMonth) {
```

6. Inside the loop, check if the current date is a Sunday, and if it is, then start a new row with a `tr` tag. Next, display a cell with the current date. If the current date is a Saturday, finish the row with a closing `tr` tag. Finally, add one to the value of the current day of the month using `setDate` to move to the next day.

```
while (currentDate.getMonth() == currentMonth) {
    if (currentDate.getDay == 0) {
        document.write("<tr>");
    }
    document.write("<td align='center'>" + ⮌
currentDate.getDate() + "</td>");
    if (currentDate.getDay() == 6) {
        document.write("</tr>");
    }
    currentDate.setDate(currentDate.getDate() + 1);
}
```

7. After all the days have been displayed, you need to see if any more empty cells are necessary to complete the last row of the table. This is done with another `for` loop:

```
for (i = currentDate.getDay(); i <= 6; i++) {
    document.write("<td> </td>");
}
```

8. Finally, close the table by outputting a closing table tag. When the script is executed, you will see the current month's calendar displayed in your browser.

```
document.write("</table>");
```

Customizing Output Using URL Variables

When you build a URL for a page, you can add a series of name-value pairs to the end of the URL in the following form:

```
http://my.url/somepage.html?name1=value1&name2=value2&...
```

Essentially, these parameters are like variables: named containers for values. In JavaScript, the document object provides the URL property that contains the entire URL for your document, and using some manipulation on this property, you can extract some or all of the URL parameters contained in the URL. The following code displays all URL parameters for the current document:

1. In a script block in the body of a document, separate the current document's URL at the question mark and store the two parts in the array urlParts:

   ```
   var urlParts = document.URL.split("?");
   ```

2. Split the part of the URL to the right of the question mark into one or more parts at the ampersand. This places each name-value pair into an array entry in the parameterParts array.

   ```
   var parameterParts = urlParts[1].split("&");
   ```

3. Output the HTML code to set up a table and display column headers for the table using the document.write method:

   ```
   document.write("<table border=1 cellpadding=3 ⊃
   cellspacing=0>");
   document.write("<tr>");
   document.write("<td><strong>Name</strong></td><td>⊃
   <strong>Value</strong></td>");
   ```

4. Start a for loop that loops through each element in the parameterParts array. This means the loop should start at 0 and count up to one less than the length of the array; this is because in an array of 10 elements, the first index is 0 and the last index is 9.

   ```
   for (i = 0; i < parameterParts.length; i ++) {
   ```

5. Output HTML to start a table row for each name-value pair:

   ```
   document.write("<tr>");
   ```

6. Separate the name-value pair at the equal sign, and store the results in the pairParts array. The first entry (at index 0) contains the name of the pair, and the second entry (at index 1) contains the value of the entry:

   ```
   var pairParts = parameterParts[i].split("=");
   ```

note

- The logic of the code in this task is simple: Split the string at the question mark, take the part to the right of the question mark and split it at each ampersand, and then take each of the resulting substrings and split them at the equal sign to split the URL parameters between their name and value parts. Using the split method of the string object helps make this process easy.

caution

- The code in this task will only work properly if there is at least one URL parameter passed to the script. When doing this, keep a couple points in mind: First, you must access the file through a Web server and not open it as a local file, and second, you must include at least one name-value pair after the question mark in the URL.

7. Display the name and value in table cells. Make sure the value of the pair is unencoded with the unescape function:

```
document.write("<td>" + pairParts[0] + "</td>");
document.write("<td>" + unescape(pairParts[1]) + "</td>");
```

8. Output HTML to close the table row, and close the loop with a closing curly bracket:

```
    document.write("</tr>");


}
```

9. Output HTML to complete the table, and then close the script with a closing script tag. The final source code should look like Listing 52-1, and when viewed in the browser, if the URL has parameters, they will be displayed in a table like the one illustrated in Figure 52-1.

```
<script language="JavaScript">
    var urlParts = document.URL.split("?");
    var parameterParts = urlParts[1].split("&");
    document.write("<table border=1 cellpadding=3 ⊃
cellspacing=0>");
    document.write("<tr>");
    document.write("<td><strong>Name</strong></td><td>⊃
<strong>Value</strong></td>");
    for (i = 0; i < parameterParts.length; i ++) {
        document.write("<tr>");
        var pairParts = parameterParts[i].split("=");
        document.write("<td>" + pairParts[0] + "</td>");
        document.write("<td>" + unescape(pairParts[1]) + ⊃
"</td>");
        document.write("</tr>");

    }
    document.write("</table>");

</script>
```

Listing 52-1: A script to display URL parameters in a table.

Figure 52-1: Displaying URL parameters as name-value pairs in a table.

tips

- One of the powerful features of any dynamic programming language for Web pages, including JavaScript, is the ability to pass data between pages and then act on that data in the target pages. One of the most common ways to pass data between pages is to use URL parameters.

- Not all characters are valid in URLs. For instance, spaces are not allowed. To handle this, URL parameter values are escaped where these special characters are replaced with codes; for instance, spaces become %20. To really work with your URL parameters, you will want to unencode the values of each parameter to change these special codes back to the correct characters. The unescape function returns a string unencoded in this way.

- To separate the URL at the question mark, use the split method of the string object, which will return the part to the left of the question mark as the first entry (entry 0) in the array and the part to the right of the question mark that contains the URL parameters as the second entry in the array (entry 1).

Dynamically Generating a Menu

To illustrate some of the power of dynamic output combine with URL parameters, this task shows how to build a simple menu system. In this example, a single JavaScript page handles a menu of five choices and renders appropriate output for each of the five choices.

This script assumes that the user's current selection is passed to the script through the URL parameter named `choice`. The actual practical implementation is as follows; this code assumes the script is in a file called `menu.html`:

1. Start a script block with the `script` tag:

   ```
   <script language="JavaScript">
   ```

2. Create a variable called `choice` to hold the user's selection; by default, the value is zero, which indicates no selection:

   ```
   var choice = 0;
   ```

3. Split the URL into the array `urlParts` at the question mark:

   ```
   var urlParts = document.URL.split("?");
   ```

4. Use the `if` statement to check if, in fact, there are any URL parameters. If there are, then the length of the `urlParts` array should be greater than 1:

   ```
   if (urlParts.length > 1) {
   ```

5. Split the list of URL parameters into their parts, and check if the pair is named `choice`; if it is, store the value of the pair in the `choice` array created earlier:

   ```
   var parameterParts = urlParts[1].split("&");

   for (i = 0; i < parameterParts.length; i++) {

      var pairParts = parameterParts[i].split("=");
      var pairName = pairParts[0];
      var pairValue = pairParts[1];

      if (pairName == "choice") {

         choice = pairValue;

      }

   }
   ```

6. Close the `if` statement with a closing curly bracket:

   ```
   }
   ```

notes

- The logic of the script is straightforward. Extract the choice parameter from the document's URL. Next, display a menu of five choices; the choices should be clickable links, except for the current selected choice. Finally, display the content for the selected choice; if this is the first visit to the page, no choice is selected and no content other than the menu in the previous step should be displayed.

- To extract the choice URL parameter, simply extract the name and value into the variables `pairName` and `pairValue`. Check if `pairName` is the choice URL parameter, and if it is, assign the value of `pairValue` to the `choice` variable.

- For each menu entry you need to check if the variable `choice` indicates that selection. If it does, display the menu entry as regular text; otherwise, make a link back to the same page, with the URL parameter `choice` set appropriately.

7. The next step is to display the menu itself. This requires five `if` statements: one for each menu entry. Each `if` statement looks like the following, adjusted for a particular choice and the appropriate output for that choice. The result is a menu that might look like Figure 53-1.

```
if (choice == 1) {
    document.write("<strong>Choice 1</strong><br>");
} else {
    document.write("<a href='menu.html?choice=1'>↵
Choice 1</a><br>");
}
```

Figure 53-1: The menu as displayed when no choice is selected.

8. Display a divider to separate the menu from the body text of the page using the `document.write` method:

```
document.write("<hr>");
```

9. Use five `if` statements, which test the value of the choice variable to display the appropriate body content. Each `if` statement should look like the following but be adjusted for the appropriate choice value and output:

```
if (choice == 1) {
    document.write("Body content for choice 1");
}
```

10. Close the script with a closing `script` tag; when viewed in a browser, a page might look like Figure 53-2:

```
</script>
```

Figure 53-2: A completed page with Choice 3 selected.

tip

▪ When working with JavaScript that manipulates URL parameters, you must be accessing the page through a Web server using a URL such as `http://my.url/test.html` and not directly using a local file path such as `c:\myfiles\test.html`. URL parameters are not available with file path access to files.

cross-reference

▪ Refer to Task 52 for a discussion of how to split a URL into its parts and extract the name-value pairs of the URL parameters.

Task 54

Replacing the Browser Document with a New Document

You can replace the browser document with a new document by using two main methods of the `document` object:

note

- In addition to outputting content into the current document stream that the browser is rendering, you can also use the `document` object to replace the currently displayed object with new content without sending the user to the server for the new document.

- `document.open`: Opens a new document stream
- `document.close`: Closes a document stream opened by `document.open`

To use these methods, you use a structure like the following:

```
document.open();
One or more document.write or document.writeln commands
document.close();
```

The following example creates a page with a JavaScript function that displays a new document using `document.open` and `document.close`. The user can click on a link to trigger the function and display the new page without accessing the server.

1. Start a script block with the `script` tag:

   ```
   <script language="JavaScript">
   ```

2. Start a new function called `newDocument`:

   ```
   function newDocument() {
   ```

3. Open a new document stream with `document.open`:

   ```
   document.open();
   ```

4. Write out the content of the new document:

   ```
   document.write("<p>This is a New Document.</p>");
   ```

5. Close the document stream with `document.close`:

   ```
   document.close();
   ```

6. Close the function with a closing curly bracket:

   ```
   }
   ```

7. Close the script with a closing `script` tag:

   ```
   </script>
   ```

8. In the body of the HTML document, include a link with an `onClick` event handler that calls the `newDocument` function; a sample final page is shown in Listing 54-1.

```
<head>
    <script language="JavaScript">
        function newDocument() {
            document.open();
            document.write("<p>This is a New Document.</p>");
            document.close();
        }
    </script>
</head>
<body>
    <p>This is the original document.</p>
    <p><a href="#" onClick="newDocument()">Display New ⤶
Document</a></p>
</body
```

Listing 54-1: This code displays a second document stream to the browser.

9. Open the document in a browser. Initially you will see the body text of the HTML document as in Figure 54-1. After clicking on the link, you should see the content output by the `newDocument` function.

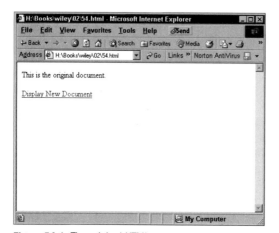

Figure 54-1: The original HTML page.

cross-reference

▪ Event handlers are discussed in Part 9. The `onClick` event handlers are introduced in Task 220.

Redirecting the User to a New Page

Unlike the `document.URL` property, which is static, the `window.location` property allows you to actually reset the location associated with a window and effectively redirect users to a new URL.

For instance, consider the following simple page:

```
<head>
   <script language="JavaScript">
      window.location = "http://www.yahoo.com/";
   </script>
</head>
<body>
   <p>You are here now</p>
</body>
```

In this case, the text "You are here now" will not even display in the browser; as soon as the page loads, the user will immediately be directed to the Yahoo! Web site.

The following script leverages the `window.location` property to allow users to enter the location they would like to visit in a form field and then takes them there when they click on the Go button:

1. Start a form with the `form` tag. This form will never be submitted anywhere, so it doesn't actually need `method` or `action` attributes:

   ```
   <form>
   ```

2. Create a text box named `url`:

   ```
   Enter a URL: <input type="text" name="url">
   ```

3. Create a button with the label "Go". This form control should be of type `button` and not type `submit`, since the button is not being used to submit the form anywhere:

   ```
   <input type="button" value="Go">
   ```

4. Add an `onClick` attribute to the button's tag. The value of this attribute is HTML code to assign the value stored in the `url` text field to the `window.location` property:

   ```
   <input type="button" value="Go" onClick="window.location ⊃
   = this.form.url.value">
   ```

5. Close the form with a closing form tag so that the complete form looks like the following:

   ```
   <form>

      Enter a URL: <input type="text" name="url">
   ```

notes

- The `window` object provides properties and methods for manipulating the current window. One of the properties is the `location` property, which contains the URL of the document displayed in the current window.

- The `onClick` attribute takes as its value JavaScript code to execute when the user clicks on the button.

```
<input type="button" value="Go" ⊃
onClick="window.location = this.form.url.value">

</form>
```

6. Store the form in an HTML file, and open that file in a Web browser. You will see a form.

7. Enter a URL in the form's text field, as illustrated in Figure 55-1.

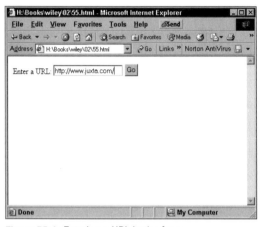

Figure 55-1: Entering a URL in the form.

8. Click on the Go button, and you will be redirected to the URL you entered, as shown in Figure 55-2.

Figure 55-2: Redirecting to the new URL.

tip

- In an event handler used for a form such as onClick, you can refer to the current form as this.form. That means this.form.url refers to the text field named url, and this.form.url. value refers to the text entered in the url text field.

cross-reference

- This task accesses data in forms and uses event handlers. Part 4 of the book addresses working with forms, while Part 9 discusses event handlers.

Creating a "Page Loading ..." Placeholder

This task looks at how to create a "page loading" placeholder that pops up in a separate window while the main document is loading. When the main document finishes loading, the placeholder window will close.

This task uses two methods of the window object plus one event handler:

- window.open: Opens a new window and loads a document in that window

- window.close: Closes a window

- onLoad: Used in the body tag to trigger JavaScript to execute when a document continues loading

The following steps create the placeholder window:

1. Create an HTML file to serve as the content of the "page loading" placeholder window. Any content you want the user to see in that window should be placed in this file. Name the file holder.html. The following is a simple file that tells the user the main page is loading:

```html
<html>
   <head>
      <title>Page Loading ...</title>
   </head>
   <body>
      <strong>
          Page Loading ... Please Wait
      </strong>
   </body>
</html>
```

2. Create the HTML file for your main document in the same directory. For this task, the file is named mainpage.html. A simple mainpage.html file might look like this:

```html
<html>
      <head>
         <title>The Main Page</title>
      </head>
      <body>
         <p>This is the main page</p>
      </body>
</html>
```

notes

- Some sites create "page loading" placeholder pages. These are typically used when loading a page that will take a long time to load either because of the amount of content being loaded or, more commonly in the case of dynamic content, when processing the page for delivery to the user will take a long time.

- You can use a number of strategies for creating a "page loading" placeholder. Such strategies can involve content being pushed from the server, or they can be entirely implemented in JavaScript on the client. This task takes the latter approach.

3. In `mainpage.html`, add a script block to the header of the document:

```
<script language="JavaScript">

</script>
```

4. In the script block, open a new window with `window.open`. This method takes three arguments: the file to load in the window, the name of the window, and a series of parameters that define the features of the window—in this case, the width and height of the window are set to 200 pixels. The method returns a reference to the window's objects so that it is possible to manipulate the window later. This reference is stored in the variable `placeHolder`:

```
var placeHolder = window.open("holder.html","⤸
holderWindow,"width=200,height=200");
```

5. Add an `onLoad` attribute to the `body` tag:

```
<body onLoad="">
```

6. As the value of the `onLoad` attribute, use `placeHolder.close()`. This closes the placeholder window once the main document finishes loading. The final `mainpage.html` code looks like Listing 56-1.

```
<html>
    <head>
        <script language="JavaScript">
            var placeHolder = ⤸
window.open("holder.html","placeholder","width=200,⤸
height=200");
        </script>
        <title>The Main Page</title>
    </head>
    <body onLoad="placeHolder.close()">
        <p>This is the main page</p>
    </body>
</html>
```

Listing 56-1: Integrating the placeholder code into an HTML document.

7. Make sure `holder.html` and `mainpage.html` are in the same directory and then load `mainpage.html` in your browser window. A window with the contents of `holder.html` should appear above the main window and then disappear as soon as the main window finishes loading.

tip

▪ This type of placeholder doesn't make much sense for a document as short as `mainpage.html`. In this case, the placeholder will appear and disappear almost immediately. You really need a long, complicated HTML document or a dynamic document that takes time to generate to make this type of placeholder worthwhile.

Part 3: Images and Rollovers

Accessing an HTML-Embedded Image in JavaScript

JavaScript makes it easy to access and manipulate images in your HTML pages. Accessing images in JavaScript is done through the Image object. An Image object is created for each image you include in your HTML code. You either access these Image objects through the images array of the document object or directly by name.

If you specify a name for an image using the name attribute of the img tag, then you can directly refer to the image as document.imageName. For example, consider the following image in your HTML document:

```
<img src="myImage.jpg" name="myImage">
```

You could refer to this in JavaScript with document.myImage.

Each Image object has numerous properties that can be used to access information about an image. These include height (the height of the image in pixels), width (the width of the image in pixels), src (the value of the src attribute of the img tag), hspace (the size of horizontal image padding in pixels), and vspace (the size of vertical image padding in pixels).

The following task illustrates how to use these properties to display an image and then provide links to display the height and width of the image in dialog boxes:

1. Use an img tag to include an image in the page; name the image myImage using the name attribute:

   ```
   <img src="image1.jpg" name="myImage">
   ```

2. Include a link for displaying the width, and add an onClick event handler to the a tag; this event handler will use the window.alert method to display the image's width in a dialog box. Notice how the image's width is obtained by referring to document.myImage .width:

   ```
   <a href="#" onClick="window.alert(document.myImage.width)
   ">Width</a><br>
   ```

3. Include a link for displaying the height, and add an onClick event handler to the a tag; this event handler will use the window.alert method to display the image's height in a dialog box. Notice how the image's height is obtained by referring to document.myImage .height. Add any necessary HTML for your preferred layout, and your final code might look something like the following:

   ```
   <img src="image1.jpg" name="myImage">
   <br>
   <a href="#" onClick="window.alert(document.myImage.width)
   ">Width</a><br>
   ```

```
<a href="#" onClick="window.alert(document.myImage.height)
">Height</a>
```

4. Save the code in an HTML file, and open it in a Web browser; you should see a page with links for displaying the width and height.

5. Click on the Width link, and the dialog box in Figure 57-1 appears.

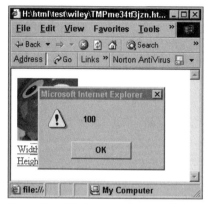

Figure 57-1: Displaying an image's width.

6. Click on the Height link, and the dialog box in Figure 57-2 appears.

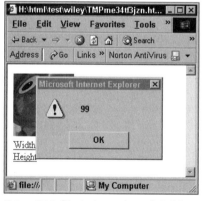

Figure 57-2: Displaying an image's height.

tip

▪ By using JavaScript's ability to manipulate images, you can achieve many different effects. These include dynamically changing images on the fly to create a slide show, creating mouse rollover effects on images, and even generating animated images or banners using JavaScript.

cross-reference

▪ The window.alert method (see Step 2) displays a dialog box with a single text message and a single button to dismiss the dialog box. It takes a single string as an argument, which should be the message to be displayed in the dialog box. This method is discussed in Task 25.

Task 58

Loading an Image Using JavaScript

In addition to creating `Image` objects by loading an image in HTML, you can create an `Image` object programmatically in JavaScript. Loading an image in JavaScript is a two-step process:

1. Create an `Image` object and assign it to a variable:

```
var myImage = new Image;
```

2. Assign a source image URL to the `src` attribute of the object:

```
myImage.src = "image URL goes here";
```

The following task illustrates the programmatic loading of an image by loading an image in this way and then providing links to display the height and width of the image in dialog boxes as in Task 57:

1. Create a script block with opening and closing `script` tags.

2. In the script, create a new `Image` object named `myImage`:

```
myImage = new Image;
```

3. Load the image by assigning its URL to the `src` attribute of `myImage`:

```
myImage.src = "image1.jpg";
```

4. In the body of the page's HTML, include a link for displaying the width and add an `onClick` event handler to the a tag; this event handler will use the `window.alert` method to display the image's width in a dialog box. The image's width is obtained by referring to `document.myImage.width`:

```
<a href="#" onClick="window.alert(document.myImage.width)⤸
">Width</a><br>
```

5. Include a link for displaying the height, and add an `onClick` event handler to the a tag; this event handler will use the `window.alert` method to display the image's height in a dialog box. The image's width is obtained by referring to `document.myImage.height`. The final page should look like the following:

```
<script language="JavaScript">

    myImage = new Image;
    myImage.src = "Tellers1.jpg";

</script>

<body>
```

caution

- As mentioned in Task 57, the `images` array contains one entry for image in the order in which the images are specified in your code. Therefore, the first image's object is `document.images[0]`, the second is `document.images[1]`, and so on. This only applies to images in your HTML document. `Image` objects created in JavaScript as shown in this task do not appear in the `images` array.

```
    <a href="#" onClick="window.alert(myImage.width)⤵
">Width</a><br>
    <a href="#" onClick="window.alert(myImage.height)⤵
">Height</a>
</body>
```

6. Save the code in an HTML file, and open the file in your browser; the page with two links should appear, but the image itself won't be displayed, as shown in Figure 58-1.

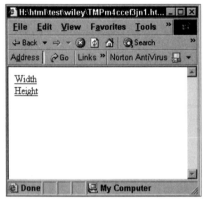

Figure 58-1: Displaying Width and Height links.

7. Click on the Width link, and a dialog box like the one in Figure 58-2 appears, showing the width of the image. Click on the Height link, and a dialog box for displaying the image's height appears.

Figure 58-2: Displaying an image's width.

tip

▪ You could create an Image object in JavaScript when you want to load an image without displaying it and then use that image later in your scripts. As an example, you might use the image in a slide show or as the rollover image when the mouse moves over an image.

cross-reference

▪ Task 57 discusses the loading of images in HTML and then accessing those images from JavaScript.

Detecting MouseOver Events on Images

Using the onMouseOver event handler, you can detect when the mouse pointer is over an image. You can then trigger actions to occur only when the mouse moves into the space occupied by the image. Typically, this is used to create rollover effects, as shown in the following tasks.

To specify an event handler, you need to use the onMouseOver attribute of the img tag to specify JavaScript to execute when the mouse rolls over the image. For example:

```
<img src="image file" onMouseOver="JavaScript code">
```

In the case where you are using an image as a link—for instance, an image serving as a button in a menu—you typically place the onMouseOver attribute in the a tag that encompasses the img tag:

```
<a href="URL" onMouseOver="JavaScript code">
    <img src="image file">
</a>
```

The following shows the use of onMouseOver in both the img and a tags and causes an appropriate message to display in a dialog box when the mouse pointer moves over an image:

1. In the body of your document, place an img tag to display the first image:

   ```
   <img src="image1.jpg">
   ```

2. Add an onMouseOver attribute to the img tag:

   ```
   <img src="image1.jpg" onMouseOver="">
   ```

3. As the value for the onMouseOver attribute, use the window.alert method to display a message when the mouse pointer moves over the image:

   ```
   <img src="image1.jpg" onMouseOver="window.alert('Over ⤶
   the Image');">
   ```

4. Add a second img tag to display another image:

   ```
   <img src="image2.jpg">
   ```

5. Place opening and closing a tags around the second image; no URL needs to be specified, and you should add an onMouseOver attribute to the a tag. As the value for the onMouseOver attribute, use the window.alert method again to display a message when the mouse pointer moves over the second image. The resulting code should look like this:

notes

* In this example, the JavaScript code is executed when the mouse pointer moves over anything inside the opening and closing a tags; in this case, only the image is inside the a block.

* The onMouseOver event is often used for rollover effects. If you are using an images as a menu button and want to display an alternate highlight image when the mouse is over the button, you will use onMouseOver. In these cases, the image will be part of a link and you will use onMouseOver in the a tag. This is the most common way the onMouseOver event is used, and it is rarely used in the img tag itself.

* The onMouseOver event is available in the a tag on any JavaScript-capable browser but is only available for the img tag in newer browsers (Netscape 6 and above or Internet Explorer 4 and above).

```
<body>
    <img src="image1.jpg" onMouseOver="alert('Over the ⟳
Image');"><br>
    <a href="#" onMouseOver="window.alert('Over the ⟳
Link');"><img src="image2.jpg"></a>
</body>
```

6. Save the code to an HTML file, and open the file in a browser. The page will look like Figure 59-1.

Figure 59-1: Displaying two images.

7. Move the mouse pointer over the first image, and a dialog box like Figure 59-2 appears. Move the mouse over the send image, and a dialog box indicating you are over the link appears.

Figure 59-2: Displaying a dialog box when the mouse moves over an image.

Detecting Click Events on Images

In much the same way as code can be specified to respond to onMouseOver events (see Task 59), you can specify action to take only when the user clicks on an image. This is done with the onClick event handler of the img tag or the a tag, depending on the situation.

You can specify an onClick attribute of the img tag:

```
<img src="image file" onClick="JavaScript code">
```

In the case where you are using an image as a link, as in an image serving as a button in a menu, you typically place the onClick attribute in the a tag that encompasses the img tag:

```
<a href="URL" onClick="JavaScript code">
    <img src="image file">
</a>
```

The following shows the use of onClick in both the img and a tags and causes an appropriate message to display in a dialog box when the mouse clicks on an image:

1. In the body of your document, place an img tag to display the first image:

   ```
   <img src="image1.jpg">
   ```

2. Add an onClick attribute to the img tag:

   ```
   <img src="image1.jpg" onClick="">
   ```

3. As the value for the onClick attribute, use the window.alert method to display a message when the mouse pointer moves over the image:

   ```
   <img src="image1.jpg" onClick="window.alert(Clicked on ⤵
   the Image');">
   ```

4. Add a second img tag to display another image:

   ```
   <img src="image2.jpg">
   ```

5. Place opening and closing a tags around the second image; no URL needs to be specified, and you should add an onClick attribute to the a tag. As the value for the onClick attribute, use the window.alert method again to display a message when the mouse pointer moves over the second image. The resulting code should look like this:

   ```
   <body>
       <img src="image1.jpg" onClick="window.alert('Click ⤵
   on the Image');"><br>
   ```

```
    <a href="#" onClick="window.alert('Clicked on the ⤶
Link');"><img src="image2.jpg"></a>
</body>
```

6. Save the code to an HTML file, and open the file in a browser. The page will look like Figure 60-1.

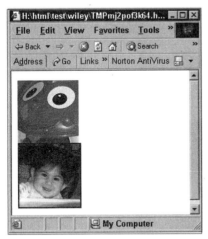

Figure 60-1: Displaying two images.

7. Click on the first image, and a dialog box indicating you clicked on the image without the link appears.

8. Click on the second image, and a dialog box like Figure 60-2 appears.

Figure 60-2: Displaying a dialog box when the mouse clicks on an image link.

Switching an Image Programatically

his task illustrates how to combine the JavaScript-based loading of images with the onMouseOver event handler to create a rollover effect. This rollover effect is typically used in the context of image-based buttons, as well as menus containing menu items built out of images.

Consider Figure 61-1. Here a single image is displayed in a Web page and the mouse pointer is not over the image. When the mouse pointer moves over the image, a rollover image replaces the original image, as in Figure 61-2. When the mouse pointer moves off the image, the image returns to the original illustrated in Figure 61-1.

Figure 61-1: When the mouse pointer is not over an image, the original image is displayed.

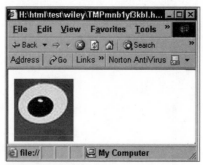

Figure 61-2: When the mouse pointer is over an image, an alternate image is displayed.

The principle of producing rollover effects in JavaScript is straightforward and involves three key pieces:

- Specify the default image in your img tag.

- Create two Image objects; in one load the default image, and in the other load the rollover image.

- Specify onMouseOver and onMouseOut event handlers to manage changing the displayed image as the mouse moves onto the image or off the image.

The following steps outline how to create a simple rollover effect for a single image in a page:

1. In the header of your page, create a script block with opening and closing `script` tags.

2. In the script, create an `Image` object named `rollImage`, and load the alternate, rollover image into it by assigning the image to the `src` property of the `rollImage` object:

```
rollImage = new Image;
rollImage.src = "rollImage1.jpg";
```

3. In the script, create an `Image` object named `defaultImage`, and load the default image to display into it.

4. In the body of your script, place the default image with an `img` tag. Use attributes of the tag to control the size and border of the image as desired, and use the `name` attribute to assign the name `myImage` to the image.

5. Wrap the `img` tag in opening and closing a tags, and specify the URL where you want users to be directed when they click on the image in the `href` attribute of the a tag. Add an `onMouseOver` attribute to the a tag, and use this to display the rollover image to the `myImage` object. This will cause the rollover image to be displayed when the mouse moves over the image. Also add an `onMouseOut` attribute to the a tag, and use this to display the default image when the mouse moves off the image. The final script should look like this:

```
<head>
   <script language="JavaScript">
      rollImage = new Image;
      rollImage.src = "rollImage1.jpg";
      defaultImage = new Image;
      defaultImage.src = "image1.jpg";
   </script>
</head>
<body>
   <a href="myUrl" onMouseOver="document.myImage.src =
rollImage.src;"
      onMouseOut="document.myImage.src = defaultImage.src;">
      <img src="image1.jpg" name="myImage" width=100
height=100 border=0>
   </a>
</body>
```

7. Save the code in an HTML file, and load it in a browser. When the mouse rolls over the image, the rollover effect should replace it with the rollover image and then switch it back to the default image when the mouse pointer leaves the space occupied by the image.

tip

- The rollover effect is designed to provide context to users, allowing them to know that the image constitutes a clickable element and showing users exactly what they are clicking on (especially in the case of numerous images in close proximity to each other in a complex layout).

62

Using Multiple Rollovers in One Page

Building on the rollover effect illustrated in Task 61, this task shows how the principle can be extended to support multiple rollovers in a single page. This is useful when you are building a menu out of rollover images.

The following steps illustrate the creation of two rollover images on a single page:

notes

- In their most basic form, multiple rollover effects require that each image have a unique name, each default image have a uniquely named Image object, and each rollover image have a uniquely named Image object.

- The onMouseOver event handler is similar to the onMouseOut event handler. It allows the programmer to specify JavaScript code to execute when the mouse pointer leaves the area occupied by a page element such as an image where onMouseOver specified code to execute when the mouse pointer entered the space occupied by a page element (see Step 4).

- In producing these rollover effects, keep in mind that an image and its alternate rollover image should usually have the same width and height in terms of the number of pixels; otherwise, one of two problems arises. First, if you don't force images to a specific size using the width and height attributes of the img tag, then the space taken by the image can change as the mouse rolls over the image, causing elements on the page around the image to move. Second, if you force the image to a specific size, one the two images will need to be distorted to match the size of the other image (see Figures).

1. In a script block in the header of a new page, create an Image object named rollImage1, and load the alternate rollover image for the first image into it by assigning the image to the src property of the rollImage1 object. Also create an Image object named defaultImage1, and load the default image for the first image into it by assigning the image to the src property of the defaultImage1 object:

```
rollImage1 = new Image; rollImage1.src = "rollImage1.jpg";
defaultImage1 = new Image; defaultImage1.src = ⤶
"image1.jpg";
```

2. Repeat the process for the second image by creating and loading rollImage2 and defaultImage2 so that the resulting script is as follows:

```
rollImage2 = new Image; rollImage2.src = "rollImage2.jpg";
defaultImage2 = new Image; defaultImage2.src = ⤶
"image2.jpg";
```

3. In the body of your script, place the two default images with img tags; use attributes of the tags to control the size and border of the image as desired, and use the name attribute to assign the names myImage1 and myImage2 to the images:

```
<img src="image1.jpg" name="myImage1" width=100 ⤶
height=100 border=0>
<img src="image2.jpg" name="myImage2" width=100 ⤶
height=100 border=0>
```

4. Wrap each img tag in opening and closing a tags, and specify the URL where you want the users to be directed when they click on the image in the href attribute of the a tag. Add an onMouseOver attribute to each a tag, and use this to display the rollover images. This will cause the rollover image to be displayed when the mouse moves over the relevant image. Also add an onMouseOut attribute to each a tag, and use this to display the default image when the mouse moves off the relevant image. The final script should look like this:

```
<head>
    <script language="JavaScript">
        rollImage1 = new Image; rollImage1.src = ⤶
"Tellers1.jpg";
        defaultImage1 = new Image; defaultImage1.src = ⤶
"lotus.jpg";
        rollImage2 = new Image; rollImage2.src = "hedi.jpg";
```

```
            defaultImage2 = new Image; defaultImage2.src = ⟲
    "ArcRV1.1.jpg";
        </script>
    </head>
    <body>
        <a href="#" onMouseOver="document.myImage1.src = ⟲
    rollImage1.src;"
          onMouseOut="document.myImage1.src = ⟲
    defaultImage1.src;">
            <img src="lotus.jpg" name="myImage1" width=100 ⟲
    height=100 border=0>
        </a>
        <a href="#" onMouseOver="document.myImage2.src = ⟲
    rollImage2.src;"
          onMouseOut="document.myImage2.src = ⟲
    defaultImage2.src;">
            <img src="ArcRV1.1.jpg" name="myImage2" width=100 ⟲
    height=100 border=0>
        </a>
    </body>
```

5. Save the code in an HTML file and load it in a browser. Two possible
    states exist: when the mouse is not over an image (Figure 62-1) and
    when the mouse is over the first image (Figure 62-2).

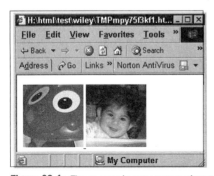

Figure 62-1: The mouse is not over any image.

Figure 62-2: The mouse is over the first image.

Task **63**

Displaying a Random Image

One application of the combination of JavaScript and images is to load a random image in a location on the page rather than the same image every time. One approach to this is to display the image entirely using JavaScript. That is, you need to use JavaScript to specify a list of possible images, select one at random, and then generate the `img` tag to display that image.

The script created in the following steps illustrates this process:

1. Create a script block with opening and closing `script` tags; the script block should be in the body of your HTML document where you want the image to be displayed:

   ```
   <script language="JavaScript">
   </script>
   ```

2. In the script, create an array named `imageList`:

   ```
   var imageList = new Array;
   ```

3. Create an entry in the array for each image you want to make available for random selection. For instance, if you have four images, assign the path and names of those images to the first four entries in the array:

   ```
   imageList[0] = "image1.jpg";
   imageList[1] = "image2.jpg";
   imageList[2] = "image3.jpg";
   imageList[3] = "image4.jpg";
   ```

4. Create a variable named `imageChoice`:

   ```
   var imageChoice;
   ```

5. Assign a random number to `imageChoice` using the `Math.random` method, which returns a random number from 0 to 1 (that is, the number will be greater than or equal to 0 but less than 1):

   ```
   var imageChoice = Math.random();
   ```

6. Extend the expression assigned to `imageChoice` by multiplying the random number by the number of entries in the `imageList` array to produce a number greater than or equal to 0 but less than 4:

   ```
   var imageChoice = Math.random() * imageList.length;
   ```

7. Extend the expression assigned to `imageChoice` further by removing any part after the decimal point with the `Math.floor` method; the result is an integer from 0 to one less than the number of entries in the array—in this case that means an integer from 0 to 3:

   ```
   var imageChoice = Math.floor(Math.random() * ↵
   imageList.length);
   ```

notes

- Each slot in an array is numbered; numbering starts at zero. This means an array with four entries has entries numbered 0 to 3.

- The `Math` object provides a number of useful methods for working with numbers and mathematical operations.

- The `length` property of an `Array` object provides the number of entries in an array. That means if an array has four entries numbered 0 to 3, then the `length` property of that array has a value of 4.

- `Math.floor` performs a function similar to rounding in that it removes the decimal part of a number. The difference is that the result of rounding can be the next highest or next lowest integer value, depending on the size of the decimal portion of the number. With `Math.floor` the result is always the next lowest integer. Therefore, rounding 2.999 would result in the integer 3, but applying `Math.floor` to the same number would result in the integer 2.

- Notice how the `img` tag is built out of two strings combined with an array variable; the combining is done with plus signs. When you are working with string values, plus signs perform concatenation of strings, as discussed in Task 15. Concatenation means that `"ab" + "cd"` results in `"abcd"`.

8. Use the `document.write` method to place an `img` tag in the HTML data stream sent to the browser. As the value of the `src` attribute of `img` tag, the random image is specified as `imageList[imageChoice]`. The final script looks like this:

```
<script language="JavaScript">

    var imageList = new Array;
    imageList[0] = "image1.jpg";
    imageList[1] = "image2.jpg";
    imageList[2] = "image3.jpg";
    imageList[3] = "image4.jpg";

    var imageChoice = Math.floor(Math.random() * ⊃
imageList.length);
    document.write('<img src="' + imageList[imageChoice] ⊃
+ '">');

</script>
```

9. Save the code in an HTML file, and display the file in a browser. A random image is displayed, as in Figure 63-1. Reloading the file should result in a different image, as illustrated in Figure 63-2 (although there is always a small chance the same random number will be selected twice in a row).

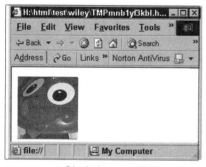

Figure 63-1: Displaying a random image.

Figure 63-2: Reloading the page will usually result in a different random image.

cross-references

- An *array* is a data type that contains multiple, numbered slots into which you can place any value. See Task 20. for a discussion of arrays.

- The `document.write` method is introduced in Task 45. It allows JavaScript code to generate output that forms part of the HTML rendered by the browser.

Displaying Multiple Random Images

The process of displaying a random image in a Web page can easily be extended to displaying multiple random images out of the same set of random images. The result is a script like the following, which displays three random images:

1. In a script block in the header of a new document, create an array named imageList:

```
var imageList = new Array;
```

2. Create an entry in the array for each image you want to make available for random selection. For instance, the following specifies the path to four images:

```
imageList[0] = "image1.jpg";
imageList[1] = "image2.jpg";
imageList[2] = "image3.jpg";
imageList[3] = "image4.jpg";
```

3. Create a function called showImage with the function keyword:

```
function showImage() {
}
```

4. In the function, create a variable named imageChoice. Assign a random number to imageChoice using the Math.random method, which returns a random number from 0 to 1 (that is, the number will be greater than or equal to 0 but less than 1). Extend the expression assigned to imageChoice by multiplying the random number by the number of entries in the imageList array to produce a number greater than or equal to zero but less than 4:

```
var imageChoice = Math.random() * imageList.length;
```

5. Extend the expression assigned to imageChoice further by removing any part after the decimal point with the Math.floor method. The result is an integer from 0 to one less than the number of entries in the array—in this case that means an integer from 0 to 3:

```
var imageChoice = Math.floor(Math.random() * ⟳
imageList.length);
```

6. Use the document.write method to place an img tag in the HTML data stream sent to the browser. As the value of the src attribute of img tag, the random image is specified as imageList[imageChoice]. The final function looks like this:

```
function showImage() {
    var imageChoice = Math.floor(Math.random() * ⟳
imageList.length);
    document.write('<img src="' + imageList[imageChoice] ⟳
+ '">');
}
```

notes

- Displaying multiple random images requires some rethinking of the script. Two script blocks are now needed: a script block in the document header that defines the array of images available and a function for displaying a single random image, along with a script block in the body of the text wherever a random image needs to be displayed. This separation of scripts, as well as the addition of a function, makes the code much more general-purpose than the code illustrated in Task 63.

- Math.floor performs a function similar to rounding in that it removes the decimal part of a number. The difference is that the result of rounding can be the next highest or next lowest integer value, depending on the size of the decimal portion of the number. With Math.floor the result is always the next lowest integer. Therefore, rounding 2.999 would result in the integer 3, but applying Math.floor to the same number would result in the integer 2.

7. In the body of the document, create a script block wherever you want to place a random image, and then invoke the showImage function there. You can invoke multiple showImage functions in the same script block. The following page shows how to display three random images in a row. Typically, the results will look like Figure 64-1. Depending on how many images are available in your array and how many random images you are displaying, there is always a chance that you will see repeat images as in Figure 64-2.

```
<head>
    <script language="JavaScript">
        var imageList = new Array;
        imageList[0] = "Tellers1.jpg";
        imageList[1] = "lotus.jpg";
        imageList[2] = "hedi.jpg";
        imageList[3] = "ArcRV1.1.jpg";
        function showImage() {
            var imageChoice = Math.floor(Math.random() *
imageList.length);
            document.write('<img src="' +
imageList[imageChoice] + '">');
        }
    </script>
</head>
<body>
    <script language="JavaScript">
        showImage();
        showImage();
        showImage();
    </script>
</body>
```

Figure 64-1: Displaying three random images.

Figure 64-2: Images may repeat.

cross-reference
- An array is a data type that contains multiple, numbered slots into which you can place any value. See Task 20 for a discussion of arrays.

Task 65

Using a Function to Create a Rollover

This task shows how to encapsulate the creation of Image objects for a rollover image into a function. The following steps show how to create the necessary function and use it to create a rollover effect for an image:

1. In the header of the document, create a script block with opening and closing script tags:

```
<script language="JavaScript">
</script>
```

2. In the script, create two variables: a source and a replacement containing the values 0 and 1, respectively. These variables allow the Image objects of each rollover array to be referred to by name: source for the default image and replacement for the rollover image.

```
var source = 0;
var replacement = 1;
```

3. Create a function named createRollOver with the function keyword. This function should take two parameters—originalImage, containing the path and name of the default image, and replacementImage, containing the path and name of the rollover image:

```
function createRollOver(originalImage,replacementImage) {
}
```

4. In the function, create an array named imageArray:

```
var imageArray = new Array;
```

5. Create a new Image object in the first element of the array, using source to specify the index, and assign originalImage as the source of that image:

```
imageArray[source] = new Image;
imageArray[source].src = originalImage;
```

6. Create a new Image object in the second element of the array, using replacement to specify the index, and assign replacementImage as the source of that image:

```
imageArray[replacement] = new Image;
imageArray[replacement].src = replacementImage;
```

7. Return the array as the value returned by the function:

```
return imageArray;
```

notes

- The task of code creation, code management, and code accuracy becomes increasingly daunting as the number of rollover images in a document increases. At some point the task of ensuring bug-free code and debugging becomes problematic. The approach in this task is aimed at mitigating this to a degree.

- Tasks 67 and 68 show how to combine these functions into a single system.

- Array elements can contain simple data types, such as numbers or strings, or complex data types, such as objects. When an array entry contains an object, the properties of that object are referred to with the notation arrayName- [index] .propertyName.

- The basis of the technique used here is to create an array of Image objects for each rollover image; each array will have two entries: one containing the Image object for the default image and the other containing the Image object for the replacement image. This combines related Image objects into a single variable (which contains the array) that can be easily accessed and referred to in a consistent way.

- When then mouse moves over the image, rollImage1- [replacement] contains the appropriate Image object, while rollImage1 [source] contains the Image object for when the mouse is not over the image.

8. After the function, invoke the `createRollOver` function to create the necessary rollover array, and assign the array returned by the function to `rollImage1`. The final script looks like this:

```
<script language="JavaScript">
   var source = 0;
   var replacement = 1;
   function createRollOver(originalImage,replacement⤸
Image) {
      var imageArray = new Array;
      imageArray[source] = new Image;
      imageArray[source].src = originalImage;
      imageArray[replacement] = new Image;
      imageArray[replacement].src = replacementImage;
      return imageArray;
   }
   var rollImage1 = createRollOver("image1.jpg","⤸
rollImage1.jpg");
</script>
```

9. In the body of the HTML, use the `img` tag to place the image, name the image `myImage1` with the `name` attribute, and place the image in an a block. The a tag must have `onMouseOver` and `onMouseOut` attributes that assign the appropriate images based on the mouse movement. The resulting source code for the body of the document looks like this:

```
<body>
   <a href="#" onMouseOver="document.myImage1.src = ⤸
rollImage1[replacement].src;"
      onMouseOut="document.myImage1.src = ⤸
rollImage1[source].src;">
      <img src="image1.jpg" width=100 name="myImage1" ⤸
border=0>
   </a>
</body>
```

10. Save the HTML file and open it in a browser. The default image is displayed as in Figure 65-1. Move the mouse over the image to see the rollover image.

Figure 65-1: When the mouse pointer is not over the image, the original image is displayed.

cross-reference

- This task and Task 66 illustrate how to encapsulate two pieces of rollover functionality: the creation of the rollover `Image` objects and the handling of image switches in event handlers.

Using a Function to Trigger a Rollover

I n addition to creating a function to handle the creation of rollover Image objects, you can encapsulate the code for handling the actual switching of images in rollovers within an event handler. This task extends the example illustrated in Task 65 and adds a function for this purpose.

The following steps show how to add the function to the code from Task 65 and build and trigger rollovers using both functions:

1. In a script block in the header of a new document, create two variables—a source and a replacement containing the values 0 and 1, respectively. These variables allow the Image objects of each rollover array to be referred to by name—source for the default image and replacement for the rollover image.

```
var source = 0;
var replacement = 1;
```

2. Create a function named createRollOver in the same way as in Task 65:

```
function createRollOver(originalImage,replacementImage) {
   var imageArray = new Array;
   imageArray[source] = new Image;
   imageArray[source].src = originalImage;
   imageArray[replacement] = new Image;
   imageArray[replacement].src = replacementImage;
   return imageArray;
}
```

3. Create a function named roll with the function keyword. This function takes two parameters—targetImage, which will be the Image object associated with the img tag for the image in question, and displayImage, which will be the Image object for the image to display:

```
function roll(targetImage,displayImage) {
}
```

4. In the function, assign the image from displayImage to the image location associated with targetImage so that the final function looks like this:

```
function roll(targetImage,displayImage) {
   targetImage.src = displayImage.src;
}
```

5. After the roll function, invoke the createRollOver function to create the necessary rollover array and assign the array returned by the function to rollImage1. The final script looks like this:

```
   var rollImage1 = createRollOver("image1.jpg"," ⤸
rollImage1.jpg");
```

6. In the body of the HTML, create an image with the `img` tag and name the image `myImage1`:

```
<img src="image1.jpg" width=100 name="myImage1" border=0>
```

7. Surround the image with opening and closing a tags:

```
<a href="myUrl">
    <img src="image1.jpg" width=100 name="myImage1" ↷
border=0>
</a>
```

8. Specify the `onMouseOver` and `onMouseOut` attributes of the a tag. These use the `roll` function to handle the switching of images.

```
<a href="#" onMouseOver="roll(myImage1,rollImage1 ↷
[replacement])" ↷
 onMouseOut="roll(myImage1, rollImage1 [source])">
    <img src="image1.jpg" width=100 name="myImage1" ↷
border=0>
</a>
```

9. Save the HTML file and open it in a browser. The default image is displayed as in Figure 66-1. Move the mouse over the image to see the rollover image, as in Figure 66-2.

Figure 66-1: When the mouse pointer is not over the image, the original image is displayed.

Figure 66-2: When the mouse pointer is over the image, the rollover image is displayed.

Task 67

Using Functions to Create Multiple Rollovers in One Page

note

- This task may seem to be more complex and use more source code than was used in Task 61 to create a rollover for a single image. This is an accurate perception; however, the benefit of this module code broken into functions is that it becomes easier to handle multiple rollovers, and code for creating and triggering each rollover becomes noticeably simpler.

The real benefits of using functions for rollovers become apparent when you try to create multiple rollover effects in a page. The following example shows how to use the functions created in Tasks 65 and 66 to create two rollover images in the same document:

1. In the script block in the header of a new document, create two variables—a source and a replacement containing the values 0 and 1, respectively. These variables allow the Image objects of each rollover array to be referred to by name: source for the default image and replacement for the rollover image:

```
var source = 0;
var replacement = 1;
```

2. Create a function named createRollOver in the same way as in Task 65:

```
function createRollOver(originalImage,replacementImage) {
    var imageArray = new Array;
    imageArray[source] = new Image;
    imageArray[source].src = originalImage;
    imageArray[replacement] = new Image;
    imageArray[replacement].src = replacementImage;
    return imageArray;
}
```

3. Create a function named roll in the same way as in Task 66:

```
function roll(targetImage,displayImage) {
    targetImage.src = displayImage.src;
}
```

4. After the roll function, invoke the createRollOver function twice to create the arrays for the two rollovers. The results are returned and stored in rollImage1 and rollImage2:

```
var rollImage1 = createRollOver("image1.jpg","⮒
rollImage1.jpg");
var rollImage2 = createRollOver("image2.jpg","⮒
rollImage2.jpg");
```

5. In the body of the document, create an image with the img tag for the first rollover, and enclose it in opening and closing a tags; use the roll function to specify appropriate image switches for the onMouseOver and onMouseOut event handlers of the a tag, and name the image myImage1 with the name attribute of the img tag:

```
<a href="#" onMouseOver="roll(myImage1,rollImage1 ⮒
[replacement])" ⮒
onMouseOut="roll(myImage1,rollImage1[source])">
```

```
    <img src="Tellers1.jpg" width=100 name="myImage1"
border=0>
</a>
```

6. In the body of the document, create an image with the `img` tag for the second rollover, and enclose it in opening and closing a tags; use the `roll` function to specify appropriate image switches for the `onMouseOver` and `onMouseOut` event handlers of the a tag, and name the image `myImage1` with the `name` attribute of the `img` tag. The final script should look like this:

```
<a href="#"
onMouseOver="roll(myImage2,rollImage2[replacement])"
 onMouseOut="roll(myImage2,rollImage2[source])">
    <img src="lotus.jpg" width=100 name="myImage2"
border=0>
</a>
```

7. Save the HTML file and open it in a browser. Two images are displayed. When the mouse pointer is not over either image, the default images are displayed, as in Figure 67-1. Move the mouse pointer over the first image to display the first rollover, as in Figure 67-2, and move over the second image to display the second rollover.

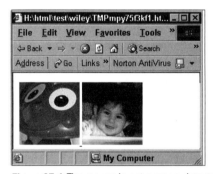

Figure 67-1:The mouse is not over any image.

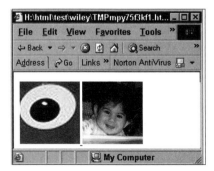

Figure 67-2:The mouse is over the first image.

tip

- The rollover effect is designed to provide context to users, allowing them to know that the image constitutes a clickable element and showing users exactly what they are clicking on (especially in the case of numerous images in close proximity to each other in a complex layout).

cross-reference

- Tasks 65 and 66 show how to use functions to modularize and simplify the code for creating and triggering rollover effects.

Creating a Simple Rollover Menu System

You have seen how moving the core rollover logic into functions can facilitate the creation of multiple rollover images. To fully leverage this, you should place the functions in a separate JavaScript file that can then be included in any document you build.

The following example illustrates how to take the functions used in Task 67, move them to an external JavaScript file, and then build a page that uses the file to create two rollover images in a page:

1. In a blank text file, create a JavaScript script, but without using script tags to open and close the script. Start the script by creating the source and replacement variables:

```
var source = 0;
var replacement = 1;
```

2. Create a function named `createRollOver`, as in Task 65:

```
function createRollOver(originalImage,replacementImage) {
   var imageArray = new Array;
   imageArray[source] = new Image;
   imageArray[source].src = originalImage;
   imageArray[replacement] = new Image;
   imageArray[replacement].src = replacementImage;
   return imageArray;
}
```

3. Create a function named `roll` in the same way as in Task 66:

```
function roll(targetImage,displayImage) {
   targetImage.src = displayImage.src;
}
```

4. Save the file as `rollover.js`.

5. In a new text file, include the `rollover.js` file by using the `src` attribute of the script tag; place this script tag in the document header:

```
<script language="JavaScript" src="rollover.js"></script>
```

6. Create a second script block in the document header.

notes

- Moving the functions to an outside file allows you to reuse the code in any page—and it vastly simplifies the pages that do use rollovers by removing the function code from those pages.

- The `.js` file extension is the standard extension for JavaScript files; you should use this extension for any files designed to contain JavaScript to be included in other HTML documents.

7. In this script, invoke the `createRollOver` function twice to create the arrays for the two rollovers. Assign the resulting arrays to `rollImage1` and `rollImage2`:

```
<script language="JavaScript">
    var rollImage1 = createRollOver("image1.jpg",↵
rollImage1.jpg");
    var rollImage2 = createRollOver("image2.jpg",↵
rollImage2.jpg");
</script>
```

8. In the body of the document, create an image with the `img` tag for the second rollover, and enclose it in opening and closing a tags. Use the `roll` function to specify appropriate image switches for the `onMouseOver` and `onMouseOut` event handlers of the a tag, and name the image `myImage1` with the `name` attribute of the `img` tag. The final script should look like this:

```
<body>
    <a href="#" onMouseOver="roll(myImage1,rollImage1↵
[replacement])"↵
      onMouseOut="roll(myImage1,rollImage1[source])">
        <img src="image1.jpg" width=100 name="myImage1" ↵
border=0>
    </a>
    <a href="#" onMouseOver="roll(myImage2,rollImage2↵
[replacement])"↵
      onMouseOut="roll(myImage2,rollImage2[source])">
        <img src="image2.jpg" width=100 name="myImage2" ↵
border=0>
    </a>
</body>
```

9. Save the HTML file and open it in a browser. When the mouse pointer is not over either image, the default images are displayed as in Figure 68-1.

Figure 68-1: The mouse is not over any image.

cross-reference

▪ Task 4 discusses the use of the `src` attribute to include outside JavaScript files in your HTML pages.

Creating a Slide Show in JavaScript

In addition to rollover effects for images, another popular use of JavaScript with images is to create slide shows in HTML pages. These slide shows can be automatic or manually controlled by the user.

This task illustrates the creation of an automatic slide show in which the image transitions happen every three seconds. The result is a slide show that starts on an initial image and then switches every three seconds. The third image is displayed after the slide show has been running for six seconds.

The following steps create the specified automatic slide show:

1. In a script block in the header of a new HTML document, create an array named `imageList`; this array will hold the `Image` objects for the slide show:

   ```
   var imageList = new Array;
   ```

2. Create a new element of the array for each slide show image and assign the path and filename of the image to the `src` attribute of the object:

   ```
   imageList[0] = new Image;
   imageList[0].src = "image1.jpg";
   imageList[1] = new Image;
   imageList[1].src = "image2.jpg";
   imageList[2] = new Image;
   imageList[2].src = "image3.jpg";
   imageList[3] = new Image;
   imageList[3].src = "image4.jpg";
   ```

3. Create a function named `slideShow` that takes a single parameter named `imageNumber`: the number of the image to display. This number is the index of a given image in the `imageList` array, and the function will display the image and then schedule the display of the next image to occur three seconds later.

   ```
   function slideShow(imageNumber) {
   }
   ```

4. In the function, display the image specified in `imageNumber` in the place of the image named `slideShow`:

   ```
   document.slideShow.src = imageList[imageNumber].src;
   ```

5. Increment `imageNumber` by one:

   ```
   imageNumber += 1;
   ```

6. Use an `if` statement to test if the new image number indicates there is another image to display; that is, `imageNumber` should be less than the length of the `imageList` array after being incremented:

   ```
   if (imageNumber < imageList.length) {
   }
   ```

notes

- The `length` property of an `Array` object provides the number of entries in an array. That means if an array has four entries numbered 0 to 3, then the `length` property of that array has a value of 4 (see Step 6).

- The `window.setTimeout` method takes two parameters: a function to call and a time in milliseconds. The function schedules an automatic call to the specified function after the specified number of milliseconds have elapsed. 3000 milliseconds is the same as 3 seconds (see Step 7).

- The `onLoad` event handler of the `body` tag is used to specify JavaScript to execute when an HTML document finishes its initial loading (see Step 8).

7. Inside the `if` block, use the `window.setTimeout` method to schedule a call to the `slideShow` function with the new value of `imageNumber` passed as a parameter. This will display the next image in three seconds:

```
window.setTimeout("slideShow(" + imageNumber + ")",3000);
```

8. Add an `onLoad` event handler to the `body` tag, and call `slideShow` with a parameter value of zero (for the first slide) from inside the event handler:

```
<body onLoad="slideShow(0)">
```

9. In the body of the document, display the first image of the slide show with an `img` tag, and use the `name` attribute to name the image `slideShow`. The final page should look like Listing 69-1.

tip

- The principle of creating a slide show is simple. First, load all the images into `Image` objects. Next, display the first image with an `img` tag. Finally, rotate the images with JavaScript until the slide show is complete.

```
<head>
    <script language="JavaScript">
        var imageList = new Array;
        imageList[0] = new Image;
        imageList[0].src = "image1.jpg";
        imageList[1] = new Image;
        imageList[1].src = "image2.jpg";
        imageList[2] = new Image;
        imageList[2].src = "image3.jpg";
        imageList[3] = new Image;
        imageList[3].src = "image4.jpg";
        function slideShow(imageNumber) {
            document.slideShow.src = ⤶
imageList[imageNumber].src;
            imageNumber += 1;
            if (imageNumber < imageList.length) {
                window.setTimeout("slideShow(" + imageNumber ⤶
+ ")",3000);
            }
        }
    </script>
</head>
<body onLoad="slideShow(0)">
    <img src="image1.jpg" width=100 name="slideShow">
</body>
```

Listing 69-1: Creating a slide show.

Randomizing Your Slide Show

As an extension to the slide show created in Task 69, this task shows how to produce a randomized slide show. The slide show continues to display random images for the list of available images as long as the page is being displayed in the browser.

The following steps create just such a random slide show:

1. In a script block in the header of a new document, create an array named imageList; this array will hold the Image objects for the slide show:

```
var imageList = new Array;
```

2. Create a new element of the array for each slide show image, and assign the path and filename of the image to the src attribute of the object:

```
imageList[0] = new Image;
imageList[0].src = "image1.jpg";
imageList[1] = new Image;
imageList[1].src = "image2.jpg";
imageList[2] = new Image;
imageList[2].src = "image3.jpg";
imageList[3] = new Image;
imageList[3].src = "image4.jpg";
```

3. Create a function named slideShow that takes a single parameter named imageNumber: the number of the image to display. This number is the index of a given image in the imageList array, and the function will display the image and then schedule the display of the next image to occur three seconds later.

```
function slideShow(imageNumber) {
}
```

4. In the function, display the image specified in imageNumber in the place of the image named slideShow:

```
document.slideShow.src = imageList[imageNumber].src;
```

5. Create a variable named imageChoice, and assign it a random number from 0 to the last index in the imageList array by using Math.floor, Math.random and imageList.length:

```
var imageChoice = Math.floor(Math.random() * ⤶
imageList.length);
```

6. Use the window.setTimeout method to schedule a call to the slideShow function with the value of imageChoice passed as a parameter. This will display the next random image in three seconds:

```
window.setTimeout("slideShow(" + imageChoice + ")",3000);
```

note

- The window.setTimeout method takes two parameters: a function to call and a time in milliseconds. The function schedules an automatic call to the specified function after the specified number of milliseconds have elapsed. 3000 milliseconds is the same as 3 seconds (see Step 6).

- The onLoad event handler of the body tag is used to specify JavaScript to execute when an HTML document finishes its initial loading (see Step 7).

7. Add an `onLoad` event handler to the `body` tag, and call `slideShow` with a parameter value of zero (for the first slide) from inside the event handler:

```
<body onLoad="slideShow(0)">
```

8. In the body of the document, display the first image of the slide show with an `img` tag, and use the `name` attribute to name the image `slideShow`. The final page should look like this:

```
<head>
    <script language="JavaScript">
        var imageList = new Array;
        imageList[0] = new Image;
        imageList[0].src = "image1.jpg";
        imageList[1] = new Image;
        imageList[1].src = "image2.jpg";
        imageList[2] = new Image;
        imageList[2].src = "image3.jpg";
        imageList[3] = new Image;
        imageList[3].src = "image4.jpg";
        function slideShow(imageNumber) {
            document.slideShow.src = ⤶
imageList[imageNumber].src;
            var imageChoice = Math.floor(Math.random() * ⤶
imageList.length);
            window.setTimeout("slideShow(" + imageChoice ⤶
+ ")",3000);
        }
    </script>
</head>
<body onLoad="slideShow(0)">
    <img src="image1.jpg" width=100 name="slideShow">
</body>
```

9. Save the page in an HTML file, and open it in a browser to display a slide show like the one in Figure 70-1.

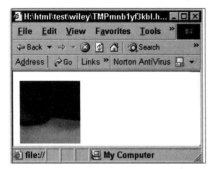

Figure 70-1: A random slide show.

cross-reference

▪ The technique in this task actually produces a simpler script than in Task 69, since it is no longer necessary to check if you have run out of images before displaying a new image. Instead, you simply keep choosing a random image and displaying it.

Triggering Slide Show Transitions from Links

notes

- Providing slide show control links requires an adjustment of the logic of the previous slide show application. Two functions are used: nextSlide to switch to the next slide and previousSlide to switch to the previous slide. The slide show will also use links in the body of the document to invoke the previousSlide and nextSlide functions.

- There are two ways to invoke JavaScript code when the user clicks on the link. The first is using javascript: JavaScript Code as the URL. The second is using the onClick attribute of the a tag. The first method is a good technique when you have a single function call to make and there is no need to follow a real URL when the link is clicked by the user.

Another useful extension of the slide show illustrated in Task 69 is to allow the user to move the slide show forward and backward by clicking on links instead of automating the transition of slides as in Tasks 69 and 70. The result is a slide show presentation that looks something like Figure 71-1.

Figure 71-1: Controlling a slide show with links in the document.

The following example creates a slide show application with these manual links for the user to control the progression of the slides:

1. In a script block in the header of a new document, create an array named imageList; this array will hold the Image objects for the slide show:

   ```
   var imageList = new Array;
   ```

2. Create an a variable named currentSlide, and set its default value to 0; this variable will be used to track the slide the user is currently viewing:

   ```
   var currentSlide = 0;
   ```

3. Create a new element of the array for each slide show image, and assign the path and filename of the image to the src attribute of the object:

   ```
   imageList[0] = new Image;
   imageList[0].src = "image1.jpg";
   imageList[1] = new Image;
   imageList[1].src = "image2.jpg";
   etc.
   ```

4. Create a function named nextSlide with the function keyword; this function will be invoked when the user wants to move forward to the next slide:

   ```
   function nextSlide() {
   }
   ```

5. In the function, use an `if` statement to check whether or not the user is already at the last slide. This is done by comparing the value stored in `currentSlide` plus 1 (for the next slide) to the length of the `imageList` array. If this is not the last slide, then there is another slide and you increment `currentSlide`:

```
if (currentSlide + 1 < imageList.length) {
    currentSlide += 1;
    document.slideShow.src = imageList[currentSlide].src;
}
```

6. Create a function named `previousSlide` with the `function` keyword; this function will be invoked when the user wants to move back to the previous slide:

```
function previousSlide() {
}
```

7. In the function, use an `if` statement to check whether or not the user is already at the first slide. This is done by comparing the value stored in `currentSlide` less 1 (for the previous slide) to zero:

```
if (currentSlide - 1 >= 0) {
}
```

8. If the previous slide is greater than or equal to zero, then the user has another slide to see and that slide is displayed and the `current Slide` value is reduced by one:

```
currentSlide -= 1;
document.slideShow.src = imageList[currentSlide].src;
```

9. In the body of the document, create two links for the previous and next slide, and in the `href` attribute, use `javascript :previousSlide()` and `javascript:nextSlide()` to invoke the appropriate functions when the user clicks on the links. Finally, include an `img` tag that displays the first image from the slide show with the name `slideShow` specified with the `name` attribute.

Including Captions in a Slide Show

In addition to rotating the images when a user clicks on a link, you can also display and rotate captions associated with the images.

This task builds on the manually controlled slide show from Task 71 and adds a caption so that the slide show looks like Figure 72-1. When the user changes images, the caption will change to match.

note

- This task provides a simple example of one way to rotate captions with images: by displaying the caption in a form's text field. This technique is universal and works on most browsers where techniques to dynamically replace HTML text directly are harder to perform in a truly browser-agnostic way.

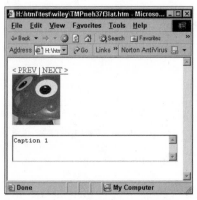

Figure 72-1: Displaying a caption with an image.

The following steps add the caption to the slide show as outlined previously:

1. In a script block in the header of a new document, create an array named `imageList`; this array will hold the `Image` objects for the slide show. At the same time, create an array named `captionList` to hold the corresponding captions:

```
var imageList = new Array;
var captionList = new Array;
```

2. Create an a variable named `currentSlide` and set its default value to 0; this variable will be used to track the slide the user is viewing:

```
var currentSlide = 0;
```

3. Create a new element of the `imageList` array for each slide show image, and assign the path and filename of the image to the `src` attribute of the object. At the same time, assign a relevant caption to the appropriate entry in the `captionList` array:

```
imageList[0] = new Image;
imageList[0].src = "image1.jpg";
captionList[0] = "Caption 1";
imageList[1] = new Image;
imageList[1].src = "image2.jpg";
captionList[1] = "Caption 2";
etc.
```

4. Create the `nextSlide` function as outlined in Task 71:

```
function nextSlide() {
    if (currentSlide + 1 < imageList.length) {
        currentSlide += 1;
        document.slideShow.src = imageList[currentSlide].src;
    }
}
```

5. In the `if` block, assign the appropriate caption to the caption text field to go along with the image:

```
function nextSlide() {
    if (currentSlide + 1 < imageList.length) {
        currentSlide += 1;
        document.slideShow.src = imageList[currentSlide].src;
        document.captionForm.caption.value = ⊃
captionList[currentSlide];
    }
}
```

6. Create the `previousSlide` function as outlined in Task 71, and add the same command as in the `nextSlide` function to handle captions. The final script should be as follows:

```
function previousSlide() {
    if (currentSlide - 1 >= 0) {
        currentSlide -= 1;
        document.slideShow.src = imageList[currentSlide].src;
        document.captionForm.caption.value = ⊃
captionList[currentSlide];
    }
}
```

7. In the body of the document, add the previous and next links and the image itself as in Task 71:

```
<a href="javascript:previousSlide()">&lt; PREV</a> |
<a href="javascript:nextSlide()">NEXT &gt;</a><br>
<img src="Tellers1.jpg" width=100 name="slideShow">
```

8. Add a form to the document and name the form `captionForm`. In the form, create a multiline text field named `caption`, and display the caption for the initial image in the text field:

```
<form name="captionForm">
    <textarea name="caption" rows=3 cols=40>Caption ⊃
1</textarea>
</form>
```

cross-reference

- Accessing form text fields and changing their values is done by assigning strings to `document.formName` `.textFieldName`. Refer to Task 79 for examples of this.

Testing If an Image Is Loaded

Sometimes when you load an image, either through the img tag or in JavaScript by creating an Image object, the loading of the image can take a long time. In these circumstances, you may want to prevent certain actions from occurring if the appropriate images have not yet loaded.

For instance, in a slide show, it might be appropriate to skip an image if it is not fully loaded when the user tries to display it. Similarly, it might be better to disable rollover effects until all relevant images have successfully loaded so that rollovers don't cause switches to incomplete or unloaded images.

This task illustrates the use of the complete property of the Image object by extending the random slide show from Task 70 so that the slide show doesn't start until all the images have fully loaded.

The following steps create this slide show application:

1. In a script block in the header of a new document, create an array named imageList; this array will hold the Image objects for the slide show. Load all the images into the array:

```
var imageList = new Array;
imageList[0] = new Image;
imageList[0].src = "image1.jpg";
imageList[1] = new Image;
imageList[1].src = "image2.jpg";
imageList[2] = new Image;
imageList[2].src = "image3.jpg";
imageList[3] = new Image;
imageList[3].src = "image4.jpg";


imageList[0] = new Image;
imageList[0].src = "image1.jpg";
imageList[1] = new Image;
imageList[1].src = "image2.jpg";
imageList[2] = new Image;
imageList[2].src = "image3.jpg";
imageList[3] = new Image;
imageList[3].src = "image4.jpg";
```

2. In the same way as in Task 70, create a function named slideShow that takes a single parameter named imageNumber, displays the specified image, randomly chooses another image, and then schedules a call to slideShow to display that image in three seconds:

```
function slideShow(imageNumber) {

    document.slideShow.src = imageList[imageNumber].src;
    var imageChoice = Math.floor(Math.random() * ⤶
imageList.length);
```

notes

- It is possible to test if an image has finished loading by checking the value of the complete property of the relevant Image object. If the value is true, then the image has finished loading.

- You can prevent the slide show from starting too early by adding a function to check if all the images have loaded. If all are loaded, the slide show starts. Otherwise, the function schedules a call to itself one second later to run the check again. This function is then called when the document has loaded to begin checking image loading status until images have loaded and the slide show can begin.

```
        window.setTimeout("slideShow(" + imageChoice + ⮌
    ")",3000);

    }
```

3. Create a function named `checkImages` with the `function` keyword:

```
function checkImages() {
}
```

4. In the function create a variable called `result` and set it to `false`:

```
var result = false;
```

5. In the function, create a `for` loop to loop through the `imageList` array:

```
for (i = 0; Ii < imageList.length; i++) {
}
```

6. In the loop, check if that image has completed loading, and if it has, make sure the result is `true`. This can be done by combining the current value of `result` with the value of the `complete` property of the related `Image` object using a boolean OR operation:

```
for (i = 0; i < imageList.length; i++) {
    result = (result || imageList[i].complete);
}
```

7. Test the result in an `if` statement, and if the result is `true`, call the `slideShow` function to start the show; otherwise, use the `window.setTimeout` method to call the `checkImages` function in one second to perform the check again:

```
if (result) {
    slideShow(0);
} else {
    window.setTimeout("checkImages()",1000);
}
```

8. In the body of the document, display the initial image with the `img` tag, and then set the `onLoad` attribute of the body tag to call the `checkImages` function:

```
<body onLoad="checkImages()">

    <img src="image1.jpg" width=100 name="slideShow">

</body>
```

Triggering a Rollover in a Different Location with a Link

R ollovers are typically triggered when a user moves the mouse over the image itself; all the examples of rollovers seen so far have worked this way. But there is nothing to prevent rollover effects to be displayed in a different place than where the mouse movement is detected.

For instance, it is possible to trap the mouse moving over a link but use this event to switch an image in a different location on the page.

This example shows how to trigger an image switch when the user moves the mouse pointer over a separate link:

note

- The onMouseOver event handler is similar to the onMouseOut event handler. It allows the programmer to specify JavaScript code to execute when the mouse pointer leaves the area occupied by a page element, such as an image where onMouseOver specified code to execute when the mouse pointer entered the space occupied by a page element (see Step 4).

1. In a script block in the header of a new document, create an Image object named originalImage and load the default image for the rollover into the object:

```
var originalImage = new Image;
originalImage.src = "image1.jpg";
```

2. Create an Image object named replacementImage, and load the rollover image for the rollover into the object. The final script block should look like this:

```
<script language="JavaScript">
    var originalImage = new Image;
    originalImage.src = "image1.jpg";

    var replacementImage = new Image;
    replacementImage.src = "rollImage1.jpg";
</script>
```

3. In the body of the document, create a link that will be used for triggering the rollover; it doesn't matter what URL is specified for the purposes of triggering the rollover:

```
<a href="myUrl">ROLLOVER THIS TEXT</a>
```

4. Add an onMouseOver attribute to the a tag, and switch the myImage object to the image in the replacementImage object; this will trigger the rollover when the mouse moves over the link:

```
<a href="#" onMouseOver="document.myImage.src = ⊃
replacementImage.src;">ROLLOVER THIS TEXT</a>
```

5. Add an onMouseOut attribute to the a tag, and switch the myImage object to the image in the originalImage object; this will return the image to the original state when the mouse moves off the link:

```
<a href="#" onMouseOver="document.myImage.src = ⊃
replacementImage.src;"
onMouseOut="document.myImage.src = ⊃
originalImage.src;">ROLLOVER THIS TEXT</a>
```

6. Add an `img` tag to the body, and display the default image. Name the image `myImage` with the `name` attribute. The final page should look like this:

```
<head>

    <script language="JavaScript">
        var originalImage = new Image;
        originalImage.src = "image1.jpg";

        var replacementImage = new Image;
        replacementImage.src = "rollimage1.jpg";
    </script>

</head>

<body>
    <a href="#" onMouseOver="document.myImage.src =
replacementImage.src;"
      onMouseOut="document.myImage.src =
originalImage.src;">ROLLOVER THIS TEXT</a><br>
    <img src="Tellers1.jpg" width=100 name="myImage">
</body>
```

7. Save the page in an HTML file, and open the file in a browser. This displays a page like Figure 74-1. When the mouse moves over the link, the rollover image will be displayed as in Figure 74-2.

Figure 74-1: Initially, the default image is displayed.

Figure 74-2: When the mouse moves over the link, the rollover image is displayed.

tip

- The rollover effect is designed to provide context to users, allowing them to know that the image constitutes a clickable element and showing users exactly what they are clicking on (especially in the case of numerous images in close proximity to each other in a complex layout).

cross-reference

- The basics of creating an image rollover effect is outlined in Task 61.

Using Image Maps and Rollovers Together

Rollovers can also be used with image maps. For instance, in Figure 75-1, an image is used to create a complex graphical menu. The individual ovals are specified in an image map and, therefore, are clickable links.

When rollovers are used with the image map, whenever the user rolls over the first oval, the image map is replaced with an alternate image highlighting that oval and providing descriptive text, as in Figure 75-2.

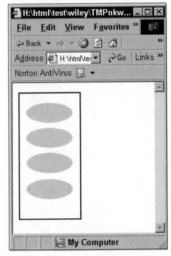

Figure 75-1: The initial image map.

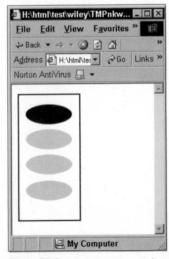

Figure 75-2: The rollover image for when the mouse pointer is over the first oval in the image map.

The following steps create a rollover effect on an image map:

1. In a script block in the header of a new document, create an `Image` object named `originalImage`, and load the default image for the rollover into the object:

```
var originalImage = new Image;
originalImage.src = "image1.jpg";
```

2. Create an `Image` object named `replacementImage`, and load the rollover image for the rollover into the object. The final script block should look like this:

```
var replacementImage = new Image;
replacementImage.src = "rollImage1.jpg";
```

3. In the header of the document, create an image map block with opening and closing `map` tags. Specify the name of the image map as `imageMap` with the `name` attribute of the `map` tag:

```
<map name="imageMap">
</map>
```

4. Use an `area` tag to specify a rectangular block for a link in the image map; use the `shape` attribute with the value `rect` and the `coords` attribute to specify the coordinates of the rectangle:

```
<area shape="rect" coords="0,0,100,100">
```

5. Add an `onMouseOver` attribute to the `area` tag to replace the image named `myImage` with `replacementImage` when the mouse rolls over the specified area. Also add an `onMouseOut` attribute to the `area` tag to replace the image named `myImage` with the `originalImage` image when the mouse rolls over the specified area:

```
<area shape="rect" coords="0,0,100,100"
  onMouseOver="document.myImage.src = ⤵
replacementImage.src;"
  onMouseOut="document.myImage.src = originalImage.src;">
```

6. In the body of the document, display the default image using an `img` tag and name the image `myImage` with the `name` attribute. Use the `usemap` attribute to associate the image with the `imageMap` image map:

```
<img src="image1.jpg" width=200 name="myImage" ⤵
usemap="#imageMap">
```

7. Save the code in an HTML file, and open it in a browser. When the mouse moves over the 100-pixel-wide and 100-pixel-deep square in the top-left corner of the image, the entire image map is replaced by the rollover image. When the mouse moves out of this area, the original image is displayed.

Generating Animated Banners in JavaScript

Many of the banner ads you see on the Web are animated. Sometimes these are done with animated GIF files, which provide a simple way to generate an animated image without resorting to any custom code.

However, GIFs have their limitations, not least of which they are not well suited to displaying photographic-style images with high color depth. That's when JPEG images come in handy. The problem is that JPEG images cannot be animated.

Using JavaScript you can animate a JPEG-based banner in much the same way that a slide show allows multiple images to be displayed. This is done by creating one JPEG image for each frame of the animation and then rotating them using JavaScript.

This task shows how you can create an animated banner with JavaScript and provide control over the amount of time between each frame transition:

1. In a script block in the header of a new document, create two arrays: `imageList` to hold the individual `Image` objects for the frames of the banner and `transitionList` to hold a list of transition times in milliseconds, specifying how long to wait after displaying one frame before displaying the next:

```
var imageList = new Array;
var transitionList = new Array;
```

2. Populate the `imageList` array with `Image` objects for the frames, and specify transition times in the `transitionList` array:

```
imageList[0] = new Image;
imageList[0].src = "frame1.jpg";
transitionList[0] = 2000;
imageList[1] = new Image;
imageList[1].src = "frame2.jpg";
transitionList[1] = 500;
imageList[2] = new Image;
imageList[2].src = "frame3.jpg";
transitionList[2] = 5000;
imageList[3] = new Image;
imageList[3].src = "frame4.jpg";
transitionList[3] = 3000;
```

3. Create a `rotateBanner` function that takes a single parameter `frameNumber` to indicate the frame that needs to be displayed:

```
function rotateBanner(frameNumber) {
}
```

note

- The `window.setTimeout` method takes two parameters: a function to call and a time in milliseconds. The function schedules an automatic call to the specified function after the specified number of milliseconds have elapsed. 3000 milliseconds is the same as 3 seconds (see Step 7).

- The `onLoad` event handler of the `body` tag is used to specify JavaScript to execute when an HTML document finishes its initial loading (see Step 9).

4. In the function, display the specified frame in the place of the Image object named banner:

```
document.banner.src = imageList[frameNumber].src;
```

5. Next, increment the frame number and assign it to a new variable called imageChoice:

```
var imageChoice = frameNumber + 1;
```

6. Check the value of imageChoice. If it is the same as the length of the imageList array, reset it to 0. This way the banner will rotate when it hits the last frame:

```
    if (imageChoice == imageList.length) ⊃
{ imageChoice = 0; }
```

7. As the last step of the function, schedule the rotateBanner function to run again after the appropriate display specified in the transitionList array:

```
window.setTimeout("rotateBanner(" + imageChoice + ⊃
")",transitionList[frameNumber]);
```

8. In the body of the document, display the first frame of the image with the img tag, and name the image banner:

```
<img src="frame1.jpg" name="banner">
```

9. In the body tag, specify the onLoad attribute to invoke rotateBanner when the document loads, passing a value of 0 to the rotateBanner function:

```
<body onLoad="rotateBanner(0)">
```

10. Save the code in an HTML, and open the file in a browser to see an animated banner as in Figure 76-1.

Figure 76-1: Displaying rotating JPEG banners with JavaScript.

Displaying a Random Banner Ad

O ne application of the combination of JavaScript and images is to load a random image in a location on the page rather than the same image every time. You can apply this to presenting random banner ads that link to the appropriate site for the ad. To do this you need to use JavaScript to specify both the location of the images and URLs associated with the images. With this data you can select one at random and display it.

The script created in the following steps illustrates this process:

1. Create a script block with opening and closing `script` tags; the script block should be in the body of your HTML document where you want the image to be displayed:

    ```
    <script language="JavaScript">
    </script>
    ```

2. In the script, create an array named `imageList`:

    ```
    var imageList = new Array;
    ```

3. Create an entry in the array for each banner's image you want to make available for random selection. For instance, if you have four images, assign the path and names of those images to the first four entries in the array:

    ```
    imageList[0] = "banner1.jpg";
    imageList[1] = "banner2.jpg";
    imageList[2] = "banner3.jpg";
    imageList[3] = "banner4.jpg";
    ```

4. Create another array to hold the URLs for each banner. The indexes in this array should correspond to the `imageList` array:

    ```
    var urlList = new Array;
    urlList[0] = "http://some.host/";
    urlList[1] = "http://another.host/";
    urlList[2] = "http://somewhere.else/";
    urlList[3] = "http://right.here/";
    ```

5. Create a variable named `imageChoice`:

    ```
    var imageChoice;
    ```

6. Assign a random number to `imageChoice` using the `Math.random` method, which returns a random number from 0 to 1 (that is, the number will be greater than or equal to 0 but less than 1):

    ```
    var imageChoice = Math.random();
    ```

7. Extend the expression assigned to `imageChoice` by multiplying the random number by the number of entries in the `imageList` array to produce a number greater than or equal to 0 but less than 4:

    ```
    var imageChoice = Math.random() * imageList.length;
    ```

notes

-   Each slot in an array is numbered; numbering starts at zero. This means an array with four entries has entries numbered 0 to 3.

-   The `Math` object provides a number of useful methods for working with numbers and mathematical operations.

-   The `length` property of an `Array` object provides the number of entries in an array. That means if an array has four entries numbered 0 to 3, then the `length` property of that array has a value of 4.

-   `Math.floor` performs a function similar to rounding in that it removes the decimal part of a number. The difference is that the result of rounding can be the next highest or next lowest integer value, depending on the size of the decimal portion of the number. With `Math.floor` the result is always the next lowest integer. Therefore, rounding 2.999 would result in the integer 3. but applying `Math.floor` to the same number would result in the integer 2.

-   Notice how the output is built out of multiple strings combined with an array variable; the combining is done with plus signs. When you are working with string values, plus signs perform concatenation of strings, as discussed in Task 15. Concatenation means that "ab" + "cd" results in "abcd".

8. Extend the expression assigned to imageChoice further by removing any part after the decimal point with the Math.floor method; the result is an integer from 0 to one less than the number of entries in the array—in this case that means an integer from 0 to 3:

```
var imageChoice = Math.floor(Math.random() * ⤴
imageList.length);
```

9. Use the document.write method to place an img tag surrounded by an a tag in the HTML data stream sent to the browser. As the value of the src attribute of img tag, the random image is specified as imageList[imageChoice], and as the value of the href attribute of the a tag, use urlList[imageChoice]. The final script looks Listing 77-1.

```
<script language="JavaScript">

    var imageList = new Array;
    imageList[0] = "image1.jpg";
    imageList[1] = "image2.jpg";
    imageList[2] = "image3.jpg";
    imageList[3] = "image4.jpg";

    var urlList = new Array;
    urlList[0] = "http://some.host/";
    urlList[1] = "http://another.host/";
    urlList[2] = "http://somewhere.else/";
    urlList[3] = "http://right.here/";

    var imageChoice = Math.floor(Math.random() * ⤴
imageList.length);
    document.write('<a href="' + urlList[imageChoice] + ⤴
'"><img src="' + imageList[imageChoice] + '"></a>');

</script>
```

Listing 77-1: Displaying a random banner ad.

10. Save the code in an HTML file, and display the file in a browser. A random banner is displayed. Reloading the file should result in a different banner (although there is always a small chance the same random number will be selected twice in a row).

cross-references

▪ An array is a data type that contains multiple, numbered slots into which you can place any value. See Task 20 for a discussion of arrays.

▪ The document.write method is introduced in Task 45. It allows JavaScript code to generate output that forms part of the HTML rendered by the browser.

Part 4: Working with Forms

Preparing Your Forms for JavaScript

In JavaScript, you can access and manipulate the content and state of fields in forms on the page. To do this, you need to give some attention to the minimum requirements needed to make your forms easily accessible in JavaScript. Primarily, you must focus on providing names for your forms and elements. The following steps walk you through the process of naming your forms and elements so you can access them using JavaScript:

1. Create a new document in your preferred editor.

2. Create a form in the body of the document. Add an input text field, a selection list, and a command button to your form:

```
<body>
    <form method="post" action="target.html">
        <input type="text">
        <select>
            <option value="1">First Choice</option>
            <option value="2">Second Choice</option>
        </select>
        <br>
        <input type="submit" value="Submit Me">
    </form>
</body>
```

This form is shown in Figure 78-1.

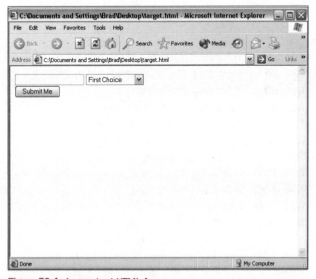

Figure 78-1: A standard HTML form.

notes

- To access a field in a form, you can use the following reference in JavaScript:

  `document.forms[0].elements[0]`

  Each form in your document is contained in the `forms` array in the order it appears in your document. The elements array, similarly, has one entry for each field in a given form in the order the fields appear in the form.

- If the form is not named, then each form is accessible in the `document.forms` array, so that the first form in the document is `document.forms[0]`, the second is `document.forms[1]`, and so on.

- If the field is not named, then each field in the form is accessible in the `document.formName.elements` array, so that the first field in the form is `document.formName.elements[0]`, the second is `document.formName.elements[1]`, and so on.

- Most of the tasks in this part use the `name` attribute to manipulate the contents of a form.

3. Name the form by adding a `name` attribute. The following code names the form `thisform`. As shown in bold, the `name` attribute is added within the `form` tag:

```
<body>
    <form method="post" action="target.html" ⤸
name="thisForm">
        <input type="text">
        <select>
            <option value="1">First Choice</option>
            <option value="2">Second Choice</option>
        </select>
        <br>
        <input type="submit" value="Submit Me">
    </form>
</body>
```

4. Name the elements within the form. Just like naming the form, this is done by adding an attribute called `name` to each field's tag. This attribute is then set to the name of the element as shown in Listing 78-1. Once you've assigned the `name` attributes, your form is ready to be easily used with JavaScript.

```
<body>

    <form method="post" action="target.html" name="thisForm">

        <input type="text" name="myText">

        <select name="mySelect">
            <option value="1">First Choice</option>
            <option value="2">Second Choice</option>
        </select>

        <br>
        <input type="submit" value="Submit Me">

    </form>
</body>
```

Listing 78-1: A JavaScript-ready form.

tips

- Naming fields and forms makes them much easier to refer to and ensures you are referring to the correct fields in your code.

- When naming forms and the elements within your forms, you should use descriptive names.

cross-reference

- Task 79 shows you how to access a text field using the assigned name.

Accessing Text Field Contents

When you create an HTML form, you are creating a series of objects, which can be accessed from within JavaScript. The form itself is an object, and then each of the fields in the form is represented by an object in JavaScript. Using these objects, you can access the values stored in form fields such as text input fields.

You can check the text that is displayed in a text input field—whether it is text that is a part of the form or text that a user has entered. To be able to access a field in JavaScript, use the following steps:

1. Create a new document in your preferred editor.

2. In the body of the document, create the form named `myForm` that contains a text input field named `myText`:

```
<body>
    <form name="myForm">
        <input type="text" name="myText">
    </form>
</body>
```

3. Create a link in your form. This link is used to display the value of the text input element in a dialog box. Specify # as the URL for the link:

```
<body>

    <form name="myForm">
        <input type="text" name="myText">
    </form>

    <a href="#">Check Text Field</a>

</body>
```

4. Use the `onClick` event handler in the link element to specify JavaScript code to execute when the user clicks on the link. To access a form field, you use the following syntax:

```
document.formName.fieldName
```

This references the object associated with the field. The object has several properties, including:

- `name`: The name of the field (as specified in the `name` attribute)

- `value`: The text displayed in the field

- `form`: A reference to the `form` object for the form in which the field exists

notes

* The following is the minimum HTML required to create a text field:

  ```
  <input type="text">
  ```

  Notice the use of # as the URL in the example. When using the `onClick` event handler to trigger the opening of a new window, you don't want to cause clicking on the link to change the location of the current window; this is a simple way to avoid this.

* If the form is not named, then each form is accessible in the `document.forms` array, so that the first form in the document is `document.forms[0]`, the second is `document.forms[1]`, and so on.

* If the field is not named, then each field in the form is accessible in the `document.formName.elements` array, so that the first field in the form is `document.formName.elements[0]`, the second is `document.formName.elements[1]`, and so on.

Therefore, the property `document.formName.formField.value` would contain a string of text as displayed in the field.

In this example, `document.myForm.myText.value` would represent the text in the text input field, so this is passed as an argument to `window.alert`. The result is that the text in the `myText` text input box is displayed in a dialog box. Listing 79-1 shows the complete listing with the JavaScript added.

```
<body>

    <form name="myForm">
        <input type="text" name="myText">
    </form>

    <a href="#" onClick="window.alert
(document.myForm.myText.value);">Check Text Field</a>

</body>
```

Listing 79-1: Accessing the value of a form text field.

5. Save the file and close it.

6. Open the file in your browser. Enter some text in the text field, and then click the link to see that text displayed in a dialog box, as illustrated in Figure 79-1.

Figure 79-1: Displaying the text field's value.

tips

- Naming forms and fields makes it much easier to refer to them and ensures you are referring to the correct fields in your code.

- In the listing in Step 4, change `document.myForm.myText.value` to `document.myForm.myText.name`. You'll see the result is that the name of the text input field is displayed instead of the value.

cross-references

- See Task 200 to learn more about the `onClick` event handler.

- For more information on naming elements and forms, see Task 78.

80 Dynamically Updating Text Fields

Using JavaScript, you can change the values in a text input field. The easiest time to make this update is when a user does something on your form. This task shows you how to dynamically update the text that is displayed in a text input field:

1. Create a new document in your preferred editor.

2. Create a form in the body of your document. Name your form `myForm`.

3. Add two text input fields to your form. Name one `myText`, which will be used to enter text. Call the other `copyText`. It will have its value dynamically changed. The following is the completed form:

```
<body>

    <form name="myForm">
        Enter some Text: <input type="text" ⤴
name="myText"><br>
        Copy Text: <input type="Text" name="copyText">
    </form>

</body>
```

4. Create a link that will be used to dynamically change the text. The user can enter text into the `myText` field and then click on the link to copy that text into the second text field; the copying is done with JavaScript. Although a link is used in this example, you could just as easily use a button click or any other event to dynamically change the text. Specify # as the URL for the link.

5. Add an `onClick` event handler to the link. This will specify the JavaScript code to execute when the user clicks on the link. The property `document.formName.formField.value` contains the value of a field in the form of a string of text. If you assign a value to the `value` property, the new value will be displayed in the text field. In this case, the value from the `myText` field will be assigned to the `copyText` field. This is done by assigning `document.myForm.myText.value` to `document.myForm.copyText.value`. Listing 80-1 shows the final form with the link and JavaScript added. Figure 80-1 shows the form.

```
<body>

    <form name="myForm">
        Enter some Text: <input type="text" name="myText"><br>
        Copy Text: <input type="text" name="copyText">
    </form>
```
(continued)

notes

■ Notice the use of # as the URL in the example. When using the `onClick` event handler to trigger the opening of a new window, you don't want to cause clicking on the link to change the location of the current window; this is a simple way to avoid this.

■ If the form is not named, then each form is accessible in the `document.forms` array, so that the first form in the document is `document.forms[0]`, the second is `document.forms[1]`, and so on.

■ If the field is not named, then each field in the form is accessible in the `document.formName.elements` array, so that the first field in the form is `document.formName.elements[0]`, the second is `document.formName.elements[1]`, and so on.

```
        <a href="#" onClick="document.myForm.copyText.value =
    document.myForm.myText.value;">Copy Text Field</a>

    </body>
```

Listing 80-1: Assigning a value to a form text field.

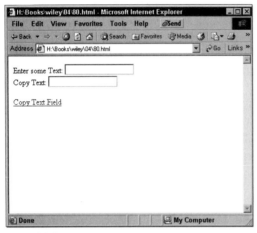

Figure 80-1: A form with two text fields.

6. Save the file and close it.

7. Open the file in your browser. You should see the form and link as shown in Figure 80-1. Enter some text in the first text field, and then click the link to see the text copied and displayed in the second field, as illustrated in Figure 80-2.

Figure 80-2: Assigning text to a text field.

tip

▪ Naming forms and fields makes it much easier to refer to them and ensures you are referring to the correct fields in your code.

cross-reference

▪ For more information on naming elements and forms, see Task 78.

Detecting Changes in Text Fields

When you create an HTML form, you are creating a series of objects that can be accessed from within JavaScript. Using these objects, you can detect changes in form fields such as text input fields.

This task shows you how to react to a change in a text input field. Text input fields are created with the `input` tag and by setting the `type` attribute equal to `text`. To make the field accessible in JavaScript, it is also best to assign a name to the field with the `name` attribute:

```
<input type="text" name="myField">
```

You can specify code to execute when a change occurs in the field with the `onChange` event handler:

```
<input type="text" name="myField" onChange="JavaScript code to ⊃
execute when the value of the field changes">
```

The following steps create a form with a text field. When a change is detected in the field, a dialog box is displayed telling the user the value in the field.

1. Create a new document in your preferred editor.

2. In the body of the document, create a form named `myForm`.

   ```
   <body>
       <form name="myForm">
       </form>
   </body>
   ```

3. In the form, create a text input field with the name `myText`:

   ```
   <body>
       <form name="myForm">
           Enter some Text: <input type="text" name="myText">
       </form>
   </body>
   ```

4. Assign an `onChange` event handler to the field. The handler should display `this.value` in a dialog box with the `window.alert` method. The final page should look like Listing 81-1.

5. Save the file and close it.

6. Open the file in your browser. You should see the form as in Figure 81-1.

7. Enter some text in the text field and then click outside the field to remove focus from the field. You should see the dialog box shown in Figure 81-2.

notes

▪ For the detection of the change to occur, most browsers (including all the major ones) don't actually consider a change to have occurred until the focus leaves the field (such as when the user clicks in another field in the form). If the user didn't do this, then every time he or she typed a character, the code in the `onChange` event handler would execute. Instead, the code only executes when a change has occurred and focus has left the field.

▪ When working in the event handler of a form field, the `this` keyword refers to the object associated with the field itself, which allows you to use `this.value` instead of `document. myForm.myText.value` to refer to the text field's value in the `onChange` event handler (see Step 4).

```
<body>
   <form name="myForm">
      Enter some Text: <input type="text" name="myText" ⮐
onChange="window.alert(this.value);">
   </form>
</body>
```

Listing 81-1: Detecting changes in text fields.

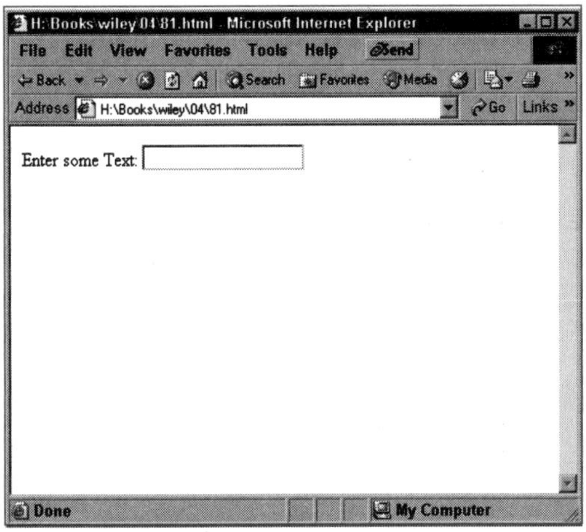

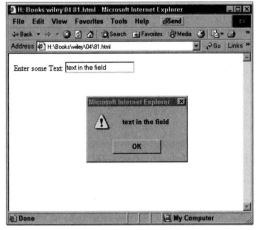

Figure 81-1: A form with a text field.

Figure 81-2: Detecting change in the text field.

cross-reference

▪ Learn about naming fields in Task 78.

Accessing Selection Lists

When you create an HTML form, you are creating a series of objects that can be accessed from within JavaScript. The form itself is an object, and then each form field is represented by an object in JavaScript. Using these objects, you can access the values stored in form fields such as selection lists. This task shows you how to check the current selection in a selection list.

The following steps create a form with a single selection list and then provide a link the user can click to display the value of the currently selected option in a dialog box. JavaScript is used to display this information in the dialog box.

1. Create a new document in your preferred editor.

2. In the body of the document, create a form named `myForm`.

3. In the form, create a selection list named `mySelect` and add a number of options:

    ```
    <body>

        <form name="myForm">
            <select name="mySelect">
                <option value="First Choice">1</option>
                <option value="Second Choice">2</option>
                <option value="Third Choice">3</option>
            </select>
        </form>

    </body>
    ```

4. After the form, create a link with # as the URL. The link will be used to display the form field's selected value in a dialog box:

    ```
    <body>

        <form name="myForm">
            <select name="mySelect">
                <option value="First Choice">1</option>
                <option value="Second Choice">2</option>
                <option value="Third Choice">3</option>
            </select>
        </form>

        <a href="#">Check Selection List</a>

    </body>
    ```

5. Use the `onClick` event handler to specify JavaScript code to execute when the user clicks on the link. In this case, `document.myForm.mySelect.value`, which represents the value of the selection option in the list, is passed as an argument to `window.alert` in

notes

- Selection lists are created with the `select` tag. You populate the list with the `option` tag:

  ```
  <select name=
  "myField">

      <option
  value="a">A</a>

      <option
  value="b">B</a>

      etc.

  </select>

  <select>

  </select>
  ```

  Notice the use of # as the URL in the example. When using the `onClick` event handler to trigger the opening of a new window, you don't want to cause clicking on the link to change the location of the current window; this is a simple way to avoid this.

- Remember that with selection lists, the text displayed for an option in the list is different than the value associated with the option. The `value` property of a selection list's object is associated with the value, and not the display text, of the currently selected option in the list.

order to display the text in a dialog box. The final page looks like
Listing 82-1.

```
<body>

   <form name="myForm">
      <select name="mySelect">
         <option value="First Choice">1</option>
         <option value="Second Choice">2</option>
         <option value="Third Choice">3</option>
      </select>
   </form>

   <a href="#" onClick="window.alert(document.
myForm.mySelect.value);">Check Selection List</a>

</body>
```

Listing 82-1: Accessing the value of a selected option in a selection list.

6. Save the file and close it.

7. Open the file in your browser. You should see the form and link as in
   Figure 82-1.

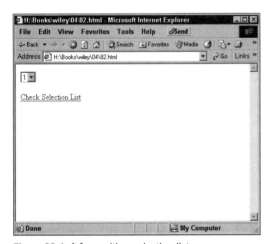

Figure 82-1: A form with a selection list.

8. Select an option from the selection list and then click the link to see
   the value of that selection displayed in a dialog box.

cross-references

▪ Task 83 shows you how to
   programmatically populate
   a selection list.

▪ Task 85 shows you how to
   detect when a selection is
   made in a selection list.

Programmatically Populating a Selection List

You can dynamically add entries to a selection list through JavaScript without ever using an `option` tag in HTML to create the selection entry. The principle is simple. The selection list object has a `length` property indicating the number of entries in the selection list. Increasing this value by 1 creates an empty entry at the end of the list, as illustrated in Figure 83-1.

* A key point here: The `length` property contains the number of elements in the list. For instance, if there are three elements, then the value is 3. But, the `options` array, like all arrays, starts counting at zero. So, the index of that last, third element is 2. You need to keep this in mind when working with selection lists dynamically from JavaScript.

* The use of the short-form `++` operator increases the operand before it by one. For instance `a++` is the same as `a = a + 1`.

* A `text` property is used to hold the text that will be displayed on the form. The `value` property is used to hold the value of the entry.

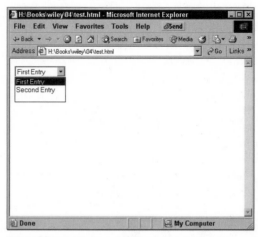

Figure 83-1: Adding a new entry to a selection list.

Once the new entry is created, you use the `options` property of the selection list to assign display text and a value to the new entry. This property is an array containing one object for each element in the array. Each of these objects has a `text` and a `value` property. To populate an entry with values, you would use the following:

```
document.formName.selectionObject.options[index of new entry].text ⤵
= "Display text";
document.formName.selectionObject.options[index of new entry].⤵
value = "Entry value";
```

The following task creates a form with a selection list with two entries and is immediately followed by JavaScript code to create a third element in the list:

1. Create a new document in your preferred editor.

2. In the body of the document, create a form named `myForm` that contains a selection list named `mySelect` with three options:

```
<form name="myForm">
  <select name="mySelect">
    <option value="First Choice">1</option>
```

```
        <option value="Second Choice">2</option>
    </select>
</form>
```

3. After the form, create a script.

4. In the script, add one to the length of the selection list:

```
<script language="JavaScript">
    document.myForm.mySelect.length++;
</script>
```

5. In the script, set the display text for the new entry:

```
document.myForm.mySelect.options[document.myForm.⏎
mySelect.length - 1].text = "3";
```

6. Set the display value for the new entry. The final page looks like
   Listing 83-1.

```
<body>
    <form name="myForm">
        <select name="mySelect">
            <option value="First Choice">1</option>
            <option value="Second Choice">2</option>
        </select>
    </form>

    <script language="JavaScript">
        document.myForm.mySelect.length++;

document.myForm.mySelect.options[document.myForm.mySelect.⏎
length - 1].text = "3";

document.myForm.mySelect.options[document.myForm.mySelect.⏎
length - 1].value = "Third Choice";
    </script>
</body>
```

Listing 83-1: Dynamically adding an entry to a selection list.

7. Save the file and open it in a browser. Expand the selection list, and
   you see three entries.

cross-references

- The ++ operators is one
  form of mathematical operation you can do with
  JavaScript. For more on
  mathematical
  operations, see Task 14.

- Task 37 shows you how to
  loop through an array.

Dynamically Changing Selection List Content

A common feature in some interactive Web forms is to change the contents of a selection list dynamically. This allows you to create intelligent forms in which a user's actions can determine what should appear in a selection list.

This is easy to do in JavaScript. The selection list object has a `length` property indicating the number of entries in the selection list. You can reset this number to the length needed based on a user's choice in another list and then populate each entry in the options array appropriately.

The following steps create a form with a selection list followed by a link. When the user clicks the link, the contents of the selection list changes.

1. In the header of a new selection list, create a script with a function called `changeList`. This function populates a selection list with new options. It takes as an argument the object associated with the selection list to change:

```
<script language="JavaScript">
function changeList(list) {
}
</script>
```

2. In the function, set the length of the list to 3:

```
list.length = 3;
```

3. Create three entries in the list:

```
function changeList(list) {
    list.length = 3;
    list.options[0].text = "First List 1";
    list.options[0].value = "First Value 1";
    list.options[1].text = "First List 2";
    list.options[1].value = "First Value 2";
    list.options[2].text = "First List 3";
    list.options[2].value = "First Value 3";
}
```

4. In the body of the document, create a form named `myForm` that contains a selection list named `mySelect` with two options:

```
<body>
    <form name="myForm">
        <select name="mySelect">
            <option value="1">First Choice</option>
            <option value="2">Second Choice</option>
        </select><br>
    </form>
</body>
```

notes

- You use the `options` property of the selection list to assign display text and a value to the new entry. This property is an array containing one object for each element in the array. Each of these objects has a `text` and a `value` property.

- To populate an entry with values, you would use the following:

  `document.formName.selectionObject.options[index of new entry].text = "Display text";`

  `document.formName.selectionObject.options[index of new entry].value = "Entry value";`

- A key point here: The `length` property contains the number of elements in the list. For instance, if there are four elements, then the value is 4. But the `options` array, like all arrays, starts counting at zero. So, the index of that last, fourth element is 3. You need to keep this in mind when working with selection lists dynamically from JavaScript.

- Notice the use of # as the URL in the example. When using the `onClick` event handler to trigger the opening of a new window, you don't want to cause clicking on the link to change the location of the current window; this is a simple way to avoid this.

5. After the form, create a link the user will use to change the items in the selection list. The link should include an `onClick` event handler. The `onClick` event handler will call `changeList` and pass the selection list object to the function:

```
<body>
    <form name="myForm">
        <select name="mySelect">
            <option value="1">First Choice</option>
            <option value="2">Second Choice</option>
        </select><br>
    </form>

    <a href="#" onClick="changeList
(document.myForm.mySelect);">Change the List</a>

</body>
```

6. Save the file and open it in a browser. The list appears, as illustrated in Figure 84-1.

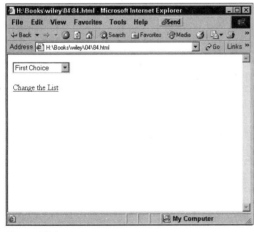

Figure 84-1: A selection list.

7. Click on the link, and the list changes to the new entries.

cross-references

- Task 83 shows you how to add a selection item to an existing selection list.

- See Task 87 to learn how to use a group of radio buttons instead of a selection list.

Detecting Selections in Selection Lists

When you create an HTML form, you are creating a series of objects that can be accessed from within JavaScript. The form itself is an object, and then each form field is represented by an object in JavaScript. Using these objects, you can detect selections made in form fields such as selection lists.

This task shows you how to react to the user selecting an option in a selection list that was created with the select tag. You can specify code to execute when a selection occurs in the field with the onChange event handler:

```
<select name="myField" onChange="JavaScript code to execute when the
value of the field changes">
```

The following steps create a form with a selection list. When a new selection is detected in the field, a dialog box is displayed that tells the user the value of the selected option.

1. Create a new document in your preferred editor.

2. In the body of the document, create a form named myForm:

```
<body>
    <form name="myForm">

    </form>
</body>
```

3. In the form, create a selection list with the name mySelect that is populated with some options:

```
<body>
    <form name="myForm">
        <select name="mySelect">
            <option value="First Choice">1</option>
            <option value="Second Choice">2</option>
            <option value="Third Choice">3</option>
        </select>
    </form>
</body>
```

4. Assign an onChange event handler to the field; the handler should display this.value in a dialog box with the window.alert method. The final page should look like Listing 85-1.

```
<body>
    <form name="myForm">

        <select name="mySelect" onChange="
window.alert(this.value);">
            <option value="First Choice">1</option>
```
(continued)

- Unlike with text fields (see Task 82), the browser will respond to selections as soon as they occur. This means as soon as the user finishes selecting an option, the code specified in the onChange event handler will execute. The only time this doesn't happen is if the user reselects the value that was already selected.

- When working in the event handler of a form field, the this keyword refers to the object associated with the field itself, which allows you to use this.value instead of document. myForm.mySelect.val ue to refer to the selection list's selected value in the onChange event handler.

```
            <option value="Second Choice">2</option>
            <option value="Third Choice">3</option>
        </select>
    </form>
</body>
```

Listing 85-1: Detecting new selections in selection lists.

5. Save the file and close it.

6. Open the file in your browser. You should see the form as in Figure 85-1.

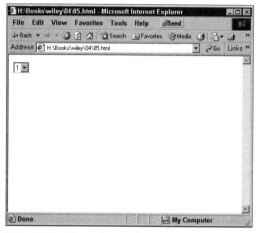

Figure 85-1: A form with a selection list.

7. Make a new selection in the list, and you should see the dialog box shown in Figure 85-2.

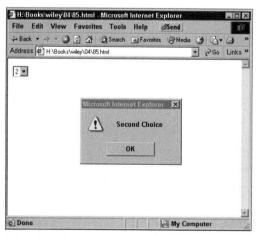

Figure 85-2: Detecting new selections.

cross-references

▪ To make the field accessible in JavaScript, it is also best to assign a name to the field with the `name` attribute. See Task 78 for information on naming fields.

▪ See Task 88 to learn how to use a group of radio buttons instead of a selection list.

Updating One Selection List Based on Selection in Another

A common feature in some interactive Web forms is for selections in one selection list to cause dynamic entries to appear in the second. This allows you to create intelligent forms in which a user's choice in one selection list can determine the available choices in a second selection list.

The following steps create a form with two selection lists. Based on the user's selection in the first list, a different set of items is displayed in the second list.

1. In the header of a new selection list, create a script that has a function called firstList. This function will populate the second list with an appropriate set of items. This function will execute if the user selects the first option in the first selection list. It takes as an argument the object associated with the second selection list.

2. In the function, set the length of the list to 3.

3. Create three entries in the list to complete the function:

```
function firstList(list) {
    list.length = 3;
    list.options[0].text = "First List 1";
    list.options[0].value = "First Value 1";
    list.options[1].text = "First List 2";
    list.options[1].value = "First Value 2";
    list.options[2].text = "First List 3";
    list.options[2].value = "First Value 3";
}
```

4. Create a second function named secondList. This function works the same as firstList, except that it creates a different set of entries for when the user chooses the second option in the first selection list:

```
function secondList(list) {
    list.length = 3;
    list.options[0].text = "Second List 1";
    list.options[0].value = "Second Value 1";
    list.options[1].text = "Second List 2";
    list.options[1].value = "Second Value 2";
    list.options[2].text = "Second List 3";
    list.options[2].value = "Second Value 3";
}
```

5. Create a third function named updateSecondSelect. It takes a form object as an argument and is called when the user makes a

notes

* A key point here: The length property contains the number of elements in the list. For instance, if there are four elements, then the value is 4. But the options array, like all arrays, starts counting at zero. So, the index of that last, fourth element is 3. You need to keep this in mind when working with selection lists dynamically from JavaScript.

* You use the options property of the selection list to assign display text and a value to the new entry.

* The selectedIndex property of a selection list's object indicates the index of the currently selected item in the list. The first item has an index 0, the second item an index 1, and so on.

* You use the options property of the selection list to assign display text and a value to the new entry. This property is an array containing one object for each element in the array. Each of these objects has a text and a value property.

* To populate an entry with values, you would use the following:

```
document.formName.
selectionObject.
options[index of
new entry].text =
"Display text";
```

```
document.formName.
selectionObject.
options[index of
new entry].value =
"Entry value";
```

selection in the first selection list. This function checks the selection that has been made and calls either `firstList` or `secondList`.

6. In the function, check if the first option is selected. If so, call `firstList`; if not, call `secondList`:

```
function updateSecondSelect(thisForm) {
    if (thisForm.firstSelect.selectedIndex == 0) {
        firstList(thisForm.secondSelect);
    } else {
        secondList(thisForm.secondSelect);
    }
}
```

7. Create a form to use your functions. In the body of the document, create a form with two selection lists named `firstSelect` and `secondSelect`. Populate the first list with two entries, and leave the second list blank. In the `body` tag, use the `onLoad` event handler to call `firstList` to populate the second list initially, and in the first `select` tag, use the `onChange` event handler to call `updateSecondSelect`:

```
<body onLoad="firstList(document.myForm.secondSelect);">
    <form name="myForm">
        <select name="firstSelect" onChange=
            "updateSecondSelect(this.form);">
            <option value="1">First Choice</option>
            <option value="2">Second Choice</option>
        </select><br>

        <select name="secondSelect">
        </select>
    </form>

    <script language="JavaScript">
        document.myForm.mySelect.length = firstList.length;
        document.myForm.mySelect.options = firstList;
    </script>
</body>
```

8. Save the file and open it in a browser. You now see two lists. The first has the first option selected, and the second displays the appropriate list for the first option.

9. Select the second option in the first list. You see the second list change.

cross-reference

- Task 83 shows you how to add a selection item to an existing selection list.

Using Radio Buttons instead of Selection Lists

Typically, selection lists, such as drop-down lists, are used to allow users to make a single selection from a list of options. However, selection lists are not the only choice of form fields available. If you plan to ask the user to make a single selection from a group of options, you can also use radio buttons. Radio buttons display a series of check box-like buttons; however, only one in a group can be selected at any time.

To create a group of radio buttons, do the following:

1. To create a radio buttons, start by creating an input tag, using radio as the value of the type attribute:

   ```
   <input type="radio">
   ```

2. Create a radio button for each option in the group:

   ```
   <input type="radio" value="1"> Option 1<br>
   <input type="radio" value="2"> Option 2<br>
   <input type="radio" value="3"> Option 3
   ```

3. Now assign a common name to all the input tags for your group of radio buttons. This common name allows the browser to associate the buttons and to ensure that the user can only select one of the radio buttons in the group:

   ```
   <input type="radio" name="myField"> Option 1<br>
   <input type="radio" name="myField"> Option 2<br>
   <input type="radio" name="myField"> Option 3
   ```

If you assign different names to each input tag, then the radio buttons are no longer a group and the user could easily select all three options, as shown in Figure 87-1.

notes

- Which type of form field to use depends on the context in which the field will be used. It is common to use radio buttons to provide selections from a small group of simple options; you often see radio buttons for choosing from pairs of options such as Male/Female, Yes/No, or True/False. By comparison, selection lists allow users to choose from long lists of options, such as choosing a state or country. Displaying these longer lists as radio buttons would make inefficient use of limited screen space.

- In option lists, you specify any text to display next to the button's input tag. The text to display is not inherent to the input tag.

- Notice the checked attribute; this indicates that this radio button will be initially selected when the form is displayed.

caution

- Just as with selection lists, each option has text that is displayed next to the button and a value, specified with the value attribute. It is the value and not the text that is tracked and manipulated from within JavaScript and submitted when you submit the form (see Step 8).

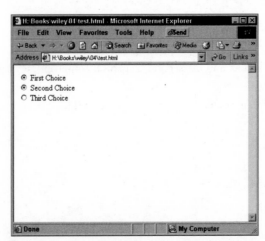

Figure 87-1: Selecting multiple radio buttons if the name is specified incorrectly.

4. Compare the use of radio buttons to a selection list. The remaining steps show you how to create a form that displays both a selection list and a set of radio buttons that show the same options. You'll see how these can be used interchangeably.

5. In a form, create a selection list named `mySelect`:

```
<select name="mySelect">

</select>
```

6. Populate the list with some options:

```
<select name="mySelect">
   <option value="Y">Yes</option>
   <option value="N">No</option>
</select>
```

7. Create a radio button for the Yes option in a radio group named `myRadio`:

```
<input type="radio" name="myRadio" value="Y" checked> Yes
```

8. Create a second radio button for the No option in the same group:

```
<input type="radio" name="myRadio" value="Y" checked> Yes
<input type="radio" name="myRadio" value="N"> No
```

9. Save the form in an HTML file.

10. Open the file in the form. You now see the same choices presented as a selection list and as a pair of radio buttons, as in Figure 87-2.

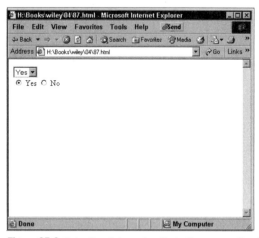

Figure 87-2: Selection lists and radio buttons can often be used for the same tasks.

cross-reference

▪ See Task 82 for a quick overview of selection lists.

Task 88

Detecting the Selected Radio Button

When you create an HTML form, you are creating a series of objects that can be accessed from within JavaScript. The form itself is an object, and an object in JavaScript also represents each form field. Using these objects, you can access the selected radio button in a group of radio buttons.

This task shows you how to check which radio button the user has selected. To access the radio button group, you use this syntax:

```
document.formName.groupName
```

This references the object associated with the radio button group. This object is actually an array containing an entry for each button in the group, and each of these entries has several properties, including two critical ones for this task:

- `checked`: Indicates if the radio button is currently selected
- `value`: Reflects the value of the `value` attribute for the radio button

Therefore, the property `document.formName.formField[0].value` would contain the value of the first radio button in a radio button group.

The following steps create a form with a group of radio buttons. The value of the currently selected radio button is displayed by clicking a link that is provided.

1. In the header of a new HTML document, create a script block with a function named `whichButton` that takes no arguments:

   ```
   <script language="JavaScript">
      function whichButton() {
      }
   </script>
   ```

2. In the function, create a variable named `buttonValue` that is initially an empty string:

   ```
   var buttonValue = "";
   ```

3. Loop through the `document.myForm.myRadio` array of radio button objects:

   ```
   for (i = 0; i < document.myForm.myRadio.length; i++) {
   }
   ```

4. In the loop, check if the current radio button item is selected:

   ```
   if (document.myForm.myRadio[i].checked) {
   }
   ```

notes

- The `checked` property has a value of `true` if it is currently selected and `false` if it is not.

- Radio button groups are created through a series of `input` tags with the same name and the type specified as `radio`:

  ```
  <input type="radio"
         name="myField"
         value="1">
  Option 1

  <input type="radio"
         name="myField"
         value="2">
  Option 2
  ```

- Arrays have a property called `length` that returns the number of items in an array, and it is used in this loop. Since arrays are zero-indexed, an array with length 5 (which contains five elements) would contain elements with indexes from 0 to 4. This is why you loop until `i` is less than, and not less than or equal to, the length of the array.

- The `checked` property of a radio button object is either `true` or `false`, which makes it sufficient as a condition for an `if` statement.

- Remember, the browser will only allow a single radio button in the group to be selected. This means that the `if` statement will be `true` only once and `buttonValue` will only ever be assigned the value of the single, selected radio button.

5. If the current button is checked, assign its value to `buttonValue`:

```
buttonValue = document.myForm.myRadio[i].value;
```

6. After the loop, return the value of `buttonValue`. Listing 88-1 presents the completed function.

```
<script language="JavaScript">
  function whichButton() {
    var buttonValue = "";
    for (i = 0; i < document.myForm.myRadio.length; i++) {
        if (document.myForm.myRadio[i].checked) {
            buttonValue = document.myForm.myRadio[i].value;
        }
    }
    return buttonValue;
  }
</script>
```

Listing 88-1: The `whichButton` function.

7. In the body of the document, create a form named `myForm` that will call your function. This should have a radio button group named `myRadio` and a link. The link should use an `onClick` event handler to display the result of calling `whichButton` in an alert dialog box. The final form should look like Listing 88-2.

```
<body>
  <form name="myForm">
    <input type="radio" name="myRadio"
        value="First Button"> Button 1<br>
    <input type="radio" name="myRadio"
        value="Second Button"> Button 2
  </form>
  <a href="#" onClick="window.alert(whichButton());">⏎
Which Radio Button?</a>
</body>
```

Listing 88-2: Detecting the selected radio button.

8. Save the file and open the file in your browser. You should see the form and link.

9. Select a radio button, and click the link to see the value displayed.

cross-reference

- For more information on using radio buttons, see Task 87

Detecting Change of Radio Button Selection

When you create an HTML form, you are creating a series of objects that can be accessed from within JavaScript. The form itself is an object, and then an object in JavaScript represents each form field. Using these objects, you can make changes in the selection of a radio button in a group of radio buttons.

This task shows you how to react to the user selecting a new radio button. To detect selection of a radio button, you can use the `onClick` event handler in each of the radio buttons in your group:

```
<input type="radio" name="myField" value="1" onClick="JavaScript ⤵
code"> Option 1
<input type="radio" name="myField" value="2" onClick="JavaScript ⤵
code"> Option 2
```

The following steps create a form with a group of radio buttons and then display an appropriate dialog box when the user selects each radio button. JavaScript is used to display these dialog boxes.

1. Create a new document in your preferred editor.

2. In the body of the document, create a form named `myForm`:

```
<body>
    <form name="myForm">
    </form>
</body>
```

3. Create a group of radio buttons called `myRadio`:

```
<body>
  <form name="myForm">
    <input type="radio" name="myRadio"
          value="First Button"> Button 1<br>
    <input type="radio" name="myRadio"
          value="Second Button"> Button 2
  </form>
</body>
```

4. Add an `onClick` event handler to each of the first radio buttons. Use the event handlers to display a dialog box when the user selects that radio button. The final page looks like Listing 89-1.

```
<body>
  <form name="myForm">
    <input type="radio" name="myRadio"
        value="First Button"
```
(continued)

notes

■ Radio button groups are created through a series of `input` tags with the same name and the type specified as `radio`:

```
<input type="radio"

        name="myField"

        value="1">
Option 1

<input type="radio"

        name="myField"

        value="2">
Option 2
```

■ Arrays have a property called `length` that returns the number of items in an array, and it is used in this loop. Since arrays are zero-indexed, an array with length 5 (which contains five elements) would contain elements with indexes from 0 to 4. This is why you loop until `i` is less than, and not less than or equal to, the length of the array.

```
onClick="window.alert('First Button selected');">Button ⤸
1<br>
        <input type="radio" name="myRadio"
          value="Second Button" ⤸
onClick="window.alert('Second Button selected');">Button 2
    </form>
</body>
```

Listing 89-1: Responding to Selection of a Radio Button.

5. Save the file and close it.

6. Open the file in a browser, and you should see the form with radio buttons, as in Figure 89-1.

Figure 89-1: A form with radio buttons.

7. Click on one of the radio buttons to see the associated dialog box, as in Figure 89-2.

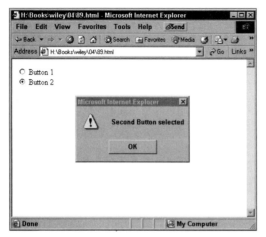

Figure 89-2: Reacting to the selection of a radio button.

cross-references

▪ See Task 81 to learn how to detect changes in text fields. Task 94 shows how to detect changes in check boxes.

▪ For more information on using radio buttons, see Task 87.

Updating or Changing Radio Button Selection

When you create an HTML form, you are creating a series of objects that can be accessed from within JavaScript. The form itself is an object, and then an object in JavaScript represents each form field. Using these objects, you can dynamically select a radio button in a group of radio buttons.

This task shows you how to select a radio button based on another action that occurs. To access the radio button group, you use the following syntax:

```
document.formName.groupName
```

This references the object associated with the radio button group. This object is actually an array containing an entry for each button in the group, and each of these entries has several properties, including two critical ones for this task:

- `checked`: Indicates if the radio button is currently selected
- `value`: Reflects the value of the `value` attribute for the radio button

Therefore, the property `document.formName.formField[0].value` would contain the value of the first radio button in a radio button group.

The following steps create a form with a pair of radio buttons and then provide two links the user can click to select the radio buttons without actually clicking directly on the radio buttons. Selecting the radio buttons is done with JavaScript.

1. In the header of a new HTML document, create a script block with a function named `selectButton` that takes a single argument containing the index of a specific radio button in the group.

2. In the function, set the `checked` property of the radio button to `true`:

```
<script language="JavaScript">
   function selectButton(button) {
      document.myForm.myRadio[button].checked = true;
   }
</script>
```

3. In the body of the document, create a form named `myForm` with a radio button group named `myRadio`:

```
<form name="myForm">
   <input type="radio" name="myRadio"
          value="First Button"> Button 1<br>
   <input type="radio" name="myRadio"
          value="Second Button"> Button 2
</form>
```

4. After the form, create a link that uses an `onClick` event handler to call the `selectButton` function to select the first radio button:

notes

- If the form is not named, then each form is accessible in the `document.forms` array, so that the first form in the document is `document.forms[0]`, the second is `document.forms[1]`, and so on. However, naming forms makes it much easier to refer to them and ensures you are referring to the correct form in your code.

- If the field is not named, then each field in the form is accessible in the `document.formName.elements` array, so that the first field in the form is `document.formName.elements[0]`, the second is `document.formName.elements[1]`, and so on. However, naming fields makes it much easier to refer to them and ensures you are referring to the correct fields in your code

- The `checked` property has a value of `true` if it is currently selected and `false` if it is not.

- Remember, the browser will only allow a single radio button in the group to be selected. When you set the `checked` property of one radio button to `true`, all other buttons in the group are automatically deselected.

- Remember, arrays are zero-indexed, so the first radio button has an index of 0.

```
<a href="#" onClick="selectButton(0);">Select First ⊃
Radio Button</a><br>
```

5. Create another link for selecting the second radio button so that the final page looks like Listing 90-1.

```
<head>
    <script language="JavaScript">
        function selectButton(button) {
            document.myForm.myRadio(button).checked = true;
        }
    </script>
</head>
<body>
    <form name="myForm">
        <input type="radio" name="myRadio"
               value="First Button"> Button 1<br>
        <input type="radio" name="myRadio"
               value="Second Button"> Button 2
    </form>

    <a href="#" onClick="selectButton(0);">Select First ⊃
Radio Button</a><br>
    <a href="#" onClick="selectButton(1);">Select Second ⊃
Radio Button</a>
</body>
```

Listing 90-1: Selecting Radio Buttons from Links.

6. Save the file and open the file in your browser. You should see the form and links as in Figure 90-1.

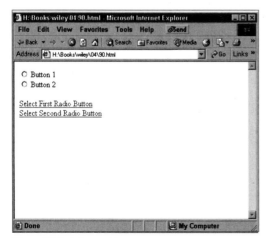

Figure 90-1: A form with radio buttons.

cross-reference

▪ See Task 84 to learn how to update options in a selection list. Task 93 shows how to change a check box's selection.

7. Select either link to select a radio button.

Creating Check Boxes

Similar to radio buttons, check boxes allow yes/no-type selections: Either the box is checked or it is not. Unlike radio buttons, however, groups of check boxes are not mutually exclusive: None can be selected, all can be selected, or any subset can be selected.

Check boxes are often used to allow users to make selections in a long list where they can choose any number of options. These lists look like Figure 91-1.

notes

- With check boxes, you specify any text to display next to the check box's input tag. The text to display is not inherent to the input tag.

- Just as with radio button, each check box has text that is displayed next to the button and a value, specified with the value attribute. It is the value and not the text that is tracked and manipulated from within JavaScript and submitted when you submit the form.

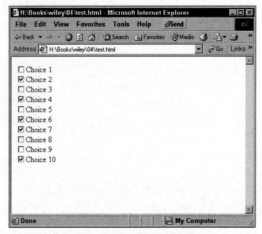

Figure 91-1: Using check boxes for long lists.

Check boxes are created with the input tag using checkbox as the value of the type attribute:

```
<input type="checkbox">
```

You can set whether a check box is selected (checked) by setting a checked property. Setting this property to true will check the box.

The following steps display a form with a series of check boxes in a list:

1. Create a new document in your editor.

2. In the body of the document, create a form:

```
<body>
   <form>

   </form>
</body>
```

3. In the form create a series of check boxes:

```
<body>
   <form>
```

```
<input type="checkbox" value="1"> First Choice<br>
<input type="checkbox" value="2"> Second Choice<br>
<input type="checkbox" value="3"> Third Choice

    </form>
</body>
```

4. Set the `checked` property so that the third option is selected by default. The final page looks like Listing 91-1.

```
<body>
    <form>

        <input type="checkbox" value="1"> First Choice<br>
        <input type="checkbox" value="2"> Second Choice<br>
        <input type="checkbox" value="3" checked = "true"> ↩
Third Choice

    </form>
</body>
```

Listing 91-1: A series of check boxes.

5. Save the file and close it.

6. Open the file in the form, and check boxes in a list appear, as shown in Figure 91-2.

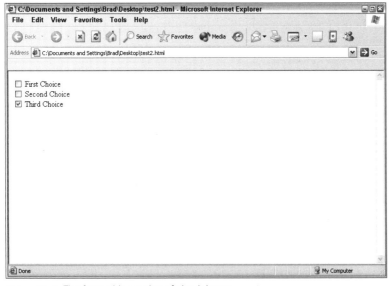

Figure 91-2: The form with a series of check boxes.

cross-reference

▪ Tasks 92, 93, and 94 show you how to use JavaScript to manipulate check boxes.

Task 92

Detecting Check Box Selections

When you create an HTML form, you are creating a series of objects that can be accessed from within JavaScript. The form itself is an object, and then an object in JavaScript represents each form field. Using these objects, you can access the selection status of check boxes.

This task shows you how to check selection status of a check box. To access the check box, you use the following syntax:

```
document.formName.fieldName
```

This references the object associated with the check box, which has several properties, including

- checked: Indicates if the check box is currently selected
- value: Reflects the value of the value attribute for the check box

Therefore, the property document.formName.formField.value would contain the value of a check box.

The following steps create a form with a check box and a link. The user can click the link to display the status of the check box selection in a dialog box. JavaScript is used to display this information in the dialog box:

1. Create a new document in your preferred editor.

2. In the body of your document, create a form named myForm:

3. In the form create a check box named myCheck:

   ```
   <input type="checkbox" name="myCheck"
           value="My Check Box"> Check Me
   ```

4. After the form create a link with the href attribute set to #. The user will use the link to check the status of the check box:

   ```
   <a href="#">Am I Checked?</a>
   ```

5. Set the onClick event handler of the link to display the current selection status by checking the checked property of the checkbox object. The final page will look like Listing 92-1.

6. Save the file and close it.

7. Open the file in your browser, and the form and link appears, as shown in Figure 92-1.

8. Click on the link to see the current selection status in a dialog box, as shown in Figure 92-2.

notes

- The checked property has a value of true if it is currently selected and false if it is not.

- Notice the use of # as the URL in the example. When using the onClick event handler to trigger the opening of a new window, you don't want to cause clicking on the link to change the location of the current window; this is a simple way to avoid this.

- The argument to window.alert requires some attention. This argument is actual a short form conditional test of the form condition ? value to return if true : value to return if false. This means if the checked property is true, then "Yes" is displayed in the dialog box; otherwise, "No" is displayed in the dialog box. The checked property of a radio button object is either true or false, which makes it sufficient as a condition for the short form conditional test used in the window.alert method.

```
<body>
  <form name="myForm">
    <input type="checkbox" name="myCheck"
           value="My Check Box"> Check Me
  </form>

  <a href="#" onClick="window.alert(document.⮑
myForm.myCheck.checked ? 'Yes' : 'No');">Am I Checked?</a>

</body>
```

Listing 92-1: Checking a check box's selection status.

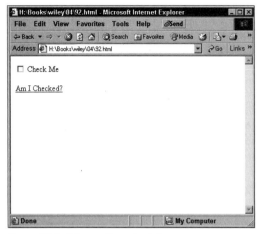

Figure 92-1: A form with a check box.

Figure 92-2: Displaying the check box's selection status.

cross-reference

- See Task 91 for more information on check boxes.

Changing Check Box Selections

When you create an HTML form, you are creating a series of objects that can be accessed from within JavaScript. The form itself is an object and then an object in JavaScript represents each form field. Using these objects you can change the selection status of check box.

This task shows you how to control selection status of a check box. To access the check box, you use the following syntax:

```
document.formName.fieldName
```

This references the object associated with the check box that has several properties including:

- `checked`: Indicates if the check box is currently selected
- `value`: Reflects the value of the `value` attribute for the check box

Therefore, the property `document.formName.formField.value` would contain the value of a check box.

The following steps create a form with a check box. A link is provided that the user can click to check or uncheck the check box. JavaScript is used to change the selection status of the check box.

1. Create a new document in your preferred editor.

2. In the body of your document, create a form named `myForm`:

```
<body>
    <form name="myForm">

    </form>
</body>
```

3. In the form, create a check box named `myCheck`:

```
<input type="checkbox" name="myCheck"
       value="My Check Box"> Check Me
```

4. After the form, create a link with the `href` attribute set to `#`. The user will use the link to select the check box:

```
<a href="#">Check the box</a>
```

5. Set the `onClick` event handler of the link to assign `true` to the `checked` property of the check box:

```
<a href="#" onClick="document.myForm.myCheck.checked = ⤶
true;">Check the box</a>
```

notes

- The `checked` property has a value of `true` if it is currently selected and `false` if it is not.

- Notice the use of `#` as the URL in the example. When using the `onClick` event handler to trigger the opening of a new window, you don't want to cause clicking on the link to change the location of the current window; this is a simple way to avoid this.

- If the field is not named, then each field in the form is accessble in the `document.formName.elements` array, so that the first field in the form is `document.formName.elements[0]`, the second is `document.formName.elements[1]`, and so on. However, naming fields makes it much easier to refer to them and ensures you are referring to the correct fields in your code.

- If the form is not named, then each form is accessible in the `document.forms` array, so that the first form in the document is `document.forms[0]`, the second is `document.forms[1]`, and so on. However, naming forms makes it much easier to refer to them and ensures you are referring to the correct form in your code.

6. Create a similar, second link to uncheck the check box but (set checked to `false` instead of `true`). The final page will look like Listing 93-1.

```
<body>
    <form name="myForm">
        <input type="checkbox" name="myCheck"
               value="My Check Box"> Check Me
    </form>

    <a href="#" onClick="document.myForm.myCheck.checked ⤵
= true;">Check the box</a><br>
    <a href="#" onClick="document.myForm.myCheck.checked ⤵
= false;">Uncheck the box</a>
</body>
```

Listing 93-1: Controlling a check box's selection status.

7. Save the file and close it.

8. Open the file in your browser, and the form and links appear, as illustrated in Figure 93-1.

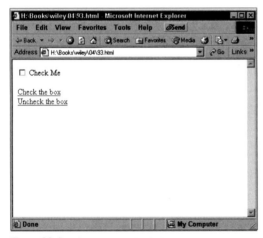

Figure 93-1: A form with a check box.

9. Click on the first link to select the check box. Click on the second link to unselect the check box.

Detecting Changes in Check Box Selections

When you create an HTML form, you are creating a series of objects that can be accessed from within JavaScript. The form itself is an object, and then an object in JavaScript represents each form field. Using these objects, you can detect changes in the selection of a check box.

This task shows you how to react to the user clicking on a check box. Check boxes are created with input tags, with the type specified as checkbox:

```
<input type="checkbox" name="myField"
        value="Some Value"> Check box text
```

To detect selection of a check box, you can use the onClick event handler:

```
<input type="checkbox" name="myField" value="Some Value" ⊃
onClick="JavaScript code to execute when the user clicks on the ⊃
checkbox"> Check box text
```

The following steps create a form with a checkbox. A dialog box is displayed each time the user clicks on the check box. JavaScript is used to display these dialog boxes.

1. Create a new document in your preferred editor.

2. In the body of the document, create a form named myForm:

```
<body>
   <form name="myForm">

   </form>
</body>
```

3. Create a group of check box named myCheck:

```
<body>
   <form name="myForm">

      <input type="checkbox" name="myCheck"
              value="My Check Box"> Check Me

   </form>
</body>
```

4. Add an onClick event handler to check box, and use it to display a dialog box when the user clicks the check box:

```
<body>
   <form name="myForm">
```

notes

■ The checked property has a value of true if it is currently selected and false if it is not.

■ The window.alert() method displays a dialog box. The value passed to this method will be displayed in the dialog box.

caution

■ Note in Step 4 that the value passed to the window.alert() method is surrounded by single quotes rather than double quotes. This is because this method is surrounded in double quotes for the onClick event. If you use double quotes, you will not get the expected results.

```
          <input type="checkbox" name="myCheck" value="My ⤶
Check Box" onClick="window.alert('You clicked the check ⤶
box');"> Check Me

     </form>
</body>
```

5. Save the file and close it.

6. Open the file in a browser, and you should see the form with the check box, as in Figure 94-1.

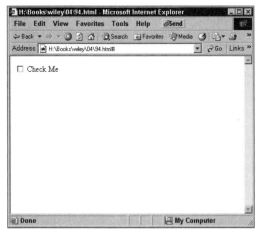

Figure 94-1: A form with a check box.

7. Click on the check box to see the associated dialog box, as in Figure 94-2.

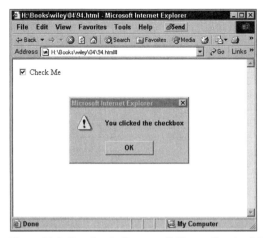

Figure 94-2: Reacting to the user clicking on the check box.

Verifying Form Fields in JavaScript

One of the main applications of JavaScript is to perform validation of the data entered into a form. One approach to form validation is to check the data entered in a field when the user attempts to move out of the field. Until valid data is entered, you prevent the user from leaving the field. The approach is simple:

- In the form field you want to validate, use the `onBlur` event handler to call a JavaScript function to test your form field.

- In the function, check the validity of the data entered. If the data is not valid, then inform the user and force the focus back to the field.

The following steps provide an example of this type of validation:

1. Create a script block in the header of a new HTML document that contains a function called `checkField`. The function takes the form field's object as an argument:

```
<script language="JavaScript">
  function checkField(field) {
  }
</script>
```

2. In the function, check if the field is empty:

```
if (field.value == "") {
}
```

3. If the field doesn't contain text, alert the user to enter text:

```
window.alert("You must enter a value in the field");
```

4. If the field contains no text, reset the focus to the field:

```
field.focus();
```

5. In the body of the document, create a form named `myForm`:

6. In the form, create a text field named `myField` and a submit button:

```
<form name="myForm" action="target.html">
    Text Field: <input type="text" name="myField"><br>
    <input type="submit">
</form>
```

7. In the `onBlur` event handler of the text field, call the `checkField` function so that the final page looks like Listing 95-1.

8. Save the file with the name `target.html` and close it.

9. Open the file in a browser. The form in Figure 95-1 appears.

```
<head>
 <script language="JavaScript">
   function checkField(field) {
     if (field.value == "") {
       window.alert("You must enter a value in the field");
       field.focus();
     }
   }
 </script>
</head>

<body>
  <form name="myForm" action="target.html">
     Text Field: <input type="text" name="myField"
        onBlur="checkField(this)"><br>
      <input type="submit">
   </form>
</body>
```

Listing 95-1: Validating a form field when the user leaves the field.

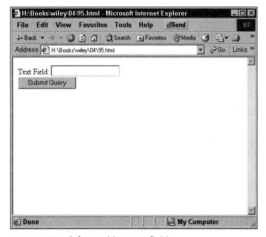

Figure 95-1: A form with a text field.

10. Click into the text field and then try to click outside the field without entering any text. An alert appears, warning you to enter text in the field, as shown in Figure 95-2, and then focus is returned to the field.

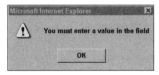

Figure 95-2: Forcing the user to enter text in a field.

cross-reference

▪ In Tasks 98 through 106 you learn how to validate specific types of information such as e-mail addresses (Task 98), phone numbers (Task 100), and passwords (Task 105).

Using the `onSubmit` Attribute of the `Form` Tag to Verify Form Fields

One of the main applications of JavaScript is to perform validation of the data entered in forms. One approach to form validation is to check the data entered in a form when the user attempts to submit the form. The approach is simple:

- In the form you want to validate, use the `onSubmit` event handler to call a JavaScript function to test your form when it is submitted.

- In the function, check the validity of the data entered in the form. If the data is not valid, then inform the user and cancel the form submission.

The following task provides an example of this type of validation. If the user attempts to submit the form without entering text in a single text field, the user will be informed that he or she must enter text or the submission will be canceled.

1. In the header of a new HTML document, create a script block with a function called `checkForm` that receives the form's object (`formObj`):

   ```
   function checkForm(formObj) {
   }
   ```

2. In the function, create a variable named `formOK` that is set to `true`:

   ```
   var formOK = true;
   ```

3. In the function, check if the field is the empty string:

   ```
   if (formObj.myField.value == "") {
   }
   ```

4. If the field contains no text, alert the user that he or she must enter text to continue. Return focus to the field and set `formOK` to `false`:

   ```
   window.alert("You must enter a value in the field");
   formObj.myField.focus();
   formOK = false;
   ```

5. Return the value of `formOK` from the function:

   ```
   return formOK;
   ```

6. In the body of the document, create a form named `myForm` that has a text field named `myField`: and a submit button:

7. In the `onSubmit` event handler of the form, call the `checkForm` function. The final page looks like Listing 96-1.

notes

- This process relies on the fact that if the JavaScript code in the `onSubmit` event handler returns false, the submission itself is canceled.

- Notice that `this` is passed as the argument to the `checkForm` function. In the event handlers for a `form` tag, `this` refers to the object for the form itself.

- The `onSubmit` event handler used here requires attention. Instead of simply calling `checkForm`, you return the value returned by `checkForm`. Since `checkForm` returns `true` if the form is OK and `false` otherwise; this allows you to cancel submission if the form is not OK and allows it to continue if the form is OK.

- This process relies on the `focus` method available for form field objects. This method sets mouse focus into a field that did not have focus before.

- The field that "has focus" is the field that is currently active. A field is often given focus when the user clicks on it or tabs to it. In this task you see how to force the focus to go to a specific field.

- Setting the `formOK` field equal to `true` assumes that the form is OK to submit.

```
<head>
 <script language="JavaScript">
   function checkForm(formObj) {
     var formOK = true;
     if (formObj.myField.value == "") {
       window.alert("You must enter a value in the field");
       formObj.myField.focus();
       formOK = false;
     }
     return formOK;
   }
 </script>
</head>

<body>
   <form name="myForm" action="target.html" onSubmit="⤴
return checkForm(this);">
       Text Field: <input type="text" name="myField"><br>
       <input type="submit">
   </form>
</body>
```

Listing 96-1: Validating a form when the user submits it.

8. Save the file with the name `target.html` and close it.

9. Open the file in a browser, and the form in Figure 96-1 appears.

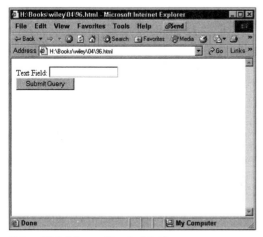

Figure 96-1: A form with a text field.

10. Try to submit the form without entering any text. You see an alert, and then focus will be returned to the field.

cross-reference

▪ Task 95 shows how to validate a single field when the
user moves away from it.

Verifying Form Fields Using INPUT TYPE="button" Instead of TYPE="submit"

One of the main applications of JavaScript is to perform validation of the data entered in forms. One approach is to check the data entered when the user attempts to submit the form, but to not use any actual submit buttons. The approach is simple:

- In the form you want to validate, use a regular button instead of a submit button to control form submission.

- In the onClick event handler of the button, call a JavaScript function to test your form when it is submitted.

- In the function, check the validity of the data entered by the user in the form. If the data isn't valid, inform the user; otherwise, submit the form.

The following task provides an example of this type of validation. If the user attempts to submit the form without entering text in a text field, an alert will state that text must be entered in the field; otherwise, the form is submitted.

1. In the header of a new HTML document, create a script block with a function called checkForm that receives the form's object (formObj):

```
function checkForm(formObj) {
}
```

2. In the function, create a variable named formOK that is set to true:

```
var formOK = true;
```

3. In the function, check to see if the text entered is the empty string:

```
if (formObj.myField.value == "") {
}
```

4. If the field is empty, alert the user that he or she must enter text to continue and then return mouse focus to the field, and set formOK to false:

```
window.alert("You must enter a value in the field");
formObj.myField.focus();
formOK = false;
```

5. Check to see if formOK is true, and if it is, submit the form:

```
if (formOK) { formObj.submit(); };
```

6. In the body of the document, create a form named `myForm` with a text field named `myField` and a regular button—not a submit button:

```
<form name="myForm" action="target.html">
   Text Field: <input type="text" name="myField"><br>
   <input type="button" value="Submit">
</form>
```

7. In the `onClick` event handler of the button, call the `checkForm` function. The final page looks like Listing 97-1.

```
<head>
 <script language="JavaScript">
   function checkForm(formObj) {
     var formOK = true;
     if (formObj.myField.value == "") {
       window.alert("You must enter a value in the field");
       formObj.myField.focus();
       formOK = false;
     }
     if (formOK) { formObj.submit(); }
   }
</script>
</head>
<body>
   <form name="myForm" action="target.html">
       Text Field: <input type="text" name="myField"><br>
       <input type="button" value="Submit"
              onClick="checkForm(this.form);">
   </form>
</body>
```

Listing 97-1: Validating a form when the user submits it.

8. Save the file with the name target.html and close it.

9. Open the file in a browser.

10. Try to submit the form without entering any text. An alert appears, and then focus is returned to the field.

cross-reference

- Task 96 shows how to do validation on a submitted form using a submit button.

Validating E-mail Addresses

When validating information on a form, you may want to test if the text in a text field conforms to a format of a valid e-mail address. This task illustrates how to do this. The method of validating an e-mail address that is used applies the following logic:

- Check if the e-mail address is empty; if it is, the field is not valid.
- Check for illegal characters, and if they occur, the field is not valid.
- Check if the @ symbol is missing; if it is, the field is not valid.
- Check for the occurrence of a dot; if there is none, the field isn't valid.
- Otherwise, the field is valid.

The following steps create a form with a single field for entering an e-mail address. When the user submits the form, the field is validated prior to submission. If validation fails, the user is informed and submission is canceled.

1. In the header of a new HTML document, create a script block containing the function `checkEmail` that receives a text string.

2. In the function, check if the e-mail address has no length, and if it does, inform the user and return `false` from the function.

3. Next, check if the following illegal characters exist: /, :, ,, or ;. If any of these characters exist, inform the user and return `false`.

4. Next, check if the @ symbol exists. If not, inform the user and return `false`.

5. Now check if a dot exists. If not, inform the user and return `false`:

6. Finally, return `true` from the function if the e-mail address passed all the tests so that the complete function looks like Listing 98-1.

7. Create another function named `checkForm` that takes a `form` object as an argument. The function should call `checkEmail` and pass it the value of the field containing the e-mail address and then return the result returned by the `checkEmail` function:

```
function checkForm(formObj) {
    return checkEmail(formObj.myField.value); }
```

8. In the body of the document, create a form that contains a field for entering the e-mail address and uses the `onSubmit` event handler to call the `checkForm` function:

```
<body>
    <form name="myForm" action="target.html"
          onSubmit="return checkForm(this);">
        E-mail: <input type="text" name="myField"><br>
        <input type="submit">
    </form>
</body>
```

notes

- There are other errors you could also check for, such as two @ symbols or a misplaced dot.

- Strings have a `length` property that returns the number of characters in the string. If the string is empty, the length will be zero.

- The `return` command can be used anywhere in a function to cease processing the function and return a value.

- The `indexOf` method of `string` objects returns the character position of a specified string within the larger string. If the string does not occur, the index is returned as -1.

- The validation is divided into two functions so it can be extended to a form with multiple fields. For instance, you could validate multiple e-mail address fields by calling `checkEmail` multiple times from `checkForm` or could perform other types of validation by adding other functions and calling them from `checkForm`. From the form, though, you still only call `checkForm`.

- Notice that `this` is passed as the argument to the `checkForm` function. In the event handlers for a `form` tag, `this` refers to the object for the form itself.

```
function checkEmail(email) {

  if (email.length == 0) {
    window.alert("You must provide an e-mail address.");
    return false;
  }

  if (email.indexOf("/") > -1) {
    window.alert("E-mail address has invalid character: /");
    return false;
  }
  if (email.indexOf(":") > -1) {
    window.alert("E-mail address has invalid character: :");
    return false;
  }
  if (email.indexOf(",") > -1) {
    window.alert("E-mail address has invalid character: ,");
    return false;
  }
  if (email.indexOf(";") > -1) {
    window.alert("E-mail address has invalid character: ;");
    return false;
  }

  if (email.indexOf("@") < 0) {
    window.alert("E-mail address is missing @");
    return false;
  }

  if (email.indexOf("\.") < 0) {
    window.alert("E-mail address is missing .");
    return false;
  }

  return true;

}
```

Listing 98-1: Function for validating an e-mail address.

9. Save the file with the name target.html, and open it in a browser.

10. Try to submit the form without a valid e-mail address and you should see an appropriate error message.

cross-reference

▪ Tasks 95, 96, and 97 illustrate how to do a very simplistic form of form validation.

Validating Zip Codes

In some cases when validating a form, you may want to test if the text in a text field conforms to a format of a zip code. This task illustrates how to validate a zip code, using the following logic:

- Check if the zip code is empty; if it is, the field is not valid.
- Remove any dashes from the zip code.
- Check the length of the zip code; if it is not 5 or 9, the field isn't valid.
- Check for any nonnumeric characters; if any occur, the field is not valid.
- Otherwise, the field is valid.

The following steps create a form with a single field for entering a zip code. When the user submits the form, the field is validated prior to submission, and if validation fails, the user is informed and submission is canceled.

1. In the header of a new HTML document, create a script block with a function called `checkZip` that takes a text string as an argument.

2. In the function check if the zip code has no length, and if it does, inform the user and return `false` from the function.

3. Next, remove any dashes from the zip code.

4. Next, check if the length of the zip code is either 5 or 9 characters. If not, inform the user and return `false` from the function:

5. Now check if any character is not a number. If any character is not a number, inform the user and return `false`. To test for nonnumeric characters, loop through each character in the string and test it.

6. Finally, return `true` from the function if the zip code passed all the tests. The complete function should look like Listing 99-1.

7. Create another function named `checkForm` that receives a `form` object. The function should call `checkZip`, and pass it the value of the field containing the zip code, and then return the result returned by the `checkZip` function:

```
function checkForm(formObj) {
    return checkZip(formObj.myField.value);
}
```

notes

- If your form is going to be used by people from countries other than the United States, you will want to apply different rules. For example, many countries allow for characters in zip codes, as well as for lengths other than 5 and 9 digits.

- Strings have a `length` property that returns the number of characters in the string. If the string is empty, the length will be zero.

- The `return` command can be used anywhere in a function to cease processing the function and return a value.

- Strings have a `replace` method that takes the string, searches for specified text (the first argument) and replaces it with specified text (the second argument), and returns the resulting string.

- The `charAt` method returns the character at the specified index location in a `string` object.

- The `onSubmit` event handler used here requires attention. Instead of simply calling `checkForm`, you return the value returned by `checkForm`. Since `checkForm` returns `true` if the form is OK and `false` otherwise, this allows you to cancel submission if the form is not OK and allows it to continue if the form is OK.

```
function checkZip(zip) {
   if (zip.length == 0) {
      window.alert("You must provide a ZIP code.");
      return false;
   }

   zip = zip.replace("-","");

   if (zip.length != 5 && zip.length != 9) {
      window.alert("ZIP codes must take the form 12345 or ⤵
12345-6789");
      return false;
   }

   for (i=0; i<zip.length; i++) {
      if (zip.charAt(i) < "0" || zip.charAt(i) > "9") {
      window.alert("ZIP codes must only contain numbers.");
      return false;
      }
   }

   return true;
}
```

Listing 99-1: Validating ZIP Codes.

tip

- You could validate multiple zip codes fields by calling checkZip multiple times from checkForm, or you could perform other types of validation by adding other functions and calling them from checkForm. From the form, though, you still only call checkForm.

8. In the body of the document, create a form that contains a field for entering the zip code and uses the onSubmit event handler to call the checkForm function:

```
<body>

   <form name="myForm" action="target.html"
         onSubmit="return checkForm(this);">

      ZIP: <input type="text" name="myField"><br>
      <input type="submit">

   </form>

</body>
```

9. Save the file as target.html and open it in a browser.

10. Try to submit the form without a valid zip code, and you should see an appropriate error message.

Validating Phone Numbers

In some cases when validating a form, you may want to test if the text in a text field conforms to a format of a valid phone number. This task illustrates how to validate a phone number using the following logic:

- Check if the phone number is empty; if it is, the field is not valid.
- Remove phone number punctuation (parentheses, dashes, spaces, and dots).
- Check the length of the phone number; if it is not 10 digits, the field is not valid.
- Check for nonnumeric characters; if any occur, the field is not valid.
- Otherwise, the field is valid.

The following steps create a form with a single field for entering a phone number. When the user submits the form, the field is validated prior to submission. If validation fails, the user is informed and submission is canceled.

1. In the header of a new HTML document, create a script block containing the function `checkPhone` that receives a text string.

2. In the function, check if the phone number has no length. If it has no length, inform the user and return `false` from the function.

3. Next, remove any phone number punctuation from the phone number. Specifically, remove dashes, spaces, parentheses, and dots.

4. Next, check if the length of the phone number is 10 characters. If not, inform the user and return `false` from the function.

5. Now check if any character is not a number. If any character is not a number, inform the user and return `false` from the function. To test for nonnumeric characters, loop through each character in the string and test it individually.

6. Finally, return `true` from the function if the phone number passed all the tests. The complete function looks like Listing 100-1.

7. Create another function named `checkForm` that takes a `form` object as an argument. The function should call `checkPhone`, pass it the value of the field containing the phone number, and then return the result returned by the `checkPhone` function:

```
function checkForm(formObj) {
    return checkPhone(formObj.myField.value); }
```

notes

- Strings have a `length` property that returns the number of characters in the string. If the string is empty, the length will be zero.

- The `return` command can be used anywhere in a function to cease processing the function and return a value.

- Strings have a `replace` method that takes the string, searches for specified text (the first argument) and replaces it with specified text (the second argument), and returns the resulting string.

- The `charAt` method returns the character at the specified index location in a `string` object.

- The `onSubmit` event handler used here requires attention. Instead of simply calling `checkForm`, you return the value returned by `checkForm`. Since `checkForm` returns `true` if the form is OK and `false` otherwise, this allows you to cancel submission if the form is not OK and allows it to continue if the form is OK.

```
function checkPhone(phone) {

   if (phone.length == 0) {
      window.alert("You must provide a phone number.");
      return false;
   }

   phone = phone.replace("-","");
   phone = phone.replace(" ","");
   phone = phone.replace("(","");
   phone = phone.replace(")","");
   phone = phone.replace(".","");

   if (phone.length != 10) {
      window.alert("Phone numbers must only include a ⊃
3-digit area code and a 7-digit phone number.");
      return false;
   }

   for (i=0; i<phone.length; i++) {
      if (phone.charAt(i) < "0" || phone.charAt(i) > "9") {
         window.alert("Phone numbers must only contain ⊃
numbers.");
         return false;
      }
   }

   return true;

}
```

Listing 100-1: The function to validate a phone number.

8. In the body of the document, create a form that contains a field for entering the phone number and uses the onSubmit event handler to call the checkForm function:

```
<body>
   <form name="myForm" action="target.html" ⊃
onSubmit="return checkForm(this);">

      Phone: <input type="text" name="myField"><br>
      <input type="submit">

   </form>
</body>
```

9. Save the file as target.html and open it in a browser.

10. Try to submit the form without a valid phone number, and you should see an appropriate error message.

tip
- You could validate multiple phone number fields by calling checkPhone multiple times from checkForm, or you could perform other types of validation by adding other functions and calling them from checkForm. From the form, though, you still only call checkForm.

cross-reference
- Task 106 shows how to validate a phone number a different way—it uses regular expressions.

Task 101

Validating Credit Card Numbers

This task illustrates how to validate a credit card number by the following logic:

- Check if the credit card number is empty; if it is, the field is not valid.
- Remove any spaces.
- Check the length of the credit card number; valid lengths are discussed in this task. If the length is wrong, the field is not valid.
- Check for nonnumeric characters; if any occur, the field is not valid.
- Otherwise, the field is valid.

The following steps create a form with a single field for entering a credit card number. When the user submits the form, the field is validated prior to submission. If validation fails, the user is informed and submission is canceled.

1. In the header of a new HTML document, create a script block with a function `checkCreditCard` that takes a text string as an argument.

2. In the function, check if the credit card number has no length. If it has no length, inform the user and return `false` from the function.

3. Next, remove any spaces from the credit card number.

4. Now check if the length of the credit card number is appropriate for the type of card. If not, inform the user and return `false`.

5. Next, check if any character is not a number. If any character isn't, inform the user and return `false`. To test for nonnumerics, loop through each character in the string and test it individually.

6. Finally, return `true` from the function if the credit card number passed all the tests. The complete function looks like Listing 101-1.

7. Create another function named `checkForm` that receives a `form` object. The function should call `checkCreditCard`, pass it the value of the field containing the credit card number, and then return the result returned by the `checkCreditCard` function:

```
function checkForm(formObj) {
    return checkCreditCard(formObj.myField.value); }
```

8. Create a form that contains a field for entering the credit card number and uses the `onSubmit` event handler to call the `checkForm` function:

```
<body>
    <form name="myForm" action="target.html"
        onSubmit="return checkForm(this);">
    Credit Card: <input type="text" name="myField"><br>
    <input type="submit">
    </form>
</body>
```

notes

- The length of a credit card number is dependent on the type of card. The type of card depends on the starting digits in the number as follows. Visa cards start with the digit 4 and have 13 or 16 digits. MasterCard cards start with 51, 52, 53, 54, or 55 and have 16 digits. American Express cards start with 34 or 37 and have 15 digits.

- The `return` command can be used anywhere in a function to cease processing the function and return a value.

- Strings have a `replace` method that takes the string, searches for specified text (the first argument) and replaces it with specified text (the second argument), and returns the resulting string.

- The `charAt` method returns the character at the specified index location in a `string` object.

- The `onSubmit` event handler used here requires attention. Instead of simply calling `checkForm`, you return the value returned by `checkForm`. Since `checkForm` returns `true` if the form is OK and `false` otherwise, this allows you to cancel submission if the form is not OK and allows it to continue if the form is OK.

```
function checkCreditCard(card) {
  if (card.length == 0) {
     window.alert("You must provide a credit card number.");
     return false;
  }

  card = card.replace(" ","");

  if (card.substring(0,1) == "4") {
     if (card.length != 13 && card.length != 16) {
        window.alert("Not enough digits in Visa number.");
          return false;
     }
  } else if (card.substring(0,1) == "5" && ⮐
(card.substring(1,2) >= "1" && card.substring(1,2) <= "5"))
  {
     if (card.length != 16) {
        window.alert("Not enough digits in MasterCard.");
        return false;
     }
  } else if (card.substring(0,1) == "3" && ⮐
(card.substring(1,2) == "4" || card.substring(1,2) == "7"))
  {
     if (card.length != 15) {
        window.alert("Not enough digits in American Expr.");
        return false;
     }
  } else {
     window.alert("This is not a valid card number.");
     return false;
  }

  for (i=0; i<card.length; i++) {
     if (card.charAt(i) < "0" || card.charAt(i) > "9") {
        window.alert("CCard must only contain numbers.");
        return false;
     }
  }
  return true;
}
```

Listing 101-1: The completed credit card validation function.

9. Save the file with the name target.html and open it in a browser.

10. Try to submit the form without a valid credit card number, and you should see an appropriate error message.

Task 101

tip

- You could validate multiple phone number fields by calling checkCreditCard multiple times from checkForm, or you could perform other types of validation by adding other functions and calling them from checkForm. From the form, though, you still only call checkForm.

Task 102

Validating Selection List Choices

In some cases when validating a form, you may want to test if the user has made a selection in a selection list.

A common approach to selection lists is to have a blank first element so as not to force the user into a default selection and then have the user choose one of the other options. Sometimes you will want to ensure the user has chosen one of those options instead of leaving the blank first choice selected.

The following steps create a form with a single selection list. When the user submits the form, the field is validated prior to submission, and if validation fails, the user is informed and submission is canceled.

1. In the header of a new HTML document, create a script block containing the function `checkList` that receives a text string:

```
function checkList(selection) {
}
```

2. In the function, check if the selected item's value has no length. If it has no length, inform the user and return `false` from the function:

```
if (selection.length == 0) {
   window.alert("You must select from the list.");
   return false;
}
```

3. Finally, return `true` from the function if the selected item passed the test so that the complete function looks like Listing 102-1.

```
function checkList(selection) {

   if (selection.length == 0) {
      window.alert("You must make a selection from the ⤶
list.");
      return false;
   }

   return true;
}
```

Listing 102-1: The completed `checkList` function.

4. Create another function named `checkForm` that takes a `form` object as an argument. The function should call `checkList`, pass it the value of the selected item in the selection list, and then return the result returned by the `checkList` function:

```
function checkForm(formObj) {
   return checkList(formObj.myField.value);
}
```

notes

- Strings have a `length` property that returns the number of characters in the string. If the string is empty, the length will be zero.

- The `return` command can be used anywhere in a function to cease processing the function and return a value.

- The validation is divided into two functions so it can be extended to a form with multiple fields. For instance, you could validate multiple selection lists by calling `checkList` multiple times from `checkForm`, or you could perform other types of validation by adding other functions and calling them from `checkForm`. From the form, though, you still only call `checkForm`.

- Notice that `this` is passed as the argument to the `checkForm` function. In the event handlers for a `form` tag, `this` refers to the object for the form itself.

- Instead of simply calling `checkForm`, you return the value returned by `checkForm`. Since `checkForm` returns `true` if the form is OK and `false` otherwise, this allows you to cancel submission if the form is not OK and allows it to continue if the form is OK.

5. Create a form that contains a selection list and uses the `onSubmit` event handler to call the `checkForm` function:

```
<body>
    <form name="myForm" action="target.html" ⊃
onSubmit="return checkForm(this);">

        Choose:
        <select name="myField">
            <option value=""></option>
            <option value="1">One</option>
            <option value="2">Two</option>
            <option value="3">Three</option>
        </select><br>
        <input type="submit">
    </form>
</body>
```

6. Save the file as `target.html` and open it in a browser. The form in Figure 102-1 appears.

Figure 102-1: A form with a selection list.

7. Try to submit the form without choosing from the selection list. You should see an appropriate error message, as in Figure 102-2.

Figure 102-2: Validating the user's selection.

cross-reference

▪ To see other ways of working with selection lists, see Tasks 82 through 86.

Task 103 Validating Radio Button Selections

In some cases when validating a form, you may want to test if the user has made a selection in a radio button group. A common approach to radio button groups is to have a radio button already selected by default. Sometimes you will want to ensure the user has chosen one of the options. The following steps create a form with a radio button group:

1. In the header of a new HTML document, create a script block containing the function checkRadio that takes a radio button:

```
function checkRadio(buttons) {
}
```

2. In the function, create a variable named radioEmpty that is assigned the value true. This assumes the user has not selected a radio button:

```
var radioEmpty = true;
```

3. Check each radio button to see if it is selected, and adjust the value of radioEmpty accordingly:

```
for (i=0; i<buttons.length; i++) {
    if (buttons[i].checked) {
        radioEmpty = false;
    }
}
```

4. Check the value of radioEmpty, and if it is true, inform the user and return false from the function:

```
if (radioEmpty) {
    window.alert("You must select from the radio ⮑
buttons.");
    return false;
}
```

5. Finally, return true from the function if the selected item passed the test so that the complete function looks like Listing 103-1.

6. Create another function named checkForm that receives a form object. The function calls checkRadio and passes it the value of the selected radio button. The checkRadio function returns the result:

```
function checkForm(formObj) {
    return checkRadio(formObj.myField.value);
}
```

7. Create a form that contains a radio button group and that uses the onSubmit event handler to call the checkForm function:

```
<body>
    <form name="myForm" action="target.html"
        onSubmit="return checkForm(this);">
        Choose:
```

notes

- The return command can be used anywhere in a function to cease processing the function and return a value.

- The validation is divided into two functions so it can be extended to a form with multiple fields. For instance, you could validate multiple radio button groups by calling checkRadio multiple times from checkForm, or you could perform other types of validation by adding other functions and calling them from checkForm. From the form, though, you still only call checkForm.

- Notice that this is passed as the argument to the checkForm function. In the event handlers for a form tag, this refers to the object for the form itself.

- The onSubmit event handler used here requires attention. Instead of simply calling checkForm, you return the value returned by checkForm. Since checkForm returns true if the form is OK and false otherwise, this allows you to cancel submission if the form is not OK and allows it to continue if the form is OK.

```
        <input type="radio" name="myField" value="1"> 1
        <input type="radio" name="myField" value="2"> 2
        <input type="radio" name="myField" value="3"> 3<br>
        <input type="submit">
    </form>
</body>
```

```
function checkRadio(buttons) {
  var radioEmpty = true;
  for (i=0; i<buttons.length; i++) {
      if (buttons[i].checked) {
          radioEmpty = false;
      }
  }

  if (radioEmpty) {
    window.alert("You must select from the radio buttons.");
    return false;
  }
    return true;
}
```

Listing 103-1: The complete `checkRadio` function.

8. Save the file and open it in a browser. Figure 103-1 shows the form.

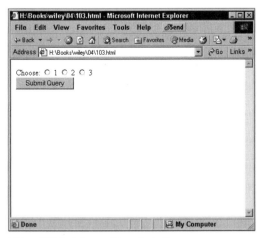

Figure 103-1: A form with radio buttons.

9. Try to submit the form without choosing a radio button, and you should see an appropriate error message.

cross-reference

▪ Tasks 88, 89, and 90 show you how to work with radio buttons in JavaScript.

Task 104

Validating Check Box Selections

In some cases when validating a form, you may want to test if the user has selected a check box. A common approach used by forms is to have the user select an optional item with a check box, and if they select the check box, require them to fill in an additional text field.

The following steps create a form with a check box and a text field. When the user submits the form, a check is made prior to submission to see if the text field is filled in if the check box is selected; if validation fails, the user is informed and submission is canceled.

1. In a new HTML document, create a script block containing the function checkCheckbox that receives a check box object:

```
function checkCheckbox(check) {
}
```

2. In the function, check if the check box is checked or not:

```
if (check.checked) {
}
```

3. If the check box is checked, check the length of the text field's text. If the length is 0, inform the user and return false from the function:

```
if (check.checked) {
    if (check.form.myText.value.length == 0) {
        window.alert("You have checked the check box; you ⤶
must provide your name.");
        return false;
    }
}
```

4. Finally, return true from the function if the form passed the test so that the complete function looks like this:

```
function checkCheckbox(check) {
    if (check.checked) {
        if (check.form.myText.value.length == 0) {
            window.alert("You have checked the check box; ⤶
you must provide your name.");
            return false;
        }
    }
    return true;
}
```

5. Create another function named checkForm that receives a form object. The function should call checkCheckbox and pass it the check box object. The checkCheckbox function should return the following result:

```
function checkForm(formObj) {
    return checkRadio(formObj.myCheck);
}
```

6. Create a form containing a check box and a text field. Use the
   onSubmit event handler to call the checkForm function:

```
<body>
    <form name="myForm" action="target.html"
            onSubmit="return checkForm(this);">
        <input type="checkbox" name="myCheck"
                value="Checked"> Check Here<br>
        If checked, enter your name:
        <input type="text" name="myText"><br>
        <input type="submit">
    </form>
</body>
```

7. Save the file and open it in a browser. The form in Figure 104-1
   appears.

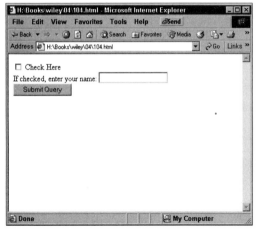

Figure 104-1: A form with a check box and text field.

8. Select the check box and try to submit the form without entering any
   text in the text field. You should see an appropriate error message, as
   in Figure 104-2.

Figure 104-2: Validating the user's selection.

cross-reference

▪ Tasks 91 through 94 present a number of ways to
   work with check boxes.

Task 105

Validating Passwords

In some cases when validating a form, you may want to test the password provided by the user. A common approach is to ask the user to specify a password of a certain length twice to ensure he or she has entered it correctly.

The following creates a form with two password fields. A check is made when the user submits to see if the two entered fields match and are at least six characters. If the checks fail, the user is informed and submission is canceled.

1. In the header of a new HTML document, create a script block containing the function checkPassword that receives two text strings:

```
function checkPassword(password,confirm) {
}
```

2. In the function, check if the passwords match, and if not, inform the user and return false from the function:

```
if (password != confirm) {
    window.alert("Passwords don't match.");
    return false;
}
```

3. Next, check if the length of the string is fewer than six characters; if it is, inform the user and return false from the function:

```
if (password.length < 6) {
    window.alert("Passwords must be 6 or more characters);
    return false;
}
```

4. Finally, return true from the function if the password passed the tests so that the complete function looks like this:

```
function checkPassword(password,confirm) {
    if (password != confirm) {
        window.alert("Passwords don't match.");
        return false;
    }
    if (password.length < 6) {
        window.alert("Passwords must be 6 or more ⊃
characters);
        return false;
    }
}
```

5. Create another function named checkForm that takes a form object as an argument. The function should call checkPassword and pass it both passwords, and then return the result returned by the checkPassword function:

```
function checkForm(formObj) {
    return checkPassword(formObj.myPassword.value,
                         formObj.myConfirm.value);
}
```

6. Create a form that contains two password fields and uses the onSubmit event handler to call the checkForm function:

```
<body>
    <form name="myForm" action="target.html"
          onSubmit="return checkForm(this);">
        Enter Password: <input type="password"
            name="myPassword"><br>
        Confirm Password: <input type="password"
            name="myConfirm"><br>
        <input type="submit">
    </form>
</body>
```

7. Save the file and open it in a browser. The form in Figure 105-1 appears.

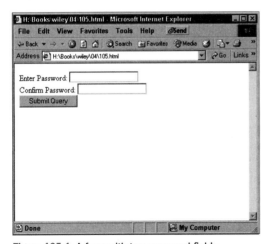

Figure 105-1: A form with two password fields.

8. Enter two mismatched passwords and submit the form. You should see an appropriate error message, as in Figure 105-2.

Figure 105-2: Validating the user's selection.

cross-reference

* Passwords are sometimes stored in cookies on the users' machines so that they don't have to enter them every time the come to a site. To learn how to create cookies, see Task 146.

Task 106

Validating Phone Numbers with Regular Expressions

notes

- Regular expressions are powerful but require you to have a lot of experience to become comfortable with them and master them. You can find an introductory tutorial on regular expressions at http://www.linuxpcug.org/lessons/regex.htm.

- When you assign a regular expression to a variable, you are creating a regular expression object. This object has a test method that allows you to test the expression against a string that is provided as an argument to the method. The method returns true if there is a match and false otherwise.

- The validation is divided into two functions so it can be extended to a form with multiple fields. For instance, you could validate multiple phone number fields by calling checkPhone multiple times from checkForm or could perform other types of validation by adding other functions and calling them from checkForm. From the form, though, you still only call checkForm.

- Notice that this is passed as the argument to the checkForm function. In the event handlers for a form tag, this refers to the object for the form itself.

In Task 100 you saw an example of how to validate a phone number in JavaScript. At the core was the checkPhone function. Unfortunately, this function shows a long, complex, and roundabout way to validate a phone number. It does have the benefit of using only a small set of simple, common JavaScript commands and constructs such as if statements and for loops, but it requires too many steps and, therefore, is prone to error: If you get the logic wrong, the validation will be incorrect.

Using regular expressions, you can greatly simplify the amount of code needed for this task. Regular expressions provide a powerful extension of the wildcard concept to allow you to specify text patterns and search for matches for those patterns. Unfortunately, regular expressions are an advanced topic beyond the scope of this task, but I will show you how to perform phone number validation using regular expressions.

Use of the regular expression is simple once you have created it. You will use it in the following format:

```
var someString ="string to test";
var regularExpression = /pattern to match/modifiers;
if (regularExpression.test(someString)) {
    Code to execute if there is a match;
}
```

The following steps create a form with a field to enter a phone number that is validated with regular expressions:

1. In the header of a new HTML document, create a script block containing the function checkPhone that returns a text string:

   ```
   function checkPhone(phone) {
   }
   ```

2. In the function, create a regular expression for matching against a phone number. Enter the following exactly as it is presented:

   ```
   var check = /^\({0,1}[0-9]{3}\){0,1}[ \-\.]{0,1}[0-9]{3}
   [ \-\.]{0,1}[0-9]{4}$/;
   ```

3. Next, test for a failure to match this pattern against the phone number. Notice that the result returned by the test method is negated. In this way, the if statement is true only when no match is found:

   ```
   if (!check.test(phone)) {
   }
   ```

4. If no match is found, inform the user and return `false` from the function:

```
if (!check.test(phone)) {
    window.alert("You must provide a valid phone number.");
    return false;
}
```

5. Finally, return `true` from the function if the phone number passed the test so that the complete function looks like this:

```
function checkPhone(phone) {
    var check = /^\({0,1}[0-9]{3}\){0,1}[ \-\.]⏎
{0,1}[0-9]{3}[ \-\.]{0,1}[0-9]{4}$/;
    if (!check.test(phone)) {
        window.alert("Provide a valid phone number.");
        return false;
    }
    return true;
}
```

6. Create another function named `checkForm` that takes a `form` object as an argument. The function should call `checkPhone` and pass it the value of the field containing the phone number and then return the result returned by the `checkPhone` function:

```
function checkForm(formObj) {
    return checkPhone(formObj.myField.value);
}
```

7. In the body of the document, create a form that contains a field for entering the phone number and uses the `onSubmit` event handler to call the `checkForm` function:

```
<body>
    <form name="myForm" action="target.html"
            onSubmit="return checkForm(this);">
        Phone: <input type="text" name="myField"><br>
        <input type="submit">
    </form>
</body>
```

8. Save the file as `target.html` and open it in a browser.

9. Try to submit the form without a valid phone number, and you should see an appropriate error message.

tip

- The regular expression for validating a phone number is as follows:

```
/^\({0,1}[0-9]
{3}\){0,1}[ \-\.]
{0,1}[0-9]{3}
[ \-\.]{0,1}[0-9]
{4}$/
```

cross-references

- In Task 100 you saw an example of how to validate a phone number in JavaScript without using regular expressions.

- Task 111 shows how to use regular expressions to validate numeric values.

Creating Multiple Form Submission Buttons Using `INPUT TYPE="button"` Buttons

note

- The `onClick` method can be used with the different HTML form controls to do something if the user has clicked on it. Here you use it with plain buttons that, without the event handler, would not perform any action.

On some Web sites you will see a form with multiple buttons that appear to be submission buttons. A common example of this is a login form: One button logs the user in, one button creates a new user account using the username entered by the user, and the third e-mails the user's password to the user in case he or she has forgotten it.

In all cases, the same form is being used, but the form is being submitted to a different URL.

By default, submit buttons always submit the form to the URL specified in the `action` attribute of the `form` tag regardless of how many appear in the form. The way around this is to use regular buttons for the extra buttons and to use the `onClick` event handlers for these buttons to reset the target URL for the form and then submit the form.

`Form` objects have an `action` property that indicates the URL where the form will be submitted. You can change this URL by assigning a new URL to the property:

```
document.formName.action = "new URL";
```

`Form` objects also have the `submit` method, which submits the form just as if the user had clicked on a submit button.

The following steps use these principles to create a login form with three buttons just like the one described previously:

1. Create a new document in your preferred browser.

2. In the body of the document, create a form; as the action, specify the page where the form should be submitted if the user is logging in:

   ```
   <body>

       <form name="myForm" action="login.html">

       </form>

   </body>
   ```

3. In the form create a `username` field:

   ```
   Username: <input type="text" name="username"><br>
   ```

4. In the form create a `password` field:

   ```
   Password: <input type="password" ⤶
   name="password"><br>
   ```

Task **107**

5. Create a submit button for the login process:

```
<input type="button" value="Login" ⊃
onClick="this.form.submit();">
```

6. Create a regular button for users who want to register new accounts:

```
<input type="button" value="Register">
```

7. In the onClick event handler for the button, set the action URL to the register page and then submit the form:

```
<input type="button" value="Register" ⊃
onClick="this.form.action = 'register.html'; ⊃
this.form.submit();">
```

8. Create a regular button for users who want to retrieve their passwords:

```
<input type="button" value="Retrieve Password">
```

9. In the onClick event handler for the button, set the action URL to the page for retrieving passwords and then submit the form. The final page looks like Listing 107-1.

```
<body>

    <form name="myForm" action="login.html">

        Username: <input type="text" name="username"><br>
        Password: <input type="password" name="password"><br>
        <input type="button" value="Login" ⊃
onClick="this.form.submit();">
        <input type="button" value="Register" ⊃
onClick="this.form.action = 'register.html'; ⊃
this.form.submit();">
        <input type="button" value="Retrieve Password" ⊃
onClick="this.form.action = 'password.html'; ⊃
this.form.submit();">

    </form>

</body>
```

Listing 107-1: Multiple buttons for submitting a form.

10. Save the file and open it in your browser. You should see a form with multiple buttons for submitting to different pages.

cross-references

▪ The onClick method is used with many of the tasks in this section.

▪ Task 105 shows you how to validate a password using JavaScript.

Reacting to Mouse Clicks on Buttons

A common use of JavaScript, as evidenced by many of the tasks in this section of the book, is to perform JavaScript tasks when the user clicks on a form button. You do this using the onClick event handler of a form button:

```
<input type="button" value="Button Label"
  onClick="JavaScript code to execute when the user clicks the ⤸
button">
```

This task illustrates using the onClick event by creating a form with a button. When the user clicks on the button, a dialog box is displayed informing the user that he or she has clicked on the button.

note
■ The onClick method can be used with the different HTML form controls to do something if the user has clicked on it.

1. Create a new HTML document in your preferred editor.

2. Create a form in the body of the document:

   ```
   <body>

       <form name="myForm" action="target.html">

       </form>

   </body>
   ```

3. In the form, create a regular button:

   ```
   <body>

       <form name="myForm" action="target.html">

           <input type="button" value="Click Me">

       </form>

   </body>
   ```

4. In the button, use an onClick event handler to display an alert dialog box when the user clicks on the button:

   ```
   <body>

       <form name="myForm" action="target.html">

           <input type="button" value="Click Me"
     onClick="window.alert('You clicked the button.');">

       </form>

   </body>
   ```

5. Save the file as `target.html` and close it.

6. Open the file in a browser, and a button appears, as shown in Figure 108-1.

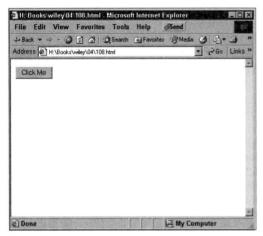

Figure 108-1: A button in a form.

7. Click on the button, and the dialog box in Figure 108-2 appears.

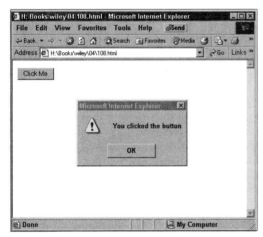

Figure 108-2: Reacting when the user clicks on the button.

cross-references

▪ The `onClick` method is used with many of the tasks in this section.

▪ You can alert a user as a response to an `onClick` event. See Task 25 for more information on alerting a user.

Using Graphical Buttons in JavaScript

HTML provides a form element type called `image` that lets you place images within a form as elements. You can apply event handlers to these images to make them a dynamic, integral part of your forms. To include an image in a form as a form element, use the `image` value for the `type` attribute of the `input` tag:

```
<input type="image" src="path to image">
```

As with other form buttons, you can specify event handlers in image buttons. For instance, the following button uses an `onClick` event handler to specify JavaScript code to execute when the user clicks on the image:

```
<input type="image" src="path to image" onClick="JavaScript code ⏎
to execute">
```

To illustrate the user of graphical buttons, the following form uses an image as a submit button. When the user clicks the button, an alert dialog box is displayed before the form is submitted.

1. Create or select an image file you will use for the image button.

2. Create a new HTML document in your preferred editor.

3. In the body of the document, create a form.

4. Place any fields you want in the form; do not include a submit button:

   ```
   <body>
       <form name="myForm" action="login.html">
           Username: <input type="text" name="username"><br>
           Password: <input type="password"
                             name="password"><br>
       </form>
   </body>
   ```

5. Create an image tag that references the image from Step 1 earlier:

   ```
   <body>
       <form name="myForm" action="login.html">
           Username: <input type="text" name="username"><br>
           Password: <input type="password"
                             name="password"><br>
           <input type="image" src="login.gif" value="Login">
       </form>
   </body>
   ```

6. Use an `onClick` event handler for the image to display a dialog box when the user clicks on the image:

   ```
   <body>
       <form name="myForm" action="login.html">
   ```

```
      Username: <input type="text" name="username"><br>
      Password: <input type="password" name="password">
      <input type="image" src="login.gif" value="Login" ⤶
  onClick="window.alert('You clicked on the image.');">
    </form>
</body>
```

7. Save the file as `login.html` and close it.

8. Open the file in a browser. The form in Figure 109-1 appears, including the image button.

tip

▪ You can create images to be used as buttons in any graphical program. This includes Microsoft Paint.

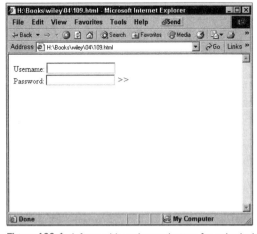

Figure 109-1: A form with an image button for submission.

9. Click on the image and the dialog box in Figure 109-2 appears.

Figure 109-2: Reacting to users clicking on the image.

cross-reference

▪ See Task 60 to learn how to detect clicks on an image in a form versus using an image as a button.

Task 110

Controlling the Form Submission URL

When you create a form in HTML, you specify what page the form should be submitted to with the action property of the form tag:

```
<form action="URL to submit the form to">
```

This is reflected in JavaScript as the action property of the form object:

```
document.formName.action
```

You can change this target URL dynamically at any point by assigning a new URL to this property:

```
document.formName.action = "new URL";
```

The following task creates a form as well as a link. If the link is clicked, the target action URL of the form is changed. When the user submits the form, the target URL is displayed in a dialog box before the form is submitted.

note

• Notice the use of # as the URL in the example. When using the onClick event handler to trigger the opening of a new window, you don't want to cause clicking on the link to change the location of the current window; this is a simple way to avoid this (see Step 5).

1. Create a form named myForm in a new document:

   ```
   <body>
       <form name="myForm" action="target.html">

       </form>
   </body>
   ```

2. In the form, create any fields you need, as well as a submit button:

   ```
   <body>
     <form name="myForm" action="target.html">
         Enter Some Text: <input type="text"
               name="myField"><br>
         <input type="submit">
     </form>
   </body>
   ```

caution

• In the example, the form is directed, or redirected, to either target.html or alternate.html. If these forms don't exist, you will get an error or a blank screen. You can change these URLs to any other URL (see Figure 110-1).

3. In the submit button, use the onClick event handler to display the action URL in a dialog box before submitting the form:

   ```
   <input type="submit" onClick="↲
   window.alert(this.form.action);">
   ```

4. After the form, create a link that targets # as the URL:

   ```
   <a href="#">Change Form Action Target</a>
   ```

5. Use an `onClick` event handler to change the target URL when the link is clicked. The complete page is presented in Listing 110-1.

```
<body>
    <form name="myForm" action="target.html">
        Enter Some Text: <input type="text" ⊃
name="myField"><br>
        <input type="submit" ⊃
onClick="window.alert(this.form.action);">
    </form>

    <a href="#" onClick="document.myForm.action = ⊃
'alternate.html';">Change Form Action Target</a>
</body>
```

Listing 110-1: The completed page.

6. Save the file and close it.

7. Open the file in a browser and you now see the form you created.

8. Submit the form without clicking on the link. It will submit to the original URL, as illustrated in Figure 110-1.

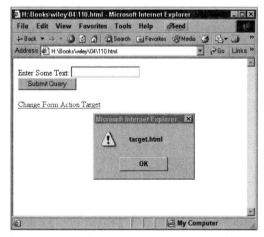

Figure 110-1: Submitting the form to the original URL.

9. Reload the file in a browser. Click on the link and then submit the form, and the form will submit to the new URL.

cross-reference

▪ Learn more about submitting forms in Task 224.

Validating a Numeric Text Field with Regular Expressions

Sometimes you will have a form where you need to limit the text entered into a text field to only particular characters. For instance, you might want to limit the text to numbers. Using regular expressions, you can easily perform this check when the user submits the form.

Regular expressions provide a powerful extension of the wildcard concept to allow you to specify text patterns and search for matches for those patterns. Unfortunately, regular expressions are an advanced topic beyond the scope of this book; however, this task shows how to perform number validation using regular expressions.

The following steps create a form with a field to enter a phone number that is validated with regular expressions:

1. In the header of a new HTML document, create a script block containing the function `checkNumber` that receives a text string:

```
<script language="JavaScript">
function checkNumber(number) {


}
</script>
```

2. In the function, create a regular expression for matching against a numeric value:

```
var check = /^[0-9]+\.?[0-9]+$/;
```

3. Next, test for a failure to match this pattern against the number:

```
if (!check.test(number)) {


}
```

4. If no match is found, inform the user and return `false` from the function:

```
if (!check.test(number)) {
   window.alert("You must provide a valid number.");
   return false;
}
```

5. Finally, return `true` from the function if the number passed the test, so that the complete function looks like this:

```
function checkNumber(number) {
   var check = /^[0-9]+\.?[0-9]+$/;
   if (!check.test(number)) {
      window.alert("You must provide a valid number.");
```

notes

- When you assign a regular expression to a variable, you are creating a regular expression object. This object has a `test` method that allows you to test the expression against a string that is provided as an argument to the method. The method returns `true` if there is a match and `false` otherwise.

- The regular expression for validating a numeric value is as follows:

  `/^[0-9]+\.?`
  `[0-9]+$/;`

- Regular expressions are powerful but require you to have a lot of experience to become comfortable with them and master them. You can find an introductory tutorial on regular expressions at http://www.linuxpcug.org/lessons/regex.htm.

- Notice that you negate the result returned by the `test` method. In this way, the `if` statement is true only when no match is found.

```
        return false;
    }
    return true;
}
```

6. Create another function named `checkForm` that takes a `form` object as an argument. The function should call `checkNumber` and pass it the value of the field containing the number and then return the result returned by the `checkNumber` function:

```
function checkForm(formObj) {
    return checkNumber(formObj.myField.value);
}
```

7. Create a form that contains a field for entering the phone number and uses the `onSubmit` event handler to call the `checkForm` function:

```
<body>
    <form name="myForm" action="target.html"
        onSubmit="return checkForm(this);">
        Enter a number: <input type="text"
                        name="myField"><br>
        <input type="submit">
    </form>
</body>
```

8. Save the file and open it in a browser. The form in Figure 111-1 appears.

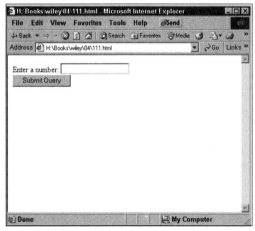

Figure 111-1: A form with a text field.

9. Try to submit the form without a valid number, and you should see an appropriate error message.

cross-reference

▪ Task 106 presents the code for using regular expressions to validate a phone number.

Encrypting Data before Submitting It

By encrypting the data in a form before submitting it across the Internet, you add a small layer of privacy to the data being transmitted. This can be achieved in JavaScript if desired by passing each form field through an encryption function before submitting the form. The principle is simple:

1. In the `form` tag, use `onSubmit` to call the encryption function before submitting the form.

2. The encryption form should work through each field in the form and encrypt the value of each field.

The encryption process can use the `elements` property of the `form` tag to easily access all the fields in a form without knowing what those fields will be in advance. This property is an array containing one entry for each object in the form. Therefore, the first field in the form can be referenced as:

```
document.formName.elements[0]
```

The following task creates a form, which is encrypted using a simple algorithm before it is transmitted. The encryption algorithm simply converts each letter in the form's fields to their numeric Unicode equivalents:

1. In the header of a new HTML document, create a script block with a function named `encrypt`. This function should take a text string as a single argument. This string will be encrypted:

```
<script language="JavaScript">
function encrypt(item) {


}
</script>
```

2. In the function, create a variable named `newItem` that will hold the encrypted string. Initially this should be an empty string:

```
var newItem = "";
```

3. Loop through each character in the original text string:

```
for (i=0; i < item.length; i++) {
}
```

4. For each character in the string, use the `charCodeAt` method of the `string` object to obtain the numerical Unicode representation of the letter and add it to the `newItem` string. Note that a dot is added after each character. This separates the characters cleanly to make it easier to decrypt later.

notes

- Strings have a `length` property that returns the number of characters in the string. If the string is empty, the length will be zero.

- The `charCodeAt` method returns the Unicode representation of the character specified by an index in the string.

- Arrays have a property called `length` that returns the number of items in an array, and it is used in this loop. Since arrays are zero-indexed, an array with length 5 (which contains five elements) would contain elements with indexes from 0 to 4. This is why you loop until `i` is less than, and not less than or equal to, the length of the array.

- The keyword `this` is used to pass the form to the function. In event handlers of the form itself, `this` refers to the object for the form itself.

- An alert has been added to the `onSubmit` event handler so that you can see the value of the encrypted text field before submitting the form. This allows you to check if the encryption is working. You wouldn't include this in a live application.

5. Return the encrypted string from the function. The `encrypt` function should look like the following:

```
function encrypt(item) {
    var newItem = "";

    for (i=0; i < item.length; i++) {
        newItem += item.charCodeAt(i) + ".";
    }
    return newItem;
}
```

6. Create a second function named `encryptForm` that takes a `form` object as an argument.

7. In the function, loop through the `elements` array. For each element, encrypt the value of the field with the encrypt function, and store the result back into the field's value:

```
function encryptForm(myForm) {

    for (i=0; i < myForm.elements.length; i++) {
        myForm.elements[i].value =
            encrypt(myForm.elements[i].value);
    }
}
```

8. In the body of the document, create a form with any needed fields. Use the `onSubmit` event handler to submit the form to the `encryptForm` function:

```
<form name="myForm" action="target.html" onSubmit="↵
encryptForm(this); window.alert(this.myField.value);">

    Enter Some Text: <input type="text" name="myField"><br>
    <input type="submit">
</form>
```

9. Save the file and open it in a browser.

10. Click on the submit button. The form is encrypted, and the encrypted value of the field is displayed in a dialog box before the form is submitted.

tips

- The idea of encrypting data in JavaScript has limited utility in terms of security. Because JavaScript code can be read by the user by viewing the source code in your browser, anyone can determine how you are encrypting the form and can easily decrypt the data. However, this approach does provide a veil of privacy; after the user submits the form, the data that is transmitted across the Internet is not immediately apparent to anyone intercepting data as it flows across the Internet. This can be helpful in some applications.

- This isn't real encryption; instead, it is just illustrative of how to tie an encryption function into a form submission process. To implement another encryption algorithm would require you to write your own encryption function and then call that function when needed.

cross-reference

- Notice the short form concatenation operator being used here: +=. Using `a += b` is the same as `a = a + b`. For more on doing math in JavaScript, see Task 14

113

Using Forms for Automatic Navigation Jumping

Sometimes you will see form selection lists used as a mechanism for providing navigation to different URLs for a page. The drop-down list will include multiple URLs, as shown in Figure 113-1. When the user selects an entry in the list, the browser is automatically sent to that URL.

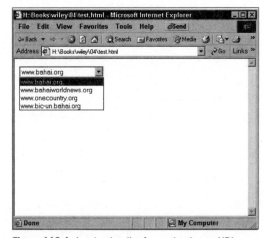

Figure 113-1: A selection list for navigating to URLs.

This navigation is achieved using two principles:

- The `onChange` event handler can detect changes in the selected item in a selection list.

- Setting `window.location` to a new URL redirects the browser.

The following task shows how to build a simple selection list with URLs. JavaScript code will redirect the user to the selected URL.

1. Create a form in the body of a new document.

2. Create a selection list with the URLs you want to allow the user to navigate to:

```
<select name="url">

  <option></option>
  <option value="http://www.juxta.com/">↵
www.juxta.com</a>
  <option value="http://www.anis.cc/">www.anis.cc</a>
  <option value="http://www.hatcher.org/">↵
www.hatcher.org</a>
  </select>
```

3. Use the onChange event handler of the select tag to redirect the browser to the URL of the selected entry (the URL is the value of each entry). Listing 113-1 shows the code.

```
<body>
  <form>
    Select a Site:

    <select name="url" onChange="window.location =
this.value;">

      <option></option>
      <option value="http://www.juxta.com/">www.juxta.com</a>
      <option value="http://www.anis.cc/">www.anis.cc</a>
      <option value="http://www.hatcher.org/">
www.hatcher.org</a>
    </select>
  </form>
</body>
```

Listing 113-1: The selection list with URLs.

4. Save the file and close it.

5. Open the file in your browser. A selection list appears, as illustrated in Figure 113-2.

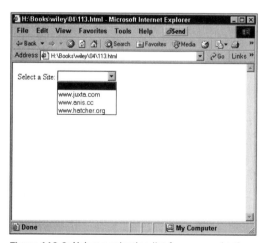

Figure 113-2: Using a selection list for user navigation.

6. Select an entry from the list. The browser is redirected to that site.

cross-references

- Task 227 shows how to take other actions when a user makes a selection.

- See Task 121 for more information on setting the location of a new browser window.

Part 5: Manipulating Browser Windows

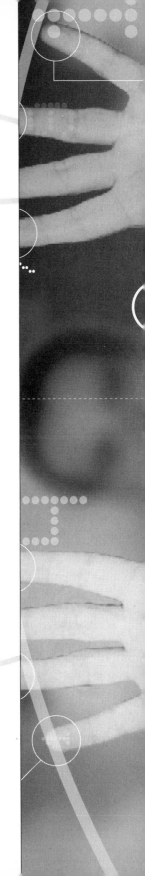

Using the `Window` **Object**

The `window` object provides access to properties and methods that can be used to obtain information about open windows, as well as to manipulate these windows and even open new windows.

This object offers properties that allow you to access frames in a window, access the window's name, manipulate text in the status bar, and check the open or closed state of the window. The methods allow the user to display a variety of dialog boxes, as well as to open new windows and close open windows.

Among the features of the `window` object are the following:

* Creating alert dialog boxes
* Creating confirmation dialog boxes
* Creating dialog boxes that prompt the user to enter information
* Opening pages in new windows
* Determining window sizes
* Controlling scrolling of the document displayed in the window
* Scheduling the execution of functions

The `window` object can be referred to in several ways:

* Using the keyword `window` or `self` to refer to the current window where the JavaScript code is executing. For instance, `window.alert` and `self.alert` refer to the same method.

* Using the object name for another open window. For instance, if a window is associated with an object named `myWindow`, `myWindow.alert` would refer to the `alert` method in that window.

The following steps illustrate how to access the `window` object by changing the text displayed in the current window's status bar:

1. In the body of the document, create a script block with opening and closing script tags:

   ```
   <script language="JavaScript">
   </script>
   ```

2. In the script block, access the `window.status` property:

   ```
   <script language="JavaScript">
      window.status
   </script>
   ```

3. Assign new text to display to the `window.status` property in the same way as assigning a text string to a variable, so that the final document looks like Listing 114-1.

```
<body>

    <script language="JavaScript">
        window.status = "A new status message";
    </script>

</body>
```

Listing 114-1: Displaying text in the status bar.

4. Save the file.

5. Open the page in a browser. A blank HTML page appears with "A new status message" displayed in the status bar, as illustrated in Figure 114-1.

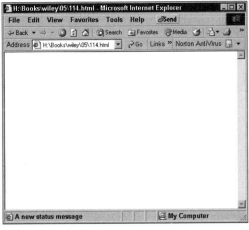

Figure 114-1: Displaying custom text in the status bar.

cross-reference

▪ The various types of dialog boxes are discussed in Tasks 25, 26, and 117.

Popping Up an Alert Dialog Box

The window object provides the alert method, which allows you to display a simple dialog box containing a text message followed by a single button the user can use to acknowledge the message and close the dialog box.

Figure 115-1 illustrates an alert dialog box in Microsoft Internet Explorer; Figure 115-2 shows the same dialog box in Netscape.

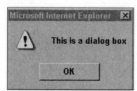

Figure 115-1: An alert dialog box in Internet Explorer.

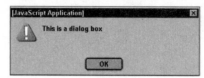

Figure 115-2: An alert dialog box in Netscape.

Creating alert dialog boxes is one of many features of the window object, which can also be used to create confirmation and prompting dialog boxes, as well as other capabilities. These include the following:

• Opening pages in new windows

• Determining window sizes

• Controlling scrolling of the document displayed in the window

• Scheduling the execution of functions

The following steps show how to display two alert dialog boxes in succession:

1. In the body of a new HTML document, create a script block with opening and closing script tags:

```
<script language="JavaScript">
</script>
```

2. Use the window.alert method to display the first dialog box:

```
window.alert("This is a dialog box");
```

3. Use the window.alert method to display the second dialog box, so that the final script looks like this:

```
<script language="JavaScript">

    window.alert("This is a dialog box");
```

```
window.alert("This is another dialog box");

</script>
```

4. Save the file.

5. Open the file in a Web browser. The first dialog box, shown in
   Figure 115-3, appears. Once the user closes the first dialog box, the
   second, shown in Figure 115-4, is displayed.

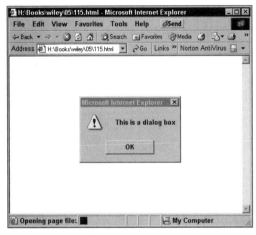

Figure 115-3: The first dialog box.

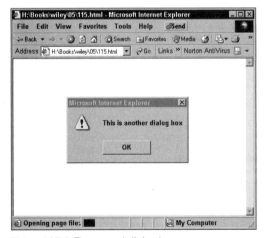

Figure 115-4: The second dialog box.

cross-reference

- The scheduling of auto-
  matic execution of a function is discussed in Tasks
  38, 39, and 40.

Task 116

Popping Up Confirmation Dialog Boxes

In addition to the `alert` method discussed in Task 115, the `window` object also provides the `confirm` method, which allows you to display a dialog box containing a text message followed by two buttons the user can use to acknowledge the message or reject it and close the dialog box. Typically these buttons are labeled OK and Cancel.

Figure 116-1 illustrates a confirmation dialog box in Microsoft Internet Explorer; Figure 116-2 shows the same dialog box in Netscape.

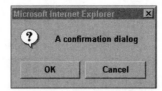

Figure 116-1: A confirmation dialog box in Internet Explorer.

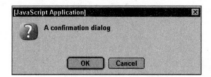

Figure 116-2: A confirmation dialog box in Netscape.

The following steps show how to display a confirmation dialog box, and then based on the user's choice, display the choice in the body of the page:

1. In the body of a new HTML document, create a script block with opening and closing `script` tags:

```
<script language="JavaScript">
</script>
```

2. Use the `window.confirm` method to display the first dialog box; the value returned by the dialog box is stored in the variable `userChoice`:

```
var userChoice = window.confirm("Click OK or Cancel");
```

3. Use an `if` statement to test the user's response to the dialog box by checking the `userChoice` variable:

```
if (userChoice) {
```

4. If the user has selected the OK button, display an appropriate message using the `document.write` method:

```
document.write("You chose OK");
```

notes

* The `window.confirm` method returns a value: `true` if the user clicks on OK or `false` if the user clicks on Cancel. This makes it easy to test the user's response to the dialog box.

* `if` statements require an expression that evaluates to true or false. Here, `userChoice` is a variable that will be either true or false, since that is the value returned by the `confirm` method. This means the expression can simply be the variable name itself.

5. If the user has selected the Cancel button, display an appropriate message. The final page should look like this:

```
<body>

    <script language="JavaScript">

        var userChoice = window.confirm("Click OK or ⏎
Cancel");
        if (userChoice) {
           document.write("You chose OK");
        } else {
           document.write("You chose Cancel");
        }

    </script>

</body>
```

6. Save the file and open it in a browser. The browser displays a confirmation dialog box like Figure 116-3. Based on the user's selection in the dialog box, the browser window will contain an appropriate message, as in Figure 116-4, where the user selected the OK button.

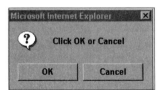

Figure 116-3: The confirmation dialog box.

Figure 116-4: The user selected OK.

cross-reference

* The window object is introduced in Task 114.

Popping Up JavaScript Prompts

In addition to the `alert` method discussed in Task 115 and the `confirm` method discussed in Task 116, the `window` object also provides the `prompt` method, which allows you to display a dialog box containing a text message followed by a text field, where the user can provide some input before closing the dialog box.

Figure 117-1 illustrates a prompt dialog box in Microsoft Internet Explorer; Figure 117-2 shows the same dialog box in Netscape.

Figure 117-1: A prompt dialog box in Internet Explorer.

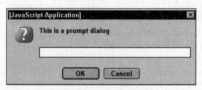

Figure 117-2: A prompt dialog box in Netscape.

The `window.prompt` method takes two arguments: The first is the text message to display, and the second is the default text to display in the text field. If you want the text field to be empty, simply use an empty string. For instance, the following example of the `window.prompt` method displays the dialog box illustrated in Figure 117-1:

```
window.prompt("Enter a value from 1 to 10","");
```

The following steps show how to use a prompt dialog box to ask the user to enter his or her name and then display the name in the body of the HTML page:

1. In the body of a new HTML document, create a script block with opening and closing `script` tags:

   ```
   <script language="JavaScript">
   </script>
   ```

2. Use the `window.prompt` method to display the dialog box; the value returned by the dialog box is stored in the variable `userName`:

   ```
   var userName = window.prompt("Please Enter Your
   Name","Enter Your Name Here");
   ```

3. Display the user's name using the `document.write` method, so that the final page looks like the following:

notes

* The `window.prompt` method returns the value entered by the user in the text field in the dialog box. By storing the result returned by the method in a variable, you can use the value later in the page.

* The `document.write` method expects a single string as an argument. In this example, two strings are concatenated (or combined) into a single string using the + operator.

```
<body>

    <script language="JavaScript">

        var userName = window.prompt("Please Enter Your ⤵
Name","Enter Your Name Here");
        document.write("Your Name is " + userName);

    </script>

</body>
```

4. Save the file.

5. Open the file in a browser. A prompt dialog box appears, as shown in Figure 117-3. After the user enters his or her name, it is displayed in the browser window, as in Figure 117-4.

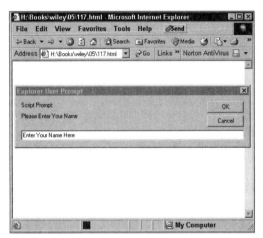

Figure 117-3: Prompting the user to enter his or her name.

Figure 117-4: Displaying the user's name.

118

Creating New Browser Windows

The window object provides the open method, which can be used to open a new browser window and display a URL in that window. In its most basic form, the open method works as follows:

```
window.open(url, window name);
```

Here, the URL is a text string of a relative or absolute URL to display in the window. The window name is a name for the window that can be used later in the target attribute of the a tag to direct a link to that window.

Opening new windows is one of many features of the window object, which can also be used for several other purposes:

- Displaying a variety of dialog boxes
- Determining window sizes
- Controlling scrolling of the document displayed in the window
- Scheduling the execution of functions

The following steps illustrate how to open a window with JavaScript. The main document will open in the current browser window, and the new window will open and display another URL:

note

- The window.open method can actually take two arguments or three arguments. For basic use, two arguments suffice. Advanced use such as controlling the size of a window when it opens relies on a third argument. This task illustrates basic use of the method.

1. In the header of a new HTML document, create a script block:

   ```
   <head>
       <script language="JavaScript">

       </script>
   </head>
   ```

2. In the script block, use the window.open method to display the URL of your choice in a new window, and name the window myNewWindow:

   ```
   <head>
       <script language="JavaScript">

           window.open("http://www.bahai.org/","myNewWindow");

       </script>
   </head>
   ```

3. In the body of the document, enter any HTML or text you want to be displayed in the initial window, so that the final page looks like Listing 118-1.

```
<head>

    <script language="JavaScript">

    window.open("http://www.bahai.org/","myNewWindow");

    </script>

</head>


<body>

    The site has opened in a new window.

</body>
```

Listing 118-1: Opening a new window.

tip
- Remember, you can't control the size of the new window using the technique from this task. Typically, the new window will be the same size as the initial window opened in your browser.

4. Save the file.

5. Open the file in a browser. The page displays, and then a new window opens to display the URL specified in the window.open method, as illustrated in Figure 118-1.

Figure 118-1: Opening a new window.

Opening a New Browser Window from a Link

notes

▪ Notice the use of # as the
URL in the example. When
using the onClick event
handler to trigger the opening of a new window, you
don't want to cause clicking on the link to change
the location of the current
window; this is a simple
way to avoid this.

▪ The window.open
method can actually take
two arguments or three
arguments. For basic use,
two arguments suffice.
Advanced use such as con-
trolling the size of a window
when it opens relies on a
third argument. This task
illustrates basic use of the
method.

One application of the window.open method described in Task 118 is to use it to open a new window when a user clicks on a link. Although it is possible to do this by simply specifying a new window name in the target attribute of the a tag, there may be reasons why this is insufficient. For instance, you may need to programmatically build the URL that needs to be displayed in a new window, and this is easier to achieve in JavaScript at the time the user clicks on the link.

To do this, you can use the window.open command in the onClick event handler of the a tag:

```
<a href="#" onClick="window.open(url,window name">Link text</a>
```

The following task illustrates how to open a window from a link using JavaScript:

1. In the body of a new HTML document, create a link:

   ```
   <body>
       <a href="">Click here</a> to open a site in a new ⤶
   window
   </body>
   ```

2. Use # as the URL for the link in the a tag:

   ```
   <body>
       <a href="#">Click here</a> to open a site in a new ⤶
   window
   </body>
   ```

3. Specify an onClick attribute to call the window.open method to open the desired URL:

   ```
   <body>
       <a href="#"
   onClick='window.open("http://www.ca.bahai.org/","⤶
   newWindow");'>Click here</a>
       to open a site in a new window
   </body>
   ```

4. Save the file.

5. Open the file in a browser. Initially, the page with the link displays, as in Figure 119-1. When the user clicks on the link, a new window is displayed with the specified URL, as in Figure 119-2.

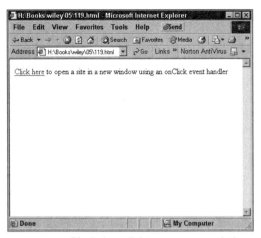

Figure 119-1: Displaying a link to open a new window.

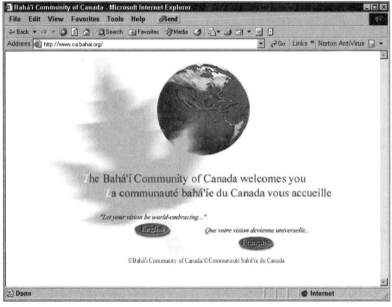

Figure 119-2: Opening a new window when the user clicks the link.

tip

• Remember, you can't control the size of the new window using the technique from this task. Typically, the new window will be the same size as the initial window opened in your browser.

Setting the Size of New Browser Windows

When using the `window.open` method, introduced in Task 118, you can actually control a number of aspects of the appearance and behavior of the window. Among the features that can be controlled is the size of the window at the time the `window.open` method opens it.

To control these features, the `window.open` method takes an optional third argument. The argument takes this form:

```
"property name=value,property name=value,etc."
```

For instance, the following example would create a window that is 500 pixels wide and 200 pixels deep, as shown in Figure 120-1:

```
window.open("http://www.onecountry.org/","myNewWindow","width=500,
height=200");
```

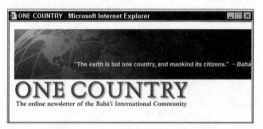

Figure 120-1: Controlling the height and width of a new window.

The following task illustrates the use of the `height` and `width` properties of new windows to open a new window that is exactly 300 pixels wide and 300 pixels tall:

1. In the header of a new HTML document, create a script block:

   ```
   <script language="JavaScript">
   </script>
   ```

2. In the script block, use the `window.open` method to display the URL of your choice in a new window, and name the window `myNewWindow`. Use the `height` and `width` properties to control the size of the window and set it to 300 by 300 pixels:

   ```
   <script language="JavaScript">

   window.open("http://www.bahai.org/","myNewWindow","
   height=300,width=300");

   </script>
   ```

3. In the body of the document, include any HTML or text you want to display in the initial window, so that the final document looks like Listing 120-1.

```
<head>
    <script language="JavaScript">
    window.open("http://www.juxta.com/","newWindow","⮐
height=300,width=300");

    </script>
</head>

<body>

    The new window is 300 by 300 pixels.

</body>
```

Listing 120-1: Controlling the size of a new window.

4. Save the file.

5. Open the file in a browser. The new window opens at the specified size, as in Figure 120-2.

Figure 120-2: Opening a 300-by-300-pixel window.

Setting the Location of New Browser Windows

notes

* This argument is a text string that contains a list of values separated by commas. These values allow you to set properties of the window being opened.

* The `window.open` method can actually take two arguments or three arguments. For basic use, two arguments suffice. Advanced use such as controlling the size of a window when it opens relies on a third argument. Task 118 illustrates the two-argument form of the method.

When using the `window.open` method, introduced in Task 118, you can actually control a number of aspects of the appearance and behavior of the window. Among the features that can be controlled is the placement on the screen of the window at the time the `window.open` method opens it.

To control the placement, the `window.open` method takes an optional third argument. The argument takes the following form:

```
"property name=value,property name=value,etc."
```

To control placement of the window, you set different properties for different browsers. For Internet Explorer, you set the `top` and `left` properties. For Netscape, you set the `screenX` and `screenY` properties. For instance, the following places a new window 200 pixels in from the left of the screen and 100 pixels down from the top of the screen, as illustrated in Figure 121-1:

```
window.open("http://www.juxta.com/","myNewWindow","width=300,
height=200,left=200,screenX=200,top=100,screenY=100");
```

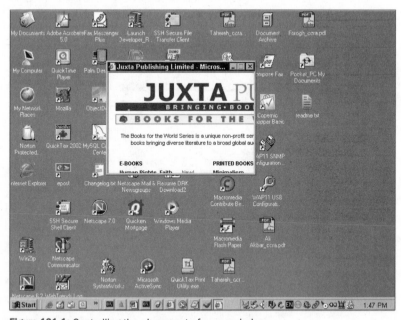

Figure 121-1: Controlling the placement of a new window.

The following task illustrates the use of these properties of new windows to open a new window that is exactly 400 pixels away from the top and left of the screen:

1. In the header of a new HTML document, create a script block:

```
<script language="JavaScript">
</script>
```

2. In the script block use the `window.open` method to display the URL of your choice in a new window, and name the window `myNewWindow`. Use the `top`, `left`, `screenX`, and `screenY` properties to control the position of the window and set it to 400 pixels from the left and top sides of the screen:

```
<script language="JavaScript">

window.open("http://www.juxta.com/","newWindow","⤵
height=300,width=500,screenX=400,screenY=400,top=400,⤵
left=400");


</script>
```

3. In the body of the document, include any HTML or text you want to display in the initial window, so that the final document looks like Listing 121-1.

```
<head>
    <script language="JavaScript">
    window.open("http://www.juxta.com/","newWindow","⤵
height=300,width=500,screenX=400,screenY=400,top=400,⤵
left=400");

    </script>
</head>

<body>

    The new window is 400 pixels from the top-left corner ⤵
    of the screen.

</body>
```

Listing 121-1: Controlling placement of a new window.

4. Save the file.

5. Open the file in a browser. The new window opens at the specified location

cross-reference

▪ Notice the use of the `width` and `height` properties to control the size of the window. These properties are discussed in Task 120.

Controlling Toolbar Visibility for New Browser Windows

When using the window.open method, introduced in Task 118, you can actually control a number of aspects of the appearance and behavior of the window. Among the features that can be controlled is whether the toolbar of the window is displayed when it is opened.

note

- Notice the use of # as the URL (see Step 2). When using the onClick event handler to trigger the opening of a new window, you don't want to cause clicking on the link to change the location of the current window; this is a simple way to avoid this.

To control the size of the window, you need to set the toolbar property value by assigning a yes or no value to it. For instance, the following example creates a window with no toolbar:

```
window.open("http://www.bahai.org/","myNewWindow","toolbar=no");
```

The following steps show how to create a page with two links. Both links open the same page in a new window, but one link opens the new window with no toolbar and the other opens it with a toolbar.

1. In the body of a new HTML document, create a link for opening a new window without a toolbar:

   ```
   <a href="">Click here</a> for a window without a toolbar
   ```

2. Use # as the URL in the a tag:

   ```
   <a href="#">Click here</a> for a window without a toolbar
   ```

3. Use the onClick attribute to call the window.open method to open a URL of your choice, and specify toolbar=no in the third argument:

   ```
   <a href='#' ⊃
   onClick='window.open("http://www.juxta.com/","⊃
   newWindow1","toolbar=no");'>Click here</a> for a window ⊃
   without a toolbar
   ```

4. Create another link for opening a new window with a toolbar:

   ```
   <a href="">Click here</a> for a window with a toolbar
   ```

5. Use # as the URL in the a tag:

   ```
   <a href="#">Click here</a> for a window with a toolbar
   ```

6. Use the onClick attribute to call the window.open method to open a URL of your choice, and specify toolbar=yes in the third argument. The final document should look like Listing 122-1.

```
<body>

    <a href='#' onClick='window.open("http://www.juxta.com/
","newWindow1","toolbar=no");'>Click here</a> for a window
without a toolbar
    <p>
<a href='#' onClick='window.open("http://www.juxta.com/","
newWindow2","toolbar=yes");'>Click here</a> for a window
with a toolbar

</body>
```

Listing 122-1: Controlling the appearance of the toolbar in new windows.

7. Save the file and open it in a browser. When the user clicks on the
   first link, a new window with no toolbar will open, as in Figure 122-1.
   When the user clicks on the second link, a new window with a toolbar will open.

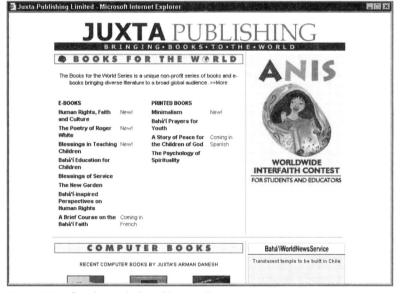

Figure 122-1: Opening a window with no toolbar.

tip

- There is no reason you cannot combine the toolbar
  property with other win-
  dow.open properties,
  such as the width and
  height properties (Task
  120) or the scrollbars
  property (Task 123). In
  order to focus strictly on
  the effect of the toolbar
  property, this task doesn't
  combine properties.

cross-reference

- To control features of the
  new window, the win-
  dow.open method takes
  an optional third argument.
  This argument is a text
  string that contains a list of
  values separated by commas. These values allow
  you to set properties of the
  window that is being
  opened. The syntax of this
  string of text is described in
  Task 120.

Task 123

Determining the Availability of Scroll Bars for New Browser Windows

note

- When a window is opened with no scroll bars, the content of the window cannot be scrolled by the user.

When using the `window.open` method, introduced in Task 118, you can actually control a number of aspects of the appearance and behavior of the window. Among the features that can be controlled is whether the scroll bars of the window are displayed when it is opened.

To control these features, the `window.open` method takes an optional third argument. This argument is a text string that contains a list of values separated by commas. These values allow you to set properties of the window that is being opened.

To control the size of the window, you need to set the `scrollbars` property value by assigning a `yes` or `no` value to it. For instance, the following example creates a window with no scroll bars:

```
window.open("http://www.bahai.org/","myNewWindow","scrollbars=no");
```

The following steps show how to create a page with two links. Both links open the same page in a small new window, but one link opens the new window with no scroll bars and the other opens it with scroll bars.

1. In the body of a new HTML document, create a link for opening a new window without a toolbar:

   ```
   <a href="">Click here</a> for a window without scrollbars
   ```

2. Use # as the URL in the a tag:

   ```
   <a href="#">Click here</a> for a window without scrollbars
   ```

3. Use the `onClick` attribute to call the `window.open` method to open a URL of your choice, and specify `scrollbars=no` in the third argument:

   ```
   <a href='#'
   onClick='window.open("http://www.juxta.com/","
   newWindow1","scrollbars=no,width=300,height=300");'>
   Click here</a> for a window without scrollbars
   ```

4. Create another link for opening a new window with scroll bars:

   ```
   <a href="">Click here</a> for a window with scrollbars
   ```

5. Use # as the URL in the a tag:

   ```
   <a href="#">Click here</a> for a window with scrollbars
   ```

6. Use the `onClick` attribute to call the `window.open` method to open a URL of your choice, and specify `scrollbars=yes` in the third argument. The final document should look like Listing 123-1.

```
<body>

    <a href='#' onClick='window.open("http://www.juxta.com/
","newWindow1","scrollbars=no,width=300,height=300");'>
Click here</a> for a window without scrollbars
    <p>
<a href='#'
onClick='window.open("http://www.juxta.com/","newWindow2
","scrollbars=yes,width=300,height=300");'>Click here</a>
for a window with scrollbars

</body>
```

Listing 123-1: Controlling the appearance of scroll bars in new windows.

7. Save the file and open it in a browser. When the user clicks on the first link, a new window with no scroll bars will open, as in Figure 123-1. When the user clicks on the second link, a new window with scroll bars will open.

Figure 123-1: Opening a window with no scroll bars.

Restricting Resizing of New Browser Windows

When using the `window.open` method, introduced in Task 118, you can actually control a number of aspects of the appearance and behavior of the window. Among the features that can be controlled is whether the window can be resized by the user after it is opened.

To control these features, the `window.open` method takes an optional third argument. This argument is a text string that contains a list of values separated by commas. These values allow you to set properties of the window that is being opened.

To control the size of the window, you need to set the `resizable` property value by assigning a `yes` or `no` value to it. For instance, the following example creates a window that cannot be resized:

```
window.open("http://www.bahai.org/","myNewWindow","resizable=no");
```

The following steps show how to create a page with two links. Both links open the same page in a small new window, but one link opens the new window so that it cannot be resized and the other opens it so that it is resizable.

1. In the body of a new HTML document, create a link for opening a new window without a toolbar:

   ```
   <a href="">Click here</a> for a window which cannot be
   resized
   ```

2. Use # as the URL in the a tag:

   ```
   <a href="#">Click here</a> for a window which cannot be
   resized
   ```

3. Use the `onClick` attribute to call the `window.open` method to open a URL of your choice, and specify `resizable=no` in the third argument:

   ```
   <a href='#'
   onClick='window.open("http://www.juxta.com/",
   "newWindow1","resizable=no,width=300,height=300");'>
   Click here</a> for a window which cannot be resized
   ```

4. Create another link for opening a new window that can be resized:

   ```
   <a href="">Click here</a> for a window which can be
   resized
   ```

5. Use # as the URL in the a tag:

   ```
   <a href="#">Click here</a> for a window which can be
   resized
   ```

note

- When a window cannot be resized, the user will not be able to grab and drag any of the edges or corners of the window. The mouse cursor should not change to resizing arrows when over the edges or corners of the window.

6. Use the `onClick` attribute to call the `window.open` method to open a URL of your choice, and specify `resizable=yes` in the third argument. The final document should look like Listing 124-1.

```
<body>

    <a href='#' onClick='window.open("http://www.juxta.com/
","newWindow1","resizable=no,width=300,height=300");'>
Click here</a> for a window which cannot be resized
    <p>
<a href='#'
onClick='window.open("http://www.juxta.com/","newWindow2
","resizable=yes,width=300,height=300");'>Click here</a>
for a window which can be resized

</body>
```

Listing 124-1: Controlling the resizing of new windows.

7. Save the file and open it in a browser. When the user clicks on the first link, a new window that cannot be resized will open, as in Figure 124-1. When the user clicks on the second link, a new window that is resizable will open.

Figure 124-1: Opening a nonresizable window.

Loading a New Document into a Browser Window

Typically, you use an a tag when you want a user to load a new document in the current browser window. However, there are times when a simple a tag is not enough. In particular, you may need to dynamically determine which page should be loaded into the browser at the time the user clicks the link. To do this, you want to use JavaScript at the time the user clicks on a link by using the onClick attribute of the a tag to set the document.location property to a new URL. For example:

```
<a href="#" onClick="document.location = new URL;">link text</a>
```

Using JavaScript to redirect the user's browser, this task shows how to build a simple page that takes the user to a new page when he or she clicks on a link:

1. In the body of a new HTML document, create a link:

   ```
   <a href="">Open New Document</a>
   ```

2. Use # as the URL in the a tag:

   ```
   <a href="#">Click here</a> for a window which cannot be resized
   ```

3. Add an onClick event handler to the a tag. In the event handler, use JavaScript to assign the URL of the new document to the document.location property. The final document should look like this:

   ```
   <body>

       <a href="#" onClick="document.location =  ⟲
   '125a.html';">Open New Document</a>

   </body>
   ```

4. Save the file and close it.

5. Create a new file containing the HTML for the second page the user will visit when he or she clicks on the link in the first document:

   ```
   <body>

       This is a new document.

   </body>
   ```

6. Save this file in the location specified by the URL in Step 3.

7. Open the first file in a browser. The browser displays a page with a link, as illustrated in Figure 125-1.

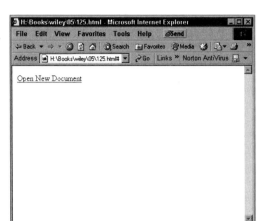

Figure 125-1: Displaying a JavaScript-based link.

8. Click on the link. The window updates to display the second page, as illustrated in Figure 125-2.

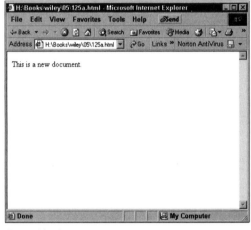

Figure 125-2: Directing the user to a new page using JavaScript.

cross-reference

▪ The document object is introduced and discussed in Task 44.

Task **125**

Controlling Window Scrolling from JavaScript

notes

* Using JavaScript, it is possible to control the vertical scroll position. That is, you can control which portion of a long document is visible in the current window.

* As an example of controlling the scroll position, consider the case where the page is 1000 pixels deep. In this case, setting `document.body.scrollTop` to 500 would scroll to halfway through the document.

* The `document.all` object exists in Internet Explorer but not in Netscape. Testing for the existence of the object is a quick, easy way to see if the user's browser is Internet Explorer.

* In an `if` statement, you can test for the existence of an object simply by making the conditional expression the name of the object.

Controlling the scroll position of a document requires a different method depending on the browser being used. In Internet Explorer, the scroll position is controlled with the `document.body.scrollTop` property. The property specifies the number of pixels down the document to place the scroll bar. The property is set with the following:

```
document.body.scrollTop = number of pixels;
```

In Netscape, the scroll position is similarly set in pixels, but the property that controls this is the `window.pageYOffset` property:

```
window.pageYOffset = number of pixels;
```

To illustrate this, the following steps show how to automatically scroll down the page by 200 pixels once the page loads:

1. In a script in the header of a new document, create a function named `scrollDocument` that takes no arguments:

   ```
   function scrollDocument() {
   }
   ```

2. In the function statement, use an `if` statement to test if the `document.all` object exists:

   ```
   if (document.all) {
   }
   ```

3. If the browser is Internet Explorer, set `document.body.scrollTop` to 200 pixels:

   ```
   if (document.all) {
      document.body.scrollTop = 200;
   }
   ```

4. If the browser is not Internet Explorer, set `window.pageYOffset` to 200 pixels, so that the final function looks like the following:

   ```
   if (document.all) {
      document.body.scrollTop = 200;
   } else {
      window.pageYOffset = 200;
   }
   ```

5. In the body tag, use the `onLoad` event handler to call the `scrollDocument` function:

   ```
   <body onLoad="scrollDocument();">
   ```

Task 126

6. In the body of the document, place your page content; there should be sufficient content to not fit in a single browser screen. The final page should look like Listing 126-1.

```html
<html>
    <head>
        <script language="JavaScript">
            function scrollDocument() {
                if (document.all) {
                    document.body.scrollTop = 200;
                } else {
                    window.pageYOffset = 200;
                }
            }
        </script>
    </head>
    <body onLoad="scrollDocument();">
        <p>
            Put lots of text here.
            Put lots of text here.
            Put lots of text here.
            etc.
        </p>
    </body>
</html>
```

Listing 126-1: Automatically scrolling a document.

7. Save the file and open it in a browser. The page should display and automatically jump down by 200 pixels, as shown in Figure 126-1.

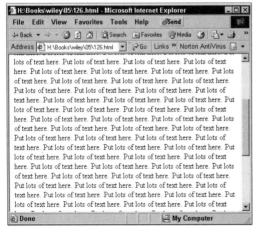

Figure 126-1: Scrolling down 200 pixels on loading.

Opening a Full-Screen Window in Internet Explorer

note
- This task only works in Internet Explorer. The window will open in Netscape but will not display the window normally.

Internet Explorer supports some interesting additional properties you can use when opening new windows with the `window.open` method. One such property allows for the creation of a full-screen window.

Typically, when you open a window with `window.open`, the new window is the same size as the window that opened it and, at a minimum, has a title bar. When you open a full-size window, it will have no window controls except scroll bars if needed and will fill the entire display.

To create a full-size window in Internet Explorer, you need to use the `fullScreen` property when opening the window:

```
window.open("URL","window name","fullScreen=yes");
```

Unlike other `window.open` properties thath work in Internet Explorer and Netscape, this property is available only in Internet Explorer browsers.

This task illustrates the use of the `fullScreen` property by creating a page with a link in it that the user can use to open a full-screen window:

1. Create a new HTML document.

2. In the body of the document, create a link that will be used for opening the full-screen window:

   ```
   <body>
       <a href="#">Open a full-screen window</a>
   </body>
   ```

3. In the `onClick` event handler of the a tag, call the `window.open` method to open the new window. Make sure you specify the `fullScreen` property for the window:

   ```
   <body>
       <a href="#" ⏎
   onClick="window.open('http://www.juxta.com/','newWindow⏎
   ','fullScreen=yes');">Open a full-screen window</a>
   </body>
   ```

4. Save the file and close it.

5. Open the file in Internet Explorer. A window with a link appears, as in Figure 127-1.

Task 127

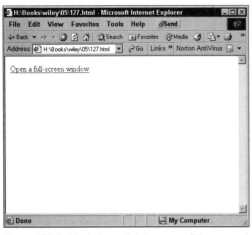

Figure 127-1: Displaying a link to open a full-screen window.

6. Click on the link, and the new full-screen window displays, as in Figure 127-2. You can close the new window with Alt+F4.

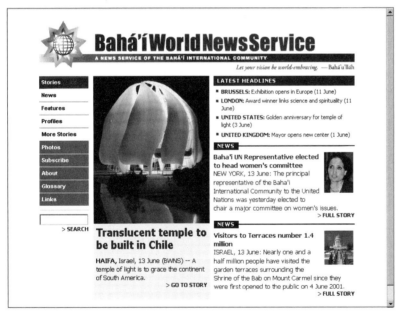

Figure 127-2: Opening a full-screen window.

Handling the Parent-Child Relationship of Windows

When the `window.open` method is used to open a new window from JavaScript, a relationship exists between the original window and the new window so that it is possible to refer to both windows from within JavaScript.

To do this, simply assign the object returned from the `window.open` method to a variable:

```
var newWindow = window.open(URL, window name);
```

Once this is done, `newWindow` refers to the `window` object for the new window.

At the same time, in the new window the `window.opener` property references the `window` object of the original window where `window.open` was called.

To illustrate this, the following example opens a new window from the first page and then provides links so that you can close the new window from the original window or close the original window from the new window:

1. In a script block in the header of a new document, open the second document in a new window and assign the object that is returned to the `newWindow` object. The final script looks like this:

   ```
   <script language="JavaScript">

       var newWindow = window.open("128a.html", "newWindow");

   </script>
   ```

2. In the body of the document, create a link for closing the new window:

   ```
   <a href="#">Close the new window</a>
   ```

3. In the `onClick` event handler for the link, call the `close` method of the `newWindow` object:

   ```
   <a href="#" onClick="newWindow.close();">Close the new ⮐
   window</a>
   ```

4. Save the file and close it.

5. In a second new file, create a link in the body for closing the original window:

   ```
   <a href="#">Close the original window</a>
   ```

6. In the `onClick` event handler for the link, call the `close` method of the `window.opener` object:

```
<a href="#" onClick="window.opener.close();">Close the ⊃
original window</a>
```

7. Save the file at the location specified in the `window.open` method in Step 2.

8. Open the first file in the browser. The second new window automatically opens. The first window contains a link to close the new window, as in Figure 128-1. The second window contains a link to close the original window, as in Figure 128-2.

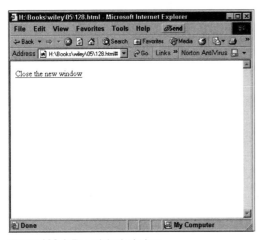

Figure 128-1: The original window.

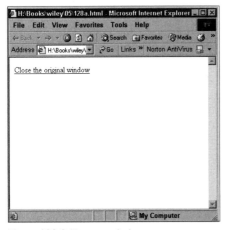

Figure 128-2: The new window.

9. Click on the link in the first window, and the new window closes. Click on the link in the new window, and the original window closes.

Updating One Window's Contents from Another

As mentioned in Task 128, when the `window.open` method is used to open a new window from JavaScript, a relationship exists between the original window and the new window so that it is possible to refer to both windows from within JavaScript.

For instance, it is possible for the original window, where the `window.open` method is called, to access the `window` object for the new window. This is made possible because the method returns a `window` object that can be stored in a variable and then used to reference the new window from JavaScript code in the original window. To do this, simply assign the object returned from the `window.open` method to a variable:

```
var newWindow = window.open(URL, window name);
```

This task illustrates how to open a new window with no page loaded and then to populate that window with content that is all created by JavaScript code in the original window.

1. In the header of a new HTML document, create a script block with opening and closing `script` tags:

```
<script language="JavaScript">
</script>
```

2. In the script, open a new window with no page loaded initially and store the object returned in the `newWindow` variable:

```
var newWindow = window.open("","newWindow");
```

3. Open a new document stream in the new window with the `document.open` method:

```
newWindow.document.open();
```

4. Output the desired content to the new window with the `document.write` method:

```
newWindow.document.write("This is a new window");
```

5. Close the document stream in the new window with the `document.close` method. The final script should look like Listing 129-1.

```
<head>

    <script language="JavaScript">

        var newWindow = window.open("","newWindow");
        newWindow.document.open();
        newWindow.document.write("This is a new window");
        newWIndow.document.close();

    </script>

</head>

<body>

    This is the original window.

</body>
```

Listing 129-1: Writing a document stream to a new window.

6. Save the file and close it.

7. Load the file in a browser. The new window automatically opens, and the text specified in the JavaScript code is displayed in the new window, as illustrated in Figure 129-1.

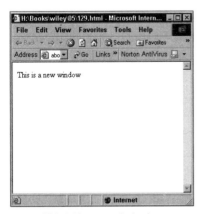

Figure 129-1: The new window's content comes from JavaScript in the original window.

Accessing a Form in Another Browser Window

When you are opening a new window in JavaScript, it is possible for the original window, where the `window.open` method is called, to access the `window` object for the new window. To do this, simply assign the object returned from the `window.open` method to a variable:

```
var newWindow = window.open(URL, window name);
```

Using this new object, you can access any part of the window or document in the new window just as you would access the original window or document.

This task illustrates how to open a new window containing a form and then provide a link in the original window, which displays the content of a field in the form in a dialog box:

1. In the body of a new HTML document, create a form and name the form `myForm` with the `name` attribute of the `form` tag:

   ```
   <form name="myForm">
   </form>
   ```

2. In the form, create a text field and name the field `myField`:

   ```
   <form name="myForm">

       <input type="text" name="myField">

   </form>
   ```

3. Save the file and close it.

4. In another new HTML file, create a script in the header of the file:

   ```
   <script language="JavaScript">
   </script>
   ```

5. In the script, use the `window.open` method to open the previous document in a new window; make sure to specify the URL for the file created in the previous steps and assign the object returned to the `newWindow` variable:

   ```
   <script language="JavaScript">

       var newWindow = window.open("130a.html","newWindow");

   </script>
   ```

6. In the body of the document, create a link for accessing the value of the form field in the new window:

   ```
   <a href="#">Check Form Field in New Window</a>
   ```

notes

- Accessing the `window` object for a new window is made possible because the `window.open` method returns a `window` object that can be stored in a variable and then used to reference the new window from JavaScript code in the original window.

- The value of a form text field is contained in the `value` property of the field's object. Hence, the reference to `myField.value` here.

7. Use the `onClick` event handler of the a tag to call the `window.alert` method:

```
<a href="#" onClick="window.alert();">Check Form Field ⊃
in New Window</a>
```

8. As the value to display in the alert dialog box, provide the value of the `myField` text field in the `myForm` form in the new window, so that the final page looks like this:

```
<a href="#" ⊃
onClick="window.alert(newWindow.document.myForm.myField.⊃
value);">Check Form Field in New Window</a>
<head>

    <script language="JavaScript">

        var newWindow = ⊃
window.open("130a.html","newWindow");

    </script>

</head>

<body>

    <a href="#" ⊃
onClick="window.alert(newWindow.document.myForm.myField.⊃
value);">Check Form Field in New Window</a>

</body>
```

9. Save the file and open it in a browser. The first window containing the link is displayed and the second window containing the form automatically opens.

10. Enter some text in the form in the new window, and then click on the link in the new window. An alert dialog box is displayed, containing the text you entered in the text field.

cross-reference

▪ As mentioned in Task 128, when the `window.open` method is used to open a new window from JavaScript, a relationship exists between the original window and the new window, so that it is possible to refer to both windows from within JavaScript.

Closing a Window in JavaScript

Every browser window has a `window` object associated with it. As mentioned in Task 114, this object offers properties that allow you to access frames in a window, access the window's name, manipulate text in the status bar, and check the open or closed state of the window. The methods allow you to display a variety of dialog boxes, as well as to open new windows and close open windows.

Among the features of the `window` object are the following:

- Creating alert dialog boxes
- Creating confirmation dialog boxes
- Creating dialog boxes that prompt the user to enter information
- Opening pages in new windows
- Determining window sizes
- Controlling scrolling of the document displayed in the window
- Scheduling the execution of functions

The `window` object can be referred to in several ways:

- Using the keyword `window` or `self` to refer to the current window where the JavaScript code is executing. For instance, `window.alert` and `self.alert` refer to the same method.
- Using the object name for another open window. For instance, if a window is associated with an object named `myWindow`, `myWindow.alert` would refer to the `alert` method in that window.

Closing a window is straightforward; just call the `close` method. For instance:

```
self.close();
```

This task illustrates this by creating a page that simply closes the current window as soon as the page is opened:

1. Create a new HTML document.

2. In the header of the document, create a script block with opening and closing `script` tags:

   ```
   <script lanauge="JavaScript">
   </script>
   ```

3. In the script call the `window.close` method. The page should look like Listing 131-1.

```
<head>

   <script lanauge="JavaScript">

      window.close();

   </script>

</head>

<body>

   This page will be closed before you see this.

</body>
```

Listing 131-1: Closing a window as soon as the document loads.

4. Save the file and close it.
5. Open the file in a browser window; the window closes immediately.

cross-reference

▪ The various types of dialog boxes are discussed in Tasks 25, 26, and 117.

Task 132 Closing a Window from a Link

Every browser window has a `window` object associated with it. As mentioned in Task 114, this object offers properties that allow you to access frames in a window, access the window's name, manipulate text in the status bar, and check the open or closed state of the window. The methods allow you to display a variety of dialog boxes, as well as to open new windows and close open windows.

Among the features of the `window` object are the following:

- Creating alert dialog boxes

- Creating confirmation dialog boxes

- Creating dialog boxes that prompt the user to enter information

- Opening pages in new windows

- Determining window sizes

- Controlling scrolling of the document displayed in the window

- Scheduling the execution of functions

The `window` object can be referred to in several ways:

- Using the keyword `window` or `self` to refer to the current window where the JavaScript code is executing. For instance, `window.alert` and `self.alert` refer to the same method.

- Using the object name for another open window. For instance, if a window is associated with an object named `myWindow`, `myWindow.alert` would refer to the `alert` method in that window.

Sometimes Web pages include a link on the page so that the user can close the page by clicking on the link, as opposed to using the window's own controls for closing the window. This is especially common in cases where a Web site pops up a new window for some specific purpose and wants to allow the user to close that new window easily. Figure 132-1 illustrates a window with this type of link from the Internet.

Figure 132-1: Offering a close link inside a window.

Providing such a "close window" link is easy to do using a `javascript:` URL in a link to call the `window.close` method:

```
<a href="javascript:window.close();">
```

The following steps show how to create a simple page with a link to close the window:

1. Create a new HTML document.

2. In the body of the document, create a link for closing the window.

3. Use a `javascript:` URL in the `href` attribute of the `a` tag to call the `window.close` method when the user clicks on the link, so that the final page looks like Listing 132-1.

```
<body>

    <a href="javascript:window.close();">Close this ⤵
Window</a>

</body>
```

Listing 132-1: Closing a window from a link.

4. Save the file and open it in a browser. A page containing a link like the one in Figure 132-2 is displayed.

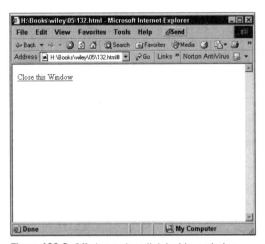

Figure 132-2: Offering a close link inside a window.

5. Click on the link and the window closes.

cross-reference

▪ The scheduling of automatic execution of a function is discussed in Tasks 38, 39, and 40.

Creating Dependent Windows in Netscape

note

• This task only works in Netscape 7. The window will open in Internet Explorer but will not display the dependent properties described here.

Netscape 7 (and Mozilla, on which it is built) supports some interesting additional properties you can use when opening new windows with the `window.open` method. One such property allows for the creation of dependent windows.

Typically, when you open a window with `window.open`, the new window is essentially independent of the window that opened it. You can minimize the windows independently, and more important, you can close windows independently. For instance, if you close the original window that issued the `window.open` command, the new window continues to stay open.

Things work differently with dependent windows, however. When you open a dependent window, its state is tied to the state of the window that opened it: Minimize the original window and the new window minimizes with it; close the original window and the new window closes with it.

Dependent windows allow you to create multiwindow applications in JavaScript in much the same way that traditional Windows or Macintosh applications may have multiple associated windows. You could use dependent windows to display control panels, data entry forms, and other tools associated with an application running in the main window, and then close them all by closing the main window.

Of course, you need to consider the fact that dependent windows don't exist in Internet Explorer, so this solution will only be of use in Netscape browsers.

To create a dependent window in Netscape, you need to use the dependent property when opening the window:

```
window.open("URL","window name","dependent");
```

This task illustrates the principle by creating a page with a link in it that the user can use to create a dependent window:

1. Create a new HTML document.

2. In the body of the document create a link that will be used for opening the dependent window:

   ```
   <a href="#">Open a dependent window</a>
   ```

3. In the `onClick` event handler of the a tag, call the `window.open` method to open the new window. Make sure you specify the dependent property for the window:

   ```
   <a href="#"
   onClick="window.open('http://www.juxta.com/','newWindow
   ','width=300,height=300,dependent');">Open a dependent
   window</a>
   ```

4. Save the file and close it.

5. Open the file in Netscape. A window with a link appears, as in Figure 133-1. Click on the link, and the new window displays, as in Figure 133-2. Minimize the original window, and you see the new window minimize with it. Close the original window, and you see the new window close with it.

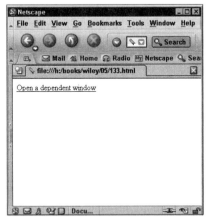

Figure 133-1: Displaying a link to open a dependent window.

Figure 133-2: Opening a dependent window.

Sizing a Window to Its Contents in Netscape

Netscape 7 (and Mozilla, on which it is built) supports some interesting additional methods you can use with windows. One such method allows for the resizing of windows based on the content they contain.

note

■ **This task only works in Netscape 7.**

Using this capability, you can reduce the size of the window to the content it contains when you can't be sure how much space the content will take up until it renders. This is useful when you want content to be perfectly framed in the window but can't predict, for instance, the size of fonts the user may be using in his or her browser.

Of course, you need to consider the fact that this window-resizing capability doesn't exist in Internet Explorer, so this solution will only be of use in Netscape browsers.

To resize window in this way with Netscape, use the `sizeToContent` method of the `window` object:

```
window.sizeToContent();
```

This task illustrates this method by creating a page that includes a link the user can use to call the `sizeToContent` method:

1. Create a new HTML document.

2. In the body of the document, create a link that will be used for resizing the window:

   ```
   <a href="#"> Resize window to the content</a>
   ```

3. In the `onClick` event handler of the a tag, call the `window.sizeToContent` method to resize the window:

   ```
   <a href="#" onClick="window.sizeToContent();">Resize ⤵
   window to the content</a>
   ```

4. Add any content to be displayed in the document. The final document could look like this:

   ```
   <body>

       <a href="#" onClick="window.sizeToContent();">Resize ⤵
   window to the content</a>
       <p>
       Put some content here for testing.

   </body>
   ```

5. Save the file and close it.

6. Open the file in Netscape. A window with a link appears, as shown in Figure 134-1. Click on the link and the window resizes to the content, as in Figure 134-2.

Figure 134-1: Displaying a link to resize the window.

Figure 134-2: Resizing the window to its content.

135

Loading Pages into Frames

HTML offers a concept called *frames* that allows you to divide the available space in a given window into subpanels into which you can load different documents.

To create frames, you use the `frameset` and `frame` tags:

```
<frameset rows="50%,*">
    <frame src="frame1.html">
    <frame src="frame2.html">
</frameset>
```

This creates a window with two horizontal frames of equal size.

The `window` object provides a way for you to access these frames in JavaScript. Each frame is associated with an object. These objects are in the `window.frames` array, so that the first array specified in your `frameset` code is `window.frames[0]`, the second is `window.frames[1]`, and so on.

In addition, frames can be named using the `name` attribute of the `frame` tag, as in the following:

```
<frameset rows="50%,*">
    <frame src="frame1.html" name="frame1">
    <frame src="frame2.html" name="frame2">
</frameset>
```

Here, the `frame` objects can be referenced as `window.frame1` and `window.frame2`.

The following example builds a frameset with two columns in a window. The right-hand frame is initially blank, while the left-hand frame contains JavaScript code to load a new document in the right-hand frame.

1. Create a new HTML document to hold the frameset, and create a `frameset` block with the `cols` attribute set to create two equal-sized columns:

   ```
   <frameset cols="50%,*">
   ```

2. In the frameset, create a `frame` tag to load the left-hand frame with the document containing the code to load a new document in the right-hand frame:

   ```
   <frame name="frame1" src="135a.html">
   ```

3. In the frameset, create a second `frame` tag to load a blank page in the right-hand frame, so that the entire document looks like this:

```
<frameset cols="50%,*">
    <frame name="frame1" src="135a.html">
    <frame name="frame2" src="about:blank">
</frameset>
```

4. Save the file and close it. Create a new HTML document, and in the header, create a script block.

5. In the script block, set the document location of the right-hand frame to the URL of the new document to load in the right-hand frame:

```
parent.frame2.document.location = "135b.html";
```

6. Provide any relevant text in the body of the document and save the file. The page should look like Listing 135-1.

```
<head>
    <script language="JavaScript">
        parent.frame2.document.location = "135b.html";
    </script>
</head>
<body>
    This is frame 1.
</body>
```

Listing 135-1: Accessing the right-hand frame from the left frame.

7. Save the file in the correct location for the URL specified in the left frame in Step 3 earlier and close it. Open a new HTML file, and place the content to be loaded in the right-hand frame, as in Listing 135-2.

```
<body>
    This is frame 2.
</body>
```

Listing 135-2: The final content of the right-hand frame.

8. Save the file so that it is in the correct location for the URL specified in Step 5 earlier and close it.

9. Load the frameset file. The page loads and the code in the left-hand frame loads the second file into the right-hand frame, so that the final window looks like Figure 135-1.

Figure 135-1: Loading a frame with JavaScript.

Task 136

Updating One Frame from Another Frame

A s outlined in Task 135, HTML offers a concept called *frames* that allows you to divide the available space in a given window into subpanels into which you can load different documents. To create frames, you use the `frameset` and `frame` tags:

```
<frameset rows="50%,*">
    <frame src="frame1.html">
    <frame src="frame2.html">
</frameset>
```

This creates a window with two horizontal frames of equal size.

The `window` object provides a way for you to access these frames in JavaScript. Each frame is associated with an object. These objects are in the `window.frames` array, so that the first array specified in your `frameset` code is `window.frames[0]`, the second is `window.frames[1]`, and so on. In addition, frames can be named using the `name` attribute of the `frame` tag, as in the following:

```
<frameset rows="50%,*">
    <frame src="frame1.html" name="frame1">
    <frame src="frame2.html" name="frame2">
</frameset>
```

Here, the `frame` objects can be referenced as `window.frame1` and `window.frame2`.

The following example builds a frameset with two columns in a window. The right-hand frame is initially blank, while the left-hand frame contains JavaScript code to write content directly into the right-hand frame.

1. Create a new HTML document to hold the frameset, and create a `frameset` block with the `cols` attribute set to create two equal-sized columns:

   ```
   <frameset cols="50%,*">
   ```

2. In the frameset, create a `frame` tag to load the left-hand frame with the document that will write output to the right-hand frame:

   ```
   <frame name="frame1" src="136a.html">
   ```

3. In the frameset, create a second `frame` tag to load a blank page in the right-hand frame, so that the entire document looks like this:

   ```
   <frameset cols="50%,*">
       <frame name="frame1" src="136a.html">
       <frame name="frame2" src="about:blank">
   </frameset>
   ```

notes

* The `rows` attribute of the `frameset` tag indicates the window is being divided into rows. The value of the attribute is a comma-separated list of row sizes specified either as a percentage of the window size or in pixels. The `*` indicates that the frame in question can take up the remainder of the window.

* The `frame` object is much like a `window` object, and a frame can contain the same objects as a window. For instance, just as a `window` object can contain a document and `document` object, so can a `frame` object.

* The `parent.frame2.document.open` reference works like this: From inside the current frame, `parent` refers to the `window` object of the window that contains the frameset. Within that `window` object, `frame2` refers to the right frame, and within that, `document.open` is the method used to open a document output stream in the frame.

4. Save the file and close it. Create a new HTML document, and in the header, create a script block.

5. In the script block, open a document output stream in the right-hand frame:

```
parent.frame2.document.open();
```

6. Using the `document.write` method, output any desired content for the second window:

```
parent.frame2.document.write("This is frame 2");
```

7. Close the document stream, so that the script looks like this:

```
<script language="JavaScript">
   parent.frame2.document.open();
   parent.frame2.document.write("This is frame 2");
   parent.frame2.document.close();
</script>
```

8. In the body of the document, place any content for the left-hand frame. The final page should look like Listing 136-1.

```
<head>
   <script language="JavaScript">
      parent.frame2.document.open();
      parent.frame2.document.write("This is frame 2");
      parent.frame2.document.close();
   </script>
</head>
<body>
   This is frame 1.
</body>
```

Listing 136-1: Writing output to another frame.

9. Save the file in the location specified for the left-hand frame in Step 3 and close it.

10. Load the frameset in a browser. The right-hand frame initially loads blank, and then immediately the left frame writes output into the frame, so that the final window looks like Figure 136-1.

Figure 136-1: Writing output into another frame.

Sharing JavaScript Code between Frames

notes

* The `rows` attribute of the `frameset` tag indicates the window is being divided into rows. The value of the attribute is a comma-separated list of row sizes specified either as a percentage of the window size or in pixels. The `*` indicates that the frame in question can take up the remainder of the window.

* The `frame` object is much like a `window` object, and a frame can contain the same objects as a window. For instance, just as a `window` object can contain a document and `document` object, so can a `frame` object.

* The `parent.frame1.doAlert` reference works like this: From inside the current frame, `parent` refers to the `window` object of the window, which contains the frameset. Within that `window` object, `frame1` refers to the right frame, and within that, `doAlert` is the function in the script block of that document.

As outlined in Task 135, HTML offers a concept called *frames* that allows you to divide the available space in a given window into subpanels into which you can load different documents.

To create frames, you use the `frameset` and `frame` tags:

```
<frameset rows="50%,*">
    <frame src="frame1.html">
    <frame src="frame2.html">
</frameset>
```

This creates a window with two horizontal frames of equal size.

The `window` object provides a way for you to access these frames in JavaScript. Each frame is associated with an object. These objects are in the `window.frames` array, so that the first array specified in your `frameset` code is `window.frames[0]`, the second is `window.frames[1]`, and so on.

In addition, frames can be named using the `name` attribute of the `frame` tag, as in the following:

```
<frameset rows="50%,*">
    <frame src="frame1.html" name="frame1">
    <frame src="frame2.html" name="frame2">
</frameset>
```

Here, the `frame` objects can be referenced as `window.frame1` and `window.frame2`.

The following example builds a frameset with two columns in a window. The left-hand frame contains JavaScript code to display a dialog box. The right-hand frame calls the code in the left-hand frame in order to display the dialog box.

1. Create a new HTML document to hold the frameset, and create a `frameset` block with the `cols` attribute set to create two equal-sized columns:

   ```
   <frameset cols="50%,*">
   ```

2. In the frameset, create a `frame` tag to load the left-hand frame with the document containing the JavaScript code to display a dialog box:

   ```
   <frame name="frame1" src="137a.html">
   ```

3. In the frameset, create a second `frame` tag to load the document that calls the dialog box code in the right-hand frame, so that the entire document looks like this:

```
<frameset cols="50%,*">
    <frame name="frame1" src="137a.html">
    <frame name="frame2" src="137b.html">
</frameset>
```

4. Save the file and close it. Create a new HTML document, and in the header, create a script block.

5. In the script block, create a function called `doAlert` that takes no arguments:

```
function doAlert() {
}
```

6. In the function, display a dialog box with your preferred message:

```
function doAlert() {
    window.alert("Frame 2 is loaded");
}
```

7. In the body of the document, place any output desired for the left frame, and save the file in the location specified for the left-hand frame in Step 2.

8. In a new HTML document, use the `onLoad` event handler of the body tag to call the `doAlert` method in the left-hand frame:

```
<body onLoad="parent.frame1.doAlert();">
    This is frame 2.
</body>
```

9. Save the file in the location indicated for the right-hand frame in Step 2 and close it.

10. Open the frameset. The two frames load as illustrated in Figure 137-1, and then the dialog box shown in Figure 137-2 appears immediately.

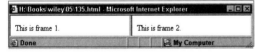

Figure 137-1: Two frames.

Figure 137-2: Calling between frames to display a dialog box.

Using Frames to Store Pseudo-Persistent Data

notes

- When you are working with frames, it is often useful to be able to store information in JavaScript variables in such a way that the variables continue to be available even as users navigate between documents in any of the frames in the window.

- Luckily with frames, you have a document that continues to exist even when the user navigates between documents in the individual frames. That persistent document is the frameset document itself.

- Since the frameset document is an HTML document, you can use JavaScript in that document like any other and, therefore, can create variables there that will not be affected by navigation within the individual frames.

Normally, if you store a variable using JavaScript code in a given document in a frame, when the user leaves that document and navigates to another in the frame, the variables are lost.

However, consider a frameset with two frames. In this case, there are three documents: the frameset document and the two documents loaded in each frame. No matter how the user navigates within the two documents, the frameset document continues to exist. Referring to variables in the frameset from code in the individual frames is straightforward:

```
parent.variableName
```

This example illustrates the use of persistent variables in the frameset document by creating a frameset in which you define a variable. In the left-hand frame, you display a document that simply outputs the persistent variable using JavaScript. In the right-hand frame, you display a document with a link that will take the user to another document that outputs the persistent variable:

1. Create a new HTML document to hold the frameset. Start the document with a script block, and set a variable named `persistentVariable` with the text of your choice in the script:

```
<script language="JavaScript">
   var persistentVariable = "This is a persistent value";
</script>
```

2. Following the script, create a frameset with two vertical frames. Load a document in the left-hand frame and a document in the right-hand frame; you will create those documents later. The final page looks like this:

```
<script language="JavaScript">
   var persistentVariable = "This is a persistent value";
</script>
<frameset cols="50%,*">
   <frame name="frame1" src="138a.html">
   <frame name="frame2" src="138b.html">
</frameset>
```

3. Save the file and close it. Create a new HTML file for loading in the left frame. In the body of the document, create a script and use the `document.write` method to output the value of `persistentVariable` in the frameset:

```
<body>
   This is frame 1. The persistent variable contains:
   <p>
```

```
<strong>
   <script language="JavaScript">
      document.write(parent.persistentVariable);
   </script>
</strong>
</body>
```

4. Save the file in the location specified in the frameset for the left-hand frame and close it. Create a new HTML file for initial loading in the right-hand frame. The body of the document should simply contain a link to a third document:

```
<body>
   This is frame 2.
   <a href="138c.html">Click here</a> to load a new ⟳
document in this frame
</body>
```

5. Save the file in the location specified in the frameset for the right-hand frame and close it. Create a new HTML for to be displayed when the user clicks on the link in the right-hand frame. The body of the document should look similar to the document loaded in the left-hand frame and display the persistent variable using the document.write method:

```
<body>
   This is a new document in frame 2. The persistent ⟳
variable contains:
   <p>
   <strong>
      <script language="JavaScript">
         document.write(parent.persistentVariable);
      </script>
   </strong>
</body>
```

6. Save the file in the location indicated in the link in Step 4, and then close the file.

7. Open the frameset in a browser. Initially, the persistent variable is displayed in the left-hand frame and a link appears in the right-hand frame. When the user clicks on the link in the right-hand frame, the value of the variable will be displayed there as well, as illustrated in Figure 138-1.

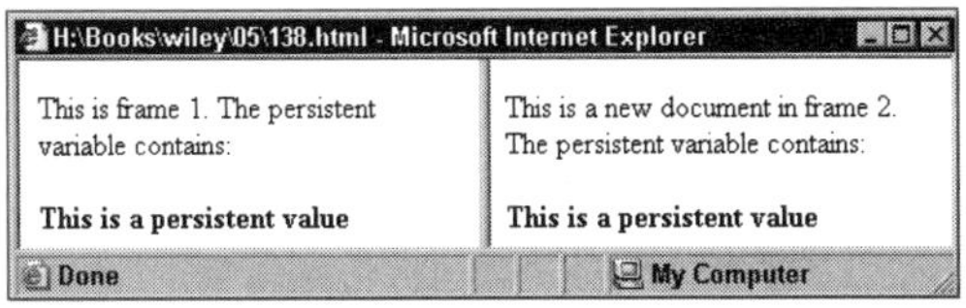

Figure 138-1: The variable is still accessible after navigating in one of the frames.

Using One Frame for Your Main JavaScript Code

notes

- When you are working with frames, it is often useful to be able to consolidate all your JavaScript functions in one frame that will not change so they are easily accessible at all times. For instance, it is not uncommon to place all the JavaScript functions in the same frame as the navigation menu, which typically will not change while the user is at the site.

- The `parent.frame1.`
`functionName` reference works like this: From inside the current frame, `parent` refers to the `window` object of the window, which contains the frameset. Within that `window` object, `frame1` refers to the left-hand frame, and within that, `functionName` is the function to invoke.

As outlined in Task 135, HTML offers a concept called *frames* that allows you to divide the available space in a given window into subpanels into which you can load different documents. Referring to functions in documents from other frames is easy:

```
parent.frameName.variableName
```

This example illustrates two frames. The left-hand frame contains two JavaScript functions, as well as links so the user can call the functions. The right-hand frame just contains two links so the user can call the functions from there as well.

1. Create a new HTML document to hold the frameset, and create a `frameset` block with the `cols` attribute set to create two equal-sized columns:

   ```
   <frameset cols="50%,*">
   ```

2. In the frameset, create a `frame` tag to load the left-hand frame with the document containing the JavaScript code containing the functions:

   ```
   <frame name="frame1" src="139a.html">
   ```

3. In the frameset, create a second `frame` tag to load the document for the right-hand frame:

   ```
   <frameset cols="50%,*">
      <frame name="frame1" src="139a.html">
      <frame name="frame2" src="139b.html">
   </frameset>
   ```

4. Save the file and close it. Create a new HTML document, and in the header, create a script block.

5. In the script block, create a function called `firstFunction` that takes no arguments.

6. In the function, use `window.alert` to display to users that they have called the first function:

   ```
   function firstFunction() {
      window.alert("This is the first function");
   }
   ```

7. Create a second function called `secondFunction` that is similar to the first:

   ```
   function secondFunction() {
      window.alert("This is the second function");
   }
   ```

8. In the body of the document, create links that use the `onClick` event handler to call the functions, and then save the file in the location specified in the frameset for the left-hand frame:

```
<body>
    <a href="#" onClick="firstFunction();">First ⮎
Function</a>
    <p>
    <a href="#" onClick="secondFunction();">Second ⮎
Function</a>
</body>
```

9. Create a new HTML file that simply contains two links that use the `onClick` event handler to call the two functions in the left-hand frame, and then save the file in the location specified for the right-hand frame in the frameset:

```
<body>
    <a href="#" ⮎
onClick="parent.frame1.firstFunction();">First ⮎
Function</a>
    <p>
    <a href="#" ⮎
onClick="parent.frame1.secondFunction();">Second ⮎
Function</a>
</body>
```

10. Open the frameset in the browser. Links appear in both frames, as illustrated in Figure 139-1. Click on the first link in the left-hand frame, and the relevant dialog box appears, as shown in Figure 139-2. Similarly, click on the second link in the right-hand frame, and the dialog box from the second function appears.

Figure 139-1: Displaying links to call functions in the left-hand frame.

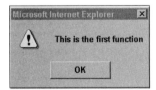

Figure 139-2: Calling a function in the left frame from a link in the left-hand frame.

Using a Hidden Frame for Your JavaScript Code

Sometimes you will want to use an additional "hidden" frame to store a document containing nothing but your JavaScript code. Creating a hidden frame is easy. Simply specify 0 pixels as the width or height of the frame in the `cols` or `rows` attribute of the `frameset` tag:

```
<frameset cols="0,50%,*">
    <frame ...>
    <frame ...>
    <frame ...>
</frameset>
```

In this example, the first frame is effectively hidden.

This task is a variation of Task 139 in that the JavaScript functions are moved to a third hidden frame and the left-hand and right-hand frames continue to offer links to allow the user to call the functions:

1. Create a new HTML document to hold the frameset, and create a `frameset` block with the `cols` attribute set to create two equal-sized columns:

   ```
   <frameset cols="0,50%,*">
   ```

2. In the frameset, create a `frame` tag to load the hidden frame with the document containing the JavaScript code containing the functions:

   ```
   <frame name="codeFrame" src="140code.html">
   ```

3. In the frameset, create second and third `frame` tags to load the documents for the visible left-hand and right-hand frames:

   ```
   <frameset cols="0,50%,*">
       <frame name="codeFrame" src="140code.html">
       <frame name="frame1" src="140a.html">
       <frame name="frame2" src="140b.html">
   </frameset>
   ```

4. Save the file and close it. Create a new HTML document, and in the header, create a script block.

5. In the script block, create a function called `firstFunction` that takes no arguments.

6. In the function, use `window.alert` to display to users that they have called the first function:

   ```
   function firstFunction() {
       window.alert("This is the first function");
   }
   ```

7. Create a second function called `secondFunction` that is similar to the first. Save the file in the location indicated in the frameset for the code document:

```
function secondFunction() {
    window.alert("This is the second function");
}
```

8. Create a new document for the left-hand frame, and in the body of the document, create links that use the `onClick` event handler to call the functions, and then save the file in the location specified in the frameset for the visible left-hand frame:

```
<body>
    <a href="#"
onClick="onClick="parent.codeFrame.firstFunction();">
First Function</a>
    <p>
    <a href="#"
onClick="onClick="parent.codeFrame.secondFunction();">
Second Function</a>
</body>
```

9. Create another new HTML file that looks the same as the document for the left-hand frame, and then save the file in the location specified for the visible right-hand frame in the frameset.

10. Open the frameset in the browser. Links appear in both frames, as illustrated in Figure 140-1. Click on the first link in the left-hand frame, and the relevant dialog box appears, as shown in Figure 140-2. Similarly, click on the second link in the right-hand frame, and the dialog box from the second function appears.

Figure 140-1: Displaying links to call functions in the hidden frame.

Figure 140-2: Calling a function in the hidden frame from a link in the left-hand frame.

Working with Nested Frames

All the examples of frames in this part of the book have dealt with a single layer of frames. That is, the window is either divided into rows or columns and that's it. But it is possible to nest framesets. For instance, start by considering a simple frameset:

```
<frameset cols="50%,*">
   <frame src="frame1.html" name="frame1">
   <frame src="frame2.html" name="frame2">
</frameset>
```

This creates two simple vertical frames. But what if you wanted the right-hand frame to be further divided into two horizontal frames? This could be done by making frame2.html into a frameset itself:

```
<frameset rows="50%,*">
   <frame src="subframe1.html" name="subframe1">
   <frame src="subframe2.html" name="subframe2">
</frameset>
```

Once you start to nest framesets in this way, the job of cross-referencing between frames using JavaScript is more complicated than you saw in simple one-level framesets. For instance, to refer to subframe2 from frame1, you would use the following:

```
parent.frame2.subframe2
```

This task illustrates the steps to create a nested frame layout like the one described previously. In subframe2, you will place a function called doAlert, and then you will provide a link in frame1 for the user to invoke that function.

1. Create a new document for the top-level frameset. In that document create a frameset with two vertical frames named frame1 and frame2:

   ```
   <frameset cols="50%,*">
      <frame src="frame1.html" name="frame1">
      <frame src="frame2.html" name="frame2">
   </frameset>
   ```

2. Save the file and close it.

3. Create a new document for frame1.html. In that document, place a link in the body of the document that calls the doAlert function in subframe2:

   ```
   <body>
      This is frame1.
      <a href="#" ⊃
   onClick="parent.frame2.subframe2.doAlert();">Click to ⊃
   see alert from subframe2.</a>
   </body>
   ```

4. Save the file and close it.

5. Create a new document for `frame2.html`. In that document, create a frameset for the nested horizontal frames in the right-hand frame, and name the frames `subframe1` and `subframe2`:

```
<frameset rows="50%,*">
    <frame src="subframe1.html" name="subframe1">
    <frame src="subframe2.html" name="subframe2">
</frameset>
```

6. Save the file and close it.

7. Create a new document for `subframe1.html`, and include any content to display in that frame:

```
<body>
    This is subframe1.
</body>
```

8. Save the file and close it.

9. Create a new document for `subframe2.html`. In the header of the document, create a script block containing the function `doAlert`, which displays an alert dialog box to the user indicating the frame where it was executed:

```
<head>
    <script language="JavaScript">
        function doAlert() { window.alert("This is ⊃
subframe2."); }
    </script>
</head>
<body>
    This is subframe2.
</body>
```

10. Save the file and close it. Open the top-level frameset in a browser, and you will see the frame layout If the user clicks on the link in the left-hand frame, he or she will see a dialog box like Figure 141-1.

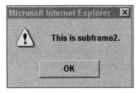

Figure 141-1: Calling a function in a nested frame.

Task 142

Updating Multiple Frames from a Link

If you have a frameset layout with multiple frames, you may want to allow several frames to update when the user clicks on a link. In this case, it is not possible to target two URLs to two frames at the same time using a simple link. Instead, it becomes necessary to leverage JavaScript to load URLs into the frames by setting the document.location property of each of the frames. This task shows how to build a frameset with three horizontal frames. A link in the top frame causes new documents to load in both of the bottom frames.

1. Create a new HTML document to hold the frameset, and create a frameset block with the rows attribute set to create three rows:

   ```
   <frameset cols="10%,45%,45%">
   ```

2. In the frameset, create three frame tags to load the three initial documents; frame1 will contain the link and the others will just contain content:

   ```
   <frameset rows="10%,45%,45%">
       <frame name="frame1" src="142a.html">
       <frame name="frame2" src="142b.html">
       <frame name="frame3" src="142c.html">
   </frameset>
   ```

3. Save the file and close it. Create a new HTML document, and in the header, create a script block.

4. In the script block, create a function named twoLinks that takes no arguments. In this function, set the document.location properties for frame2 and frame3 to new documents:

   ```
   function twoLinks() {
       parent.frame2.document.location = "142bnew.html";
       parent.frame3.document.location = "142cnew.html";
   }
   ```

5. In the body of the document, create a link to call the twoLinks function:

   ```
   <body>
       <a href="#" onClick="twoLinks();">Update frame2 and ⤸
   frame3</a>
   </body>
   ```

6. Save the file in the location indicated for frame1 in the frameset earlier. Next, create two simple HTML files for the initial documents for frame2 and frame3. For instance, frame2's document could look like this:

   ```
   <body>
      This is frame 2.
   </body>
   ```

7. Next, create two simple HTML files for the new documents for frame2 and frame3. These are the documents that are loaded in the

notes

▪ Typically, if you want to use a link in one frame to cause a new document to load in another frame, you use the target attribute of the a tag to specify the name of the frame where the document indicated in the URL should load.

▪ frame1 will contain the link, while frame2 and frame3 will be the frames that will be updated.

▪ The parent.frame2.document.location reference works like this: From inside the current frame, parent refers to the window object of the window that contains the frameset. Within that window object, frame2 refers to the right-hand frame, and within that, document.location is the URL of the document loaded in that frame.

▪ Make sure the documents indicate the frame so you can see what is happening.

`twoLinks` function discussed earlier. For instance, `frame3`'s document could look like this:

```
<body>
   This is a new document in frame3.
</body>
```

8. Load the frameset file. The page loads as shown in Figure 142-1. Click on the link, and the two bottom frames update as shown in Figure 142-2.

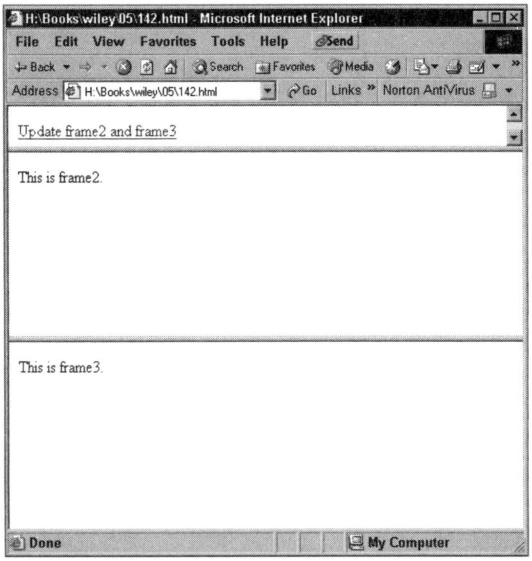

Figure 142-1: Three frames in a window.

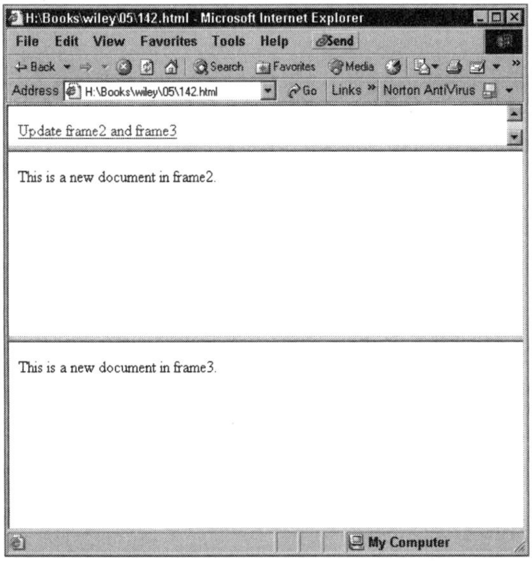

Figure 142-2: Updating the two bottom frames from a link.

143

Dynamically Creating Frames in JavaScript

In the previous tasks dealing with frames, all the examples have statically defined a frameset. This task shows that you can use JavaScript to create a frameset so that, ultimately, you can make programmatic decisions about the layout and documents displayed in a frameset.

The principle is simple: In a script, use `document.write` to output the `frameset` and `frame` tags, and if necessary, dynamically specify the value of attributes when doing this. For instance, if the name of a document to display in a frame is contained in a variable, you could output that frame's tag with the following:

```
document.write("<frame src='" + frameUrl + "'>");
```

The following steps illustrate creating a frameset in JavaScript that then displays two simple HTML files in the frames:

1. Create a new document to hold the frameset code. In that document, create a script block:

   ```
   <script language="JavaScript">
   ```

2. In the script, open a new document output stream with `document.open`:

   ```
   document.open();
   ```

3. Use `document.write` to output the frameset code to the browser, and close the stream with `document.close`, so the script looks like Listing 143-1.

   ```
   <script language="JavaScript">

       document.open();
       document.write("<frameset cols='50%,*'>");
       document.write("<frame src='143a.html'>");
       document.write("<frame src='143b.html'>");
       document.write("</frameset>");
       document.close();

   </script>
   ```

   Listing 143-1: Creating a frameset using JavaScript.

4. Save the file and close it.

note

- Be careful in the use of quotation marks when outputting HTML with `document.write`. If you enclose the string being output in double quotes, then your attributes should really use single quotes. Otherwise, you need to escape your double quotes with backslashes (`\"`).

5. Create an HTML document for displaying in the left-hand frame:

```
<body>

   This is frame 1.

</body>
```

6. Save the file in the location specified in the frameset for the left-hand frame and close it.

7. Create an HTML document for displaying in the left-hand frame:

```
<body>

   This is frame 2.

</body>
```

8. Save the file in the location specified in the frameset for the right-hand frame and close it.

9. Open the frameset file in your browser, and you see the two documents loaded in the two frames, as illustrated in Figure 143-1.

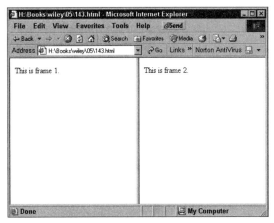

Figure 143-1: Creating two frames in a script.

tip

- This technique of dynamically creating HTML from within JavaScript is flexible and not limited to frames alone. Any HTML tag could be dynamically delivered so that its attributes can be dynamically specified from within JavaScript.

cross-reference

- The document.write method and its use are discussed further in Task 9.

Task 144 Dynamically Updating Frame Content

When working inside a document in a frame, you are essentially working in exactly the same environment you would be working in if your document was loaded straight into a window.

For instance, documents loaded into a window have a `document` object associated with them, and you access them with the following:

```
document.method()
```

or

```
document.property
```

Similarly, when a document is loaded in a frame, the document also has a `document` object associated with it, and accessing it from code within that page is exactly the same.

To illustrate this principle, this task shows how to load documents into two frames. Each document has a link that invokes JavaScript to change the content displayed in the frame using `document.write`.

1. Create a new HTML document to hold the frameset, and create a `frameset` block with the `cols` attribute set to create two equal-sized columns:

   ```
   <frameset cols="50%,*">
   ```

2. In the frameset, create a `frame` tag to load the document for the left-hand frame:

   ```
   <frame name="frame1" src="144a.html">
   ```

3. In the frameset, create a second `frame` tag to load the documents for the right-hand frame:

   ```
   <frameset cols="50%,*">
      <frame name="frame1" src="144a.html">
      <frame name="frame2" src="144b.html">
   </frameset>
   ```

4. Save the file and close it. Create a new HTML document, and in the body, create a link for the user to click to display new content:

   ```
   <a href="#">Click here for new content</a>
   ```

5. In the `onClick` event handler for the a tag, use `document.write` to write new content to the window:

```
<a href="#" onClick="document.write('New ⤴
Content<br>');">Click here for new content</a>
```

6. Save the file in the location specified for the left-hand frame and close it.

7. Create a new HTML document for the right-hand frame, and duplicate the content of the document specified for the left-hand frame:

```
<body>
    <a href="#" onClick="document.write('New ⤴
Content<br>');">Click here for new content</a>
</body>
```

8. Save the file in the location specified for the right-hand frame and close it.

9. Open the frameset file in your browser. You should see two identical frames, as illustrated in Figure 144-1. Click on either of the links, and that frame should update with new content. In Figure 144-2, the user has clicked the right-hand link, and the right-hand frame was updated.

tip

- By default, the `document.write` method writes its output into the frame or window in which the code exists—that is, the frame or window in which the document containing the `document.write` code is loaded.

Figure 144-1: Both frames offer links to update their content.

Figure 144-2: Updating the right-hand frame with new content.

Task **145**

Referring to Unnamed Frames Numerically

In all the previous examples in this part of the book, we have referred to frames by the names specified in the name attribute of the frame tag. For instance, consider the following frameset:

```
<frameset rows="50%,*">
    <frame src="frame1.html" name="frame1">
    <frame src="frame2.html" name="frame2">
</frameset>
```

Here, the first frame is referred to as window.frame1 from within the frameset document or parent.frame1 from within one of the two frames. But what if no name attributes were specified? Consider the following frameset:

```
<frameset rows="50%,*">
    <frame src="frame1.html">
    <frame src="frame2.html">
</frameset>
```

Here, the frame name approach used in the previous example will not work. So you need another approach. The following task shows how to create two frames; in each frame there is a function called doAlert that displays a dialog box. You call these functions through links from the other frame using the frames array instead of frame names.

1. Create a new HTML document to hold the frameset, and create a frameset block with the rows attribute set to create two equal-sized columns:

   ```
   <frameset rows="50%,*">
   ```

2. In the frameset, create a frame tag to load the document for the top frame:

   ```
   <frame name="frame1" src="145a.html">
   ```

3. In the frameset, create a second frame tag to load the documents for the bottom frame:

   ```
   <frameset rows="50%,*">
       <frame name="frame1" src="145a.html">
       <frame name="frame2" src="145b.html">
   </frameset>
   ```

4. Save the file and close it. Create a new HTML document for the top frame. In the header of the document, create a script block, and in the script block, place a function called doAlert to display a message to the user indicating the current frame:

notes

- Notice the use of 0 and 1 as the array indexes for the first and second frame. In JavaScript, arrays start counting at 0, so the first element is indexed 0, the second is indexed 1, and so on.

- Luckily, the objects associated with each frame are stored in an array in the frames property of the window object for the frameset. Now you can refer to window.frames[0] and window.frames[1]. Similarly, from within the frames themselves, you can refer to parent.frames[0] and parent.frames[1]. The objects in the frames array appear in the order in which the frame tags appear in the frameset.

```
<script language="JavaScript">
    function doAlert() { window.alert("This is the top ⊃
frame"); }
</script>
```

5. In the body of the text, create a link for calling the function in the bottom frame:

```
<a href="#">Call the bottom frame</a>
```

6. In the `onClick` event handler for the `a` tag, call the `doAlert` function in the bottom frame:

```
<a href="#" onClick="parent.frames[1].doAlert();">Call ⊃
the bottom frame</a>
```

7. Save the file in the location specified in the frameset for the top frame. Create a similar document for the bottom frame, but alter the message displayed in the dialog box and make the link call the function in the top frame:

```
<script language="JavaScript">
    function doAlert() { window.alert("This is the ⊃
bottom frame"); }
</script>
<body>
    <a href="#" onClick="parent.frames[0].doAlert();">⊃
Call the top frame</a>
</body>
```

8. Save the file in the location specified in the frameset for the bottom frame.

9. Open the frameset in a browser. You see two frames with links, as illustrated in Figure 145-1. Click on the link in the top frame to see the dialog box shown in Figure 145-2.

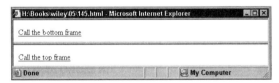

Figure 145-1: Two unnamed frames.

Figure 145-2: Calling the bottom frame from the top.

Part 6: Manipulating Cookies

Creating a Cookie in JavaScript

JavaScript cookies are stored in the `document.cookie` object and are created by assigning values to this object. When creating a cookie, you typically specify a name, value, and expiration date and time for that cookie. The cookie will then be accessible in your scripts every time the user returns to your site until the cookie expires. These cookies will also be sent to your server every time the user requests a page from your site.

The simplest way to create a cookie is to assign a string value to the `document.cookie` object, which looks like this:

```
name=value;expires=date
```

The name is a name you assign to the cookie so that you can refer to it later when you want to access it. The value is any text string that has been escaped as if it were going to appear in a URL (you do this in JavaScript with the `escape` function).

The following steps outline how to create a new cookie in JavaScript:

1. In the header of a new document, create a script block with opening and closing `script` tags:

   ```
   <head>
      <script language="JavaScript">

      </script>
   </head>
   ```

2. In the script, type **document.cookie** followed by an equal sign to begin assigning a value to the `document.cookie` object:

   ```
   document.cookie =
   ```

3. Type an opening double quotation followed by a name for the cookie followed by an equal sign. In this case, the name is `myCookie`:

   ```
   document.cookie = "myCookie=
   ```

4. Close the double quotation, and type a plus sign:

   ```
   document.cookie = "myCookie=" +
   ```

5. Enter the value you wish to assign to the cookie as the argument to the `escape` function. In this case, the value of the cookie is "`This is my Cookie`":

   ```
   document.cookie = "myCookie=" + escape("This is my  ⏎
   Cookie")
   ```

notes

- Normally, cookies are simple variables set by the server in the browser and returned to the server every time the browser accesses a page on the same server. They are typically used to carry persistent information from page to page through a user session or to remember data between user sessions. With JavaScript, though, you can create and read cookies in the client without resorting to any server-side programming.

- The `escape` function takes a string and escapes any characters that are not valid in a URL. Escaping involves replacing the character with a numeric code preceded by a percent sign. For instance, spaces become %20 (see Step 5).

6. Type a semicolon to end the command. The final result is that you will have JavaScript code like that in Listing 146-1.

```
<head>
    <script language="JavaScript">

        document.cookie = "myCookie=" + escape("This is my ⏎
Cookie");

    </script>
</head>
```

Listing 146-1: Creating a Cookie.

7. For testing purposes, you can see the exact string you are assigning to the document.cookie object by using the window.alert method to display the same string in a simple dialog box. The result looks like Figure 146-1.

```
<head>
    <script language="JavaScript">

        document.cookie = "myCookie=" + escape("This is my⏎
Cookie");
        window.alert("myCookie=" + escape("This is my   ⏎
Cookie"));

    </script>
</head>
```

Figure 146-1: Displaying a cookie in a dialog box.

cross-reference

• Task 25 discusses the creation of alert dialog boxes using the window.alert method. The method takes a single string argument. In this case, you are building a string by concatenating two strings.

Task 147

Accessing a Cookie in JavaScript

If the current document has a single cookie associated with it, then the `document.cookie` object contains a single string with all the details of the cookie. A typical `document.cookie` string looks like this:

```
myCookie=This%20is%20my%20Cookie
```

You probably noticed that there is no indication of the expiration date. When you access the `document.cookie` object, it contains a cookie only if there is a cookie available for the site in question that has not expired. This determination is handled automatically in the background, and it is unnecessary to include the actual expiration date in the string returned by the `document.cookie` object.

To access a cookie, you need to separate the name and value using the `split` method of the `String` object, as outlined in the following steps:

1. In the header of a new HTML document, create a script block with opening and closing `script` tags:

```
<head>
    <script language="JavaScript">

    </script>
</head>
```

2. Assign the `document.cookie` object to a new variable. In this case, the object is assigned to the string `newCookie`:

```
var newCookie = document.cookie;
```

3. Split the cookie at the equal sign and assign the resulting array to a new variable. You do this with the `split` method of the `String` object, which takes as an argument the character that serves the delimiter where you want to split the string. The resulting parts of the string are returned in an array. In this case, the array is stored in a variable called `cookieParts`:

```
var cookieParts = newCookie.split("=");
```

4. Assign the first entry in the array to a variable; this entry in the array contains the name of the cookie. In this case, the name is stored in the variable `cookieName`:

```
var cookieName = cookieParts[0];
```

5. Assign the second entry in the array to a variable; this entry in the array contains the value of the cookie. At the same time, unescape the string with the `unescape` function. In this case, the end result is that the unescaped value of the cookie stored in the `cookieValue` variable. The resulting JavaScript code is shown in Listing 147-1.

note

- Cookies are just small text files stored by your browser and then returned to the server, or a JavaScript script, when necessary. There are complaints that cookies pose security or privacy risks. Cookies are not really a security risk, and privacy implications of cookies are debatable. They are, however, very useful for any Web applications that span more than one page (see Step 5).

```
<head>
   <script language="JavaScript">
      var newCookie = document.cookie;
      var cookieParts = newCookie.split("=");
      var cookieName = cookieParts[0];
      var cookieValue = unescape(cookieParts[1]);
   </script>
</head>
```

Listing 147-1: Splitting a cookie into its name and value parts.

6. You can test the cookie results by using the `window.alert` method to display each variable in turn in a simple dialog box; these dialog boxes are illustrated in Figures 147-1 and 147-2.

```
<head>
   <script language="JavaScript">
      var newCookie = document.cookie;
      var cookieParts = newCookie.split("=");
      var cookieName = cookieParts[0];
      var cookieValue = unescape(cookieParts[1]);
      window.alert(cookieName);
      window.alert(cookieValue);
   </script>
</head>
```

Figure 147-1: Displaying the cookie name in a dialog box.

Figure 147-2: Displaying the cookie value in a dialog box.

Task 148

Displaying a Cookie

note

- As indicated in Task 146, it is a good idea to escape cookie values in order to remove characters that are not valid in cookies. This means you need to unescape the cookies when accessing them so that you end up with the original, intended value instead of a value with a number of escaped characters.

A common use of a cookie is to include the value in the Web page being displayed. If a cookie stores a user's username, you might want to display a login form with the username field filled in with the user's username. The following illustrates this by creating a simple login form with two fields for the username and password and displaying the username in the username field, if available. The username will be stored in a cookie named `loginName`, if it has been set:

1. In a separate script block at the start of the body of your page, extract the name and value of the cookie to two variables; refer to Task 147 for a summary of this process. In this case, the name of the cookie is stored in `cookieName`, and the value in `cookieValue` and the script block should look like Listing 148-1.

```
<script language="JavaScript"
    var newCookie = document.cookie;
    var cookieParts = newCookie.split("=");
    var cookieName = cookieParts[0];
    var cookieValue = unescape(cookieParts[1]);
</script>
```

Listing 148-1: Extract the cookie's name and value in separate script block.

2. After the script, enter a `form` tag to start the form; make sure the form is being submitted to an appropriate location for processing:

```
<form method="post" action="doLogin.cgi">
```

3. Start a new script block with the `script` tag:

```
<script language="JavaScript">
```

4. Enter an `if` command to test that the name of the cookie is `loginName` and the value is not the empty string:

```
if (cookieName == "loginName" && cookieValue != "") {
```

5. Display a username text field that includes the user's username from the cookie. Display this with the `document.write` command:

```
document.write('Username: <input type="text" ⊃
name="username" value="' + cookieValue + '">');
```

6. Enter an `else` command:

```
} else {
```

7. Display a username text field without the user's username for the case where no cookie is available. Display this with the `document.write` command:

```
document.write('Username: <input type="text" ⊃
name="username">');
```

8. Close the `if` block, and close the script block with a closing `script` tag:

```
}
</script>
```

9. Enter an `input` tag to create a password entry field:

```
Password: <input type="password" name="password">
```

10. Close the form with a closing `form` tag. The resulting form code should look like Listing 148-2, and the form, when displayed, should look like Figure 148-1.

```
<form method="post" action="doLogin.cgi">
    <script language="JavaScript">
        if (cookieName == "loginName" && cookieValue != "") {
            document.write('Username: <input type="text" ⤺
name="username" value="' + cookieValue + '">');
        } else {
            document.write('Username: <input type="text" ⤺
name="username">');
        }
    </script>
    Password: <input type="password" name="password">
</form>
```

Listing 148-2: The code to dynamically display a username in a form.

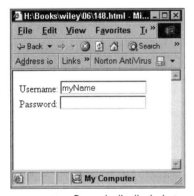

Figure 148-1: Dynamically displaying a username in a form.

tip
- You need to test the cookie's name and value before using it for two reasons. First, there is a chance that the cookie contained in `document.cookie` is a different cookie. Second, if the cookie is an empty string, then no username is available (see Step 4).

cross-reference
- Task 9 discusses generating output to the browser from JavaScript using the `document.write` method. The method takes a single string argument. In this case, you are building a string by concatenating two strings.

Controlling the Expiry of a Cookie

When you create a cookie, you may want to set an expiration date and time. If you set a cookie without an expiry, the cookie will expire at the end of the user's browser session and you will lose the ability to access the cookie across multiple user sessions. To create a cookie with an expiration date, you need to append an expiration date to the cookie string so that the cookie string looks like the following:

```
name=value;expires=date
```

The expiration date is optional and is typically represented as a string in Greenwich Mean Time, which you can generate with the toGMTString method of the Date object.

The following steps outline the process of creating a cookie with an expiration date:

1. Create a Date object for the date and time when you want the cookie to expire; this is done by assigning a new instance of the Date object to a variable and passing the date information as an argument to the Date object. In this case, the resulting Date object is stored in the variable myDate and the date for the object is set to April 14, 2005, at 1:15 P.M.:

```
var myDate = new Date(2005,03,14,13,15,00);
```

2. Type **document.cookie** followed by an equal sign to begin assigning a value to the document.cookie object:

```
document.cookie =
```

3. Type an opening double quotation followed by a name for the cookie followed by an equal sign. In this case, the name is myCookie:

```
document.cookie = "myCookie=
```

4. Close the double quotation, and type a plus sign:

```
document.cookie = "myCookie=" +
```

5. Enter the value you wish to assign to the cookie as the argument to the escape function, and follow the escape function with a plus sign. In this case, the value of the cookie is "This is my Cookie":

```
document.cookie = "myCookie=" + escape("This is my ⊃
Cookie") +
```

6. Type an opening double quotation following by a semicolon followed by **expires**, and follow this with an equal sign, a closing quotation mark, and then another plus sign:

```
document.cookie = "myCookie=" + escape("This is my ⊃
Cookie") + ";expires=" +
```

Task 149

7. Type **myDate.toGMTString()** to add the specified date and time as a properly formatted string to the cookie, and end the command with a semicolon. Your code should now look like Listing 149-1.

```
<head>
    <script language="JavaScript">
        var myDate = new Date(2005,03,14,13,15,00);
        document.cookie = "myCookie=" + escape("This is my ⤶
Cookie") + ";expires=" + myDate.toGMTString();
    </script>
</head>
```

Listing 149-1: Creating a cookie in JavaScript.

tip

▪ When creating dates, remember that in JavaScript months are numbered starting at 0. This means January is month 0, February is month 1, March is month 2, April is month 3, and so on (see Step 1).

8. For testing purposes, you can see the exact string you are assigning to the `document.cookie` object by using the `window.alert` method to display the same string a simple dialog box. The result looks like Figure 149-1.

```
<head>
    <script language="JavaScript">
        var myDate = new Date(2005,03,14,13,15,00);
        document.cookie = "myCookie=" + escape("This is my ⤶
Cookie") + ";expires=" + myDate.toGMTString();
        window.alert("myCookie=" + escape("This is my Cookie")
+ ";expires=" + myDate.toGMTString());
    </script>
</head>
```

Microsoft Internet Explorer

⚠ myCookie=This%20is%20my%20Cookie;expires=Thu, 14 Apr 2005 20:15:00 UTC

OK

Figure 149-1: Displaying a cookie in a dialog box.

Using a Cookie to Track a User's Session

A common application of cookies is to track user-specific information across a user's session with a Web site. This might mean tracking the user's latest preference selections, a user's search query, or a session ID, which allows your script to determine additional information for displaying the page appropriately for the user. In all cases, a session is considered to have ended after a certain amount of time without user activity has expired.

The way this is done is to set the appropriate cookie with an expiration date and time that will cause the cookie to elapse when the session should end. For instance, if a session should end after a 20-minute period of inactivity, the cookie's expiry should be 20 minutes in the future. Then, on each page the user accesses in the site, the session cookie should be reset with a new expiry 20 minutes in the future.

To do this, include the following code at the start of each page in your Web application; this example is generic and works for any single cookie that needs to be maintained across a user's session:

1. Obtain the name and value of the cookie as outlined in Task 147; here the name and value will be stored in the variables `cookieName` and `cookieValue`:

   ```
   var newCookie = document.cookie;
   var cookieParts = newCookie.split("=");
   var cookieName = cookieParts[0];
   var cookieValue = unescape(cookieParts[1]);
   ```

2. Create a new `Date` object, but don't set the date. Here the `Date` object is assigned to the variable `newDate`:

   ```
   var newDate = new Date();
   ```

3. Set the expiration date to the appropriate number of minutes in the future. You do this by using the `setTime` method of the `newDate` object. This method takes the time as a number of milliseconds. To set the time into the future, get the current time with the `getTime` method and then add the number of milliseconds. For instance, 20 minutes is 1200000 milliseconds:

   ```
   newDate.setTime(newDate.getTime() + 1200000);
   ```

4. Type **document.cookie** followed by an equal sign to begin assigning a value to the `document.cookie` object:

   ```
   document.cookie =
   ```

5. Type **cookieName** followed by a plus sign followed by an equal sign in quotation marks:

```
document.cookie = cookieName + "="
```

6. Type a plus sign followed by the `escape` function with `cookieValue` as the argument, followed by a plus sign:

```
document.cookie = cookieName + "=" + escape(cookieValue) +
```

7. Type an opening double quotation followed by a semicolon followed by expires; then follow this with an equal sign and a closing quotation mark and then another plus sign:

```
document.cookie = cookieName + "=" + escape(cookieValue) + ⊃
";expires=" +
```

8. Type **newDate.toGMTString()** to add the specified date and time as a properly formatted string to the cookie, and end the command with a semicolon. Your JavaScript code should look like Listing 150-1.

```
<head>
    <script language="JavaScript">
        var newCookie = document.cookie;
        var cookieParts = newCookie.split("=");
        var cookieName = cookieParts[0];
        var cookieValue = unescape(cookieParts[1]);
        var newDate = new Date();
        newDate.setTime(newDate.getTime() + 1200000);
        document.cookie = cookieName + "=" + ⊃
escape(cookieValue) + ";expires=" + newDate.toGMTString();
    </script>
</head>
```

Listing 150-1: Creating a new session cookie at the start of every page in an application.

cross-references

- Task 47 discusses the use of the `Date` object to obtain and display the current date.

- Task 146 discusses the creation of cookies and the use of the `document.cookie` property in that process.

Using a Cookie to Count Page Access

One use of cookies is to provide a personal page counter. This is different than a global access counter, which displays the total number of visits to a site by any visitor. Instead, a personal hit counter displays the user's personal access count. The approach is simple: Create a cookie with a long expiration date, and each time the user accesses the page, retrieve the cookie, increment it by 1, display the value, and then resave the cookie with a new expiration date and time. The following generates a personal hit counter using a cookie named myHits:

1. Create a script block at the start of your page with an opening script tag:

```
<script language="JavaScript">
```

2. Obtain the name and value of the cookie as outlined in Task 147; here the name and value will be stored in the variables cookieName and cookieValue:

```
var newCookie = document.cookie;
var cookieParts = newCookie.split("=");
var cookieName = cookieParts[0];
var cookieValue = unescape(cookieParts[1]);
```

3. Assign the cookie value to a variable named previousCount:

```
var previousCount = cookieValue;
```

4. Use an if statement to check if the cookieName is not myHits or the cookieValue is a null value (in other words, no cookie existed), and if either condition is true, set previousCount to zero:

```
if (cookieName != "myHits" || cookieValue == null) {
   previousCount = 0;
}
```

5. Increment the value of previousCount by 1, and assign it the variable newCount:

```
var newCount = parseInt(previousCount) + 1;
```

6. Create a new Date object, but don't set the date. Here the Date object is assigned to the variable newDate:

```
var newDate = new Date();
```

7. Set the expiration date to the appropriate number of minutes in the future. You do this by using the setTime method of the newDate object. This method takes the time as a number of milliseconds. To set the time into the future, get the current time with the getTime method and then add the number of milliseconds. For instance, 30 days is 30 days times 24 hours per day times 60 minutes per hour times 60 seconds per minute times 1000 milliseconds per second, or 2592000000 milliseconds:

```
newDate.setTime(newDate.getTime() + 2592000000);
```

8. Reset the cookie by assigning the value of `newCount` to the `document.cookie` object with an expiration date as specified in `newDate`. (This process was described in Task 149.)

```
document.cookie = "myHits=" + newCount + ";expires=" + ⤸
newDate.toGMTString();
```

9. Close the script block with a closing `script` tag, so that the result-ing script block looks like Listing 151-1.

```
<script language="JavaScript">
    var newCookie = document.cookie;
    var cookieParts = newCookie.split("=");
    var cookieName = cookieParts[0];
    var cookieValue = unescape(cookieParts[1]);
    var previousCount = cookieValue;
    if (cookieName != "myHits" || cookieValue == null) {
        previousCount = 0;
    }
    var newCount = parseInt(previousCount) + 1;
    var newDate = new Date();
    newDate.setTime(newDate.getTime() + 2592000000);
    document.cookie = "myHits=" + newCount + ";expires=" + ⤸
newDate.toGMTString();
</script>
```

Listing 151-1: Incrementing and resaving a counter cookie at the start of a page.

10. In the body of your text, when you want to display the current count, create a new script block and use the `document.write` method to display the value of the `newCount` variable. You will see the results in your browser.

```
<script language="JavaScript">
    document.write("You have visited this page " + ⤸
newCount + " time(s).");
</script>
```

cross-reference

• Task 9 discusses generat-ing output to the browser from JavaScript using the `document.write` method. The method takes a single string argument. In this case, you are building a string by concatenating two strings.

Deleting a Cookie

Sometimes you will want to delete a cookie so that subsequent attempts to read the cookie return nothing. For instance, you may want to remove a username cookie if the user logs out or explicitly asks not to save his or her username in a cookie. To do this, you reset the cookie but set the expiration date to a time in the past. This causes the browser to drop the cookie and the cookie will cease to be returned, effectively deleting it.

The following example illustrates how to delete a cookie name `myCookie`:

1. In the head of a new HTML document, create a script block with opening and closing `script` tags:

   ```
   <head>
       <script language="JavaScript">

       </script>
   </head>
   ```

2. In the script, create a new `Date` object, but don't set the date. Here the `Date` object is assigned to the variable `newDate`:

   ```
   <head>
       <script language="JavaScript">

           var newDate = new Date();

       </script>
   </head>
   ```

3. Set the expiration date to some time in the past; for instance, you might set the date to one day in the past. You do this by using the `setTime` method of the `newDate` object. This method takes the time as a number of milliseconds. To set the time into the past, get the current time with the `getTime` method and then subtract the number of milliseconds. For instance, one day is 86400000 milliseconds:

   ```
   <head>
       <script language="JavaScript">

           var newDate = new Date();
           newDate.setTime(newDate.getTime() - 86400000);

       </script>
   </head>
   ```

4. Type **document.cookie** followed by an equal sign to begin assigning a value to the `document.cookie` object:

   ```
   document.cookie =
   ```

note

- Task 146 discusses the creation of cookies and the use of the `document.cookie` property in that process. The deletion of a cookie involves setting a cookie with an expiration date that is not in the future.

5. Type an opening double quotation followed by a name for the cookie followed by an equal sign. In this case, the name is `myCookie`:

```
document.cookie = "myCookie=
```

6. Type a semicolon followed by **expires**, and follow this with an equal sign and a closing quotation mark, and then a plus sign:

```
document.cookie = "myCookie=;expires=" +
```

7. Type **newDate.toGMTString()** to add the specified date and time as a properly formatted string to the cookie, and end the command with a semicolon. Your JavaScript code should look like Listing 152-1.

```
<head>
    <script language="JavaScript">

        var newDate = new Date();
        newDate.setTime(newDate.getTime() - 86400000);
        document.cookie = "myCookie=;expires=" + ⤸
newDate.toGMTString();

    </script>
</head>
```

Listing 152-1: Deleting a cookie.

8. For testing purposes, you can display the current cookie using the `window.alert` method to ensure no cookie exists with the name `myCookie`:

```
<head>
    <script language="JavaScript">

        var newDate = new Date();
        newDate.setTime(newDate.getTime() - 86400000);
        document.cookie = "myCookie=;expires=" + ⤸
newDate.toGMTString();
        window.alert(document.cookie);

    </script>
</head>
```

cross-reference

- Task 25 discusses the creation of alert dialog boxes using the `window.alert` method.

Task 153

Creating Multiple Cookies

note

- The escape function takes a string and escapes any characters that are not valid in a URL. Escaping involves replacing the character with a numeric code preceded by a percent sign. For instance, spaces become %20.

Within limits, it is possible to create multiple cookies for a Web page. This allows you to set and track multiple values throughout your Web application or between user sessions. There are limitations, however. Most Web browsers set limits on the number of cookies that can be set or the total number of bytes that can be consumed by the cookies from one site. When these thresholds are set, the oldest cookies for a site are automatically expired as you attempt to create new ones even if their expiration date and time has not been reached.

To create multiple cookies from JavaScript, you simply assign each cookie in turn to the document.cookie object and ensure that each cookie has a different name. The same ability to set expiration date and time exists for each cookie as when setting a single cookie, and each cookie may have a different expiration date and time.

The following example illustrates the creation of two cookies named myFirstCookie and mySecondCookie:

1. Type **document.cookie** followed by an equal sign to begin assigning a value to the document.cookie object:

   ```
   document.cookie =
   ```

2. Type an opening double quotation followed by a name for the cookie followed by an equal sign. In this case, the name is myFirstCookie:

   ```
   document.cookie = "myFirstCookie=
   ```

3. Close the double quotation and type a plus sign:

   ```
   document.cookie = "myFirstCookie=" +
   ```

4. Enter the value you wish to assign to the first cookie as the argument to the escape function. In this case, the value of the cookie is "This is my first Cookie":

   ```
   document.cookie = "myFirstCookie=" + escape("This is my ⏎
   first Cookie")
   ```

5. Type a semicolon to end the command. For the first cookie, your JavaScript code should look like Listing 153-1.

   ```
   document.cookie = "myFirstCookie=" + escape("This is my ⏎
   first Cookie");
   ```

Listing 153-1: Creating the first cookie in JavaScript.

6. Continue to create the second cookie on a new line of your script by typing **document.cookie** followed by an equal sign to begin assigning a value to the `document.cookie` object:

```
document.cookie =
```

7. Type an opening double quotation followed by a name for the cookie followed by an equal sign. In this case, the name is `mySecondCookie`:

```
document.cookie = "mySecondCookie=
```

8. Close the double quotation and type a plus sign:

```
document.cookie = "mySecondCookie=" +
```

9. Enter the value you wish to assign to the first cookie as the argument to the `escape` function. In this case, the value of the cookie is "This is my first Cookie":

```
document.cookie = "mySecondCookie=" + escape("This is ⏎
my second Cookie")
```

10. Type a semicolon to end the command. Your JavaScript code for the two cookies should now look like Listing 153-2.

```
<script language="JavaScript">
    document.cookie = "myFirstCookie=" + escape("This is ⏎
my first Cookie");
    document.cookie = "mySecondCookie=" + escape("This is ⏎
my second Cookie");
</script>
```

Listing 153-2: Creating two cookies from a single script in JavaScript.

tip

- In theory, browsers should store at least 300 cookies of at least 4096 characters in size and should allow each individual server host or domain name to create at least 20 cookies. In practice, Netscape and Internet Explorer do not always adhere to these standards. In fact, Internet Explorer allows you to indicate the maximum percentage of your hard drive that cookies are allowed to fill.

cross-reference

- Task 146 discusses the creation of cookies and the use of the `document.cookie` property in that process. The same process applies for each cookie regardless of the number of cookies you are creating.

Task 154

Accessing Multiple Cookies

If a page has multiple cookies associated with it, then accessing one, or all, of those cookies is a little more complicated than illustrated in Task 147. This is because when you access document.cookie, you will now see a series of cookies separated by semicolons like this:

```
firstCookieName=firstCookieValue;secondCookieName=secondCookieValue;
etc.
```

This means to extract a cookie from a page with multiple cookies requires two steps: separating the string returned by document.cookie into multiple pieces using the semicolon to determine where to break the string, and then treating each cookie individually.

The following example assumes you have two cookies on the page: myFirstCookie and mySecondCookie. These steps extract both cookies and display them in dialog boxes using the window.alert method.

1. Use the indexOf method of the String object to locate the character where the string "myFirstCookie=" appears in the string returned by the document.cookie object. This value is assigned to the variable first:

   ```
   var first = document.cookie.indexOf("myFirstCookie=");
   ```

2. Use the indexOf method once more to find where the cookie ends (by looking for a semicolon), and assign this location to the variable firstEnd. Searching starts after the location where "myFirstCookie=" was found:

   ```
   var firstEnd = document.cookie.indexOf(";", first + 1);
   ```

3. Check to see whether or not a semicolon was found by checking if firstEnd has the value -1. If the value is -1, it means that this cookie is the last cookie and firstEnd should be set to the last character in the document.cookie string:

   ```
   if (firstEnd == -1) { firstEnd = document.cookie.length; }
   ```

4. Extract the value of the first cookie by taking the substring starting at the character after "myFirstCookie=" and ending at the semicolon. This is done with the substring method of the String object, and the resulting substring is passed to unescape to remove any escaped characters. The results are stored in the variable firstCookie. Note that first + 14 is used as the first character of the substring; this represents the first character after the equal sign after myFirstCookie (since "myFirstCookie=" is 14-characters long). The resulting code for extracting myFirstCookie looks like Listing 154-1.

```
var first = document.cookie.indexOf("myFirstCookie=");
var firstEnd = document.cookie.indexOf(";", first + 1);
if (firstEnd == -1) { firstEnd = document.cookie.length; }
var firstCookie = ⤸
unescape(document.cookie.substring(first+14,firstEnd));
```

Listing 154-1: Extracting a cookie from multiple cookies.

5. Repeat the process for the second cookie, but search for mySecondCookie and store the results in new variables named second, secondEnd and secondCookie:

```
var second = document.cookie.indexOf("mySecondCookie=");
var secondEnd = document.cookie.indexOf(";", second + 1);
if (secondEnd == -1) { secondEnd = document.cookie.length;
}
var secondCookie = ⤸
unescape(document.cookie.substring(second+15,secondEnd));
```

6. Display each of the cookie values in turn using the window.alert method. You should see dialog boxes like Figures 154-1 and 154-2.

```
window.alert(firstCookie);
window.alert(secondCookie);
```

Figure 154-1: Displaying the first cookie.

Figure 154-2: Displaying the second cookie.

Task 155

Using Cookies to Present a Different Home Page for New Visitors

With cookies you can track if a user has visited your site previously (or, at least, if he or she has visited recently). This can be done by simply setting a cookie indicating the user has visited and then giving it a long expiration time. Then each time the user returns to the site, you can update the expiration time to ensure that the cookie is unlikely to ever expire.

Meanwhile, each time a user accesses a page in your site, you can test for the existence of the cookie, and if it isn't there, you can direct the user to a default start page where you want new users to begin their experience of your site. Alternately, you can test the cookie only when a user accesses the home page and direct new users to a specialized home page just for them.

The following outlines the code you need to build into every page on your site, or just into your home page, to achieve this. In this example, the cookie named visitCookie will exist and be set to a value of 1 if the user has previously visited the site.

1. Create a new Date object, but don't set the date. Here the Date object is assigned to the variable newDate:

   ```
   var newDate = new Date();
   ```

2. Set the expiration date to be an appropriate distance in the future; for instance, you might set the date to six months in the future. You do this by using the setTime method of the newDate object. This method takes the time as a number of milliseconds. To set the time into the future, get the current time with the getTime method and then add the number of milliseconds. For instance, six months (or 26 weeks) is 26 weeks times 7 days per week times 24 hours per day times 60 minutes per hour times 60 seconds per minute times 1000 milliseconds per seconds, for a total of 15724800000 milliseconds:

   ```
   newDate.setTime(newDate.getTime() + 15724800000);
   ```

3. Search the document.cookie string to see whether or not "visitCookie=" exists. This is done with the indexOf method of the String object, and the return value is the index of the first occurrence of "visitCookie=", which is stored here in the variable firstVisit:

   ```
   var firstVisit = document.cookie.indexOf("visitCookie=");
   ```

4. Use an if command to test if a visitCookie cookie exists:

   ```
   if (firstVisit == -1) {
   ```

5. If the cookie does not exist, you want to set a `visitCookie` cookie, using the date and time stored in `newDate` to set the expiration date for the cookie:

```
document.cookie = "visitCookie=1;expires=" +
newDate.toGMTString();
```

6. After setting the `visitCookie` cookie for new visitors, redirect them to the special home page for new visitors by setting a new value for the `window.location` property:

```
window.location = "http://myurl.com/new.html"
```

7. Close the `if` block with a closing curly bracket:

```
}
```

8. If processing reaches this point, then the user is a returning user and has not been redirected to the new page. In this case, the `visitCookie` needs to be reset with the new expiration date and time indicated in `newDate`. The final script looks like Listing 155-1.

```
<script language="JavaScript">
    var newDate = new Date();
    newDate.setTime(newDate.getTime() + 15724800000);
    var firstVisit = document.cookie.indexOf("visitCookie=");
    if (firstVisit == -1) {
        document.cookie = "visitCookie=1;expires=" +
newDate.toGMTString();
        window.location = "http://myurl.com/new.html"
    }
    document.cookie = "visitCookie=1;expires=" +
newDate.toGMTString();
</script>
```

Listing 155-1: Redirecting new users to a custom home page.

tip

- There are some flaws to this cookie-based approach to determining if a user has previously viewed your site. Namely, users may choose to explicitly turn off cookies in their browsers.

cross-references

- Task 154 illustrates how to search for and identify specific cookies in the set of accessible cookies.

- Task 55 shows how to redirect the user's browser to another URL using the `window.location` object.

Task 156

Creating a Cookie Function Library

notes

- The `getCookie` function adds some extra logic. First it checks to make sure at least one cookie exists by testing the length of the `document.cookie` string, and then it only retrieves a value for the cookie if a matching cookie is found. If there is no matching cookie, then an empty string is returned by the function.

- Task 146 discusses the creation of cookies and the use of the `document.cookie` property in that process. The deletion of a cookie involves setting a cookie with an expiration date that is not in the future (see Step 6).

As you probably noted in the previous tasks dealing with cookies, working with cookies requires a lot of string and date manipulation, especially when accessing existing cookies when multiple cookies have been set. To address this, you should create a small cookie function library for yourself so that you can create, access, and delete cookies without needing to rewrite the code to do this every time.

Most cookie libraries include three functions:

- `getCookie`: Retrieves a cookie based on a cookie name passed in as an argument.

- `setCookie`: Sets a cookie based on a cookie name, cookie value, and expiration date passed in as arguments.

- `deleteCookie`: Deletes a cookie based on a cookie name passed in as an argument.

The following steps outline how to create these functions for yourself. You can then include them in any pages where you need to work with cookies in JavaScript.

1. Start the `getCookie` function with the `function` keyword, and define a single argument named `cookieName`:

```
function getCookie(cookieName) {
```

2. Based on the technique outlined in Task 154, retrieve the text for the cookie named in the `cookieName` argument, as shown in Listing 156-1.

```
function getCookie(cookieName) {
    var cookieValue = "";
    if (document.cookie.length > 0) {
        var cookieStart = document.cookie.indexOf(cookieName
+ "=");
        if (cookieStart != -1) {
            var cookieEnd = document.cookie.indexOf(";",
cookieStart + 1);
            if (cookieEnd == -1) { cookieEnd =
document.cookie.length; }
            var cookieValue =
unescape(document.cookie.substring(cookieStart+cookieName.
length+1,cookieEnd));
        }
    }
    return cookieValue;
}
```

Listing 156-1: The `getCookie` function.

3. Start the `setCookie` function with the `function` keyword, and define three arguments named `cookieName`, `cookieValue`, and `expiryDate`:

```
function setCookie(cookieName,cookieValue,expiryDate) {
```

4. Based on the technique outlined in Task 147, create the cookie by assigning the appropriate string to the `document.cookie` object, so that the final function looks like Listing 156-2.

```
function setCookie(cookieName,cookieValue,expiryDate) {
    document.cookie = cookieName + "=" + escape↩
(cookieValue) + ";expires=" + expiryDate.toGMTString();
}
```

Listing 156-2: The `setCookie` function.

5. Start the `deleteCookie` function with the `function` keyword, and define a single argument named `cookieName`:

```
function deleteCookie(cookieName) {
```

6. Based on the technique outlined in Task 152, delete the cookie named in the `cookieName` argument, so that the final function looks like Listing 153-3.

```
function deleteCookie(cookieName) {
    var newDate = new Date();
    newDate.setTime(newDate.getTime() - 86400000);
    document.cookie = cookieName + "=deleted;expires=" + ↩
newDate.toGMTString();
}
```

Listing 156-3: The `deleteCookie` function.

7. Include these three functions in pages that must manipulate cookies, and then simply invoke the functions. For instance, the following code sets a new `myCookie` function, retrieves it, displays the value, and then deletes it:

```
var newDate = new Date();
newDate.setTime(newDate.getTime() + 86400000);
setCookie("myCookie","This is My Cookie",newDate);
var cookieValue = getCookie("myCookie");
window.alert(cookieValue);
deleteCookie("myCookie");
```

cross-reference

• The `getCookie` function returns a value using the `return` keyword. This technique is discussed in Task 29.

Task 157

Allowing a Cookie to be Seen for all Pages in a Site

When a cookie is created by JavaScript, by default it is only accessible from other pages in the same directory on the server. You can, however, define which directory path on the server is allowed to access a cookie you create.

For instance, you could create a cookie in the page /dir/subdir/mypage. html and do any number of things, including the following:

- That the cookie is accessible from the parent directory and from all its children (in other words, everywhere below /dir)

- Indicate that the cookie is accessible only in the current directory and in its children (in other words, everywhere below /dir/subdir/)

- Indicate that the cookie is accessible anywhere on the same site (in other words, everywhere below /).

You do this by extending your cookie definition when you create the cookie and adding a path clause to the cookie, so that the cookie now looks like this:

```
name=value;expires=expiryDate;path=accessPath
```

For example, the following steps create the cookie myCookie and make it accessible to all pages on the same site:

1. Create a Date object for the date and time when you want the cookie to expire; this is done by assigning a new instance of the Date object to a variable and passing the date information as an argument to the Date object. In this case, the resulting Date object is stored in the variable myDate and the date for the object is set to April 14, 2005, at 1:15 P.M.:

```
var myDate = new Date(2005,03,14,13,15,00);
```

2. Type **document.cookie** followed by an equal sign to begin assigning a value to the document.cookie object:

```
document.cookie =
```

3. Type an opening double quotation followed by a name for the cookie followed by an equal sign. In this case, the name is myCookie:

```
document.cookie = "myCookie=
```

4. Close the double quotation and type a plus sign:

```
document.cookie = "myCookie=" +
```

note

- The escape function takes a string and escapes any characters that are not valid in a URL. Escaping involves replacing the character with a numeric code preceded by a percent sign. For instance, spaces become %20 (see Step 5).

5. Enter the value you wish to assign to the cookie as the argument to the escape function, and follow the escape function with a plus sign. In this case, the value of the cookie is "This is my Cookie":

```
document.cookie = "myCookie=" + escape("This is my ⏎
Cookie") +
```

6. Type an opening double quotation following by a semicolon followed by **expires**, and follow this with an equal sign and a closing quotation mark and then another plus sign:

```
document.cookie = "myCookie=" + escape("This is my ⏎
Cookie") + ";expires=" +
```

7. Type myDate.toGMTString() to add the specified date and time as a properly formatted string to the cookie, and follow that with a plus sign:

```
document.cookie = "myCookie=" + escape("This is my ⏎
Cookie") + ";expires=" + myDate.toGMTString() +
```

8. Type an opening double quotation followed by a semicolon followed by path, and follow this with an equal sign and a forward slash, and finally close the double quotation and end the command with a semicolon:

```
document.cookie = "myCookie=" + escape("This is my ⏎
Cookie") + ";expires=" + myDate.toGMTString() + ";path=/";
```

9. On another page in another directory on the site, attempt to retrieve the cookie and display it in a dialog box with the window.alert method. Figure 157-1 shows the result.

```
var newCookie = document.cookie;
var cookieParts = newCookie.split("=");
var cookieName = cookieParts[0];
var cookieValue = unescape(cookieParts[1]);
window.alert(cookieValue);
```

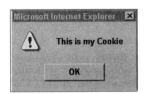

Figure 157-1: Displaying a cookie set in a different directory.

Part 7:   DHTML and Style Sheets

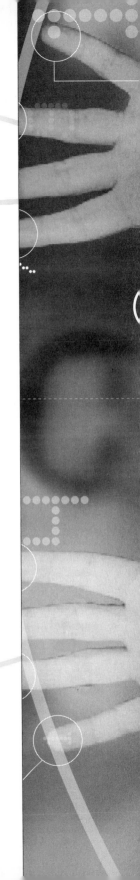

Controlling Line Spacing

E very element of your page has an object associated with it that can be accessed through JavaScript. For instance, you can manipulate an element's line spacing window using this object.

The line spacing information is part of the `style` property of the object. The `style` property is an object reflecting all the cascading style sheet (CSS) style settings for an object, including the `line-height` attribute. This means you can specify the line height of an object, typically in pixels, with the following property:

```
object.style.line-height
```

To reference the element's object, you use the `document.getElementById` method. For each object in your document that you want to manipulate through JavaScript, you should assign an ID using the `id` attribute of the element's tag. For instance, the following has the ID `myLayer`:

```
<div id="myLayer"> </div>
```

From this, you can obtain a reference to the layer's object with the following:

```
var layerRef = document.getElementById("myLayer");
```

`layerRef` would then refer to the object for the layer element (`myLayer`) of your document, and you could change its line height with this:

```
layerRef.style.lineHeight = "15px";
```

The following steps show how to build a page with a layer element and a link. When the user clicks the link, the line height in the layer increases.

1. In the header of a new document, create a script block containing a function named `moreSpace`. The function should take one argument containing the ID of the element to work with:

   ```
   function moreSpace(objectID) {
   }
   ```

2. Create a variable named `thisObject`, and associate it with the ID object specified in the function's argument. Use `document.getElementById`:

   ```
   var thisObject = document.getElementById(objectID);
   ```

3. Increase the value of the `lineHeight` attribute of the element's `style` object so that the final function looks like:

   ```
   thisObject.style.lineHeight =
       parseInt(thisObject.style.lineHeight) + 5 + "px";
   ```

notes

- The `style` object referred to here and the `document.getElementByID` method are only available in newer browsers with robust support for the Domain Object Model. This means this task will only work in Internet Explorer 5 and later or Netscape 6 and later.

- The `parseInt` function is used here in resetting the line height because `lineHeight` returns a string such as `18px`. `parseInt` converts this string into a numeric value, such as `18`, to which you can safely add 5 pixels.

- Notice the use of a `javascript:` URL in the link. This URL causes the specified JavaScript code to execute when the user clicks on the link.

- When you call the `moreSpace` function, you pass in the object ID as a string; that is why `myObject` is contained in single quotes.

4. In the body of the document, create a layer and position it where you are using the `style` attribute of the `div` tag. Specify an initial line height for the object, and specify `myObject` as the ID for the layer:

```
<div id="myObject" style="position: absolute; left:
50px; top: 50px; width: 150px; font-size: 14px; line-
height: 18px; background-color: #cccccc;">This is my
object and it has lots of text for us to experiment
with.</div>
```

5. Create a link the user can click to call the `moreSpace` function, so the final page looks like Listing 158-1.

```
<head>
  <script language="JavaScript">
    function moreSpace(objectID) {
      var thisObject = document.getElementById(objectID);
      thisObject.style.lineHeight =
        parseInt(thisObject.style.lineHeight) + 5 + "px";
    }
  </script>
</head>
<body>

    <div id="myObject" style="position: absolute; left:
50px; top: 50px; width: 150px; font-size: 14px; line-
height: 18px; background-color: #cccccc;">This is my
object and it has lots of text for us to experiment
with.</div>

    <a href="javascript:moreSpace('myObject');">
Increase the line spacing.</a>
</body>
```

Listing 158-1: Changing an element's line height.

6. Save the file and close it.

7. Open the file in a browser, and you see the link and the text object.

8. Click on the link, and the layer's line height increases. Keep clicking and the line height keeps increasing.

cross-reference

■ This task shows you how to change line spacing in text. Tasks 174 and 175 show you how to manipulate the font characteristics of text.

Determining an Object's Location

Every element of your page has an object associated with it that can be accessed through JavaScript. For instance, you can determine an object's location in the browser window using this object.

The location information is part of the `style` property of the object. The `style` property includes the `left` and `top` attributes. You can determine the location of an object with the following two properties:

```
object.style.left
object.style.top
```

To reference the element's object, you use the `document.getElementById` method. For each object in your document that you want to manipulate through JavaScript, you should assign an ID using the `id` attribute of the element's tag. For instance, the following image has the ID `myImage`:

```
<img src="image.gif" id="myImage">
```

Then, you could obtain a reference to the image's object with the following:

```
var imageRef = document.getElementById("myImage");
```

This means `imageRef` would then refer to the object for the image element of your document, and you could reference the position of the image with this:

```
imageRef.style.left
imageRef.style.top
```

The following steps show how to build a page with a layer element and a link. When the user clicks the link, he or she sees a dialog box reporting the coordinate locations of the object.

1. In the header of a new document, create a script block containing a function named `getLocation`. The function should take one argument containing the ID of the element to work with:

   ```
   function getLocation(objectID) {
   }
   ```

2. Create a variable named `thisObject`, and associate it with the `ID` object specified in the function's argument. Use `document.getElementById`:

   ```
   var thisObject = document.getElementById(objectID);
   ```

3. Create the variables `x` and `y` and store the `left` and `top` properties of the object in them:

   ```
   var x = thisObject.style.left;
   var y = thisObject.style.top;
   ```

notes

- Values for the `top` and `left` properties are usually set in pixels.

- The `style` object referred to here and the `document.getElementByID` method are only available in newer browsers with robust support for the Domain Object Model. This means this task will only work in Internet Explorer 5 and later or Netscape 6 and later.

- In Step 6 notice the use of a `javascript:` URL in the link. This URL causes the specified JavaScript code to execute when the user clicks on the link.

- When you call the `getLocation` function, you pass in the object ID as a string; that is why `myObject` is contained in single quotes.

4. Display the information in a dialog box for the user using
   `window.alert` so that the final function looks like this:

   ```
   window.alert("Object Location: (" + x + "," + y + ")");
   ```

5. In the body of the document, create a layer and position it wherever
   you want using the `style` attribute of the `div` tag. Specify
   `myObject` as the ID for the layer:

   ```
   <div id="myObject" style="position: absolute; left: ⊃
   50px; top: 200px; background-color: #cccccc;">My Object⊃
   </div>
   ```

6. Create a link the user can click to call the `getLocation` function, so
   the final page looks like Listing 159-1.

```
<head>
  <script language="JavaScript">
  function getLocation(objectID) {

      var thisObject = document.getElementById(objectID);
      var x = thisObject.style.left;
      var y = thisObject.style.top;

      window.alert("Object Location: (" + x + "," + y + ⊃
")");
    }
  </script>
</head>

<body>
    <div id="myObject" style="position: absolute; left: ⊃
50px; top: 200px; background-color: #cccccc;">My ⊃
Object</div>

    <a href="javascript:getLocation('myObject');">Where is ⊃
the object?</a>
</body>
```

Listing 159-1: Determining the location of an object.

7. Save the file and close it.

8. Open the file in a browser, and you see the link and object.

9. Click on the link to see the object's location in a dialog box.

cross-reference

- See Task 249 for issues
  that may arise regarding
  object placement when
  working with different
  browsers.

Placing an Object

E very element of your page has an object associated with it that can be accessed through JavaScript. For instance, you can determine an object's location in the browser window using this object.

The location information is part of the style property of the object. The style property includes the left and top attributes. You can specify the location of an object, typically in pixels, with the following two properties:

```
object.style.left
object.style.top
```

To reference the element's object, you use the document.getElementById method. For each object in your document that you want to manipulate through JavaScript, you should assign an ID using the id attribute of the element's tag. For instance, the following image has the ID myImage:

```
<img src="image.gif" id="myImage">
```

Then, you could obtain a reference to the image's object with the following:

```
var imageRef = document.getElementById("myImage");
```

This means imageRef would then refer to the object for the image element of your document, and you could assign a new location to the picture with the following:

```
imageRef.style.left = 100;
imageRef.style.top = 200;
```

This code positions the image at 100 pixels from the left of the browser window and 200 pixels from the top of the browser window.

The following steps show how to build a page with a layer element and a link. When the user clicks the link, the object moves to a new location.

1. In the header of a new document, create a script containing a function named moveObject. The function should take one argument that contains the ID of the element to work with:

   ```
   function moveObject(objectID) {
   }
   ```

2. Create a variable named thisObject, and associate it with the object specified in the function's argument. Use document.getElementById:

   ```
   var thisObject = document.getElementById(objectID);
   ```

notes

- The style object referred to here and the document. getElementByID method are only available in newer browsers with robust support for the Domain Object Model. This means this task will only work in Internet Explorer 5 and later or Netscape 6 and later.

- Here the left and top of the object are specified as simple numbers; these are treated as pixels.

- In Step 5 notice the use of a javascript: URL in the link. This URL causes the specified JavaScript code to execute when the user clicks on the link.

- When you call the moveObject function, you pass in the object ID as a string; that is why myObject is contained in single quotes.

3. Assign new locations to the `left` and `top` attributes of the element's `style` object:

```
thisObject.style.left = 300;
thisObject.style.top = 100;
```

4. In the body of the document, create a layer and position it wherever you want, using the `style` attribute of the `div` tag. Specify `myObject` as the ID for the layer:

```
<div id="myObject" style="position: absolute; left:
50px; top: 200px; background-color: #cccccc;">My
Object</div>
```

5. Create a link the user can click to call the `moveObject` function, so the final page looks like Listing 160-1.

```
<head>
  <script language="JavaScript">

  function moveObject(objectID) {
      var thisObject = document.getElementById(objectID);

      thisObject.style.left = 300;
      thisObject.style.top = 100;

  }
  </script>
</head>

<body>
    <div id="myObject" style="position: absolute; left:
50px; top: 200px; background-color: #cccccc;">My Object</div>

    <a href="javascript:moveObject('myObject');">Move
Object to (300,100).</a>
</body>
```

Listing 160-1: Moving a page element.

6. Save the file and close it.

7. Open the file in a browser, and you see the link and object.

8. Click on the link, and the element moves to a new location

cross-references

- In this task, you set the location of an object. In Task 159 you can learn how to retrieve the location of an object.

- See Tasks 166 and 167 to learn how to center an item on your page.

Moving an Object Horizontally

Every element of your page has an object associated with it that can be accessed through JavaScript. For instance, you can determine an object's location in the browser window using this object. The location information is part of the `style` property of the object.

To reference the element's object, you use the `document.getElementById` method. For each object in your document that you want to manipulate through JavaScript, you should assign an ID using the `id` attribute of the element's tag. Then, you could obtain a reference to the object with the following:

```
var tagRef = document.getElementById("TagID");
```

With this, `objRef` refers to the object for the `TagID` element of your document. You could assign a new location to the element using the `left` and `top` attributes:

```
objRef.style.left = 100;
objRef.style.top = 200;
```

This code positions the element at 100 pixels from the left of the browser window and 200 pixels from the top of the browser window.

The following steps show how to build a page with a layer element and a link. When the user clicks the link, the object moves 10 pixels to the right; the user can click on the link repeatedly to keep moving the object further to the right.

1. In the header of a new document, create a script block containing a function named `moveRight`. The function should take one argument that contains the ID of the element to work with:

   ```
   function moveRight(objectID) {
   }
   ```

2. Create a variable named `thisObj`, and associate it with the object specified in the function's argument. Use `document.getElementById`:

   ```
   var thisObj = document.getElementById(objectID);
   ```

3. Assign a new location to the `left` attribute of the element's `style` object:

   ```
   thisObj.style.left = parseInt(thisObj.style.left) + 10;
   ```

4. In the body of the document, create a layer and position it wherever you want using the `style` attribute of the `div` tag. Specify `myObject` as the ID for the layer:

   ```
   <div id="myObject" style="position: absolute; left: 50px; ⤶
   top: 200px; background-color: #cccccc;">My Object</div>
   ```

5. Create a link the user can click to call the moveRight function, so the final page looks like Listing 161-1.

```
<head>
 <script language="JavaScript">
  function moveRight(objectID) {

   var thisObj = document.getElementById(objectID);
   thisObj.style.left = parseInt(thisObj.style.left) + 10;
  }
 </script>
</head>

<body>
     <div id="myObject" style="position: absolute; left: ⮎
50px; top: 200px; background-color: #cccccc;">My ⮎
Object</div>

      <a href="javascript:moveRight('myObject');">Move ⮎
Object to the right.</a>
</body>
```

Listing 161-1: Moving a page element.

6. Save the file and close it.

7. Open the file in a browser, and you see the link and object, as shown in Figure 161-1.

Figure 161-1: A layer and a link.

8. Click on the link several times, and the element moves progressively further to the right.

cross-references

▪ Task 162 shows you how to move an object vertically.

▪ Task 159 shows you how to determine the current location of an object.

Moving an Object Vertically

Every element of your page has an object associated with it that can be accessed through JavaScript. For instance, you can determine an object's location in the browser window using this object. The location information is part of the `style` property of the object.

To reference the element's object, you use the `document.getElementById` method. For each object in your document that you want to manipulate through JavaScript, you should assign an ID using the `id` attribute of the element's tag. Then, you could obtain a reference to an object with the following:

```
var objRef = document.getElementById("TagID");
```

With this, `objRef` would then refer to the object for the `TagID` element of your document. You could assign a new location to the element using the `left` and `top` attributes:

```
objRef.style.left = 100;
objRef.style.top = 200;
```

This code positions the image at 100 pixels from the left of the browser window and 200 pixels from the top of the browser window.

The following steps show how to build a page with a layer element and a link. When the user clicks the link, the object moves 10 pixels down; the user can click on the link repeatedly to keep moving the object further down.

1. In the header of a new document, create a script block containing a function named `moveDown`. The function should take one argument, which contains the ID of the element to work with:

   ```
   function moveDown(objectID) {
   }
   ```

2. Create a variable named `thisObj`, and associate it with the object specified in the function's argument. Use `document.getElementById`:

   ```
   var thisObj = document.getElementById(objectID);
   ```

3. Assign a new location to the `top` attribute of the element's `style` object:

   ```
   thisObj.style.top = parseInt(thisObj.style.top) + 10;
   ```

4. In the body of the document, create a layer and position it wherever you want using the `style` attribute of the `div` tag. Specify `myObject` as the ID for the layer:

   ```
   <div id="myObject" style="position: absolute; left: ⊃
   50px; top: 200px; background-color: #cccccc;">My ⊃
   Object</div>
   ```

notes

- The `style` object referred to here and the `document.getElementByID` method are only available in newer browsers with robust support for the Domain Object Model. This means this task will only work in Internet Explorer 5 and later or Netscape 6 and later.

- The `parseInt` function is used here in resetting the top position because `top` returns a string such as `100px`. `parseInt` converts this string into a numeric value, such as `100`, to which you can safely add 10 pixels.

- In Step 5 notice the use of a `javascript:` URL in the link. This URL causes the specified JavaScript code to execute when the user clicks on the link.

- When you call the `moveDown` function, you pass in the object ID as a string; that is why `myObject` is contained in single quotes.

- The `style` property is actually an object reflecting all the CSS style settings for an object. This includes the `left` and `top` attributes:

  `object.style.left`

  `object.style.top`

5. Create a link the user can click to call the moveDown function, so the final page looks like Listing 162-1.

```
<head>
  <script language="JavaScript">
  function moveDown(objectID) {

    var thisObj = document.getElementById(objectID);
    thisObj.style.top = parseInt(thisObj.style.top) + 10;
  }
  </script>
</head>

<body>
  <div id="myObject" style="position: absolute; left: ⊃
50px; top: 200px; background-color: #cccccc;">My Object</div>

  <a href="javascript:moveDown('myObject');">Move ⊃
Object down.</a>
</body>
```

Listing 162-1: Moving a page element.

6. Save the file and close it.

7. Open the file, and you see the link and object, as shown in Figure 162-1.

Figure 162-1: A layer and a link.

8. Click on the link several times, and the element moves progressively further down.

cross-reference

- Task 159 shows you how to determine the current location of an object.

Moving an Object Diagonally

very element of your page has an object associated with it that can be accessed through JavaScript. For instance, you can determine an object's location in the browser window using this object. The location information is part of the `style` property of the object.

To reference the element's object, you use the `document.getElementById` method. For each object in your document that you want to manipulate through JavaScript, you should assign an ID using the `id` attribute of the element's tag. Then, you could obtain a reference to the object with the following:

```
var objRef = document.getElementById("TagID");
```

With this, `objRef` would then refer to the object for the `TagID` element of your document, and you could assign a new location to the element with this:

```
objRef.style.left = 100;
objRef.style.top = 200;
```

This code positions the image at 100 pixels from the left of the browser window and 200 pixels from the top of the browser window.

The following steps show how to build a page with a layer element and a link. When the user clicks the link, the object moves 10 pixels down and 10 pixels to the right; the user can click on the link repeatedly to keep moving the object.

1. In the header of a new document, create a script block containing a function named `moveDiagonally`. The function should take one argument that will contain the ID of the element to work with:

   ```
   function moveDiagonally(objectID) {
   }
   ```

2. Create a variable named `thisObj`, and associate it with the object specified in the function's argument. Use `document.getElementById`:

   ```
   var thisObj = document.getElementById(objectID);
   ```

3. Assign a new location to the `left` attribute of the element's `style` object:

   ```
   thisObj.style.left = parseInt(thisObj.style.left) + 10;
   ```

4. Assign a new location to the `top` attribute of the element's `style` object so that the final function looks like this:

   ```
   thisObj.style.top = parseInt(thisObj.style.top) + 10;
   ```

- The `style` object referred to here and the `document.getElementByID` method are only available in newer browsers with robust support for the Domain Object Model. This means this task will only work in Internet Explorer 5 and later or Netscape 6 and later.

- The `parseInt` function is used here in resetting the left position because `left` returns a string such as `100px`. `parseInt` converts this string into a numeric value, such as `100`, to which you can safely add 10 pixels.

- In Sep 6 notice the use of a `javascript:` URL in the link. This URL causes the specified JavaScript code to execute when the user clicks on the link.

- When you call the `moveDiagonally` function, you pass in the object ID as a string; that is why `myObject` is contained in single quotes.

- The `style` property is actually an object reflecting all the CSS style settings for an object. This includes the `left` and `top` attributes:

   `object.style.left`

   `object.style.top`

5. In the body of the document, create a layer and position it wherever you want using the `style` attribute of the `div` tag. Specify `myObject` as the ID for the layer:

```
<div id="myObject" style="position: absolute; left: 50px; ⤵
top: 200px; background-color: #cccccc;">My Object</div>
```

6. Create a link the user can click to call the `moveDiagonally` function, so the final page looks like Listing 163-1.

```
<head>
 <script language="JavaScript">
  function moveDiagonally(objectID) {
   var thisObj = document.getElementById(objectID);

   thisObj.style.left = parseInt(thisObj.style.left) + 10;
   thisObj.style.top = parseInt(thisObj.style.top) + 10;
   }
 </script>
</head>

<body>
<div id="myObject" style="position: absolute; left: ⤵
50px; top: 200px; background-color: #cccccc;">My Object</div>

 <a href="javascript:moveDiagonally('myObject');">Move ⤵
Object diagonally.</a>
</body>
```

Listing 163-1: Moving a page element.

7. Save the file and close it.

8. Open the file in a browser, and you see the link and object.

9. Click on the link several times, and the element moves progressively further along the diagonal.

cross-reference

▪ Task 161 shows you how to move an object horizontally, while Task 162 shows you how to move an object vertically.

Controlling Object Movement with Buttons

The following steps show how to build a page with a layer element and four buttons. The buttons move the layer element up, down, right, or left.

notes

- The parseInt function is used here in resetting the top position because top returns a string such as 100px. parseInt converts this string into a numeric value, such as 100, to which you can safely add 10 pixels.

- When you call the moveDiagonally function, you pass in the object ID as a string; that is why myObject is contained in single quotes.

1. In the header of a new document, create a script block containing a function named moveUp. The function should take one argument that contains the ID of the element to work with and should subtract 10 pixels from the top property of the element's style object:

```
function moveUp(objectID) {
    var thisObj = document.getElementById(objectID);
    thisObj.style.top = parseInt(thisObj.style.top) - 10;
}
```

2. Create another function called moveDown. The function should work just like moveUp, except that it adds 10 pixels to the top property:

```
thisObj.style.top = parseInt(thisObj.style.top) + 10;
```

3. Create another function called moveRight. The function should work just like moveUp, except that it adds 10 pixels to the left property:

```
thisObj.style.left = parseInt(thisObj.style.left) + 10;
```

4. Create another function called moveLeft. The function should work like moveUp, except that it subtracts 10 pixels from the left property:

```
thisObj.style.left = parseInt(thisObj.style.left) - 10;
```

5. In the body of the document, create a layer and position it wherever you want using the style attribute of the div tag. Specify myObject as the ID for the layer:

```
<div id="myObject" style="position: absolute; left: 50px; ⊃
top: 200px; background-color: #cccccc;">My Object</div>
```

6. Create four buttons using the input tag. Each button should display a symbol (using the value attribute), indicating which direction it moves the object in and should use the onClick event handler to call the appropriate function specified earlier.

7. Use a table to position the buttons in a diamond layout so that the final page looks like Listing 164-1.

```
<head>
 <script language="JavaScript">
   function moveUp(objectID) {
     var thisObj = document.getElementById(objectID);
```
                                                        (continued)

```
      thisObj.style.top = parseInt(thisObj.style.top) - 10;
    }
    function moveDown(objectID) {
      var thisObj = document.getElementById(objectID);
      thisObj.style.top = parseInt(thisObj.style.top) + 10;
    }
    function moveRight(objectID) {
      var thisObj = document.getElementById(objectID);
      thisObj.style.left = parseInt(thisObj.style.left) + 10;
    }
    function moveLeft(objectID) {
      var thisObj = document.getElementById(objectID);
      thisObj.style.left = parseInt(thisObj.style.left) - 10;
    }
    </script>
</head>

<body>
<div id="myObject" style="position: absolute; left: ⤵
50px; top: 200px; background-color: #cccccc;">My Object</div>
 <table>
  <tr valign="bottom">
    <td colspan="2" align="center">
        <input type="button" value="^" ⤵
onClick="moveUp('myObject');">
    </td></tr>
  <tr valign="middle">
    <td align="right">
        <input type="button" value="<" ⤵
onClick="moveLeft('myObject');">
    </td>
    <td align="left">
        <input type="button" value=">" ⤵
onClick="moveRight('myObject');">
    </td></tr>
  <tr valign="top">
    <td colspan="2" align="center">
        <input type="button" value="v" ⤵
onClick="moveDown('myObject');">
    </td></tr>
  </table>
</body>
```

Listing 164-1: Controlling element placement using buttons.

8. Save the file and open it in a browser. You now see the buttons and object.

9. Click repeatedly on the buttons, and the element moves in the directions indicated by the buttons.

cross-reference

* See Task 163 for more background information on the style object and the other variables used in this task.

Creating the Appearance of Three-Dimensional Movement

Every element of your page has an object associated with it that can be accessed through JavaScript. For instance, you can determine an object's location in the browser window using this object as well as its size.

The following steps show how to build a page with a layer element that starts in the top left at 100 by 100 pixels and moves down and to the right while progressively increasing in size, until it has moved 100 pixels from its original starting position. The result is an effect of a square moving closer to the user.

1. In the header of a new document, create a script block containing a function named moveObject. The function should take one argument that contains the ID of the element to work with:

```
function moveObject(objectID) {
}
```

2. Create a variable named thisObj, and associate it with the object specified in the function's argument. Use document.getElementById:

```
var thisObj = document.getElementById(objectID);
```

3. Assign new locations to the left and top attributes of the style object:

```
thisObj.style.left = parseInt(thisObj.style.left) + 10;
thisObj.style.top = parseInt(thisObj.style.top) + 10;
```

4. Assign new values to the height and width attributes of the element's style object. Increase the size by 10 percent in each direction each time by multiplying the current height and width by 1.1:

```
thisObj.style.width = parseInt(thisObj.style.width) * 1.1;
thisObj.style.height = parseInt(thisObj.style.height) *
1.1;
```

5. As the last step in the function, you have to decide if the object should move again. Test the current location, and if the left position of the object is less than 200 pixels, use the window.setTimeout method to schedule the function run again. The final function looks like this:

```
function moveObject(objectID) {
    thisObj = document.getElementById(objectID);
    thisObj.style.left = parseInt(thisObj.style.left) + 10;
    thisObject.style.top = parseInt(thisObject.style.
top) + 10;
    thisObj.style.width = parseInt(thisObj.style.width)
* 1.1;
```

notes

- This task illustrates a very crude implementation of an object moving in three dimensions toward the user. It is meant to illustrate that you can precisely control the positioning and height of page elements dynamically in JavaScript to create whatever visual effects you require in your applications.

- The parseInt function is used here in resetting the position because the properties return a string such as 100px. parseInt converts this string into a numeric value, such as 100, to which you can safely add 10 pixels.

- The window.set Timeout method takes two arguments: the function to call and the number of millisecond to wait before calling the function. In specifying the function, you need to specify its arguments as well. This is done here so that the actual function call will look like this: moveObject- ('myObject').

- When you call the moveObject function, you pass in the object ID as a string; that is why myObject is contained in single quotes (see Step 7).

- The onLoad event handler specifies JavaScript code to execute once the page completes loading. This way, once the page is loaded and the page element exists, you will animate, you begin the animation of the element.

```
thisObj.style.height = parseInt(thisObj.style.height) *
1.1;

    if (parseInt(thisObj.style.left) < 200) {
        window.setTimeout("moveObject('" + objectID +
"')",150);
    }
}
```

6. In the body of the document, create a layer named myObject, and
   position it wherever you want using the style attribute of the
   div tag:

```
<div id="myObject" style="position: absolute; left: 50px;
top: 200px; background-color: #cccccc;">My Object</div>
```

7. In the onLoad event handler of the body tag, call the moveObject
   function to start the animation. The final page is in Listing 165-1.

```
<head>
 <script language="JavaScript">
  function moveObject(objectID) {
   thisObj = document.getElementById(objectID);
   thisObj.style.left = parseInt(thisObj.style.left) + 10;
   thisObj.style.top = parseInt(thisObj.style.top) + 10;
   thisObj.style.width = parseInt(thisObj.style.width) ⤶
* 1.1;
   thisObj.style.height = parseInt(thisObj.style.height) ⤶
* 1.1;

    if (parseInt(thisObj.style.left) < 200) {
       window.setTimeout("moveObject('" + objectID + ⤶
         "')",150);
    }
  }
 </script>
</head>

<body onLoad="moveObject('myObject');">
<div id="myObject" style="position: absolute; left: 50px; ⤶
top: 50px; height: 50px; width: 50px; background-color: ⤶
#cccccc;"></div>
</body>
```

Listing 165-1: Animating an object in apparent three dimensions.

8. Save the file and open it in a browser. You now see the initial page
   block element. The element animates, moving down and to the right
   and growing larger until it reaches its final position.

Centering an Object Vertically

With JavaScript, you can determine the dimensions of the working area of the browser window. Using this information, you can precisely position elements in the center of the browser window. This means you can center a page element vertically if needed.

To do this, you need to know the height of the working area of the window. The way you do this depends on the browser you are using:

- In Netscape 6 and higher, the `window.innerHeight` property indicates the height of the working area of the browser window in pixels.

- In Internet Explorer, the `document.body.clientHeight` property indicates the height in pixels.

To center an object vertically, you will also need to know its height and be able to reset its height. The height of a page element is obtained from the `height` property of the `style` object associated with the element.

To reference the element's object, you use the `document.getElementById` method. You obtain a reference to an object with the following:

```
var objRef = document.getElementById("elementName");
```

This means `objRef` would then refer to the object for the element named `elementName`, and you could reference its height with this:

```
objRef.style.height
```

The following task creates a layer on the page along with a link. When the user clicks the link, the object will be centered vertically in the browser window:

1. In the header of a new document, create a script block containing a function named `centerVertically`. The function should take one argument called `objectID`, which contains the ID of the element to work with.

2. Create a variable named `thisObj`, and associate it with the object ID specified in the function's argument. Use `document.getElementById`:

   ```
   var thisObj = document.getElementById(objectID);
   ```

3. Create a variable named `height`, and store the height of the working area of the browser window in a variable:

   ```
   var height = (window.innerHeight) ? window.↵
   innerHeight : document.body.clientHeight;
   ```

notes

- The `style` object referred to here and the `document.getElementByID` method are only available in newer browsers with robust support for the Domain Object Model. This means this task will only work in Internet Explorer 5 and later or Netscape 6 and later.

- Here you can see an example of short-form conditional evaluation. This takes the form `(condition) ? value if true : value if false`. What the condition in this example says is this: ""If `window.innerHeight` exists, then assign that value to `height`; otherwise, assign `document.body.clientHeight` to `height`."

- The formula for placing the page element vertically in the center has to determine where to place the top edge of the object. You know that the object takes up some amount of space, and exactly half of the remaining space in the window should be above the object. Therefore, you subtract the height of the object from the height of the window and divide by two to find out where to place the top edge of the page element.

- When you call the `centerVertically` function, you pass in the object ID as a string; that is why `myObject` is contained in single quotes.

4. Assign the height of the object to it a variable named
   `objectHeight`:

   ```
   var objectHeight = parseInt(thisObject.style.height);
   ```

5. Calculate the correct placement of the top of the object, and store it
   in the variable `newLocation`:

   ```
   var newLocation = (height - objectHeight) / 2;
   ```

6. Assign this new location to the `height` attribute of the element's
   `style` object:

   ```
   thisObj.style.top = newLocation;
   ```

7. In the body of the document, create a layer named `myObject`, and
   position it wherever you want using the `style` attribute of the
   `div` tag:

   ```
   <div id="myObject" style="position: absolute; left: ⤶
   50px; top: 200px; background-color: #cccccc;">My ⤶
   Object</div>
   ```

8. Create a link the user can click to call the `centerVertically` function, so the final page looks like Listing 166-1.

   ```
   <head>
    <script language="JavaScript">
     function centerVertically(objectID) {
       var thisObj = document.getElementById(objectID);
       var height = (window.innerHeight) ? window.innerHeight⤶
          : document.body.clientHeight;
       var objectHeight = parseInt(thisObj.style.height);
       var newLocation = (height - objectHeight) / 2;
       thisObj.style.top = newLocation;
     }
    </script>
   </head>

   <body>
   <div id="myObject" style="position: absolute; left: 50px; ⤶
   top: 200px; background-color: #cccccc;">My Object</div>

   <a href="javascript:centerVertically('myObject');">Center ⤶
   object vertically.</a>
   </body>
   ```

Listing 166-1: Centering an object vertically.

9. Open the file in a browser, and you now see the link and object. Click
   on the link and the object repositions to the vertical center of the
   document area of the browser window.

Task 167

Centering an Object Horizontally

With JavaScript, you can determine the dimensions of the working area of the browser window. Using this information, you can precisely position elements in the center of the browser window. This means you can center a page element horizontally if needed.

To do this, you need to know the width of the working area of the window. The way you do this depends on the browser you are using:

- In Netscape 6 and higher, the window.innerWidth property indicates the width of the working area of the browser window in pixels.

- In Internet Explorer, the document.body.clientWidth property indicates the width in pixels.

To center an object horizontally, you will also need to know its width and be able to reset its width. The width of a page element is obtained from the width property of the style object associated with the element.

To reference the element's object, you use the document.getElementById method. You could obtain a reference to an object with the following:

```
var objRef = document.getElementById("elementName");
```

This means objRef would then refer to the object for the element named elementName, and you could reference the width of the layer with this:

```
objRef.style.width
```

The following task creates a layer on the page along with a link. When the user clicks the link, the object will be centered horizontally in the browser window.

1. In the header of a new document, create a script block containing a function named centerHorizontally. The function should take one argument called objectID, which contains the ID of the element to work with.

2. Create a variable named thisObj, and associate it with the object ID specified in the function's argument. Use document.getElementById:

   ```
   var thisObj = document.getElementById(objectID);
   ```

3. Create a variable named width, and store the height of the working area of the browser window in the variable:

   ```
   var height = (window.innerWidth) ? window.innerWidth : ⤶
   document.body.clientWidth;
   ```

notes

- The style object r eferred to here and the document.getElement ByID method are only available in newer browsers with robust support for the Domain Object Model. This means this task will only work in Internet Explorer 5 and later or Netscape 6 and later.

- Here you can see an example of short-form conditional evaluation. This takes the form (condition) ? value if true : value if false. What the condition in this example says is this: "If win dow.innerWidth exists, then assign that value to width; otherwise, assign document.body. clientWidth to width."

- The formula for placing the page element horizontally in the center has to deter mine where to place the left edge of the object. You know that the object takes up some amount of space, and exactly half of the remaining space in the window should be to the left of the object. Therefore, you subtract the width of the object from the width of the window and then divide by two to find out where to place the left edge of the page element (see Step 5).

- In Step 8 notice the use of a javascript: URL in the link. This URL causes the specified JavaScript code to execute when the user clicks on the link.

Task **167**

4. Assign the width of the object to a variable named `objectWidth`:

```
var objectWidth = parseInt(thisObj.style.width);
```

5. Calculate the correct placement of the left of the object, and store it in the variable `newLocation`:

```
var newLocation = (width - objectWidth) / 2;
```

6. Assign this new location to the `width` attribute of the element's `style` object:

```
thisObj.style.left = newLocation;
```

7. Create a layer and position it wherever you want using the `style` attribute of the `div` tag. Specify `myObject` as the ID for the layer:

```
<div id="myObject" style="position: absolute; left: ⊃
50px; top: 200px; background-color: #cccccc;">My ⊃
Object</div>
```

8. Create a link the user can click to call the `centerHorizontally` function, so the final page looks like Listing 167-1.

```
<head>
 <script language="JavaScript">
   function centerHorizontally(objectID) {
     var thisObj = document.getElementById(objectID);
     var width = (window.innerWidth) ? window.innerWidth :
        document.body.clientWidth;
     var objectWidth = parseInt(thisObj.style.width);
     var newLocation = (width - objectWidth) / 2;
     thisObj.style.left = newLocation;
   }
 </script>
</head>

<body>
<div id="myObject" style="position: absolute; left: 50px; ⊃
top: 200px; background-color: #cccccc;">My Object</div>

<a href= "javascript:centerHorizontally('myObject');"> ⊃
Center object horizontally.</a>
</body>
```

Listing 167-1: Centering an object horizontally.

9. Open the file in a browser, and you now see the link and object. Click on the link, and the object repositions to the horizontal center of the document area of the browser window.

Controlling Line Height in CSS

As browser support for cascading style sheets has improved, so too has the ability of Web designers to control all aspects of their pages' appearance through Dynamic HTML.

One of the aspects of the appearance of your pages that can be controlled through style sheets is the line spacing used for text. This is controlled with the `line-height` attribute:

```
<div style="line-height: 20px;">
   Text goes here
</div>
```

The following task illustrates this attribute by displaying text with a variety of spacing set:

1. Create a new HTML document in your preferred editor.

2. In the body of your document, create a layer containing text. Set the line spacing tightly:

```
<div style="font-size: 24px; line-height: 18px;">This
is a paragraph with really tight line spacing as you
can see.</div>
```

3. Create another layer, and set the line spacing moderately:

```
<div style="font-size: 24px; line-height: 30px;">This
is a paragraph with pretty standard line spacing as you
can see.</div>
```

4. Create another layer, and set the line spacing loosely. The final page should look like Listing 168-1.

```
<body>

    <div style="font-size: 24px; line-height: 18px;">This
is a paragraph with really tight line spacing as you can
see.</div>

    <hr>
```

(continued)

notes

- Dynamic HTML is the combination of JavaScript, cascading style sheets, and the Domain Object Model, which together make it possible to build sophisticated interactive user interfaces and applications that run in the browser.

- You only need to specify these style attributes to enforce them. For instance, if you don't want extra line spacing, you can normally leave out `line-height`.

```
        <div style="font-size: 24px; line-height: 30px;">This
is a paragraph with pretty standard line spacing as you
can see.</div>

        <hr>

        <div style="font-size: 24px; line-height: 48px;">This
is a paragraphy with pretty loose line spacing as you can
see.</div>

</body>
```

Listing 168-1: Changing line spacing.

5. Save the file and close it.

6. Open the file in your browser, and you should see three blocks of text with different line spacing, as in Figure 168-1.

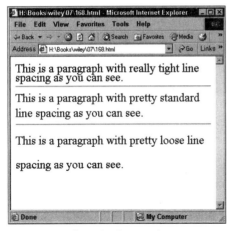

Figure 168-1: Changing line spacing

cross-reference

- Task 158 shows you how to control the line spacing using JavaScript.

Creating Drop Shadows with CSS

As browser support for cascading style sheets has improved, so too has the ability for you to implement special visual effects purely in Dynamic HTML code. One such effect is a drop shadow, such as the one in Figure 169-1.

Figure 169-1: A drop shadow down with absolute positioning.

Drop shadows on rectangular page elements is simple: You need one layer to be positioned behind and slightly offset from another. For example, the following creates a block box with a 5-pixel-wide gray shadow:

```
<div style="background-color: #cccccc; width: 100px; height: ⤷
100px; position: absolute; left: 105px; top: 105px;"> </div>
<div style="background-color: #000000; width: 100px; height: ⤷
100px; position: absolute; left: 100px; top: 100px;"> </div>
```

The problem with this approach is that it requires absolute and precise positioning of both the shadow and the main layer. Relative positioning in the flow of a document is not possible. Consider the following code:

```
<div style="background-color: #cccccc; width: 100px; height: ⤷
100px; position: relative; left: 105px; top: 105px;"> </div>
<div style="background-color: #000000; width: 100px; height: ⤷
100px; position: relative; left: 100px; top: 100px;"> </div>
```

This fails to create the drop shadow, as illustrated in Figure 169-2.

The solution lies in embedded layers. The outer `div` tag specifies the dimensions and color of the shadow. Inside the `div` block, a second `div` block specifies the dimensions, color, and relative placement of the front layer. Then, the outer `div` tag can be positioned using absolute or relative positioning, and the entire unit will be placed together. A drop shadow is illustrated in the following steps:

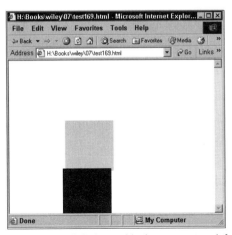

Figure 169-2: Relative positioning may not work for drop shadows.

1. In a new document, create a body block with a layer for the shadow. Specify the height, width, and color of the shadow:

```
<body>
<div style="width: 100px; height: 100px; position: ⏎
relative; background: #cccccc;"> </div>
</body>
```

2. Inside the layer for the shadow, create the layer to sit on top of the shadow. In addition to the dimensions and color of the layer, use relative positioning to position that layer to the left and slightly up from the shadow, so that the final document looks like Listing 169-1.

```
<body>
  <div style="width: 100px; height: 100px; position: ⏎
relative; background: #cccccc;">
      <div style="width: 100px; height: 100px; background: ⏎
#00ffff; position: relative; left: -4px; top: -4px;">
      This box has a drop shadow.
      </div>
   </div>
</body>
```

Listing 169-1: Creating a drop shadow.

3. Save the file and close it.

4. Open the file in a browser, and you now see a box with a drop shadow.

cross-reference

- In Task 170, you'll see how to modify a drop shadow.

Task 170

Modifying a Drop Shadow

The ability of Web designers to implement visual effects purely in their Dynamic HTML code has improved thanks to browser support for cascading style sheets. One such effect is a drop shadow, such as the one shown in Figure 170-1.

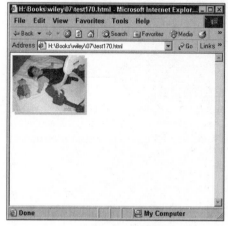

Figure 170-1: A displayed drop shadow.

In this task, you will see how to manipulate the visual attributes of your drop shadow from JavaScript once the shadow is in place. You can manipulate any style attribute of the shadow by providing an ID for the shadow's layer and then accessing the `style` property of the layer's object.

This task creates a drop shadow and then provides two links: When the user clicks the first link, the color of the shadow changes, and when the user clicks the second link, the width of the shadow changes.

1. In the header of a new document, create a script block containing a function named `changeDropColor`. The function should take one argument, which contains the ID of the element to work with:

    ```
    function changeDropColor(dropID) {
    }
    ```

2. Create a variable named `dropObject`, and associate it with the object specified in the function's argument. Use `document.getElementById`:

    ```
    var dropObject = document.getElementById(dropID);
    ```

3. Change the color assigned to the background attribute of the element's `style` object:

    ```
    dropObject.style.background = "#000000";
    ```

notes

- You can refer to an object's background color with `object.style.background`.

- To reference the element's object, you use the `document.getElementById` method:

  ```
  var objectRef =
  document.getElementById(
      "element ID");
  ```

  The variable `objectRef` then refers to the object associated with the element specified in the ID.

- The `style` object referred to here and the `document.getElementById` method are only available in newer browsers with robust support for the Domain Object Model. This means this task will only work in Internet Explorer 5 and later or Netscape 6 and later.

- By increasing the width and height of the shadow by 5 pixels each, you make the shadow stick that much further out from behind the front layer, which makes the shadow seem thicker.

- In Step 7 notice the use of a `javascript:` URL in the link. This URL causes the specified JavaScript code to execute when the user clicks on the link.

- When you call the `changeDropColor` function, you pass in the object ID as a string; that is why `myObject` is contained in single quotes.

4. Create another function named `changeDropWidth`. The function should take one argument containing the ID of the element to work with. The function should work in the same way as `changeDropColor`, except that the dimensions of the element are changed instead of the background color (see Listing 170-1).

5. In the body of the document, create your drop shadow. Make sure the outer layer has the ID `myDrop`.

6. Create a link the user can click to call the `changeDropColor` function.

7. Create another link the user can click to call the `changeDropWidth` function, so the final page looks like Listing 170-1.

cross-reference

■ The method for creating this type of drop shadow with cascading style sheets is discussed in depth in Task 169. This task is based on the principles from Task 169.

```
<head>
    <script language="JavaScript">
        function changeDropColor(dropID) {
            var dropObject = document.getElementById(dropID);
            dropObject.style.background = "#000000";
        }
        function changeDropWidth(dropID) {
            var dropObject = document.getElementById(dropID);
            dropObject.style.width = 105;
            dropObject.style.height = 105;
        }
    </script>
</head>

<body>
    <div id="myDrop" style="width: 100px; height: 100px; ⊃
position: relative; left: 0px; top: 0px; background: ⊃
#cccccc;">
        <div style="width: 100px; height: 100px; background: ⊃
#00ffff; position: relative; left: -4px; top: -4px;">
            This box has a drop shadow.
        </div>
    </div>
    <a href="javascript:changeDropColor('myDrop');">Change ⊃
Color of the Drop Shadow</a><br>
    <a href="javascript:changeDropWidth('myDrop');">Change ⊃
Width of the Drop Shadow</a>
</body>
```

Listing 170-1: Changing the appearance of a drop shadow.

8. Save the file and open it in a browser. You now see the drop shadow that was illustrated in Figure 170-1.

9. Clicking the first link changes the shadow's color to black. Clicking the second increases the width of the shadow by 5 pixels.

Removing a Drop Shadow

The ability of Web designers to implement visual effects purely in their Dynamic HTML code has improved thanks to browser support for cascading style sheets. One such effect is a drop shadow, such as the one shown in Figure 171-1.

notes

- You can refer to an object's background color with `object.style.background`.

- To reference the element's object, you use the `document.getElement ById` method:

```
var objectRef =
document.getElement
ById(
    "element ID");
```

The variable `objectRef` then refers to the object associated with the element specified in the ID.

- The `style` object referred to here and the `document.getElement ById` method are only available in newer browsers with robust support for the Domain Object Model. This means this task will only work in Internet Explorer 5 and later or Netscape 6 and later.

- By setting the `background` style property to `none`, you effectively remove the background color and make the drop shadow layer transparent.

- In Step 5 notice the use of a `javascript:` URL in the link. This URL causes the specified JavaScript code to execute when the user clicks on the link.

- When you call the `removeDrop` function, you pass in the object ID as a string; that is why `myObject` is contained in single quotes.

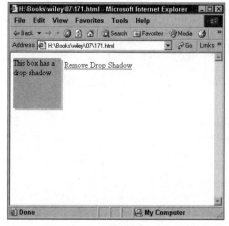

Figure 171-1: A displayed drop shadow.

In this task, you will see how to manipulate the visual attributes of your drop shadow from JavaScript in order to remove the shadow. You can manipulate any style attribute of the shadow by providing an ID for the shadow's layer and then accessing the `style` property of the layer's object.

This task creates a drop shadow and then provides a link. When the user clicks the link, the drop shadow disappears.

1. In the header of a new document, create a script block containing a function named `removeDrop`. The function should take one argument that contains the ID of the element to work with:

```
function removeDrop(dropID) {
}
```

2. Create a variable named `dropObject`, and associate it with the object specified in the function's argument. Use `document.getElementById`:

```
var dropObject = document.getElementById(dropID);
```

3. Change the color assigned to the background attribute of the element's `style` object to `none` so that the final function looks like this:

```
function changeDropColor(dropID) {
   var dropObject = document.getElementById(dropID);
   dropObject.style.background = "none";
}
```

4. In the body of the document, create your drop shadow. Make sure the outer layer has the ID myDrop:

```
<div id="myDrop" style="width: 100px; height: 100px; ⤵
position: relative; left: 0px; top: 0px; background: ⤵
#cccccc;">
    <div style="width: 100px; height: 100px; background: ⤵
#00ffff; position: relative; left: -4px; top: -4px;">
        This box has a drop shadow.
    </div>
</div>
```

5. Create a link the user can click to call the removeDrop function, so the final page looks like Listing 171-1.

```
<head>
    <script language="JavaScript">
        function removeDrop(dropID) {
            var dropObject = document.getElementById(dropID);
            dropObject.style.background = "none";
        }
    </script>
</head>

<body>
    <div id="myDrop" style="float: left; width: 100px; ⤵
height: 100px; position: relative; background: #cccccc;">
        <div style="float: left; width: 100px; height: ⤵
100px; background: #00ffff; position: relative; left: ⤵
-4px; top: -4px;">
            This box has a drop shadow.
        </div>
    </div>

    <a href="javascript:removeDrop('myDrop');">Remove Drop ⤵
Shadow</a>
</body>
```

Listing 171-1: Removing a drop shadow.

6. Save the file and open it in a browser. You now see the drop shadow.

7. Click on the link and the shadow disappears.

Task 172

Placing a Shadow on a Nonstandard Corner

notes

- Dynamic HTML is the combination of JavaScript, cascading style sheets, and the Domain Object Model, which together make it possible to build sophisticated interactive user interfaces and applications that run in the browser.

- The drop shadow effect described in this task will work on newer browsers such as Internet Explorer 5 and higher or Netscape 6 and higher.

As browser support for cascading style sheets has improved, so too has the ability for you to implement special visual effects purely in their Dynamic HTML code. One such effect is a drop shadow. In this task, you will see how you can make the "drop" shadow actually protrude from any corner of the element simply by adjusting the style attributes assigned to the inner layer of your drop shadow effect.

Task 169 shows how the typical drop shadow effect is created. In that task, you can see that the critical attributes that control the way the drop shadow works are the `left` and `top` style attributes on the inner `div` tag. The inner `div` tag specifies the front layer, which is positioned relative to the position of the shadow. Therefore, the following positioning rules apply to these two attributes:

- Use a negative value for the `left` attribute to make the shadow appear on the right of the element.

- Use a positive value for the `left` attribute to make the shadow appear on the left of the element.

- Use a negative value for the `top` attribute to make the shadow appear on the bottom of the element.

- Use a positive value for the `top` attribute to make the shadow appear on the top of the element.

The following task applies these principles to create three identical drop shadow effects, except that the shadow appears on a different, nonstandard corner of the element in each instance:

1. Create an element with a drop shadow in the top left using positive values for the `left` and `top` style attributes on the inner layer:

    ```
    <div style="width: 100px; height: 100px; position: ⮌
    relative; background: #cccccc;">
        <div style="width: 100px; height: 100px; ⮌
    background: #00ffff; position: relative; left: 4px; ⮌
    top: 4px;">
            This box has a drop shadow.
        </div></div>
    ```

2. Create an element with a drop shadow in the bottom left using a positive value for the `left` style attribute and a negative value for the `top` style attribute on the inner layer.

3. Finally, create an element with a drop shadow in the top right using a negative value for the `left` style attribute and a positive value for the `top` style attribute on the inner layer. The final page should look like Listing 172-1.

```
<body>
    <div style="width: 100px; height: 100px; position:
relative; background: #cccccc;">
        <div style="width: 100px; height: 100px; background:
#00ffff; position: relative; left: 4px; top: 4px;">
            This box has a Top/Left drop shadow.
    </div></div> <br>
    <div style="width: 100px; height: 100px; position:
relative; background: #cccccc;">
        <div style="width: 100px; height: 100px; background:
#00ffff; position: relative; left: 4px; top: -4px;">
            This box has a Bottom/Left drop shadow.
    </div></div> <br>
    <div style="width: 100px; height: 100px; position:
relative; background: #cccccc;">
        <div style="width: 100px; height: 100px; background:
#00ffff; position: relative; left: -4px; top: 4px;">
            This box has a Top/Right drop shadow.
    </div></div>
</body>
```

Listing 172-1: Placing the shadow on any nonstandard corner.

4. Save the file and close it.

5. Open the file in a browser, and you now see the drop shadow effects, as illustrated in Figure 172-1.

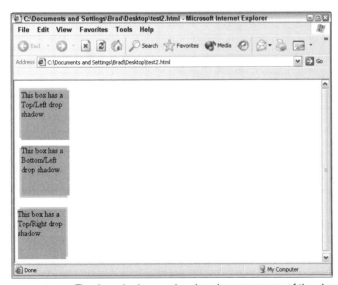

Figure 172-1: The drop shadow can be placed on any corner of the element.

Managing Z-Indexes in JavaScript

Using cascading style sheets, you can control the relative stacking order of layers. The stacking order of layers determines which layers appear on top of other layers when they overlap with each other. You control this stacking order with the z-index style attribute, which takes a numeric value. The larger the value, the higher a layer is in the stack.

The layer ordering information is part of the style property of the object. You can determine the layer order position of an object by using object.style. zindex. The following steps create two overlapping layers with links to adjust which layer is on top:

1. In the header of a new document, create a script block containing a function named swapLayer that takes two arguments named topTarget (which will contain the layer ID for the layer to move to the top) and bottomTarget (which will contain the layer ID for the layer to move to the bottom):

```
function swapLayer(topTarget,bottomTarget) {    }
```

2. In the function, set the stacking order for the desired top layer to 2 and for the bottom layer to 1:

```
document.getElementById(topTarget).style.zIndex = 2;
document.getElementById(bottomTarget).style.zIndex = 1;
```

3. In the body of the document, create a layer named firstLayer with a stacking order of 1:

```
<div id="firstLayer" style=" ... z-index: 1;"> </div>
```

4. In the layer, create a link to call swapLayer designed to move the layer to the top of the stack; specify 'firstLayer' as the first argument and 'secondLayer' as the second argument:

```
<p><a href= ⤵
"javascript:swapLayer('firstLayer','secondLayer')">
Move to top</a></P>
```

5. Create a second layer named secondLayer with a stacking order of 2:

```
<div id="secondLayer" style=" ... z-index: 2;"> </div>
```

6. In the layer, create a link to call swapLayer design to move the layer to the top of the stack; specify 'secondLayer' as the first argument and 'firstLayer' as the second argument. The final page should look like Listing 173-1.

notes

- By default, layers stack on top of each other in the order in which they appear in the HTML file.

- To reference the element's object, you use the document.getElement ById method:

```
var objectRef =
document.getElement
ById(
   "element ID");
```

The variable objectRef then refers to the object associated with the element specified in the ID.

- See Listing 173-1 for the rest of the style attributes defined in Steps 3 and 5.

- The style object r eferred to here and the document.getElement ByID method are only available in newer browsers with robust support for the Domain Object Model. This means this task will only work in Internet Explorer 5 and later or Netscape 6 and later.

- Simply resetting one layer's stacking order doesn't alter another page element's stacking order. In order to cause the layers to flip positions in the stack as in this example, you need to change both layers' stacking order positions.

```
<head>
 <script language="JavaScript">
  function swapLayer(topTarget,bottomTarget) {
    document.getElementById(topTarget).style.zIndex = 2;
    document.getElementById(bottomTarget).style.zIndex = 1;
  }
 </script>
</head>
<body>
    <div id="firstLayer" style="position: absolute; left: ⏎
10px; top: 10px; width: 100px; height: 100px; background-⏎
color: yellow; z-index: 1;">
       <p><a href= ⏎
    "javascript:swapLayer('firstLayer','secondLayer')">⏎
    Move to top</a></P> </div>
    <div id="secondLayer" style="position: absolute; left: ⏎
60px; top: 60px; width: 100px; height: 100px; background-⏎
color: lightgrey; z-index: 2;">
       <p><a href=⏎
    "javascript:swapLayer('secondLayer','firstLayer')">⏎
    Move to top</a></P> </div>
</body>
```

Listing 173-1: Changing stacking order with JavaScript.

7. Save the file and close it. Open the file in a browser, and you now see two overlapping layers, as illustrated in Figure 173-1.

Figure 173-1: Overlapping layers.

8. Click on the Move to Top link in the bottom layer, and it moves to the top of the stack. Click on the Move to Top link in the other layer, and you should return to the original state of the page.

Setting Fonts for Text with CSS

A s browser support for cascading style sheets has improved, so too has the ability for you to control all aspects of your pages' appearance through Dynamic HTML. One of the aspects of the appearance of your pages that can be controlled through style sheets is the font used for text. You can control this with the `font-family` style attribute. For instance, the following sets all text in a layer to Arial:

```
<div style="font-family: Arial;">
    Text goes here
</div>
```

Similarly, you can change a font inline using the `span` tag:

```
<p>
    This is text. Some of it <span style="font-family: Arial;">is
in Arial.</span>
</p>
```

This results in the text shown in Figure 174-1.

Figure 174-1: Changing font inline with a style sheet.

When specifying fonts, you have no way to guarantee the user will have the fonts on his or her browser. For this reason, you typically specify a list of fonts such as the following:

```
font-family: Arial, Helvetica, SANS-SERIF;
```

Here, if the user doesn't have Arial installed, his or her browser will use Helvetica. If Helvetica isn't installed, then SANS-SERIF is used. SANS-SERIF is one of a special group of font names provided in cascading style sheets. It indicates that the browser should use its default sans serif font instead of a specific font.

The following task illustrates the `font-family` attribute by displaying text in three different fonts:

1. In the body of your document, create a layer containing text. Specify `Times, SERIF` as the `font-family` style:

```
<div style="font-family: Times, SERIF;">This type is ⮐
Times</div>
```

2. Create another layer containing text. This time specify `Arial, SANS-SERIF`:

```
<div style="font-family: Arial, SANS-SERIF;">This type ⮐
is Arial</div>
```

3. Create another layer containing text. This time specify `Courier, MONOSPACE`. The final page should look like Listing 174-1.

```
<body>
    <div style="font-family: Times, SERIF;">This type is ⮐
Times</div>
    <div style="font-family: Arial, SANS-SERIF;">This type ⮐
is Arial</div>
    <div style="font-family: Courier, MONOSPACE;">This type ⮐
is Courier</div>
</body>
```

Listing 174-1: Changing font family.

4. Save the file and close it.

5. Open the file in your browser, and you should see three blocks of text in different fonts, as in Figure 174-2.

Figure 174-2: Changing fonts with `font-family`.

tip
- Two other special font names you might want to use are SERIF (the browser's default serif font) and MONOSPACE (the browser's default mono-spaced font).

cross-reference
- Task 175 shows you how to control the style for text (such as size and bolding).

Setting Font Style for Text with CSS

As browser support for cascading style sheets has improved, so too has the ability of Web designers to control all aspects of their pages' appearance through Dynamic HTML.

One of the aspects of the appearance of your pages that can be controlled through style sheets is the style used for text. For instance, you can control the following:

- Use the `font-style` style attribute to control the italicization of text. The following makes text italic:

```
<div style="font-style: italic;">
    Text goes here
</div>
```

- Use the `font-weight` style attribute to control the boldness of text. The following makes text bold:

```
The following text is bold: <span style="font-weight: ⤸
bold;">This is bold</span>
```

- Use the `font-size` style attribute to control the size of text. You can specify sizes in points (such as `24pt`), in pixels (such as `18px`), or as some fraction of the default font size (such as `1.5em`). Typically, you will use points or pixels (which are more consistent between browsers and operating systems), as in the following:

```
<div style="font-size: 18px;">
    Text goes here
</div>
```

- Use the `text-decoration` attribute to control underlining of text. The following makes text underlined:

```
The following text is underlined: <span style="text-⤸
decoration: underline;">This is underlined</span>
```

The following task illustrates these attributes by displaying text in all four styles, as well as combining the styles:

1. In the body of your document, create a layer containing text. Make the text italic:

```
<div style="font-style: italic;">This type is ⤸
Italics</div>
```

2. Create another layer and make the text bold:

```
<div style="font-weight: bold;">This type is Bold</div>
```

notes

- Dynamic HTML is the combination of JavaScript, cascading style sheets, and the Domain Object Model, which together make it possible to build sophisticated interactive user interfaces and applications that run in the browser.

- You only need to specify these style attributes to enforce them. For instance, if you don't want bold text, you can normally leave out `font-weight`.

3. Create another layer and make the text 24 point:

```
<div style="font-size: 24pt;">This type is 24pt</div>
```

4. Create another layer and make the text underlined:

```
<div style="text-decoration: underline;">This type is ⏎
Underlined</div>
```

5. Create another layer containing text, and apply all four styles from the previous layers. The final page should look like Listing 175-1.

```
<body>
    <div style="font-style: italic;">This type is ⏎
Italics</div>
    <div style="font-weight: bold;">This type is Bold</div>
    <div style="font-size: 24pt;">This type is 24pt</div>
    <div style="text-decoration: underline;">This type is ⏎
Underlined</div>
    <div style="font-style: italic; font-weight: bold; ⏎
font-size: 24pt; text-decoration: underline;">This type ⏎
has all four styles</div>
</body>
```

Listing 175-1: Changing font styles.

6. Save the file and close it.

7. Open the file in your browser, and you should see five blocks of text in different styles, as in Figure 175-1.

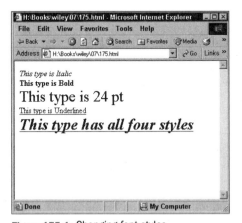

Figure 175-1: Changing font styles.

cross-reference

- Task 174 shows you how to change the font used on text.

Controlling Text Alignment with CSS

As browser support for cascading style sheets has improved, so too has the ability of Web designers to control all aspects of their pages' appearance through Dynamic HTML.

One of the aspects of the appearance of your pages that can be controlled through style sheets is alignment of text. You can control this with the `text-align` style attribute. For instance, the following sets all text in a layer to be centered:

```
<div style="text-align: center;">
    Text goes here
</div>
```

This results in the text shown in Figure 176-1.

notes

• Dynamic HTML is the combination of JavaScript, cascading style sheets, and the Domain Object Model, which together make it possible to build sophisticated interactive user interfaces and applications that run in the browser.

• Normally, you will only apply text alignment to layers (`div` tags, as well as standard HTML elements such as `h1`, `p`, and so on) but not to inline text (`span` tags).

Figure 176-1: Changing font alignment to centered.

The following task illustrates the `text-align` attribute by displaying text in three different alignments:

1. Create a new HTML document in your preferred editor.

2. In the body of your document, create a layer containing text. Specify `left` as the `text-align` style:

```
<div style="text-align: left;">This type is left-
aligned</div>
```

3. Create another layer containing text. This time specify `center`:

```
<div style="text-align: center;">This type is
centered</div>
```

4. Create another layer containing text. This time specify `right`. The final page should look like Listing 176-1.

```
<body>

    <div style="text-align: left;">This type is left-
aligned</div>

    <div style="text-align: center;">This type is
centered</div>

    <div style="text-align: right;">This type is right-
aligned</div>

</body>
```

Listing 176-1: Changing text alignment.

5. Save the file and close it.

6. Open the file in your browser, and you should see three blocks of text with different alignments, as in Figure 176-2.

Figure 176-2: Changing alignment with `text-align`.

cross-reference

■ Task 174 shows you how to change the font for text, while Task 175 shows you how to change the styles (such as bolding and size).

Task 177

Controlling Spacing with CSS

notes

- Dynamic HTML is the combination of JavaScript, cascading style sheets, and the Domain Object Model, which together make it possible to build sophisticated interactive user interfaces and applications that run in the browser.

- You only need to specify these style attributes to enforce them. For instance, if you don't want extra letter spacing, you can normally leave out `letter-spacing`.

As browser support for cascading style sheets has improved, so too has the ability of Web designers to control all aspects of their pages' appearance through Dynamic HTML.

One of the aspects of the appearance of your pages that can be controlled through style sheets is the spacing used for text. For instance, you can control the following:

- Use the `letter-spacing` style attribute to control the spacing of letters. You can specify spacing in pixels (such as `10px`) or as some fraction of the width of the letter "m" in the font you are using (such as `2.0em`):

```
<div style="letter-spacing: 20px;">
    Text goes here
</div>
```

- Use the `word-spacing` style attribute to control the spacing between words in pixels or em units:

```
The following text has larger word spacing: <span
style="word-spacing: 3.0em;">This has bigger word
spacing</span>
```

The following task illustrates these attributes by displaying text with a variety of spacing set:

1. Create a new HTML document in your preferred editor.

2. In the body of your document, create a layer containing text. Set the letter spacing using pixels:

```
<div style="letter-spacing: 10px;">These letters are 10
pixels apart</div>
```

3. Create another layer and set the letter spacing as a fraction of the width of the letter "m":

```
<div style="letter-spacing: 2em;">These letters are
2 m's apart</div>
```

4. Create another layer and set the word spacing using pixels:

```
<div style="word-spacing: 30px;">These words are 30
pixels apart</div>
```

5. Create another layer and set the word spacing as a fraction of the
   width of the letter "m." The final page should look like Listing 177-1.

```
<body>

    <div style="letter-spacing: 10px;">These letters are ⤷
10 pixels apart</div>

    <div style="letter-spacing: 2em;">These ⤷
letters are 2 m's apart</div>

    <div style="word-spacing: 30px;">These words are 30 ⤷
pixels apart</div>

    <div style="word-spacing: 5em;">These words are 5 m's ⤷
apart</div>

</body>
```

Listing 177-1: Changing text spacing.

6. Save the file and close it.

7. Open the file in your browser, and you should see four blocks of text
   with different spacing, as in Figure 177-1.

Figure 177-1: Changing text spacing.

cross-reference

- In addition to spacing, you
  may want to control the
  alignment of your text. Task
  176 shows how to set the
  alignment.

Task 178

Controlling Absolute Placement with CSS

As browser support for cascading style sheets has improved, so too has the ability of Web designers to control all aspects of their pages' appearance through Dynamic HTML.

One of the aspects of the appearance of your pages that can be controlled through style sheets is the placement of layers. You can place layers in an absolute fashion by using the `position: absolute` style setting. You then use the `left` and `top` style attribute to specify the position of a layer relative to the top left corner of the document section of the browser window. Typically, you will set these values in pixels. For instance, consider the following layer:

```
<div style="position: absolute; left: 100px; right: 100px;">
   Text goes here
</div>
```

This results in text positioned 100 pixels below and to the right of the top left corner, as illustrated in Figure 178-1.

notes

- Dynamic HTML is the combination of JavaScript, cascading style sheets, and the Domain Object Model, which together make it possible to build sophisticated interactive user interfaces and applications that run in the browser.

- Layers are created with `div` tags and can contain any valid HTML in them. They are simply containers for the HTML to which you can apply styles for the whole layer.

- With absolute positioning, the order of layers really doesn't matter. In this example, the second layer visually appears in the flow of the page as being before the first layer.

Figure 178-1: Changing layer positioning.

The following task illustrates absolute positioning by displaying two absolutely positioned layers:

1. Create a new HTML document in your preferred editor.

2. In the body of your document, create a layer containing text and place it 200 pixels in and down from the top left corner:

```
<div style="position: absolute; top: 200px; left:
200px;">This text is placed 200 pixels from the top and
300 pixels from the left of the window</div>
```

3. Create another layer containing text, and place it right at the top left corner. The final page should look like Listing 178-1.

```
<body>

    <div style="position: absolute; top: 200px; left: ⟲
200px;">This text is placed 200 pixels from the top and ⟲
300 pixels from the left of the window</div>

    <div style="position: absolute; top: 0px; left: ⟲
0px;">This text is placed right in the top-left corner of ⟲
the window</div>

</body>
```

Listing 178-1: Controlling layer positioning.

4. Save the file and close it.

5. Open the file in your browser, and you should see the two layers, as in Figure 178-2.

Figure 178-2: Controlling layer positioning with absolute positioning.

cross-reference

■ More information on controlling the order of layers can be found in Task 173.

Controlling Relative Placement with CSS

As browser support for cascading style sheets has improved, so too has the ability of Web designers to control all aspects of their pages' appearance through Dynamic HTML.

One of the aspects of the appearance of your pages that can be controlled through style sheets is the placement of layers. Layers are created with `div` tags and can contain any valid HTML in them. They are simply containers for the HTML to which you can apply styles for the whole layer.

You can place layers in a relative fashion by using the `position: relative` style setting. This means that any positioning you specify is relative to where you would normally have expected the layer to appear in your document given its placement in the flow of HTML in your document.

You then use the `left` and `top` style attribute to specify the position of a layer relative to its normal place in the flow of the document. Typically, you will set these values in pixels. For instance, consider the following layer:

```
<div style="position: relative; left: 100px; right: 100px;">
   Text goes here
</div>
```

The following task illustrates relative positioning by creating a document that starts with a paragraph and then follows that with a relatively positioned layer:

1. Create a new HTML document in your preferred editor.

2. In the body of your document, create a paragraph:

   ```
   <p>
   Here is some text
   </p>
   ```

3. Create a relatively positioned layer to follow the paragraph. The final page should look like Listing 179-1.

```
<body>

    <p>Here is some text</p>

    <div style="position: relative;
        left: 50px;
        top: 100px;">
    This text is indented 50 pixels relative to the text
    before it and shifted down by 100 pixels
    </div>

</body>
```

Listing 179-1: Controlling layer positioning.

4. Save the file and close it.

5. Open the file in your browser, and you should see the two layers, as in Figure 179-1.

Figure 179-1: Controlling layer positioning with relative positioning.

cross-reference

■ Relative positioning can also be used in creating shadows. See Tasks 169 through 172 for more information on shadows.

Task 180

Adjusting Margins with CSS

notes

- Layers are created with `div` tags and can contain any valid HTML in them. They are simply containers for the HTML to which you can apply styles for the whole layer.

- When you are specifying all four margin widths with the `margin` attribute, the first value is for the top margin and then the values proceed clockwise, with the right margin, the bottom margin, and finally the left margin.

- This outer layer with a border is presented for visual purposes. It allows you to see where the margin occurs as the space between the visible edge of an inner layer and the border (see Step 2).

- The inner layer has a background color to show where the visible part of the layer ends and the margins start (see Step 3).

- By default, layers have no margins; so if you don't need a margin, you don't have to specify any margin-related style attributes (see Step 5).

As browser support for cascading style sheets has improved, so too has the ability for you to control all aspects of your pages' appearance through Dynamic HTML. One of the aspects of the appearance of your pages that can be controlled through style sheets is the margin of a layer.

To understand margins and their meaning in style sheets, you need to learn about the box model used in cascading style sheets. The box model defines a layer's outer components, as shown in Figure 180-1.

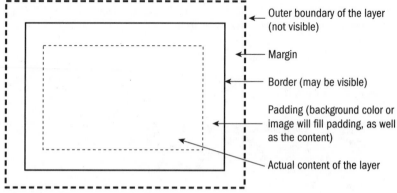

Figure 180-1: The CSS box model.

You control the width of the margin in one of several ways:

- Use the `margin` attribute to set the same margin width for all sides. The following creates 5-pixel margins on all sides of the layer:

```
<div style="margin: 5px;">
   Text goes here
</div>
```

- Use the `margin` attribute to set different widths for the different sides:

```
<div style="margin: 5px 10px 15px 20px;">
   Text goes here
</div>
```

- Specify distinct margins individually using the `margin-top`, `margin-bottom`, `margin-right`, and `margin-left` attributes. For instance, the following only creates margins on the top and to the right of the layer:

```
<div style="margin-top: 5px; margin-right: 5px;">
   Text goes here
</div>
```

Task **180**

The following task illustrates how margins work by displaying the same layer with two different margin settings:

1. In the body of your document, create a layer with a border:

   ```
   <div style="border-style: solid; border-width: 1px;">
   </div>
   ```

2. In this layer, create another layer with a margin:

   ```
   <div style="background-color: #cccccc; margin: 10px;">
   10 pixel margins</div>
   ```

3. Create another layer with a border, and inside that, create a layer without a margin, so that the final page looks like Listing 180-1.

   ```
   <body>
    <div style="border-style: solid; border-width: 1px;">
     <div style="background-color: #cccccc; margin: 10px;"
   >10 pixel margins</div>
    </div>
    <br>
    <div style="border-style: solid; border-width: 1px;">
     <div style="background-color: #cccccc;">No margins</div>
    </div>
   </body>
   ```

   Listing 180-1: Using margins.

4. Save the file and close it.

5. Open the file in your browser, and you should see the two layers, as in Figure 180-2.

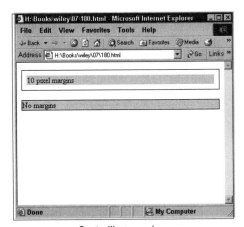

Figure 180-2: Controlling margins.

Applying Inline Styles

Task 181

With cascading style sheets, there are a number of ways you can apply styles to text. One way is to use inline style definitions. These allow you to specify styles in the `style` attribute of any HTML tag.

For instance, you might specify a style attribute specifically for one paragraph:

```
<p style="style definition">A paragraph<p>
```

Similarly, you might specify style settings for a layer that can contain lots of HTML:

```
<div style="style definition">Lots of HTML</div>
```

Finally, you can specify inline styles that override styles just for a given span of text, as in the following:

```
<p>
    This is text and <span style="style definition">this is ⊃
inline</span>
</p>
```

The following task illustrates the use of inline style assignments:

1. Create a new HTML document in your preferred editor.

2. In the body of your document, create a level 1 heading:

   ```
   <h1>A Stylized Headline</h1>
   ```

3. Apply styles to the heading:

   ```
   <h1 style="font-family: Arial; font-size: 18px;">A ⊃
   Stylized Headline</h1>
   ```

4. After the heading, create a layer with some HTML in it:

   ```
   <div>
      <h1>A Layer</h1>
      This layer has <strong>style</strong>. It also has ⊃
   some inline text.
   </div>
   ```

5. Add a style specification to the layer:

   ```
   <div style="background-color: #cccccc; color: red;">
      <h1>A Layer</h1>
      This layer has <strong>style</strong>. It also has
      some inline text.
   </div>
   ```

6. Specify a style definition for some of the text in the layer, using a span tag, so that the final document looks like Listing 181-1.

Task 181

```
<body>

    <h1 style="font-family: Arial; font-size: 18px;">A ⤶
Stylized Headline</h1>

    <div style="background-color: #cccccc; color: red;">
       <h1>A Layer</h1>
       This layer has <strong>style</strong>. It also has ⤶
       some <span style="color: white; background-color: ⤶
       black;">inline text</span>.
    </div>

</body>
```

Listing 181-1: Using inline style definitions.

7. Save the file and close it.

8. Open the file in a browser to see the styles, as in Figure 181-1.

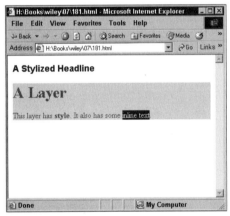

Figure 181-1: Applying inline styles.

cross-reference

▪ You can set a number of different style values. For example, Tasks 174 and 175 show you how to set some of the text characteristics, and Task 176 shows you how to control alignment.

Using Document Style Sheets

With cascading style sheets, there are a number of ways you can apply styles to text. One way is to use a style sheet specified in the header of your document. You can then refer to and reuse these styles throughout your document.

A document style sheet is specified between opening and closing `style` tags in the header of your document:

```
<head>
   <style type="text/css">
   </style>
</head>
```

To build your style sheet, just define the styles in the style block. You can define three types of style definitions:

- HTML element definitions, which specify a default style for different HTML elements (in other words, for different HTML tags)
- Class definitions, which can be applied to any HTML tag by using the class attribute common to all tags
- Identity definitions, which apply to any page elements that have a matching ID

The following steps show you how to create a style sheet in a document and then use the styles:

1. In the header of a new document, create a style block:

    ```
    <style type="text/css">
    </style>
    ```

2. In the style block, create a style definition for the p tag:

    ```
    P {
       font-family: Arial, Helvetica, SANS-SERIF;
       color: #ff0000;  }
    ```

3. Next, create a style definition for the myClass class:

    ```
    .myClass {
       font-size: 24pt;
       font-style: italic;  }
    ```

4. Finally, create a style definition for elements with the myID ID:

    ```
    #myID { background-color: #cccccc;  }
    ```

5. In the body of your document, create a level 1 heading and apply the myClass class to it:

    ```
    <h1 class="myClass"> This is a headline </h1>
    ```

notes

- You can combine as many different style definitions as needed into a single style sheet.

- You must specify a type in the style tag, and the type should always be text/css.

- Using a class overrides any existing defaults for the HTML element. Therefore, the default font, size, and so on used by the browser for level 1 heads will be completely ignored in this case, and only the specified style rules will affect the visual appearance of the header.

6. Create a paragraph:

```
<p>This is a plain old paragraph. </p>
```

7. Finally, create a layer with the ID myID and place some HTML in it, so that the final page looks like Listing 182-1.

```
<head>
    <style type="text/css">
        P { font-family: Arial, Helvetica, SANS-SERIF;
            color: #ff0000;   }
        .myClass { font-size: 24pt;
                   font-style: italic;    }
        #myID { background-color: #cccccc; }
    </style>
</head>
<body>
    <h1 class="myClass">This is a headline</h1>
    <p>This is a plain old paragraph.</p>
    <div id="myID">
        This layer has the ID myID.
    </div>
</body>
```

Listing 182-1: Using a document style sheet.

8. Save the file and close it.

9. Open the file in your browser, and you now see the document styles applied to the displayed text, as in Figure 182-1.

Figure 182-1: Using a document style sheet.

cross-references

- In Task 183 you learn how to make a global style sheet that can be used by many of your documents.

- Task 190 shows how to manipulate style sheet settings using JavaScript. Task 189 shows how to access the settings using JavaScript.

Creating Global Style Sheet Files

Typically, you will not only want to reuse styles with different elements on your page, but you will also want to use the same style definitions in different documents. You can do this by defining your styles in a global style sheet file and then including that file in any of the documents in your site that need to use the styles.

To build a global style sheet file, just define the styles in a separate file. You can define three types of style definitions:

- HTML element definitions, which specify a default style for different HTML elements (in other words, for different HTML tags). For instance, the following defines a style for level 1 headers in HTML:

```
h1 {
    font-family: Arial, Helvetica, SANS-SERIF;
    font-size: 18px;  }
```

- Class definitions, which can be applied to any HTML tag by using the class attribute common to all tags:

```
.className {
    font-family: Arial, Helvetica, SANS-SERIF;
    font-size: 18px;  }
```

- Identity definitions, which apply to any page elements that have a matching ID:

```
#ID {
    font-family: Arial, Helvetica, SANS-SERIF;
    font-size: 18px;  }
```

Once you have a style sheet file, the easiest way to include it in your documents is with the link tag in the header of your document:

```
<link rel="stylesheet" href="path to style sheet file">
```

The following steps show how to create a global style sheet file and then include it and use it in an HTML file:

1. Create a new document in your preferred editor. This file will be the style sheet file.

2. In the file, create a style definition for the p tag:

```
P {   background-color: #cccccc;
        font-size: 24pt;  }
```

3. In the file, also create a style definition for a class named myClass:

```
.myClass {
    font-weight: bold;
    font-family: Arial, Helvetica, SANS-SERIF;  }
```

notes

- You can combine as many definitions as needed into a single style sheet file.

- Typically, you will save the style sheet file with a .css extension.

4. Save the file as `style.css`.

5. In a new HTML file, create a `link` tag in the header to include the style sheet file you just saved:

```
<head>
   <link rel="stylesheet" href="style.css">
</head>
```

6. In the body of the document, create a plain paragraph of text:

```
<p>This is a paragraph with some style.</p>
```

7. Follow the paragraph with a layer that uses the `myClass` class, so that the final page looks like Listing 183-1.

```
<head>
   <link rel="stylesheet" href="style.css">
</head>
<body>
   <p>This is a paragraph with some style.</p>
   <div class="myClass">This is a layer with some ↵
style.</div>
</body>
```

Listing 183-1: Using a global style sheet file.

8. Save the file and close it.

9. Open the HTML file, and you should see the styles from the global style sheet file applied to your document as in Figure 183-1.

Figure 183-1: Styles from the global style sheet file apply to your documents.

cross-reference

▪ See Task 184 to learn how to override a style that has been set.

Overriding Global Style Sheets for Local Instances

Typically, you will not only want to reuse styles with different elements on your page, but you will also want to use the same style definitions in different documents. You can do this by defining your styles in a global style sheet file and then including that file in any of the documents in your site that need to use the styles.

To build a global style sheet file, just define the styles in a separate file. Task 183 shows you how to define three types of style definitions:

- HTML element definitions, which specify a default style for different HTML elements (in other words, for different HTML tags)

- Class definitions, which can be applied to any HTML tag using the class attribute common to all tags

- Identity definitions, which apply to page elements having a matching ID

One you have a style sheet file, the easiest way to include it in your documents is with the `link` tag in the header of your document:

```
<link rel="stylesheet" href="path to style sheet file">
```

You can then use the styles in your document, but also override individual style attributes as needed by using the style attribute in any tag. For instance, the following layer uses a `style` class but then specifies a local font size that overrides any font size that may be specified in the class:

```
<div class="class name" style="font-size: 24pt;">
   Text goes here   </div>
```

The following steps show how to create a global style sheet file, and then include it and use it in an HTML file and override individual style attributes:

1. In a new file create a style definition for the p tag:

   ```
   P {    background-color: #cccccc;
      font-size: 24pt;   }
   ```

2. In the file also create a style definition for a class named `myClass`:

   ```
   .myClass {
      font-weight: bold;
      font-family: Arial, Helvetica, SANS-SERIF;   }
   ```

3. Save the file as `style.css`. This will be your style sheet file.

4. In a new HTML file, create a `link` tag in the header to include the style sheet file you just saved:

   ```
   <head><link rel="stylesheet" href="style.css"></head>
   ```

notes

- Typically, you will save the style sheet file with a `.css` extension.

- You can combine as many definitions as needed into a single style sheet file.

5. In the body of the document, create a plain paragraph of text:

   ```
   <p>This is a paragraph with some style.</p>
   ```

6. Set a local style for the paragraph to specify the font size and make the text italic:

   ```
   <p style="font-size: 14pt; font-style: italic;">This is ⮐
   a paragraph with some style.</p>
   ```

7. Follow the paragraph with a layer that uses the `myClass` class:

   ```
   <div class="myClass">This is a layer with some ⮐
   style.</div>
   ```

8. Override the font weight for the layer. Listing 184-1 shows the page.

   ```
   <head><link rel="stylesheet" href="style.css"></head>

   <body>
       <p style="font-size: 14pt; font-style: italic;">This ⮐
   is a paragraph with some style.</p>
       <div class="myClass" style="font-weight: normal;">This ⮐
   is a layer with some style.</div>
   </body>
   ```

   Listing 184-1: Overriding global styles.

9. Save the file and open it in your browser. You should see the styles from the global style sheet file, with the specific local styles overriding them, applied to your document, as in Figure 184-1.

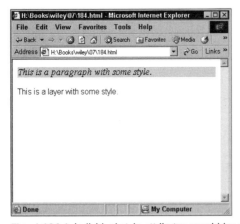

Figure 184-1: Individual style attributes overridden with local style definitions.

cross-reference

▪ See Task 182 for additional information on creating individual styles.

Creating a Drop Cap with Style Sheets

One of the aspects of the appearance of your pages that can be controlled through style sheets is the appearance of the first letter of a block of text. Using this ability, you can create special effects such as drop caps (large first letters of a paragraph, page, or document).

To control this, you typically use a document style sheet in the header of your document. In the style sheet, a style for a class should be defined; it should specify the normal appearance of text for the class.

Next, a special selector can be used to override the appearance of just the first letter of text to which this class is applied. The class and selector style definitions are defined as follows:

```
.myClass { style definition }
.myClass:first-letter { style definition for the first letter only }
```

The following task creates a paragraph of text with a drop cap:

1. In the header of a new HTML document, create a style block:

   ```
   <style type="text/css">

   </style>
   ```

2. Create a style definition for the myClass class. This defines the normal text appearance for the paragraph:

   ```
   .myClass {
       font-size: 24px;
   }
   ```

3. Create a style definition for the first letter of the myClass class:

   ```
   .myClass:first-letter {
       float: left;
       font-size: 72px;
       margin-right: 10px;
       margin-bottom: 10px;
   }
   ```

4. In the body of the document, create a layer that is assigned the myClass class, and put a paragraph of text in the layer. The final page should look like Listing 185-1.

notes

- Cascading style sheets has a range of special selectors, including selectors for when the mouse is hovering over a given HTML element, for the first letter of the element, for the first line of an element, for only links in an element, and so on.

- Notice the `float` attribute. Essentially this says that the element to which the attribute is applied should be placed at the left and other text and elements on the page should wrap around it to the right. This allows you to specify that the text of the paragraph should wrap around the drop cap. Otherwise, the large letter will sit on the first line and extend up above the first line.

- There is no need to apply any special styling to the first letter itself in the text. The style sheet, with the `first-letter` selector, will handle that job.

```
<head>
   <style type="text/css">
      .myClass {
         font-size: 24px;
      }
      .myClass:first-letter {
         float: left;
         font-size: 72px;
         margin-right: 10px;
         margin-bottom: 10px;
      }
   </style>
</head>

<body>
   <div class="myClass">
      This is a big paragraph with lots of text. The goal ⤸
      is to see what happens to the first character as a ⤸
      so-called drop cap. Should be interesting.
   </div>
</body>
```

Listing 185-1: Creating a drop cap.

5. Save the file and close it.

6. Open the file in your browser, and you should see the paragraph with the drop cap, as in Figure 185-1.

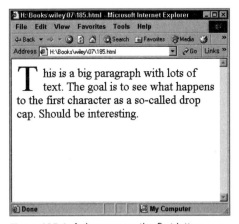

Figure 185-1: A drop cap on the first letter.

cross-reference

▪ Task 182 discusses document style sheets.

Customizing the Appearance of the First Line of Text

As browser support for cascading style sheets has improved, so too has the ability of Web designers to control all aspects of their pages' appearance through Dynamic HTML.

One of the aspects of the appearance of your pages that can be controlled through style sheets is the appearance of the first line of a block of text. To control this, you typically use a document style sheet in the header of your document. In the style sheet, a style for a class should be defined; it should specify the normal appearance of text for the class.

Next, a special selector can be used to override the appearance of just the first line of text to which this class is applied. The class and selector style definitions are defined as follows:

```
.myClass { style definition }
.myClass:first-line { style definition for the first line only }
```

The following task creates a paragraph of text with a special first-line style:

1. In the header of a new HTML document, create a style block:

   ```
   <style type="text/css">
   </style>
   ```

2. Create a style definition for the myClass class. This will define the normal text appearance for the paragraph:

   ```
   .myClass {
       font-size: 24px;
   }
   ```

3. Create a style definition for the first line of the myClass class:

   ```
   .myClass:first-letter {
       font-size: 48px;
       color: #999999;
       font-style: italic;
   }
   ```

4. In the body of the document, create a layer that is assigned the myClass class, and put a paragraph of text in the layer. The final page should look like Listing 186-1.

5. Save the file and close it.

6. Open the file in your browser, and you should see the paragraph with the drop cap, as in Figure 186-1.

notes

- Dynamic HTML is the combination of JavaScript, cascading style sheets, and the Domain Object Model, which together make it possible to build sophisticated interactive user interfaces and applications that run in the browser.

- Cascading style sheets have a range of special selectors, including selectors for when the mouse is hovering over a given HTML element, for the first letter of the element, for the first line of an element, for only links in an element, and so on.

- The nice thing about the first-line selector is that it always affects the first line regardless of changes in the window dimensions. If you have a very narrow window with fewer words on the first line than a wider window, then only those words are affected by the style.

- There is no need to apply any special styling to the first line itself in the text. The style sheet, with the first-line selector, will handle that job.

```
<head>
   <style type="text/css">
      .myClass {
         font-size: 24px;
      }
      .myClass:first-line {
         font-size: 48px;
         color: #999999;
         font-style: italic;
      }
   </style>
</head>

<body>
   <div class="myClass">
      This is a big paragraph with lots of text.
      The goal is to see what happens to the first
      line of the paragraph. Should be interesting.
   </div>
</body>
```

Listing 186-1: Creating a first-line effect.

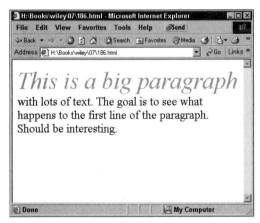

Figure 186-1: A special style on the first line.

7. Resize your browser window to a different width. Even though the number of words on the first line changes, it is always just the first line that displays the special style.

187

Applying a Special Style to the First Line of Every Element on the Page

One of the aspects of the appearance of your pages that can be controlled through style sheets is the appearance of the first line of a block of text. To control this, you typically use a document style sheet in the header of your document.

A special selector can be used to override the appearance of just the first line of any element in the page as follows:

```
:first-line { style definition for first line of all elements }
```

The following task creates a document with a special first-line style and shows how it applies to any element in the page:

1. In the header of a new HTML document, create a style block:

   ```
   <style type="text/css">
   </style>
   ```

2. Create a style definition for the first line of elements:

   ```
   :first-letter {
       font-size: 48px;
       color: #999999;
       font-style: italic;
   }
   ```

3. Create a layer with a paragraph of text in the body of the document:

   ```
   <div>
       This is a big paragraph with lots of text. The goal ⤶
       is to see what happens to the first line of the ⤶
       paragraph. Should be interesting.
   </div>
   ```

4. Create a paragraph and place text in it:

   ```
   <p>This is a big paragraph...</p>
   ```

5. Create a level 1 header and place text in it:

   ```
   <h1>This is a big paragraph...</h1>
   ```

6. Finally, place a paragraph of text outside any element. The final page should look like Listing 187-1.

   ```
   <head>
     <style type="text/css">
       :first-line {
   ```
   (continued)

notes

- Cascading style sheets has a range of special selectors, including selectors for when the mouse is hovering over a given HTML element, for the first letter of the element, for the first line of an element, for only links in an element, and so on.

- The nice thing about the first-line selector is that it always affects the first line regardless of changes in the window dimensions. If you have a very narrow window with fewer words on the first line than a wider window, then only those words are affected by the style.

- The first-line effect will not apply to the last paragraph, since the last paragraph is not in a page element.

```
                font-size: 48px;
                color: #999999;
                font-style: italic;  }
      </style>
   </head>

   <body>
      <div>
         This is a big paragraph with lots of text. The goal ⊃
         is to see what happens to the first line of the ⊃
         paragraph. Should be interesting.
      </div>
      <p>This is a big paragraph with lots of text. The goal ⊃
         is to see what happens to the first line of the ⊃
         paragraph. Should be interesting.</p>
      <h1>This is a big paragraph with lots of text. The ⊃
         goal is to see what happens to the first line of ⊃
         the paragraph. Should be interesting.</h1>
      This is a big paragraph with lots of text. The goal ⊃
      is to see what happens to the first line of the ⊃
      paragraph. Should be interesting.
   </body>
```

Listing 187-1: Creating a first-line effect.

7. Save the file and close it.

8. Open the file in your browser, and you should see the four paragraphs, as in Figure 187-1.

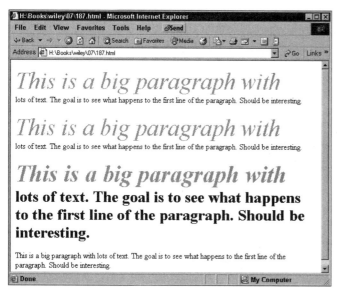

Figure 187-1: A special style on the first line.

188

Applying a Special Style to All Links

O ne of the aspects of the appearance of your pages that can be controlled through style sheets is the appearance of all links in the document. To control this, you typically use a document style sheet in the header of your document.

A special selector can be used to override the appearance of any link in the page as follows:

```
:link { style definition for all links }
```

The following task creates a document with a special link style and shows how it applies to any link in the page:

1. In the header a new HTML document, create a style block:

   ```
   <style type="text/css">

   </style>
   ```

2. Create a style definition for links:

   ```
   :link {
      background-color: #999999;
      color: red;
      font-style: italic;
   }
   ```

3. In the body of the document, create a layer with a link in it:

   ```
   <div>
      This is a layer with <a href="#">a link</a>.
   </div>
   ```

4. Create a level 1 header and put a link in it:

   ```
   <h1>
      This is a header with <a href="#">a link</a>.
   </h1>
   ```

5. Finally, place a paragraph of text outside any element and include a link in it. The final page should look like Listing 188-1.

```
<head>
   <style type="text/css">
      :link {
         background-color: #999999;
         color: red;
         font-style: italic;
      }
   </style>
</head>

<body>
   <div>
      This is a layer with <a href="#">a link</a>.
   </div>

   <h1>
      This is a header with <a href="#">a link</a>.
   </h1>

   This is floating text with <a href="#">a link</a>.
</body>
```

Listing 188-1: Creating a link effect.

6. Save the file and close it.

7. Open the file in your browser, and you should see the links with the special style, as in Figure 188-1.

Figure 188-1: A special style for links.

Task 189

Accessing Style Sheet Settings

The beauty of Dynamic HTML is that it allows you to integrate JavaScript and cascading style sheets. Your styles are not just static visual definitions that are fixed once the page is rendered. Instead, you can actually access all these style attributes from within your JavaScript code.

Every page element has an object associated with it that you can access in JavaScript. These objects have a `style` property. The `style` property is actually an object reflecting all the CSS style settings for an object.

To reference the element's object, you use the `document.getElementById` method. You obtain a reference to the object with the following:

```
var objRef = document.getElementById("elementID");
```

This means `objRef` would then refer to the object for the `elementID` element.

The following steps show how to build a page with a layer element and a form that can be used to enter the name of any style attribute and then display that attribute's value in a dialog box:

1. In the script block of a new document, create a function named `displayStyle` that takes two arguments—the ID of the element to work with and a style name:

   ```
   function displayStyle(objected,styleName) {  }
   ```

2. In the function, create a variable named `thisObj`, and use `document.getElementById` to associate this with the object for the ID specified in the function's argument:

   ```
   var thisObj = document.getElementById(objectID);
   ```

3. Create a variable named `styleValue`, and assign the style's value to it:

   ```
   var styleValue = eval("thisObj.style." + styleName);
   ```

4. Display the information in a dialog box using `window.alert`:

   ```
   window.alert(styleName + "=" + styleValue);
   ```

5. Create a layer and position it wherever you want using the `style` attribute of the `div` tag. Specify `myObject` as the ID for the layer:

   ```
   <div id="myObject" style="position: absolute; left: ⤵
   50px; top: 200px; background-color: #cccccc;">My ⤵
   Object</div>
   ```

6. Create a form with a text input field named `styleText`:

   ```
   <form>Style: <input type="text" name="styleText"> </form>
   ```

notes

- The actual style sheet attribute names do not translate directly to style attribute names in JavaScript. Two rules apply:

  - If a style sheet attribute name is a single word with no dash, then the same name applies in JavaScript.

  - If the style sheet attribute name has one or more dashes, remove each dash and capitalize the letter that follows the dash. Therefore, `margin-left` would become `marginLeft` in JavaScript.

- The `style` object referred to here and the `document.getElementById` method are only available in newer browsers with robust support for the Domain Object Model. This means this task will only work in Internet Explorer 5 and later or Netscape 6 and later.

caution

- If you don't enter a value into the form that is presented when you run Listing 189-1, you may get a JavaScript runtime error.

Task **189**

7. In the form, add a button. Use the `onClick` event handler to invoke the `displayStyle` function, so that the final page looks like Listing 189-1.

```
<head>
 <script language="JavaScript">
  function displayStyle(objectID,styleName) {
    var thisObj = document.getElementById(objectID);
    var styleValue = eval("thisObj.style." + styleName);
    window.alert(styleName + "=" + styleValue);
  }
 </script>
</head>
<body>
   <div id="myObject" style="position: absolute; left: ⤸
50px; top: 200px; background-color: #cccccc;">My Object</div>
   <form>
       Style: <input type="text" name="styleText">
       <input type="button" value="Display Style" ⤸
onClick="displayStyle('myObject',this.form.styleText.⤸
value);">
   </form>
</body>
```

Listing 189-1: Displaying a layer's style attributes.

8. Save the file and open it in a browser. You now see the form and object, as illustrated in Figure 189-1.

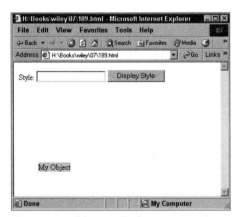

Figure 189-1: A layer and a form.

9. Enter a style name in the form (such as `backgroundColor`), and click the button to see the style value displayed in a dialog box.

Manipulating Style Sheet Settings

The beauty of Dynamic HTML is that it allows you to integrate JavaScript and cascading style sheets. Your styles, therefore, are not just static visual definitions that are fixed once the page is rendered. Instead, you can actually manipulate all these style attributes from within your JavaScript code.

Every page element has an object associated with it that you can access in JavaScript. These objects have a `style` property. The `style` property is actually an object reflecting all the CSS style settings for an object.

To reference the element's object, you use the `document.getElementById` method. You could obtain a reference to the object with the following:

```
var objRef = document.getElementById("elementID");
```

This means `objRef` would then refer to the object for the `elementID` element.

The following steps show how to build a page with a layer element and a form the user can use to enter the name of any style attribute and a value, and then apply it to the layer:

1. In the script block of a new document, create a function named `changeStyle`. The function should take three arguments that contain the ID of the element to work with, a style name, and a style value, respectively:

   ```
   function changeStyle(objected,styleName,styleValue) {  }
   ```

2. In the function, create a variable named `thisObj`, and use `document.getElementById` to associate this with the object for the ID specified in the function's argument:

   ```
   var thisObj = document.getElementById(objectID);
   ```

3. Assign the new value to the specified style:

   ```
   eval("thisObj.style." + styleName + "='" + styleValue ⤶
   + "'");
   ```

4. In the body of the document, create a layer and position it wherever you want using the `style` attribute of the `div` tag. Specify `myObject` as the ID for the layer.

5. Create a form with two text input fields named `styleText` and `styleValue`:

   ```
   <form>
       Style: <input type="text" name="styleText"><br>
       Value: <input type="text" name="styleValue"><br>
   </form>
   ```

6. In the form add a button. Use the `onClick` event handler to invoke the `changeStyle` function, so that the final page looks like Listing 190-1.

```
<head>
 <script language="JavaScript">
   function changeStyle(objectID,styleName,styleValue) {
       var thisObj = document.getElementById(objectID);
       eval("thisObj.style." + styleName + "='" +
          styleValue + "'");     }
</script>
</head>
<body>
   <div id="myObject" style="position: absolute; left: ⊃
50px; top: 200px; background-color: #cccccc;">My Object</div>
   <form>
       Style: <input type="text" name="styleText"><br>
       Value: <input type="text" name="styleValue"><br>
       <input type="button" value="Display Style" ⊃
onClick="changeStyle('myObject',this.form.styleText.⊃
value,this.form.styleValue.value);">
   </form>
</body>
```

Listing 190-1: Changing a layer's style attributes.

7. Save the file and open it in a browser, and you now see the form and object, as illustrated in Figure 190-1.

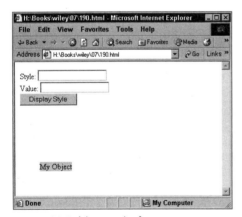

Figure 190-1: A layer and a form.

8. Enter a style name and value in the form, and click the button to see the style value applied to the layer.

Hiding an Object in JavaScript

Every element of your page has an object associated with it that can be accessed through JavaScript. For instance, you can determine an object's visibility in the browser using this object. The visibility information is part of the `style` property of the object.

To reference the element's object, you use the `document.getElementById` method. For each object in your document that you want to manipulate through JavaScript, you should assign an ID using the `id` attribute of the element's tag. Then, you could obtain a reference to an object with the following:

```
var objRef = document.getElementById("TagID");
```

This means `objRef` would then refer to the object for the `TagID` element of your document, and you could reference the visibility of the image with this:

```
objRef.style.visibility
```

The following steps show how to build a page with a layer element and a link. When the user clicks the link, the object disappears.

1. In the header of a new document, create a script block containing a function named `hideObject` that takes one argument containing the ID of the element to work with:

   ```
   function hideObject(objectID) {
   }
   ```

2. Create a variable named `thisObject`, and associate it with the object specified in the function's argument. Use `document.getElementById`:

   ```
   var thisObject = document.getElementById(objectID);
   ```

3. Set the `visibility` property of the element's `style` object to `hidden`, so that final function looks like this:

   ```
   function hideObject(objectID) {
     var thisObject = document.getElementById(objectID);
     thisObject.style.visibility = "hidden";
   }
   ```

4. In the body of the document, create a layer and position it wherever you want using the `style` attribute of the `div` tag. Specify `myObject` as the ID for the layer:

   ```
   <div id="myObject" style="position: absolute; left: ⊃
   50px; top: 200px; background-color: #cccccc;">My ⊃
   Object</div>
   ```

notes

- The `style` property is actually an object reflecting all the CSS style settings for an object, including the `visibility` attribute. This means you can determine the visibility of an object with `object.style.visibility`.

- The `style` object referred to here and the `document.getElementByID` method are only available in newer browsers with robust support for the Domain Object Model. This means this task will only work in Internet Explorer 5 and later or Netscape 6 and later.

- In Step 5 notice the use of a `javascript:` URL in the link. This URL causes the specified JavaScript code to execute when the user clicks on the link.

- When you call the `hideObject` function, you pass in the object ID as a string; that is why `myObject` is contained in single quotes.

5. Create a link the user can click to call the `hideObject` function, so the final page looks like Listing 191-1.

```
<head>
 <script language="JavaScript">
   function hideObject(objectID) {
      var thisObject = document.getElementById(objectID);
      thisObject.style.visibility = "hidden";
   }
   </script>
</head>

<body>
  <div id="myObject" style="position: absolute; left: ⟳
50px; top: 200px; background-color: #cccccc;">My Object</div>

   <a href="javascript:hideObject('myObject');">Hide the ⟳
object</a>
   </body>
```

Listing 191-1: Hiding an object.

6. Save the file and close it.

7. Open the file in a browser, and you now see the link and object, as illustrated in Figure 191-1.

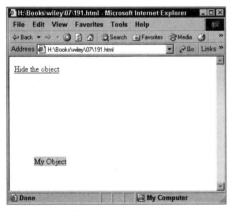

Figure 191-1: A layer and a link.

8. Click on the link to see the object disappear.

cross-reference

▪ Task 192 shows how to make an object visible.

Displaying an Object in JavaScript

Every element of your page has an object associated with it that can be accessed through JavaScript. For instance, you can determine an object's visibility in the browser using this object. The visibility information is part of the `style` property of the object.

To reference the element's object, you use the `document.getElementById` method. For each object in your document that you want to manipulate through JavaScript, you should assign an ID using the `id` attribute of the element's tag. Then, you could obtain a reference to an object with the following:

```
var objRef = document.getElementById("TagID");
```

This means `objRef` would then refer to the object for the `TagID` element of your document, and you could reference the visibility of the image with this:

```
objRef.style.visibility
```

The following steps show how to build a page with a layer element and a link. The layer element will initially not be visible, and when the user clicks the link, the object will appear.

1. In the header of a new document, create a script block containing a function named `showObject`. The function should take one argument that contains the ID of the element to work with:

   ```
   function showObject(objectID) {
   }
   ```

2. Create a variable named `thisObject`, and associate it with the object specified in the function's argument. Use `document.getElementById`:

   ```
   var thisObject = document.getElementById(objectID);
   ```

3. Set the `visibility` property of the element's `style` object to `visible`, so that final function looks like this:

   ```
   function showObject(objectID) {
       var thisObject = document.getElementById(objectID);
       thisObject.style.visibility = "visible";
   }
   ```

4. In the body of the document, create a layer and position it wherever you want using the `style` attribute of the `div` tag. Specify `myObject` as the ID for the layer; make sure that the layer is hidden:

   ```
   <div id="myObject" style="position: absolute; left: ⊃
   50px; top: 200px; background-color: #cccccc; visibility: ⊃
   hidden;">My Object</div>
   ```

notes

- The `style` property is actually an object reflecting all the CSS style settings for an object, including the `visibility` attribute. This means you can determine the visibility of an object with `object.style.visibility`.

- The `style` object referred to here and the `document.getElementByID` method are only available in newer browsers with robust support for the Domain Object Model. This means this task will only work in Internet Explorer 5 and later or Netscape 6 and later.

- In Step 5 notice the use of a `javascript:` URL in the link. This URL causes the specified JavaScript code to execute when the user clicks on the link.

- When you call the `showObject` function, you pass in the object ID as a string; that is why `myObject` is contained in single quotes.

5. Create a link the user can click to call the `showObject` function, so the final page looks like Listing 192-1.

```
<head>
 <script language="JavaScript">
   function showObject(objectID) {
       var thisObject = document.getElementById(objectID);
       thisObject.style.visibility = "visible";
   }
 </script>
 </head>

<body>
     <div id="myObject" style="position: absolute; left: ⊃
50px; top: 200px; background-color: #cccccc; visibility: ⊃
hidden;">My Object</div>

     <a href="javascript:showObject('myObject');">Show ⊃
the object</a>
 </body>
```

Listing 192-1: Showing an object.

6. Save the file and close it.

7. Open the file in a browser, and you now see the link, as illustrated in Figure 192-1.

Figure 192-1: A link, but the layer is hidden.

8. Click on the link to see the object appear.

cross-reference

- Task 191 shows how to hide an object.

Detecting the Window Size

Using JavaScript, you can determine the dimensions of the working area of the browser window. The way you do this depends on the browser you are using:

- In Netscape 6 and higher, the `window.innerHeight` property indicates the height of the working area of the browser window in pixels. Similarly, `window.innerWidth` indicates the width.

- In Internet Explorer, the `document.body.clientHeight` property indicates the height in pixels. Similarly, the `document.body.clientWidth` property indicates the width.

The following task shows you how to display this information in the browser window:

1. Create a new HTML document in your preferred editor.

2. In the body of the document, include any introductory text:

   ```
   <body>

       The window has the following dimensions:

   </body>
   ```

3. Create a script block after the introductory text:

   ```
   <script language="JavaScript">

   </script>
   ```

4. In the script, create a variable named `width`, and assign the width of the window to it:

   ```
   var width = (window.innerWidth) ? window.innerWidth : ↵
   document.body.clientWidth;
   ```

5. Next, create the variable named `height`, and assign the height of the window to it:

   ```
   var height = (window.innerHeight) ? window.innerHeight : ↵
   document.body.clientHeight;
   ```

6. Finally, use the `document.write` method to display the dimensions in the browser window. The final page should look like Listing 193-1.

note

- In Step 4 you can see an example of short-form conditional evaluation. This takes the form `(condition) ? value if true : value if false`. What the condition in this example says is this: "If `window.innerWidth` exists, then assign that value to `width`; otherwise, assign `document.body.clientWidth` to `width`."

```
<body>

    The window has the following dimensions:

    <script language="JavaScript">

        var width = (window.innerWidth) ? window.⊃
innerWidth : document.body.clientWidth;
        var height = (window.innerHeight) ? window.⊃
innerHeight : document.body.clientHeight;
        document.write(width + " by " + height + " pixels");

    </script>

</body>
```

Listing 193-1: Obtaining the browser's dimensions.

7. Save the file and close it.

8. Open the file in a browser, and you now see the window's dimensions, as illustrated in Figure 193-1.

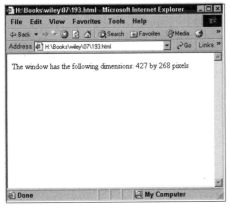

Figure 193-1: The browser's dimensions.

tip

- You can use the information presented in this task to do a number of interesting things. For example, using the information in Tasks 178 or 179, you can place items in certain locations in the Window. For instance, you can determine the center of the window by dividing the width and height in half.

cross-reference

- In addition to detecting the size of a window, you can also detect other information. For example, see Task 195 to discover the steps for detecting the number of colors.

Task 194

Forcing Capitalization with Style Sheet Settings

As browser support for cascading style sheets has improved, so too has the ability for you to control all aspects of your pages' appearance through Dynamic HTML.

One of the aspects of the appearance of your pages that can be controlled through style sheets is the capitalization used for text. You can control this with the `text-transform` style attribute. For instance, the following sets all text in a layer to uppercase:

```
<div style="text-transform: uppercase;">
   Text goes here
</div>
```

Similarly, you can change to all lowercase inline using the `span` tag:

```
<p>
   This is text. Some of it <span style="text-transform: ⤴
lowercase;">is in Arial.</span>
</p>
```

The `text-transform` attribute has three possible values:

- `uppercase`: All letters are converted to uppercase.
- `lowercase`: All letters are converted to lowercase.
- `capitalize`: Capitalization is converted to a title style where the first letter of each word is capitalized.

The following task illustrates the `text-transform` attribute by displaying text in all three capitalization styles:

1. Create a new HTML document in your preferred editor.

2. In the body of your document, create a layer containing text. Specify uppercase as the `text-transform` style:

   ```
   <div style="text-transform: uppercase;">This text is ⤴
   uppercase</div>
   ```

3. Create another layer containing text. This time specify `capitalize`:

   ```
   <div style="text-transform: capitalize;">This ⤴
   text is capitalized</div>
   ```

note

- Dynamic HTML is the combination of JavaScript, cascading style sheets, and the Domain Object Model, which together make it possible to build sophisticated interactive user interfaces and applications that run in the browser.

4. Create another layer containing text. This time specify lowercase:

```
<div style="text-transform: lowercase;">This text is ⟳
lowercase</div>
```

5. Create another layer containing text. This time don't specify the text-transform attribute. The final page should look like Listing 194-1.

```
<body>

    <div style="text-transform: uppercase;">This text is ⟳
uppercase</div>

    <div style="text-transform: capitalize;">This text is ⟳
capitalized</div>

    <div style="text-transform: lowercase;">This text is ⟳
lowercase</div>

    <div>This text is normal</div>

</body>
```

Listing 194-1: Changing capitalization.

6. Save the file and close it.

7. Open the file in your browser, and you should see four blocks of text in different capitalization styles, as in Figure 194-1.

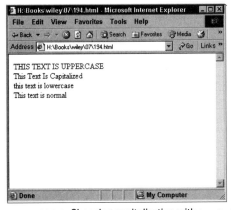

Figure 194-1: Changing capitalization with text-transform.

Detecting the Number of Colors

Every user's display settings has a color depth associated with it. The color depth is usually specified in bits (such as 8-bit or 16-bit) and refers to the size of the number used to specify each pixel's color: the larger the color depth, the more colors the display can render.

Using JavaScript, you can determine the color depth of the user's display. This is done with the `window.screen.colorDepth` property, which returns the number of bits of the color depth.

The following task shows you how to display this information in the browser window:

1. Create a new HTML document in your preferred editor.

2. In the body of the document, include any introductory text:

   ```
   <body>

       The display has the following color depth:

   </body>
   ```

3. Create a script block after the introductory text:

   ```
   <script language="JavaScript">

   </script>
   ```

4. In the script, create a variable named `depth`, and assign the color depth to it:

   ```
   var depth = window.screen.colorDepth;
   ```

5. Next, create the variable named `colors`, and assign the number of colors to it:

   ```
   var colors = Math.pow(2,depth);
   ```

6. Finally, use the `document.write` method to display the depth and number of colors in the browser window. The final page should look like Listing 195-1.

notes

■ The color depth information could be used to select and display an appropriate image for the user. For users with a large color depth, you could provide a richly textured color image, while other users would get a simpler visual with fewer colors.

■ If a user has 8-bit color, then the number of colors that can be displayed is 2^8. Similarly, 16-bit means 2^{16} colors.

■ The `Math.pow` method is used to calculate exponent values. Here you calculate 2 to the power of the color depth.

```
<body>

    The display has the following color depth:

    <script language="JavaScript">

        var depth = window.screen.colorDepth;
        var colors = Math.pow(2,depth);

        document.write(depth + " bits which means " + ⮐
colors + " colors");

    </script>

</body>
```

Listing 195-1: Obtaining the color depth.

7. Save the file and close it.

8. Open the file in a browser, and you now see the display's color information, as illustrated in Figure 195-1.

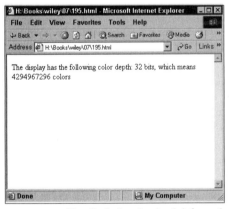

Figure 195-1: The display's color depth information.

cross-reference

- You can detect other values as well. For example, see Task 193 to learn how to detect the size of the current browser window.

Adjusting Padding with CSS

As browser support for cascading style sheets has improved, so too has the ability of Web designers to control all aspects of their pages' appearance through Dynamic HTML.

One of the aspects of the appearance of your pages that can be controlled through style sheets is the padding of a layer. To understand padding and its meaning in style sheets, you need to learn about the box model used in cascading style sheets. The box model defines a layer's outer components, as shown in Figure 196-1.

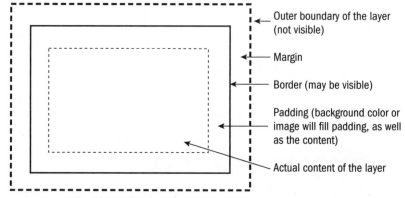

Figure 196-1: The CSS box model.

notes

• Layers are created with `div` tags and can contain any valid HTML in them. They are simply containers for the HTML to which you can apply styles for the whole layer.

• When you are specifying all four padding widths with the `padding` attribute, the first value is for the top padding and then the values proceed clockwise with the right padding, the bottom padding, and finally the left padding.

• The layer has a background color to show where padding is happening.

• By default, layers have no padding, so if you don't need any padding, you don't have to specify any padding-related style attributes.

You control the width of the padding in one of several ways:

• Use the `padding` attribute to set the same padding width for all sides. The following creates 5-pixel padding on all sides of the layer:

```
<div style="padding: 5px;">
   Text goes here
</div>
```

• Use the `padding` attribute to set different margin widths for the different sites:

```
<div style="padding: 5px 10px 15px 20px;">
   Text goes here
</div>
```

• Specify distinct margins individually using the `padding-top`, `padding-bottom`, `padding-right`, and `padding-left` attributes. For instance, the following only creates padding on the top and to the right of the layer:

```
<div style="padding-top: 5px; padding-right: 5px;">
   Text goes here
</div>
```

The following task illustrates how margins work by displaying the same layer with two different padding settings:

1. Create a new HTML document in your preferred editor.

2. Create a layer with padding in the body of the document:

```
<div style="background-color: #cccccc; padding: 10px;"↩
>10 pixel margins</div>
```

3. Create another layer without any padding, so that the final page looks like Listing 196-1:

```
<body>

    <div style="background-color: #cccccc; padding: 10px;"↩
>10 pixel padding</div>

    <br>

    <div style="background-color: #cccccc;">No padding</div>

</body>
```

Listing 196-1: Using padding.

4. Save the file and close it.

5. Open the file in your browser, and you should see the two layers, as in Figure 196-2.

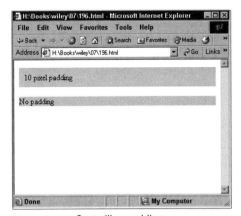

Figure 196-2: Controlling padding.

Part 8: Dynamic User Interaction

Creating a Simple Pull-Down Menu

With JavaScript, you can create dynamic user interfaces. One interface is a pull-down menu that might initially appear closed in a Web page. But when the user moves the mouse pointer over the menu, the pull-down menu appears, as in Figure 197-1.

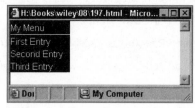

Figure 197-1: The menu in its open position.

This task outlines how to build an extremely simple pull-down menu. The principle is simple. Given an object named `myObject`, you can specify the top of the object in pixels relative to the browser window with the following:

```
myObject.top = pixel placement relative to top of window;
```

The following steps show how to create a simple pull-down menu in the top left corner of the browser window with three menu items in the menu:

1. In the header of your HTML document, create a script block with opening and closing `script` tags.

2. In the script block, create a function named `menuToggle` that takes a single attribute called `target`, which is the name of the object containing the menu:

   ```
   function menuToggle(target) {
   }
   ```

3. In the function, create a variable named `targetMenu` and set it to the appropriate object with the specified object name in `target`:

   ```
   targetMenu = (document.getElementById) ?
   document.getElementById(target).style : eval
   ("document." + target);
   ```

4. Finish the function by assigning the appropriate top value to the top property of the `targetMenu` object:

   ```
   targetMenu.top = (parseInt(targetMenu.top) == 22)
   ? -2000 : 22;
   ```

5. Also in the header, create a style sheet block with opening and closing `style` tags:

notes

- Drop-down menus work in much the same way as menu in most Windows applications; when the user moves the mouse over the menu (or clicks on the menu in some cases), the menu appears.

- Notice the use of the conditional based on `document.getElementById`. In Internet Explorer, this method is available, and you use it to access the `style` property of the target object. But in Netscape, this method is not available and the correct object to work with is the object itself and not a `style` property. By testing for the existence of the `getElementById` method, you can determine what browser you are using.

6. Create three style classes: `menu`, `menuTitle`, and `menuLink`. `menu` is for the menu block itself and should have an absolute top position of -2000 pixels so the menu is initially hidden. `menuTitle` is for the menu header and should have an absolute position of 0 pixels to place the menu's header at the top of the screen. Finally, `menuEntry` specifies the appearance and behavior of individual items in the menu.

```
.menu { position:absolute;
    font:15px arial, helvetica, sans-serif;
    background-color:#020A33;
    line-height: 20px; top: -2000px; }
.menuTitle { position:absolute;
    font:15px arial, helvetica, sans-serif;
    background-color:#020A33;
    line-height: 21px; top: 0px;
    text-decoration:none; color:#FFFFFF; }
.menuEntry { text-decoration:none; color:#FFFFFF; }
.menuEntry:link { color:#FFFFFF; }
.menuEntry:hover { background-color:#CCCCCC; ⮐
color:#020A33; }
```

7. In the body of the document, use opening and closing `div` tags to create the menu title block:

```
<div class="menuTitle" style="left:0px; width:100px;"
 onMouseover="menuToggle('myMenu');"
 onMouseout="menuToggle('myMenu');">My Menu</div>
```

8. In the body of the document, use opening and closing `div` tags to create the menu block:

```
<div id="myMenu" class="menu" style="left:0px; ⮐
width:100px;"
 onMouseout="menuToggle('myMenu')">
</div>
```

9. In the div block create one link for each entry. The link should use the `menuEntry` style class and should be followed by a `br` tag. This div block can be placed anywhere in the body of the document:

```
<div id="myMenu" class="menu" style="left:0px; ⮐
width:100px;"
 onMouseout="menuToggle('myMenu')">
    <a href="http://someurl/" class="menuEntry">First ⮐
Entry</a><br>
    <a href="http://anotherurl/" class="menuEntry">Second ⮐
Entry</a><br>
    <a href="http://onemoreurl/" class="menuEntry">Third ⮐
Entry</a>
</div>
```

Creating Two Pull-Down Menus

In Task 197 you saw how to create a simple pull-down menu. In this task, this is extended to displaying two pull-down menus simultaneously. Here the same principle is repeated, allowing the same JavaScript and style sheets to be used for multiple menus and, in fact, can be extended to any number of menus.

The result is that two menus are displayed. Either one of the menus can be expanded at a given time, as illustrated in Figure 198-1.

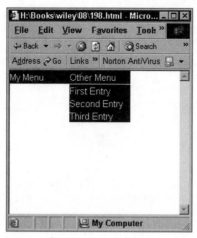

Figure 198-1: Opening the second menu.

Use the following steps to create two menus in the top left corner of the browser window:

1. In the header of your HTML document, create a script block and place the menuToggle function from Task 197 in the block:

```
<script language="JavaScript">
<!--
    function menuToggle(target) {
        targetMenu = (document.getElementById) ?
document.getElementById(target).style : eval
("document." + target);
        targetMenu.top = (parseInt(targetMenu.top) == 22)
? -2000 : 22;
    }
// -->
</script>
```

2. In the header of your HTML document, create a style block and include the same menu, menuTitle, and menuEntry styles as in Task 197:

```
.menu { position:absolute;
    font:15px arial, helvetica, sans-serif;
```

```
        background-color:#020A33;
        line-height: 20px; top: -2000px; }
    .menuTitle { position:absolute;
        font:15px arial, helvetica, sans-serif;
        background-color:#020A33;
        line-height: 21px; top: 0px;
        text-decoration:none; color:#FFFFFF; }
    .menuEntry { text-decoration:none; color:#FFFFFF; }
    .menuEntry:link { color:#FFFFFF; }
    .menuEntry:hover { background-color:#CCCCCC; ⊃
color:#020A33; }
```

3. In the body of the document, create the title block for the first menu's header:

```
<div class="menuTitle" style="left:0px; width:100px;"⊃
 onMouseover="menuToggle('myMenu');"⊃
 onMouseout="menuToggle('myMenu');">My Menu</div>
```

4. In the body of the document, create the menu block for the first menu:

```
<div id="myMenu" class="menu" style="left:0px; ⊃
width:100px;"
 onMouseout="menuToggle('myMenu')">
    <a href="http://someurl/" class="menuEntry">First ⊃
Entry</a><br>
    <a href="http://anotherurl/" class="menuEntry">Second ⊃
Entry</a><br>
    <a href="http://onemoreurl/" class="menuEntry">Third ⊃
Entry</a>
</div>
```

5. In the body of the document, create the title block for the second menu's header; notice that the left side of the menu is placed at 100 pixels, which is just to the right of the first, 100-pixel-wide menu:

```
<div class="menuTitle" style="left:100px; width:100px;"⊃
 onMouseover="menuToggle('otherMenu');"⊃
 onMouseout="menuToggle('otherMenu');">Other Menu</div>
```

6. In the body of the document, create the menu block for the second menu and, again, set the left side of the menu to 100 pixels:

```
<div id="otherMenu" class="menu" style="left:100px; ⊃
width:100px;"
 onMouseout="menuToggle('otherMenu')">
    <a href="http://someurl/" class="menuEntry">First ⊃
Entry</a><br>
    <a href="http://anotherurl/" class="menuEntry">Second ⊃
Entry</a><br>
    <a href="http://onemoreurl/" class="menuEntry">Third ⊃
Entry</a>
</div>
```

cross-reference

■ This task is a simple extension of the code in Task 197.

Detecting and Reacting to Selections in a Pull-Down Menu

In Tasks 197 and 198, you saw how to create simple pull-down menus in which the individual menu items point to URLs for other pages. Two techniques can be used to trigger JavaScript code from a menu entry in these menus: Use a `javascript:` URL in the `href` attribute of each menu entry's link, or use the `onClick` event handler for each menu entry's link. This task uses the first technique to extend the simple menu from Task 197 to cause a dialog box to be displayed when the user selects a menu entry instead of following a URL.

1. In the header of your HTML document, create a script block and place the `menuToggle` function from Task 197 in the block:

```
<script language="JavaScript">
<!--
   function menuToggle(target) {
      targetMenu = (document.getElementById) ? ⤸
document.getElementById(target).style : eval("document." ⤸
+ target);
      targetMenu.top = (parseInt(targetMenu.top) == 22) ⤸
? -2000 : 22;
   }
// -->
</script>
```

2. In the header of your HTML document, create a style block and include the same menu, menuTitle, and menuEntry styles as in Task 197:

```
<style type="text/css">
   .menu {
      position:absolute; background-color:#020A33;
      font:15px arial, helvetica, sans-serif;
      line-height: 20px; top: -2000px;
   }
   .menuTitle {
      position:absolute; background-color:#020A33;
      font:15px arial, helvetica, sans-serif;
      line-height: 21px; top: 0px;
      text-decoration:none; color:#FFFFFF;
   }
   .menuEntry {
      text-decoration:none; color:#FFFFFF;
   }
   .menuEntry:link {
      color:#FFFFFF;
   }
   .menuEntry:hover {
```

```
        background-color:#CCCCCC; color:#020A33;
    }
</style>
```

3. In the body of the document, create the title block for the menu's header:

```
<div class="menuTitle" style="left:0px; width:100px;"
 onMouseover="menuToggle('myMenu');"
 onMouseout="menuToggle('myMenu');">My Menu</div>
```

4. In the body of the document, create the menu block for the menu:

```
<div id="myMenu" class="menu" style="left:0px;
 width:100px;" onMouseout="menuToggle('myMenu')">
</div>
```

5. Create the menu links, using the menuEntry style class. For each link, use a javascript: URL to display a dialog box when the user selects the menu entry:

```
<div id="myMenu" class="menu" style="left:0px;
 width:100px;" onMouseout="menuToggle('myMenu')">
    <a href="javascript:alert('You chose the first
entry');" class="menuEntry">First Entry</a><br>
    <a href="javascript:alert('You chose the second
entry');" class="menuEntry">Second Entry</a><br>
    <a href="javascript:alert('You chose the third
entry');" class="menuEntry">Third Entry</a>
</div>
```

6. Save the file and open it in a browser. The menu is displayed closed, as in Figure 199-1.

Figure 199-1: The menu displays closed by default.

7. Select an entry from the menu. The browser displays a dialog box, as illustrated in Figure 199-2.

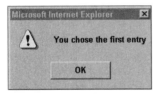

Figure 199-2: Displaying a dialog box when a user selects an entry.

tip

▪ There is no practical limit to the JavaScript code you can execute when the user selects a menu entry. Of course, to make your code manageable, what you want to do is place the code you want to execute for a menu entry into a function and then call that function from the onClick event handler or the javascript: URL.

cross-reference

▪ This task is a simple extension of the code in Task 197.

Task 200

Generating a Drop-Down Menu with a Function

This task shows how to simplify the creation of menus by encapsulating most of the work into functions and then simply invoking the functions. The following steps outline how to extend the basic menu from Task 197 to use a function to create the menu:

1. In the header of your HTML document, create a script block and place the `menuToggle` function from Task 197 in the block:

```
<script language="JavaScript">
<!--
    function menuToggle(target) {
        targetMenu = (document.getElementById) ? ⤶
document.getElementById(target).style : eval("document." ⤶
+ target);
        targetMenu.top = (parseInt(targetMenu.top) == 22) ⤶
? -2000 : 22;
    }
// -->
</script>
```

2. In the script block, create a second function named `createMenu`. This function takes five parameters: a name for the menu object, a display title for the menu, an array containing menu entries, and the horizontal placement and width of the menu in pixels:

```
function
createMenu(menuName,menuTitle,menuEntries,left,width) {
}
```

3. In the function, create a variable named `numEntries` containing the number of entries in the `menuEntries` array:

```
numEntries = menuEntries.length;
```

4. Use the `document.write` method to output the menu title block; use the `menuName` variable to pass the name of the `menuObject` in the calls to `menuToggle` in the `onMouseover` and `onMouseout` event handlers, as well as `menuTitle` as the title text in the block:

```
document.write('<div class="menuTitle" style="left:0px; ⤶
width:100px;"');
document.write('onMouseover="menuToggle(\'' + menuName ⤶
+ '\');"');
document.write('onMouseout="menuToggle(\'' + menuName + ⤶
'\');">');
document.write(menuTitle);
document.write('</div>');
```

5. To finish the function, use the `document.write` method to output the menu block. You will need to use a `for` loop to output one link for each entry in the `menuEntries` array:

```
document.write('<div id="myMenu" class="menu"
style="left:0px; width:100px;"');
document.write('onMouseout="menuToggle(\'' + menuName +
'\')">');
for (i = 0; i < numEntries; i++) {
    document.write('<a href="' + menuEntries[i].url + '"
class="menuEntry">' + menuEntries[i].entry + '</a><br>');
}
document.write('</div>');
```

6. In the header of your HTML document, create a style block and include the same `menu`, `menuTitle`, and `menuEntry` styles as in Task 197.

7. In the body of the document, create a script block with opening and closing `script` tags.

8. In the script, create an array named `myMenu`:

```
var myMenu = new Array();
```

9. Create array entries for each entry in the menu. Notice that each entry is an object containing two properties named `entry` (the display text for the entry) and `url` (the URL for the entry's link):

```
myMenu[0] = { entry: "Entry 1", url: "http://someurl/" };
myMenu[1] = { entry: "Entry 2", url: "http://anotherurl/
" };
myMenu[2] = { entry: "Entry 3", url: "http://otherurl/" };
```

10. As the last line of the script, call the `createMenu` function, providing `myMenu` as the object name for the menu, "My Menu" as the display header for the menu, the `myMenu` array as the array of entries, and positioning to place the menu at the left side of the window. This code produces a menu like Figure 200-1.

```
createMenu("myMenu","My Menu",myMenu,0,100);
```

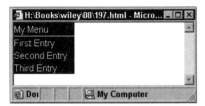

Figure 200-1: The menu in its expanded state.

201 # Placing Menu Code in an External File

In Task 200, you saw how to encapsulate the creation of a menu into functions. However, for the task to be really useful, you will want to be able to reuse the menu system in any of your HTML files and applications. To do this, you need to move the relevant JavaScript code and style sheets to external files that can simply be included in your HTML documents. The following steps outline how to do this:

1. Create a new file to contain the JavaScript code, and place the code for the createMenu and menuToggle functions in that file. The code looks like Listing 201-1.

notes

- Placing menu creation in functions effectively creates a menuing system in which the developer doesn't need to understand the JavaScript to create this type of dynamic drop-down menu.

- The link tag allows you to create certain types of relationships to external files. One type of relationship is to style sheets, effectively including the style sheet file in the current document.

```
function
createMenu(menuName,menuTitle,menuEntries,left,width) {
    numEntries = menuEntries.length;
    document.write('<div class="menuTitle" style="left:0px;
width:100px;"');
    document.write('onMouseover="menuToggle(\'' + menuName
+ '\');"');
    document.write('onMouseout="menuToggle(\'' + menuName
+ '\');">');
    document.write(menuTitle);
    document.write('</div>');
    document.write('<div id="myMenu" class="menu"
style="left:0px; width:100px;"');
    document.write('onMouseout="menuToggle(\'' + menuName
+ '\')">');
    for (i = 0; i < numEntries; i++) {
        document.write('<a href="' + menuEntries[i].url + '"
class="menuEntry">' + menuEntries[i].entry + '</a><br>');
    }
    document.write('</div>');
}

function menuToggle(target) {
    targetMenu = (document.getElementById) ?
document.getElementById(target).style : eval("document."
+ target);
    targetMenu.top = (parseInt(targetMenu.top) == 22) ?
-2000 : 22;
}
```

Listing 201-1: The menu.js file.

2. Save the file as `menu.js` and close it.

3. Create a new file to contain the styles for the menu, and place the style sheet code in it.

4. Save the file as `menu.css` and close it. Make sure it is in the same directory as `menu.js`.

5. Create a new file for the main HTML document that will display the menu.

6. In the header of the document, use the `script` tag to include `menu.js`:

```
<script language="JavaScript" src="menu.js">
</script>
```

7. In the header of the document, use the `link` tag to include `menu.css`:

```
<link rel="stylesheet" href="menu.css">
```

8. In the body of the document, include a script block to build an array of menu entries and call the `createMenu` function:

```
<body>
    <script language="JavaScript">
        var myMenu = new Array();
        myMenu[0] = { entry: "Entry 1", url: ⊃
"http://someurl/" };
        myMenu[1] = { entry: "Entry 2", url: ⊃
"http://anotherurl/" };
        myMenu[2] = { entry: "Entry 3", url: ⊃
"http://otherurl/" };
        createMenu("myMenu","My Menu",myMenu,0,100);
    </script>
</body>
```

Inserting a Prebuilt Drop-Down Menu

In Tasks 197 to 201, you saw how to build and manage your own simple drop-down menu system. However, the menus created in these tasks are quite simple. Using more advanced JavaScript, it is possible to create extremely sophisticated menu systems. These menus can offer improved visual effects, can create multitiered menus, and can do much more.

In this task, you will see how to use a complex prebuilt menu system. The menu in question is Top Navigational Bar IV from dynamicdrive.com and can be downloaded from `www.dynamicdrive.com/dynamicindex1/topmen4/index.htm`.

This system offers a flexible, robust system for creating navigation menu bars across the top of the page. These menus can be two levels deep and offer the ability to include icons in the menu entries and apply fading effects to the displaying of menus. The menu looks like Figure 202-1. Figure 202-2 illustrates one of the menus in the open state.

Figure 202-1: The Top Navigational Bar IV.

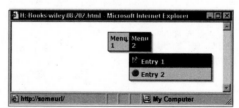

Figure 202-2: Opening a menu.

Creating this type of menu is quite complex. This menu system has more than 900 lines of dense code, which makes it clear that you are better off using a prebuilt system than creating your own.

The following steps outline how to build your own simple menu using this menu system:

1. Download the Top Navigation Bar IV; the code comes in a ZIP file.

2. Unzip the file to a directory in your Web site. The menu includes a number of image files, plus two JavaScript files (`mmenu.js` and `menu_array.js`), plus a sample HTML file (`menu.htm`).

3. In your HTML file, use `script` tags to include the two JavaScript files; these tags should be the first ones to appear in the body of your document:

```
<script language=JavaScript src="menu_array.js" ⮐
type=text/javascript></script>
<script language=JavaScript src="mmenu.js" ⮐
type=text/javascript></script>
```

4. Open the file menu_array.js in your editor.

5. Scroll down to the section that starts with the following text:

```
//////////////////////////////////
// Editable properties START here //
//////////////////////////////////
```

6. Make any changes to the visual style settings in this section of the file. The role of these settings is well documented in the file itself.

7. In the next section of the file, replace the series of addmenu function calls with your own to create your own hierarchy of menus. The meaning of the parameters to addmenu is described in the menu_array.js file. The following calls create a menu bar with two menus.

```
addmenu(menu=[⮐
"mainmenu",20,200,,1,,style1,1,"left",effect,,1,,,,,,,,,,⮐
,"Menu 1  ","show-menu=menu1",,"",1⮐
,"Menu 2  ","show-menu=menu2",,"",1⮐
])
addmenu(menu=["menu1",⮐
,,120,1,"",style1,,"left",effect,,,,,,,,,,,,⮐
,"Entry 1","http://someurl/",,,1⮐
,"Entry 2","http://otherurl/",,,1⮐
,"Entry 3","show-menu=submenu1",,,1⮐
])
addmenu(menu=["submenu1",⮐
,,170,1,"",style1,,"left",effect,,,,,,,,,,,,⮐
,"SubEntry1","http://anotherurl/",,,0⮐
])
addmenu(menu=["menu2",⮐
,,170,1,"",style1,,"left",effect,,,,,,,,,,,,⮐
,"<img src=newsimage.gif border=0> Entry ⮐
1","http://someurl/",,,1⮐
,"<img src=newsimage.gif border=0> Entry ⮐
2","http://otherurl/",,,1⮐
])
```

8. Ensure the last line of the file is as follows:

```
dumpmenus()
```

9. Save the file and open the main HTML file in your browser to view the menu.

Creating a Floating Window

At times, it is necessary to create a window that floats above another window at all times; even if the user attempts to bring the rear window to the foreground, you want the floating window to remain in front.

Creating these floating windows is fairly easy. From your main document, you create the new floating window, and then in the floating window, you trap any attempt to remove focus from the floating window and return focus to the window. The following steps outline the creation of a simple floating window:

1. Create a new document in your HTML editor. This document will serve as the document for the main, background window.

2. In the document header, create a new script block with opening and closing `script` tags.

3. In the script, create a function called `floatingWindow`, which will be used to display the floating window. Use the `function` keyword to create the function:

```
function floatingWindow(){
}
```

4. In the function, use the `window.open` method to open a new window of your preferred height; in the window, load the file `floatingWindow.html`. Here the window is 300 by 175 pixels, and the resulting `window` object is stored in the variable `floater`:

```
function floatingWindow(){
    floater = ⏎
window.open("floatingWindow.html","","height=175,⏎
width=300,scrollbars=no");
}
```

5. In the `onLoad` event handler of the `body` tag, call the `floatingWindow` function so that the final document looks like Listing 203-1.

6. Save and close the file, and open a new file in your editor to contain the content of the floating window.

7. In the `body` tag of file, use the `onBlur` event handler to call the `self.focus` method to force the window to come back to the front if the user attempts to remove focus from the window:

```
<body onBlur="self.focus()">

    Floating Window

</body>
```

notes

- There are numerous reasons why you might want to create floating windows as described here. For example, you might want a permanent toolbar or control panel window that provides controls that must be accessible to the user at all times; placing them in a floating window can help ensure this. Similarly, if loading a page takes a long time, you may want a floating window to appear during loading to provide other information or a status report to the user.

- The technique described here works on Internet Explorer and on Netscape Communicator 4.7x. It does not work on newer versions of Netscape. In these newer Netscape browsers, the window doesn't stay on top if the user brings the rear window to the foreground. This doesn't prevent you from using the floating window code outlined here to create a pop-up window, however.

```
<head>
<script language="JavaScript">
<!--
function floatingWindow(){
    floater = ⟳
window.open("floatingWindow.html","","height=175,⟳
width=300,scrollbars=no");
}
//-->
</script>
</head>

<body onLoad="floatingWindow()">
    Main Document Goes Here.
</body>
```

Listing 203-1: Creating a floating window.

8. Save the file as floatingWindow.html.

9. Open the background file and you should see the floating window displayed in the front, as in Figure 203-1.

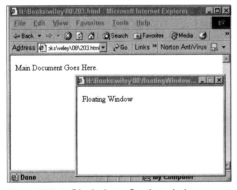

Figure 203-1: Displaying a floating window.

Closing a Floating Window

As described in Task 203, sometimes the goal of a floating window is to present a temporary placeholder while a larger, time-consuming document loads in a rear window. In this situation, it is necessary to be able to close the floating window programmatically once the rear window is ready.

JavaScript makes this easy by allowing you to reference the floating window from the main window that created it. This task shows how to close the floating window from the main window by automatically closing the floating window five seconds after it is displayed.

1. Create a new document in your HTML editor. This document will serve as the document for the main, background window.

2. In the document header, create a new script block with opening and closing `script` tags.

3. In the script, create a function called `floatingWindow`, which will be used to display the floating window. Use the `function` keyword to create the function. In the function, use the `window.open` method to open a new window of your preferred height; in the window, load the file `floatingWindow.html`. Here the window is 300 by 175 pixels, and the resulting `window` object is stored in the variable `floater`:

```
function floatingWindow(){
    floater = ⤸
window.open("floatingWindow.html","","height=175,⤸
width=300,scrollbars=no");
}
```

4. In the `onLoad` event handler of the `body` tag, call the `floatingWindow` function, and then use the `setTimeout` function to call `floater.close` five seconds after the floating window is displayed:

```
<body onLoad="floatingWindow(); setTimeout⤸
('floater.close()',5000);">
    Main Document Goes Here.
</body>
```

5. Save and close the file, and open a new file in your editor to contain the content of the floating window.

6. In the `body` tag of file, use the `onBlur` event handler to call the `self.focus` method to force the window to come back to the front if the user attempts to remove focus from the window:

```
<body onBlur="self.focus()">
    Floating Window
</body>
```

notes

- The technique described here works on Internet Explorer and on Netscape Communicator 4.7x. It does not work on newer versions of Netscape. In these newer Netscape browsers, the window doesn't stay on top if the user brings the rear window to the foreground. This doesn't prevent you from using the floating window code outlined here to create a popup window, however.

- The `setTimeout` function allows you to schedule a function or method call for future execution. The function takes two parameters: the function or method call to invoke and the number of milliseconds to wait before executing the function call.

- When you call `floater.close`, you are calling the `close` method of the `floater` object; `floater` is the `window` object associated with the floating window so this function call closes the floating window.

7. Save the file as `floatingWindow.html`.

8. Open the background file and you should see the floating window displayed in the front, as in Figure 204-1. Five seconds later the floating window should disappear, as illustrated in Figure 204-2.

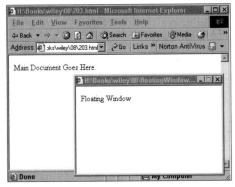

Figure 204-1: Displaying a floating window.

Figure 204-2: Closing the floating window.

Resizing a Floating Window

In Task 203, you saw how to create a floating window. Sometimes you will want to manipulate that floating window after it has been displayed. Among the ways in which a floating window can be manipulated is to resize it.

In this task, you learn how to resize a floating window using JavaScript code executed in the main, rear window. To do this, you rely on the `resizeTo` method of the `window` object.

The following task shows how to automatically resize the floating window to 400 by 300 pixels five seconds after it is displayed:

1. Create a new document in your HTML editor. This document will serve as the document for the main, background window.

2. In the document header, create a new script block with opening and closing `script` tags.

3. In the script, create a function called `floatingWindow`, which will be used to display the floating window. Use the `function` keyword to create the function. In the function, use the `window.open` method to open a new window of your preferred height; in the window, load the file `floatingWindow.html`. Here the window is 300 by 175 pixels, and the resulting `window` object is stored in the variable `floater`:

```
function floatingWindow(){
    floater = ⤶
window.open("floatingWindow.html","","height=175, ⤶
width=300,scrollbars=no");
}
```

4. In the script, create a second function called `resizeFloatingWindow`. The function should call `floater.resizeTo` to resize the floating window:

```
function resizeFloatingWindow() {
    floater.resizeTo(400,300);
}
```

5. In the `onLoad` event handler of the `body` tag, call the `floatingWindow` function, and then use the `setTimeout` function to call `resizeFloatingWindow` five seconds after the floating window is displayed:

```
<body onLoad="floatingWindow(); setTimeout(resize⤶
FloatingWindow()',5000);">
    Main Document Goes Here.
</body>
```

notes

* This method takes two parameters, the width and height of the window, and changes the window dimensions to match: *windowObject*.resizeTo (*width*,*height*); (see Step 3).

* The technique described here works on Internet Explorer and on Netscape Communicator 4.7x. It does not work on newer versions of Netscape. In these newer Netscape browsers, the window doesn't stay on top if the user brings the rear window to the foreground. This doesn't prevent you from using the floating window code outlined here to create a pop-up window, however.

* The setTimeout function allows you to schedule a function or method call for future execution. The function takes two parameters: the function or method call to invoke and the number of milliseconds to wait before executing the function call (see Step 5).

6. Save and close the file, and open a new file in your editor to contain the content of the floating window.

7. In the `body` tag of file, use the `onBlur` event handler to call the `self.focus` method to force the window to come back to the front if the user attempts to remove focus from the window:

```
<body onBlur="self.focus()">
    Floating Window
</body>
```

8. Save the file as `floatingWindow.html`.

9. Open the background file and you should see the floating window displayed in the front, as in Figure 205-1. Five seconds later the floating window should resize, as illustrated in Figure 205-2.

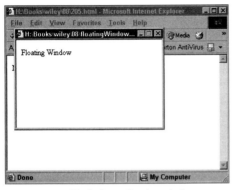

Figure 205-1: Displaying a floating window.

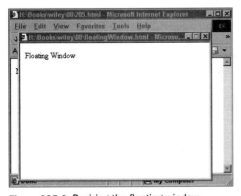

Figure 205-2: Resizing the floating window.

Moving a Floating Window

In the last task, you saw how to resize a floating window programatically. Sometimes you will want to manipulate that floating window in other ways after it has been displayed. Among the other ways in which a floating window can be manipulated is that you can move the window to a new location in the display.

In this task, you learn how to move a floating window using JavaScript code executed in the main, rear window. To do this, you rely on the `moveBy` method of the `window` object.

The following task shows how to automatically move the floating window to the right and down by 200 pixels in each direction five seconds after it is displayed:

1. Create a new document in your HTML editor. This document will serve as the document for the main, background window.

2. In the document header, create a new script block with opening and closing `script` tags.

3. In the script, create a function called `floatingWindow`, which will be used to display the floating window. Use the `function` keyword to create the function. In the function, use the `window.open` method to open a new window of your preferred height; in the window, load the file `floatingWindow.html`. Here the window is 300 by 175 pixels, and the resulting `window` object is stored in the variable `floater`:

```
function floatingWindow(){
    floater = ⤸
window.open("floatingWindow.html","","height=175,⤸
width=300,scrollbars=no");
}
```

4. In the script, create a second function called `moveFloatingWindow`. The function should call `floater.moveBy` to move the floating window:

```
function moveFloatingWindow() {
    floater.moveBy(200,200);
}
```

5. In the onLoad event handler of the `body` tag, call the `floatingWindow` function, and then use the `setTimeout` function to call `moveFloatingWindow` five seconds after the floating window is displayed:

```
<body onLoad="floatingWindow(); setTimeout('move⤸
FloatingWindow()',5000);">
    Main Document Goes Here.
</body>
```

6. Save and close the file, and open a new file in your editor to contain the content of the floating window.

notes

- This task takes two parameters, the horizontal and vertical offsets for moving the window: *windowObject*.moveBy (*horizontalOffset,vertical Offset*). The `moveBy` method moves a window relative to its current location. Negative values are possible to move a window to the left or up.

- Closely related to the `moveBy` method is the `moveTo` method; the critical difference is that the `moveTo` method allows you to specify an absolute position on the screen in pixels.

- The `moveBy` and `moveTo` methods are available in both Internet Explorer and Netscape browsers starting with version 4.

- The technique described here works on Internet Explorer and on Netscape Communicator 4.7x. It does not work on newer versions of Netscape. In these newer Netscape browsers, the window doesn't stay on top if the user brings the rear window to the foreground. This doesn't prevent you from using the floating window code outlined here to create a pop-up window, however.

- The `setTimeout` function allows you to schedule a function or method call for future execution. The function takes two parameters: the function or method call to invoke and the number of milliseconds to wait before executing the function call.

7. In the `body` tag of file, use the `onBlur` event handler to call the `self.focus` method to force the window to come back to the front if the user attempts to remove focus from the window:

```
<body onBlur="self.focus()">
   Floating Window
</body>
```

8. Save the file as `floatingWindow.html`.

9. Open the background file and you should see the floating window displayed in the front, as in Figure 206-1. Five seconds later the floating window should move, as illustrated in Figure 206-2.

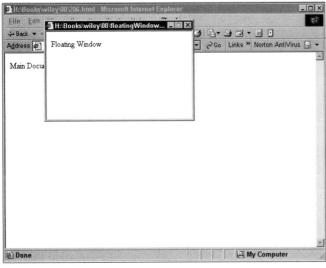

Figure 206-1: Displaying a floating window.

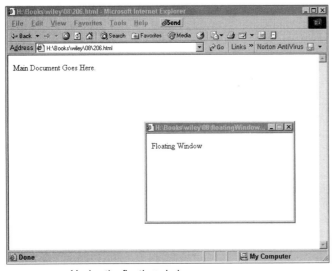

Figure 206-2: Moving the floating window.

Changing the Content of a Floating Window

In Task 205 you learned how to resize a floating window, and in Task 206 you saw how to move a floating window. Another useful manipulation of a floating window is to be able to change the contents of the window programmatically as events occur in the main, background window.

In this task, you learn how to change the content of a floating window using JavaScript code executed in the main, rear window. To do this, you rely on three methods of the document object: open, write, and close.

The following task shows how to automatically change the content of the floating window five seconds after it is displayed:

1. Create a new document in your HTML editor. This document will serve as the document for the main, background window.

2. In the document header, create a new script block with opening and closing script tags.

3. In the script, create a function called floatingWindow, which will be used to display the floating window. Use the function keyword to create the function. In the function, use the window.open method to open a new window of your preferred height; in the window, load the file floatingWindow.html. Here the window is 300 by 175 pixels, and the resulting window object is stored in the variable floater:

```
function floatingWindow(){
    floater = ⤶
window.open("floatingWindow.html","","height=175,⤶
width=300,scrollbars=no");
}
```

4. In the script, create a second function called newFloatingWindow. The function should use the document object to display new content in the floating window:

```
function newFloatingWindow() {
    floater.document.open();
    floater.document.write("New Floating Window Content");
    floater.document.close();
}
```

5. In the onLoad event handler of the body tag, call the floatingWindow function, and then use the setTimeout function to call newFloatingWindow five seconds after the floating window is displayed:

notes

- The technique described in this task is particularly useful if unexpected events happen when loading the background and the floating window is a placeholder while that loading takes place. Another use would be to change the contents of a toolbar or control panel displayed in the floating window as the contents of the main window change.

- The open method creates a new document stream in a specific window, the write method outputs text or HTML to the document stream, and the close method closes the document stream.

- Notice the use of floater.document.methodName. The document object is a property of the window object, and floater refers to the window object for the floating window.

- The setTimeout function allows you to schedule a function or method call for future execution. The function takes two parameters: the function or method call to invoke and the number of milliseconds to wait before executing the function call.

```
<body onLoad="floatingWindow(); setTimeout(new
FloatingWindow()',5000);">
    Main Document Goes Here.
</body>
```

6. Save and close the file, and open a new file in your editor to contain the content of the floating window.

7. In the `body` tag of file, use the `onBlur` event handler to call the `self.focus` method to force the window to come back to the front if the user attempts to remove focus from the window:

```
<body onBlur="self.focus()">
    Floating Window
</body>
```

8. Save the file as `floatingWindow.html`. Open the background file and you should see the floating window displayed in the front, as in Figure 207-1. Five seconds later the floating window should display the new content, as illustrated in Figure 207-2.

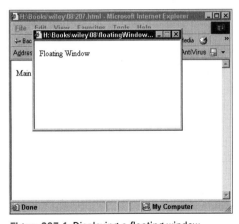

Figure 207-1: Displaying a floating window.

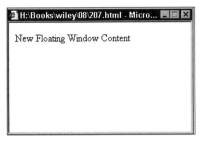

Figure 207-2: Changing the content of the floating window.

cross-reference

▪ The use of the document object for outputting to the browser is discussed in detail in Part 2.

Detecting Drag and Drop

Microsoft Internet Explorer provides a special set of events for detecting and responding to drag-and-drop events. This task discusses the basic application of these events to detecting drag-and-drop events in Internet Explorer.

The Microsoft event model provides seven events related to drag-and-drop activity:

- onDragStart: This event fires when the user presses the mouse button and begins dragging an object. This event is specified and trapped in the source object that is being dragged, and this is where you want to save information about the object that is being dragged.

- onDrag: This event fires repeatedly as an object continues to be dragged. It is specified and trapped in the source object that is being dragged.

- onDragEnter: This event fires when an object is dragged over a possible drop target. It is specified and trapped in the drop target object.

- onDragOver: This event fires repeatedly as an object is being dragged over a possible drop target. It is specified and trapped in the drop target object.

- onDragLeave: This event fires when an object is dragged out of a possible drop target. It is specified and trapped in the drop target object.

- onDragEnd: This event fires when an object that is being dragged is dropped anywhere. It is specified and trapped in the source object that is being dragged.

- onDrop: This event fires when an object is dropped in a possible drop target. It is specified and trapped in the drop target object.

There are a few catches to using these events. First, unless you are dropping on a text box, the onDrop event will not be triggered unless the default behavior for the onDragLeave and onDragEnd event handlers is canceled. This is done by setting event.returnValue to false for these events in the tag for the drop target object, as in the following:

```
<div onDragLeave="event.returnValue = false;" onDragEnd=⊃
"event.returnValue=false;">
```

The following steps show how to create a simple drag-and-drop example. In this example, the user can drag selected text over a target blue box. When the user drops the object, a dialog box will confirm the name of the object that was dragged and the name of the object where it was dropped.

1. Create a new document and create a script block in the header. In the script block, define the variable sourceObject as a new Object that will be a placeholder to store the object the user drags:

```
var sourceObject = new Object();
```

notes

- For a more detailed discussion of drag and drop in Internet Explorer, consult the article "Drag and Drop in Internet Explorer" at http://webreference.com/programming/javascript/dragdropie/.

- Notice the reference to the event object. The event object exists for each event handler and includes information about the event. One of the properties of this object is the returnValue property used here. Another useful property is the srcElement property, which points to the object where the event fired.

- Notice that event.src Element is used here. This allows you to store the object being dragged in sourceObject for later use when the object is dropped.

- The id attribute of an object contains the name specified in the id attribute of the tag that created the object.

2. In the body of the document, use span tags to specify the text for dragging. Name the block dragThis with the id attribute, and use the onDragStart event handler to assign the source object to sourceObject when the user starts dragging the text:

```
<span id="dragThis"⤵
onDragStart="sourceObject = event.srcElement;">
   Drag This
</span>
```

3. Create the blue target box, using a div tag. Name the box dropHere, and cancel onDragEnter and onDragOver as outlined earlier in this task. Finally, use onDrop to display a dialog box naming the object that was dragged and where it was dropped.

```
<div id="dropHere"
 onDragEnter="event.returnValue = false;"
 onDragOver="event.returnValue = false;"
 onDrop="alert(sourceObject.id + ' was dropped on '⤵
+ event.srcElement.id);"
 style="height:100;width:100;left:500;position:absolute;⤵
background-color:blue;">
    
</div>
```

4. Save the file and open it in your browser.

5. Select the text, and drag it and drop it on the blue box. A dialog box like Figure 208-1 appears.

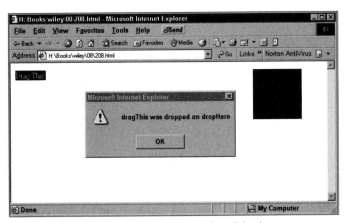

Figure 208-1: Dropping the text displays an alert dialog box.

Moving a Dragged Object in Drag and Drop

In Task 208 you saw the basics of drag and drop. This task shows you how to move a dragged object in Internet Explorer. For instance, consider Figure 209-1. In this case, the goal is to allow the user to drag the text into the blue square and drop it to leave it in the square and remove the original text, as in Figure 209-2.

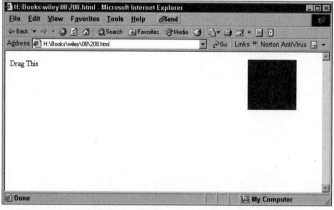

Figure 209-1: Preparing to move the text.

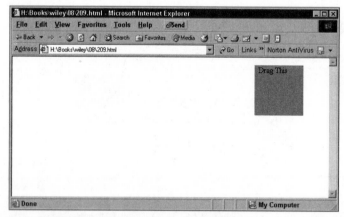

Figure 209-2: Moving the text after dragging and dropping.

Doing this requires several steps:

1. When the user starts dragging the object, save the object for future use.

2. When the user drops the object on the blue box, insert the HTML from the source object into the body of the blue box.

3. Remove the original object from the page.

The following steps build this example:

1. Create a new document and create a script block in the header. In the script block, define the variable `sourceObject` as a new `Object` that will be a placeholder to store the object the user drags:

```
var sourceObject = new Object();
```

2. Add a function to the script block named `moveObject` that takes two arguments: `source` and `destination`, which are the source object being dragged and the target object where the source object was dropped:

```
function moveObject(source,destination) {
}
```

3. In the function, add the complete HTML of the source object to the inside of the destination object, and then set the `display` style of the source object to `none` to hide it. This duplicates the source object in the inside of the destination drop target object and then hides the original:

```
function moveObject(source,destination) {
    destination.innerHTML += source.outerHTML;
    source.style.display = "none";
}
```

4. In the body of the document, use `span` tags to specify the text for dragging. Name the block `dragThis` with the `id` attribute, and use the `onDragStart` event handler to assign the source object to `sourceObject` when the user starts dragging the text:

```
<span id="dragThis"↵
onDragStart="sourceObject = event.srcElement;">
    Drag This
</span>
```

5. Create the blue target box, using a `div` tag. Name the box `dropHere`, and cancel `onDragEnter` and `onDragOver` as outlined earlier in this task. Finally, use `onDrop` to call the function `moveObject` with `sourceObject` and `event.srcElement` as the two arguments.

```
<div id="dropHere"
  onDragEnter="event.returnValue = false;"
  onDragOver="event.returnValue = false;"
  onDrop="moveObject(sourceObject,event.srcElement);"
  style="height:100;width:100;left:500;position:absolute;↵
background-color:blue;"> </div>
```

6. Save the file, and open it in a browser to test the drag-and-drop code.

Task 210

Changing Cursor Styles

Sometimes it is useful to be able to override the default cursor to provide information to the user about the object the mouse is over . This is achieved in Internet Explorer using the `cursor` style attribute in cascading style sheets. This allows you to specify the state of the cursor while it is over an object, and this is useful to control the cursor while an object is being dragged. The basic syntax to use this attribute is as follows:

```
.styleName { cursor: cursorName; }
```

The possible cursor names include the following:

- `auto`: Allows the browser to automatically choose a cursor
- `all-scroll` (Internet Explorer 6): Arrows pointing in all four directions with a dot in the middle
- `col-resize` (Internet Explorer 6): Arrows pointing left and right separated by a vertical bar
- `crosshair`: A simple crosshair
- `default`: The default cursor (usually an arrow)
- `hand`: The hand cursor, which is typically used when the pointer hovers over a link
- `help`: An arrow with a question mark
- `move`: Crossed arrows
- `no-drop` (Internet Explorer 6): A hand with a small circle with a line through it
- `not-allowed` (Internet Explorer 6): A circle with a line through it
- `pointer` (Internet Explorer 6): The hand cursor, which is typically used when the pointer hovers over a link
- `progress` (Internet Explorer 6): An arrow with an hourglass next to it
- `row-resize` (Internet Explorer 6): Arrows pointing up and down separated by a horizontal bar
- `text`: An I-bar
- `vertical-text` (Internet Explorer 6): A horizontal I-bar
- `wait`: An hourglass

note

- There are a number of reasons why you might want to change the cursor. For instance, if an object has help information associated with it, you might want a cursor with a question mark to appear when the mouse is over the object. Similarly, an object that can be moved should display a crosshair cursor when the mouse is over it.

The following example shows three boxes on the page, and each displays a different cursor (a hand, an hourglass, and a crosshair) when the mouse rolls over the box:

1. Create a new document in your editor.

2. In the body of the document, use a `div` tag to create a box. Set the cursor attribute to `hand`. In this example, the box has a border and is 100 pixels by 100 pixels:

```
<div style="border-style: solid; width: 100; height: ⊃
100; cursor: hand;"> </div>
```

3. Create a second box and set the cursor attribute to `wait` for an hourglass:

```
<div style="border-style: solid; width: 100; height: ⊃
100; cursor: wait;"> </div>
```

4. Create a third box and set the cursor attribute to `crosshair`.

```
<div style="border-style: solid; width: 100; height: ⊃
100; cursor: crosshair;"> </div>
```

5. Save the file and open it in a browser. The page shows three boxes, as in Figure 210-1. Move the mouse over the three boxes to view the three cursors.

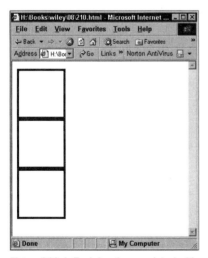

Figure 210-1: Each box is associated with a different cursor.

cross-reference

▪ The use of the `div` tag is discussed in Task 169.

Determining the Current Scroll Position

U sing JavaScript, you can determine how far down the page the user has scrolled. Consider Figure 211-1, for example. Here the window is quite narrow, so the user must scroll further down the window to see the same text as in a wide window, where scrolling would be minimized.

notes

- JavaScript allows you to determine the scroll position by allowing you to check how many pixels down the scroll bar the user has scrolled. This means that the scroll distance is related to the size of the window.

- When you are working with frames, keep in mind that the `parent` object in a frame refers to the parent frameset. This object has a `frames` property that is an array of frame objects referring to all frames in the frameset. With two horizontal frames, the top frame will be `frames[0]` and the bottom frame will be `frames[1]`.

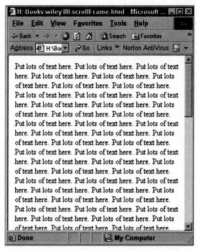

Figure 211-1: A long document in a narrow window.

To determine the vertical position of the scroll bar, you need to use different techniques in Internet Explorer and Netscape. In Internet Explorer, the `scrollTop` property of the `body` object points to the current scroll position:

```
document.body.scrollTop
```

In Netscape, the `pageYOffset` property of the `window` object provides the same information:

```
window.pageYOffset
```

The following steps illustrate how to use this capability to create a two-frame HTML page in which the bottom frame contains a document the user can scroll and the top frame contains a button the user can click to view the current scroll position in a dialog box:

1. Create a new document to hold the contents of the bottom frame.

2. In the header of the document, create a script block. In the script block, create a function named `scrollCheck` that doesn't take any arguments:

   ```
   function scrollCheck() {
   }
   ```

3. In the function, use an `if` statement to check if the user is using Internet Explorer; this is achieved by checking if `document.all`

exists (it won't exist in Netscape). Based on this, use the `alert` method to display the current vertical scroll position:

```
function scrollCheck() {
    if (document.all) {
        alert(document.body.scrollTop);
    } else {
        alert(window.pageYOffset);
    }
}
```

4. In the body of the document, put lots of text so that the document is likely to stretch beyond the bottom of the average browser window.

5. Save the file as `scrollFrame.html` and close it. Create another new file to hold the top frame.

6. Create a button in the body of the document, using the `input` tag, and display the text "`Scroll Position`".

```
<input type="button" value="Scroll Position">
```

7. Add an `onClick` event handler to the button, and use that to call the `scrollCheck` function in the other frame:

```
<input type="button" value="Scroll Position" ⟳
onClick="parent.frames[1].scrollCheck();">
```

8. Save the file as `scrollButton.html` and close it. Create another new file to hold the frameset.

9. Create a frameset with `scrollButton.html` in the top frame and `scrollFrame.html` in the bottom frameset:

```
<frameset rows="50,*">
    <frame src="scrollButton.html">
    <frame src="scrollFrame.html" id="mainFrame">
</frameset>
```

10. Save the file and open it in your browser. The two frames are displayed. Scroll the bottom frame to the desired location, and then click the Scroll Position button in the top frame. The current scroll position of the bottom frame is displayed in a dialog box, as in Figure 211-2.

Figure 211-2: Checking the scroll position of the bottom frame.

Creating an Expanding/Collapsing Menu

This task shows how to quickly build a simple expanding/collapsing menu with a minimum of JavaScript code required. The menu you will build allows for a hierarchical menu to be defined as a series of embedded unordered lists. In fully expanded form, the menu might look like Figure 212-1, but it is possible to expand or collapse any tree of the hierarchy.

notes

- In the case of parent-child relationships, when the child is hidden, the space taken by the child is removed; this allows the menu outlined above to collapse automatically. The `display` attribute is simple to use: no value means the object is displayed; `none` means the object is hidden.

- Notice the use of the conditional based on `document.getElementById`. In Internet Explorer, this method is available and you use it to access the `style` property of the target object. But in Netscape, this method is not available and the correct object to work with is the object itself and not a `style` property. By testing for the existence of the `getElementById` method, you can determine what browser you are using.

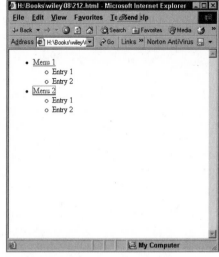

Figure 212-1: The menu fully expanded.

The principle behind this task is two-fold:

1. Objects on the page have parents and children. If one object is contained within another's opening and closing tags, then the object is the child.

2. Objects can have a style attribute named `display` that controls whether the object is displayed.

The following task builds a page containing such an expanding and collapsing menu:

1. Create a new file and place a script block in the header of the document, using opening and closing `script` tags:

2. In the script block, create a function called `toggleMenu` that takes a single argument—the name of the object to display or hide:

```
function toggleMenu(target) {
}
```

3. In the function, create a variable named `targetLayer` to select the appropriate object to use in manipulating the display `style` attribute:

```
targetLayer = (document.getElementById) ? document.
getElementById(target).style : eval("document." + target);
```

4. Use a conditional expression to hide or display the object in question. This is done by checking if the `display` attribute is set to `none`. If it is, the attribute is set to an empty string. Otherwise, it is set to `none`. The result of this logic is that the `display` attribute toggles between none and an empty string each time the function is called. The resulting function is as follows:

```
function toggleMenu(target) {
    targetLayer = (document.getElementById) ? document.⤴
getElementById(target).style : eval("document." + target);
    targetLayer.display = (targetLayer.display == "none") ⤴
? "" : "none";
}
```

5. In the body of the document, create your menu hierarchy with unordered lists:

```
<ul>
    <li>
        Menu 1
        <ul>
            <li>Entry 1</li>
            <li>Entry 2</li>
        </ul>
    </li>
    <li>
        Menu 2
        <ul>
            <li>Entry 1</li>
            <li>Entry 2</li>
        </ul>
    </li>
</ul>
```

6. In the `ul` tags for the child lists, assign names with the `id` attribute, and use the `style` attribute to set `display` to none. For the first menu, you might use the following:

```
<ul id="menu1" style="display:none">
```

7. Turn the entries in the parent list into links. Each link should use a `javascript:` URL to call `toggleMenu` and pass it the name of the appropriate child list. As an example, the entry for the first menu might be as follows:

```
<a href="javascript:toggleMenu('menu1');">Menu 1</a>
```

8. Save the file and open it in a browser to test the menu.

213

Creating a Highlighting Menu Using Just Text and CSS—No JavaScript

Sometimes the simplest interactive menus are those that require the least effort to create. This task shows how to create a simple menu bar where the menu entries highlight when the mouse hovers over them—without any JavaScript or other dynamic scripting. Instead, only the cascading style sheets side of Dynamic HTML is used.

This task relies on effective use of style sheets. The key is that any style entry, such as a class, can have a special case defined for when the mouse hovers over an element on the page as a link. For instance, consider the following simple example:

```
<head>
   <style type="text/css">
       .item { text-decoration: none; }
       .item:hover {text-decoration: underline; }
   </style>
</head>

<body>
   <a href="http://someurl" class="item">The Link</a>
</body>
```

Here one style class named item is created. It is defined so that when a link using that class is in its normal state, it is not underlined, as shown in Figure 213-1. However, when the mouse hovers over the link, the underlining appears.

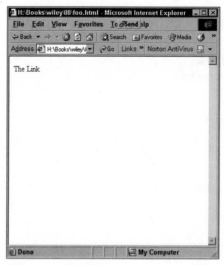

Figure 213-1: The link is normally not underlined.

The following steps show how to create a menu bar consisting of three gray buttons. When the mouse pointer is over the button, it switches color to a dark blue.

1. Create a new HTML document in your editor.

2. In the header of the document, create a style block with opening and closing `style` tags.

3. In the style block, create a style class named `menuEntry`. Make sure the height and width and background color of the style are specified. Here the buttons will be 100 by 25 pixels with a gray background. In addition, you can optionally set a border style, text styles, and so on.

```
.menuEntry {
    width: 100px;
    height: 25px;
    background-color: #CCCCCC;
    border-style: solid;
    border-width: 1px;
    border-color: black;
    text-align: center;
    text-decoration: none;
    color: #020A33;
}
```

tip
▪ When defining the style for `menuEntry`, you are free to use any valid style attributes and settings to achieve the effect you are aiming for.

4. In the style block, create a special hover style for the `menuEntry` class. This should change the color of the background and text to create the highlighting effect:

```
.menuEntry:hover {
    background-color: #020A33;
    color: yellow;
}
```

5. In the body of the document, create three links that use the `menuEntry` class. Use the `style` attribute to position these links at even intervals across the top of the page:

```
<a href="http://someurl/" class="menuEntry" style=⊃
"top: 1; left: 1;">Entry 1</a>
<a href="http://someurl/" class="menuEntry" style=⊃
"top: 1; left: 52;">Entry 2</a>
<a href="http://someurl/" class="menuEntry" style=⊃
"top: 1; left: 103;">Entry 3</a>
```

cross-reference
▪ Style sheets are one of the main subjects of Part 7.

6. Save the file and open it in a browser to use the menu.

Creating a Highlighting Menu Using Text, CSS, and JavaScript

This task shows how to use JavaScript to implement a hover effect instead of simply using CSS. The possible advantages of this include being able to execute any JavaScript code that is necessary when the mouse pointer hovers over an entry in the menu.

This task relies on the `borderStyle` property of objects in JavaScript, which allows you to reset the border style of an object programmatically in code. When set to `outset`, the object will have a three-dimensional border as in Figure 214-1. Setting the property to `none` removes the border.

note

- Notice the use of the conditional based on `document.getElementById`. In Internet Explorer, this method is available and you use it to access the `style` property of the target object. But in Netscape, this method is not available and the correct object to work with is the object itself and not a `style` property. By testing for the existence of the `getElementById` method, you can determine what browser you are using.

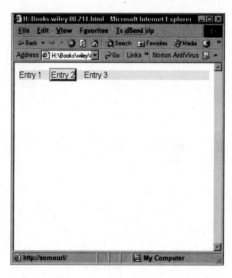

Figure 214-1: Highlighting a menu element with a three-dimensional border.

The following steps build the menu illustrated previously:

1. Create a new document.

2. In the header of the document, create a style block. In the style block, define a `menuItems` class with the visual style that is desired. Make sure border color and size is specified but that the border style is set to none:

```
<style type="text/css">
    .menuitems {
        border-size:2.5px;
        border-style:none;
        border-color:#FFF2BF;
        text-decoration:none;
        color:blue;
        font-family:Arial,Helvetica,SANS-SERIF;
    }
</style>
```

3. In the header of the document, create a script block with opening and closing `script` tags.

4. In the script, create a function called `toggleMenu`. The function should take two arguments: `target`, which contains the name of the object to toggle, and `border`, which contains the desired border style as a string:

```
function toggleMenu(target,border) {
}
```

5. In the function, define a variable named `targetLayer` that will point to the object you can use to manipulate the visual style of the object named in `target`:

```
targetLayer = (document.getElementById) ?
document.getElementById(target).style : eval
("document." + target); @
```

6. Complete the function by setting the object's border style to the style specified in the `border` argument:

```
function toggleMenu(target,border) {
    targetLayer = (document.getElementById) ?
document.getElementById(target).style : eval
("document." + target);
    targetLayer.borderStyle = border;
}
```

7. In the body of the document, create a layer with a `div` tag:

```
<div style="background-color:#FFF2BF;">
</div>
```

8. Inside the layer, create one or more links that use the class `menuItems` and are named with the `id` attribute. Use the `onMouseover` and `onMouseout` event handlers to call `toggleMenu` to switch the border style:

```
<div style="background-color:#FFF2BF;">
    <a href="http://someurl/" class="menuItems" id=
"entry1" onMouseover="toggleMenu('entry1','outset');"
onMouseout="toggleMenu('entry1','none');">Entry 1</a>
  
    <a href="http://someurl/" class="menuItems" id=
"entry2" onMouseover="toggleMenu('entry2','outset');"
onMouseout="toggleMenu('entry2','none');">Entry 2</a>
  
    <a href="http://someurl/" class="menuItems" id=
"entry3" onMouseover="toggleMenu('entry3','outset');"
onMouseout="toggleMenu('entry3','none');">Entry 3</a>
</div>
```

cross-reference
- The use of the `div` tag is discussed in Task 169.

9. Save the file and open it in a browser to test the menu.

Placing Content Offscreen

With JavaScript it is easy to hide content offscreen until you need it. This is an alternative to using the visibility of layers to hide and display content. Using JavaScript, in fact, you can control the placement of the top and left of any element on your page. With this in mind, you can use a negative pixel value to place an element off the top of the screen.

The principle is simple. Given an object named myObject, you can specify the top of the object in pixels relative to the browser window with the following:

```
myObject.top = pixel placement relative to top of window;
```

For instance, if you want the object to be placed 100 pixels down from the top of the window, use this:

```
myObject.top = 100;
```

Similarly, you can specify the left of the object, as in the following example, which places an object 2000 pixels off the left side of the browser window:

```
myObject.left = -2000;
```

The question at hand is how to identify the appropriate object to apply the top or left property to. In Internet Explorer, objects have a style property that contains a style object. Therefore, for an object on the page named myObject, in Internet Explorer, you refer to myObject.style.top and myObject.style.left. In Netscape, the top and left properties are directly accessible from the object as myObject.top and myObject.left.

The following task shows how to display text in a layer and allow users to hide the text when they click on a link:

1. Create a new document.

2. In the header of the document, create a script block with opening and closing script tags.

3. In the script, create a function named hideLayer that takes a single attribute target; target will represent the name of the object that will by hidden when the user clicks on the link:

```
function hideLayer(target) {
}
```

4. In the function, create a variable named targetLayer to hold the object you will work with; this will be dependent on the browser being used:

```
targetLayer = (document.getElementById) ? document.⤴
getElementById(target).style : eval("document." + target);
```

notes

- Notice the use of the conditional based on document. getElementById. In Internet Explorer, this method is available and you use it to access the style property of the target object. But in Netscape, this method is not available and the correct object to work with is the object itself and not a style property. By testing for the existence of the getElementById method, you can determine what browser you are using.

- To hide menus, you set the top of the menu object to -2000 pixels. This should be large enough to hide any menu that fits on the screen, since most screen resolutions do not exceed 2000 pixels in depth.

- Notice the use of the position: absolute style attribute in the div tag. This is necessary to allow absolute placement of the object when you reset the top of the layer.

5. Use the `targetLayer` object to set the top of the object to -2000 pixels to move it off the screen. The function looks like this:

```
function hideLayer(target) {
    targetLayer = (document.getElementById) ?
document.getElementById(target).style : eval
("document." + target);
    targetLayer.top = -2000;
}
```

6. In the body of the document, use opening and closing `div` tags to create a layer named `myLayer`:

```
<div id="myLayer" style="position: absolute;">
</div>
```

7. In the layer, place any text you want to display, followed by a link that uses a `javascript:` URL to call the `hideLayer` function, and pass in the name of the layer as string:

```
<div id="myLayer" style="position: absolute;">
    <p>Here is some text in a layer.</p>
    <p><a href="javascript:hideLayer('myLayer')">
Click here to hide the layer</a></P>
</div>
```

8. Save the file and open it in your browser. The text and link appears, as in Figure 215-1.

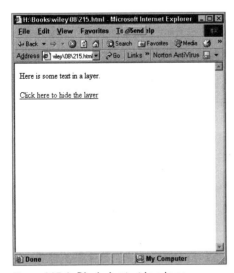

Figure 215-1: Displaying text in a layer.

9. Click on the link, and the text and link in the layer disappears.

Sliding Content into View

By extending the principle of hiding objects offscreen, you can build a system to slide an object into view from outside the browser window. The idea is simple: Place an object offscreen and then gradually change its placement until it is fully displayed in the window.

The simple approach to this would be to place the object offscreen and then use a loop to move the object onto the screen pixel by pixel. For instance, you could use a simple `for` loop to move the object `myObject` onscreen from 200 pixels above the top of the window into the window.

The problem with this is that the loop moves so quickly, the object effectively appears onscreen instantly. Instead, it may be necessary to pause between each change in the location of the object. This can be achieved using the `setTimeout` method, which allows a scheduled call to a function. For instance, the following code causes each move to happen one-tenth of a second apart:

```
function moveLayer(target,newTop) {
    targetLayer = (document.getElementById) ? document.↵
getElementById(target).style : eval("document." + target);
    targetLayer.top = newTop;
    if (newTop < 0) {
        setTimeout("moveLayer('" + target + "'," + ↵
(newTop+1) + ")",100);
    }
}
moveLayer('myObject',-200);
```

The following task shows a complete page where the text of the page scrolls onto the screen using this technique:

1. Create a new document in your editor.

2. In the header of the document, create a script block with opening and closing `script` tags.

3. In the script, create a variable named `slideSpeed` that indicates the speed at which the content should slide onto the screen. The lower the value of `slideSpeed`, the faster the content will move when sliding:

   ```
   var slideSpeed = 1;
   ```

4. Create the `moveLayer` function as outlined earlier in this task. Notice that the time specified in the `setTimeout` function uses `slideSpeed` as a multiplier to set the number of milliseconds between each call to the `moveLayer` function:

   ```
   function moveLayer(target,newTop) {
       targetLayer = (document.getElementById) ? document.↵
   getElementById(target).style : eval("document." + target);
   ```

notes

- In this task things move much slower; in fact, they may move too slowly. This can be adjusted by changing the 100 in the `setTimeout` function call to a smaller value.

- Notice the use of the `setTimeout` function. Here you are essentially scheduling a recursive call to the same function and rebuilding the function arguments with the new top point set 1 pixel lower than it was on the current call. This is allowed to repeat until the top of the object is at 0 pixels, which means it is just inside the window.

- Notice the use of the conditional based on `document.getElementById`. In Internet Explorer, this method is available and you use it to access the `style` property of the target object But in Netscape, this method is not available and the correct object to work with is the object itself and not a `style` property. By testing for the existence of the `getElementById` method, you can determine what browser you are using.

```
        targetLayer.top = newTop;
        if (newTop < 0) {
            setTimeout("moveLayer('"+target+"','"+(newTop+1)+")",⤴
slideSpeed * 25);
        }
    }
```

5. In the `body` tag, use the `onLoad` event handler to call `moveLayer` when the page loads. The sliding animation will start at 100 pixels above the top of the window, since this is where the layer in question will be placed initially:

```
<body onLoad="moveLayer('myLayer',-100);">
```

6. Create a layer using opening and closing `div` tags, and name the layer `myLayer` with the `id` attribute.

7. Set the style attribute of the `div` tag to apply absolute positioning, and position the layer 100 pixels beyond the top of the window:

```
<div id="myLayer" style="position: absolute; top: -100;">
```

8. Place any text desired in the layer:

```
<div id="myLayer" style="position: absolute; top: -100;">
    <p>
        Place the text of the page here.
        Place the text of the page here.
        Place the text of the page here.
        Place the text of the page here.
        Place the text of the page here.
    </p>
</div>
```

9. Save the file and open it in your browser. Initially, nothing will be displayed. Gradually, the content of the page will slide down into the window, as illustrated in Figure 216-1. Finally, the entire text will be displayed, and sliding will stop when the text reaches the top of the window.

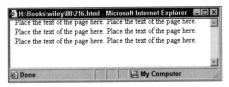

Figure 216-1: The content will slide down.

Creating a Sliding Menu

Extending the technique outlined in Task 216, you can create a menu that slides into view when it is needed and then is hidden when it is not needed. This task shows how to create a menu that only displays a small link initially. When the user clicks the link, the menu slides into view horizontally, as shown in Figure 217-2. When the user is finished with the menu, he or she can click on the link at the far right to hide the menu and it will slide back to the left to be hidden.

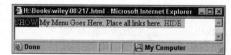

Figure 217-1: The menu slides into view when it is needed.

The following steps create a page that implements this menu:

1. In the header of the HTML file, create a script block and define three variables: `slideSpeed` (the delay factor between slide increments; the lower the number the faster the slide effect), `menuWidth` (the width in pixels the menu will require), and `leftPosition` (the left position where the menu should end up after sliding into the window):

```
var slideSpeed = 1;
var menuWidth = 300;
var leftPosition = 51;
```

2. Create a function called `showLayer` designed to slide the menu into view; this function will resemble the function used in Task 216. The function takes two arguments—the name of the layer containing the menu and the left position where the layer should be moved to:

```
function showLayer(target,newLeft) {
    targetLayer = (document.getElementById) ? document.
getElementById(target).style : eval("document." + target);
    targetLayer.left = newLeft;
    if (newLeft < leftPosition) {
        setTimeout("showLayer('"+target+"',"+
(newLeft+1)+")",slideSpeed * 10);
    }
}
```

3. Create a function called `hideLayer` designed to slide the menu out of view:

```
function hideLayer(target,newLeft) {
    targetLayer = (document.getElementById) ? document.
getElementById(target).style : eval("document." + target);
```

```
        targetLayer.left = newLeft;
        if (newLeft > -menuWidth) {
            setTimeout("hideLayer('"+target+"','"+
(newLeft-1)+")",slideSpeed * 10);
        }
    }
}
```

4. In the body of the document, create a layer with a `div` tag to display the link users will use to slide the menu into view:

```
<div style="position: absolute; top: 0; left: 0; width:
50; background: #020A33; z-index: 1;">
</div>
```

5. In the layer, create a link to call the `showLayer` function when it is clicked; start moving from the negative value of `menuWidth`:

```
<div style="position: absolute; top: 0; left: 0; width:
50; background: #020A33; z-index: 1;">
    <a style="color: yellow; text-decoration: none;"
href="javascript:showLayer('myLayer',-menuWidth);
">SHOW</a>
</div>
```

6. Create a layer with a `div` tag to hold the menu itself. The layer should be named `myLayer`:

```
<div id="myLayer" style="position: absolute; top: 0;
left: -300; width: 300; background: #CCCCCC; color:
black; z-index: 0;">
</div>
```

7. In the layer, create your menu and include a link that uses a `javascript:` URL to call the `hideLayer` function so the user can hide the menu:

```
<div id="myLayer" style="position: absolute; top: 0;
left: -300; width: 300; background: #CCCCCC; color:
black; z-index: 0;">
    My Menu Goes Here. Place all links here.
    <a style="text-decoration: none;" href="javascript:
hideLayer('myLayer',leftPosition);">HIDE</a>
</div>
```

8. Save the file and open it in a browser to use the menu.

Auto-Scrolling a Page

This task extends the ability to read a page's scroll position outlined in Task 211 and provides a simple mechanism to automatically scroll a page from top to bottom once it is loaded. This task relies on the principle that not only can the scroll position be read, it can also be written.

In Internet Explorer, the scroll position is controlled through the `document. body.scrollTop` property, while in Netscape, it is controlled by `window. pageYOffset`.

The following steps set up a page that automatically scrolls from top to bottom once loaded:

1. Create a new document and place a script block in the header of the document:

   ```
   <script language="JavaScript">
   </script>
   ```

2. In the script, create a function named `scrollPage` that takes no arguments. This function will move the scroll bar down 1 pixel, and if the page is not yet at the bottom schedule, it will make another call to itself to move the scroll bar further down:

   ```
   function scrollPage() {
   }
   ```

3. Start the scroll by creating the variables `origScroll` and `newScroll` to hold values later in the function:

   ```
   var origScroll = 0;
   var newScroll = 0;
   ```

4. Test for the existence of `document.all` to determine whether or not the browser is Internet Explorer:

   ```
   if (document.all) {
   ```

5. If the browser is Internet Explorer, first store the current scroll position in `origScroll`, then add 1 to `document.body.scrollTop` to move the scroll bar down 1 pixel, and, finally, store the new scroll position in `newScroll`:

   ```
   if (document.all) {
      origScroll = document.body.scrollTop;
      document.body.scrollTop += 1;
      newScroll = document.body.scrollTop;
   }
   ```

notes

- The notion behind comparing `newScroll` and `origScroll` is that even if the current scroll position is increased by 1, if the page is at the bottom, the scroll position value will not actually change.

- The `setTimeout` function allows you to schedule a function or method call for future execution. The function takes two parameters: the function or method call to invoke and the number of milliseconds to wait before executing the function call.

6. If the browser is Netscape, perform the same steps as for Internet Explorer but use `window.pageYOffset` for the scroll position:

```
if (document.all) {
    origScroll = document.body.scrollTop;
    document.body.scrollTop += 1;
    newScroll = document.body.scrollTop;
} else {
    origScroll = window.pageYOffset;
    window.pageYOffset+=1;
    newScroll = window.pageYOffset;
}
```

7. Test if `newScroll` is bigger than `origScroll`. If it is, then the scrolling hadn't reached the bottom of the page and `setTimeout` is used to schedule a new call to the `scrollPage` function:

```
if (newScroll > origScroll) {
    setTimeout("scrollPage()",25);
}
```

8. In the `body` tag, use the `onLoad` event handler to call the `scrollPage` function once the page loads:

```
<body onLoad="scrollPage()">
```

9. Place any text for the page in the body of the document and save the page.

10. Load the page in your browser, and it automatically starts scrolling, as in Figure 218-1.

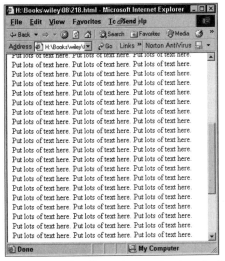

Figure 218-1: Scrolling a document automatically.

Part 9: Handling Events

Task **219**

Responding to the onMouseOver **Event**

Javascript provides an event model that allows you to script actions to take in response to events. These event handlers consist of JavaScript to execute only when the event occurs. Most events are associated with user actions executed with items in the visible HTML page, and most of these event handlers can be specified through attributes of HTML tags.

One event that is commonly used in JavaScript is the onMouseOver event. This event is triggered when the user moves the mouse pointer over an element in a page such as a link or an image. It is common to use the onMouseOver event with images.

The basic structure of an event handler looks like the following, illustrated with an a tag:

```
<a href="some url" onMouseOver="some JavaScript">link text</a>
```

While you can string together multiple JavaScript commands, separating them by commas, in the onMouseOver attributes, typically you will want to create a JavaScript function elsewhere in your document and then call that function from the onMouseOver attribute to keep your HTML code clean and simple to follow.

The following steps display an alert dialog box when the user rolls over a link in an HTML document:

1. Start a script block with the script tag:

   ```
   <script language="JavaScript">
   ```

2. Start a function named doMouseOver to be the function you will call when the user triggers the onMouseOver event; the function takes a single parameter named message that will contain a string intended to be displayed in the alert dialog box:

   ```
   function doMouseOver(message) {
   ```

3. Use the alert method of the window object to display the message in an alert dialog box:

   ```
   window.alert(message);
   ```

4. End the function with a closing curly bracket:

   ```
   }
   ```

note

- The onMouseOver event is commonly used to produce rollover effects. When the pointer moves over an image, it changes (see Step 6). See Task 61 for an example of how to implement a rollover.

5. Close the script block with the closing `script` tag:

```
</script>
```

6. In the body of your HTML document, add an `onMouseOver` attribute to the a tag you want to trigger the `onMouseOver` event. Make the value of the attribute `doMouseOver('You Rolled Over the Link')`, as in the following code. Figure 219-1 shows a simple document containing the script block and a link with the `onMouseOver` event specified. When the mouse moves over the link, an alert dialog box like the one in Figure 219-2 is displayed.

```
<a href="http://my.url/" onMouseOver="doMouseOver('You ⤶
Rolled Over the Link')">Roll Over this Link</a>
```

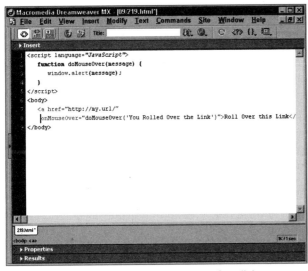

Figure 219-1: Using the `onMouseOver` event for a link.

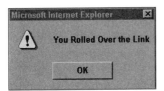

Figure 219-2: Displaying an alert dialog box when the user moves the mouse over a link.

tip

▪ The `window.alert` method takes a single argument that should be a text string. It then displays that text string in a dialog box (see Step 6).

cross-reference

▪ Refer to Task 25 for information on how to create an alert dialog box.

Taking Action When the User Clicks on an Object

U sing the JavaScript event model, you can run JavaScript code when a user clicks on an object. This is done using the onClick event handler. The onClick event handler is commonly used with form buttons and links, but you can apply it to other objects as well.

The onClick event handler is commonly used in forms to perform verification of the form data before allowing the form to be submitted. This is done by using the onClick attribute in the input tag for the button that submits the form.

Another popular use of this event handler is to perform an action when a link is clicked. For instance, you might confirm the user wants to follow a link before allowing he or she to follow it. If a link will take the user to a page that performs some type of irreversible action such as deleting data, you could confirm the user's choice before allowing the user to proceed.

Used in a link, the onClick event handler looks like the following:

```
<a href="some url" onClick="some JavaScript">link text</a>
```

The following example illustrates how you can confirm a user wants to follow a link before actually allowing the user's browser to follow the link. To do this, you will use the window.confirm method, which looks like Figure 220-1 in Internet Explorer and Figure 220-2 in Netscape.

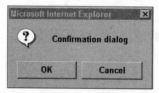

Figure 220-1: A confirmation dialog box in Internet Explorer.

Figure 220-2: A confirmation dialog box in Netscape.

The following steps show how to use the window.confirm method to confirm users want to follow a link:

1. Create a regular link like the following:

```
<a href="http://my.url/">Click Here</a>
```

2. Add the `onClick` attribute to the a tag:

```
<a href="http://my.url/" onClick="">Click Here</a>
```

3. As the value for the `onClick` attribute first enter **"return"**:

```
<a href="http://my.url/" onClick="return">Click Here</a>
```

4. The value to return is the return value of the `window.confirm` method. Therefore, the return command should be followed by the `window.confirm` method:

```
<a href="http://my.url/" onClick="return window.
confirm('Do you want to follow the link?')">Click Here</a>
```

5. When the user clicks on the link, the browser displays a confirmation dialog box like Figure 220-3.

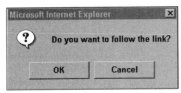

Figure 220-3: Displaying a confirmation dialog box when the user clicks on a link.

tip

▪ The `window.confirm` method takes a single argument that should be a text string. It then displays that text string in a dialog box, along with an OK and Cancel button. It returns a boolean value based on the button the user clicks (see Step 4).

cross-reference

▪ Refer to Task 26 for information on how to create a confirmation dialog box using the `window.confirm` method.

Responding to Changes in a Form's Text Field

U sing JavaScript's event handlers combined with forms provides a powerful but simple mechanism for creating dynamic forms that react to user input in the client without having to be submitted to the server. These types of forms can be used to create calculator applications, to prompt users for data, and for other applications.

One of the event handlers that you can use to create dynamic forms that react to user actions is the onChange event handler. When used with a text field, the onChange event handler is invoked each time the text in the field changes and then the cursor leaves the text field. Used with a text field, the onChange event handler looks like this:

```
<input type="text" name="textField" onChange="Some JavaScript">
```

The following example illustrates a dynamic form in which a user enters a number in one text field and the square of the number is automatically displayed in a second text field once the user's cursor leaves the first text field:

1. Start a script block with the script tag:

   ```
   <script language="JavaScript">
   ```

2. Start a function named doSquare that takes a single parameter containing a pointer to the field where a change occurred:

   ```
   function doSquare(formField) {
   ```

3. Calculate the square of the number, and assign that value to a temporary variable named square:

   ```
   var square = formField.value * formField.value;
   ```

4. Assign the value of the variable square to the form field named squareValue:

   ```
   formField.form.squareValue.value = square;
   ```

5. End the function with a closing curly bracket:

   ```
   }
   ```

6. Close the script block with the closing script tag:

   ```
   </script>
   ```

7. In the body of your HTML document, start a form; the form tag doesn't need to have a method or action attribute:

   ```
   <form>
   ```

8. Create a text field named `number` that should have an `onChange` event handler that calls the function `doSquare` and passes in a pointer to this form field:

```
<input type="text" name="number" ⤶
onChange="doSquare(this)">
```

9. Create a text field named `squareValue` that will be used to display the square of the value entered by the user:

```
<input type="text" name="squareValue">
```

10. Add any descriptive text to help the user understand the form, and close the form with a closing `form` tag. The final page should look like the following:

```
<script language="JavaScript">
    function doSquare(formField) {
        var square = formField.value * formField.value;
        formField.form.squareValue.value = square;
    }
</script>
<body>
    <form>
        <input type="text" name="number" ⤶
onChange="doSquare(this)">
        squared is
        <input type="text" name="squareValue">
    </form>
</body>
```

A sample form with real values is illustrated in Figure 221-1.

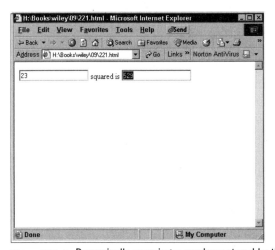

Figure 221-1: Dynamically squaring a number entered by the user.

cross-reference

• Task 81 discusses the `onChange` event handler and detecting change in text fields in forms.

Responding to a Form Field Gaining Focus with onFocus

U sing the onFocus event handler, you can trigger JavaScript code to execute whenever a form field gains focus. Gaining focus means, for instance, that the cursor is placed in a text field.

This event handler is commonly used in forms where the designer of the form displays prompt text for a field inside the field; when the user clicks in the field, the prompt text disappears and the user can begin typing his or her desired input.

The onFocus event handler can also be used to prevent editing of a text field when the rest of the form is in a particular state. For instance, you could make a form field uneditable except when a second text field contains an appropriate value.

The following example shows how you can create a text field with a prompt in the field that disappears once the user places the cursor in the text field:

1. Start your form with an appropriate form tag:

   ```
   <form method="post" action="http://my.url/">
   ```

2. Create a text field with a default initial value; this initial value should be prompt text for the field. The form field can have any name; the text field should look like Figure 222-1 when it is first displayed to the user.

   ```
   <input type="text" name="myField" value="Enter Your Name">
   ```

note

- When you are working with a form field's object for a text field, keep in mind that the value property contains the current text in the field (see Step 4).

Figure 222-1: Displaying a prompt in a text field.

3. Add an onFocus attribute to the text field:

```
<input type="text" name="myField" value="Enter Your ⤵
Name" onFocus="">
```

4. Set the value of the onFocus attribute to this.value = '' in order to clear the text field when the field gains focus; when the user clicks in the field, the prompt text will disappear, as illustrated in Figure 222-2.

```
<input type="text" name="myField" value="Enter Your ⤵
Name" onFocus="this.value = ''">
```

tip

▪ The value stored in text fields are strings. When you want to change the value of a text field, you need to assign a string value to the text field's value property. In this case, you assign an empty string to clear the text field.

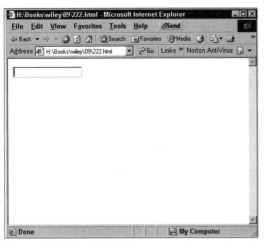

Figure 222-2: The text field clears when the user gives it cursor focus.

5. Add any additional fields and close the form with a closing form tag; your final form might look something like this:

```
<form method="post" action="http://my.url/">
    <input type="text" name="myField" value="Enter Your ⤵
Name" onFocus="this.value = ''">
    <input type="submit" value="Submit">
</form>
```

cross-reference

▪ Tasks 79 and 80 discuss how to access the value displayedin a form's text fields.

Taking Action When a Form Field Loses Focus with `onBlur`

A corollary to `onFocus` is the `onBlur` event handler. This event handler is invoked when a form field loses cursor focus. Using this event handler, you could verify form field data right after a user enters it and prevent the user from continuing if the data he or she entered is invalid. Similarly, you could extend the example from Task 222, and when a user removes cursor focus from a form field, you could redisplay the original prompt if the user hasn't entered any text of his or her own in the field.

The logic of this in-field prompt works like this:

- When first displayed, the text field contains default text that serves as a prompt.

- When the user places the cursor in the text field, the default text disappears.

- When the user removes the cursor from the text field, the default text reappears if no text has been entered by the user.

The following example extends the example from Task 222 to provide this complete logic:

1. Start your form with an appropriate `form` tag:

   ```
   <form method="post" action="http://my.url/">
   ```

2. Create a text field with a default initial value; this initial value should be prompt text for the field. The form field can have any name:

   ```
   <input type="text" name="myField" value="Enter Your Name">
   ```

3. Add an `onFocus` attribute to the text field:

   ```
   <input type="text" name="myField" value="Enter Your ⤶
   Name" onFocus="">
   ```

4. Set the value of the `onFocus` attribute to `this.value = ''` in order to clear the text field when the field gains focus; when the user clicks in the field, the prompt text will disappear:

   ```
   <input type="text" name="myField" value="Enter Your ⤶
   Name" onFocus="this.value = ''">
   ```

5. Add an `onBlur` attribute to the text field:

   ```
   <input type="text" name="myField" value="Enter Your ⤶
   Name" onFocus="this.value = ''" onBlur="">
   ```

6. Set the value of the `onBlur` attribute to `if (this.value == '')` `{ this.value = 'Enter Your Name' }` in order to redisplay the original prompt if the user leaves the field without entering any text:

```
<input type="text" name="myField" value="Enter Your ⤸
Name" onFocus="this.value = ''" onBlur="if (this.value ⤸
== '') { this.value = 'Enter Your name' }">
```

7. Add any additional fields and close the form with a closing `form` tag; the final page should look like Listing 223-1. When the user clicks outside the field without entering any text in the field, the prompt will reappear, as shown in Figure 223-1.

```
<form method="post" action="http://my.url/">
    <input type="text" name="myField" value="Enter Your ⤸
Name" onFocus="this.value = ''" onBlur="if (this.value ⤸
== '') { this.value = 'Enter Your name' }">
    <input type="submit" value="Submit">
</form>
```

Listing 223-1: In-field prompting.

Figure 223-1: The prompt returns if the field is still empty when the field loses focus.

cross-references

▪ Task 222 provides an example of the `onFocus` event handler.

Post-Processing Form Data with onSubmit

A powerful application of JavaScript event handlers is to process form data before it is submitted to ensure the validity of the data. Using this, you can ensure that required fields have been completed and that fields contain valid types of data (for instance, if you are asking for a phone number in a text field, it shouldn't contain a generic string). By validating data in the client with JavaScript, you can prompt the user to fix the problems before submitting the form and thus eliminate an unnecessary transaction with the server, which consumes bandwidth and server resources.

The simplest way to post-process form data is to trap form submission by using the onSubmit event handler in the form tag. The JavaScript code executed by the onSubmit event handler must return either a true or false value.

The following example illustrates a form with two text fields. The fields are validated before form submission to ensure that the first is not empty and that the second is not empty and contains a numeric value.

1. Start a script block with the script tag:

   ```
   <script language="JavaScript">
   ```

2. Create a function named processForm that takes a single argument called targetForm that contains the form object to process:

   ```
   function processForm(targetForm) {
   ```

3. Set a temporary variable to track if the form validated successfully; initially, it is assumed that validation will succeed:

   ```
   var success = true;
   ```

4. Test the first form field named text1 to see if it is empty, and if it is, alert the user and set success to false:

   ```
   if (targetForm.text1.value == "") {
     success = false;
     window.alert("The first form field must not be empty");
   }
   ```

5. Test the second form field named text2 to see if it contains a number and if not alert the user and set success to false:

   ```
   if (typeof(targetForm.text2.value) != "number") {
     success = false;
     window.alert("The second form field must contain a ⤶
   number");
   }
   ```

notes

notes

- When you are using onSubmit, if true is returned by the JavaScript run when the event is triggered, then the form will be submitted; otherwise, the form will not be submitted. This allows you to perform form field validation and return false if there is a problem, which means the user can continue editing the form before trying to submit it again.

- In event handlers inside the form tag, the this keyword refers to the object associated with the form itself. In this case, that allows you to pass the object associated with the form to the processForm function (see Step 9).

Task **224**

6. Return the success value, and close the function and script block so that the script block looks like this:

```
<script language="JavaScript">
    function processForm(targetForm) {
        var success = true;
        if (targetForm.text1.value == "") {
            success = false;
            window.alert("The first form field must not be ⤶
empty");
        }
        if (typeof(targetForm.text2.value) != "number") {
            success = false;
            window.alert("The second form field must ⤶
contain a number");
        }
        return success;
    }
</script>
```

7. In the body of your document, create the form containing the two text fields:

```
<form method="post" action="http://my.url">
    First field:
    <input type="text" name="text1"><br>
    Second field:
    <input type="text" name="text2"><br>
    <input type="submit" value="submit">
</form>
```

8. Add an onSubmit attribute to the form tag:

```
<form method="post" action="http://my.url" onSubmit="">
```

9. Set the value of the onSubmit attribute to return processForm(this):

```
<form method="post" action="http://my.url" ⤶
onSubmit="return processForm(this)">
```

10. When the user submits the form, if it is not completed properly, the user will see one or two error messages, as shown in Figure 224-1, and the form will not be submitted to the server.

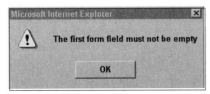

Figure 224-1: Incomplete forms will generate errors when submitted.

Creating Code to Load When a Page Loads with `onLoad`

note

- The `Date` object offers a number of methods to access parts of the date. The `getFullYear`, `getMonth`, and `getYear` methods return the year, month, and day numerically (see Step 4).

Often you need to execute some JavaScript code just after a page loads, but you want to ensure the code doesn't execute before the page has loaded completely. The simplest form of executing code at load time is to place it in a script block but not inside a function, as shown in the following high-level overview of an HTML page:

```
<head>
   <script language="JavaScript">
      Code to execute at load time
   </script>
</head>
<body>
   Body of the document
</body>
```

The problem here is that the JavaScript may execute before the body of the document has finished loading. This can cause problems if your code refers to page elements that have not been loaded when the code executes; in fact, the code will throw errors in this case.

The solution to the problem lies in the use of the `onLoad` event handler. Used in conjunction with the `body` tag, the `onLoad` event handler is executed once the entire body of a document has been loaded. If you place the code to execute at load time in a function, the preceding code is transformed into the following using `onLoad`:

```
<head>
   <script language="JavaScript">
      function startFunction() {
         Code to execute at load time
      }
   </script>
</head>
<body onLoad="startFunction()">
   Body of the document
</body>
```

The following example uses `onLoad` to populate a form text field with the current date at the time the page is loaded into the browser by the client:

1. Start a script block with the `script` tag:

   ```
   <script language="JavaScript">
   ```

2. Create a function named `start` that takes no arguments:

```
function start() {
```

3. Create a new date object, and assign it to the variable `now`:

```
var now = new Date();
```

4. Set the value of the `date` text field in the first form in the document to the current date:

```
document.forms[0].date.value = now.getFullYear() + "/" ↵
+ now.getMonth() + "/" + now.getDay();
```

5. Close the function with a curly bracket:

```
}
```

6. In the `body` tag of your HTML document, add an `onLoad` attribute with the value `start()`:

```
<body onLoad="start()">
```

7. Create a form with a text field named date with no initial default value:

```
<form method="post" action="http://my.url">
    <input type="text" name="date">
</form>
```

8. Load the page in your browser; the form field should contain the current date, as illustrated in Figure 225-1.

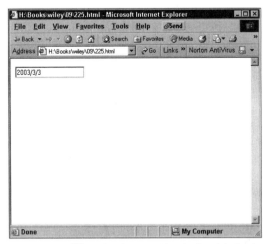

Figure 225-1: When the document loads, the date is placed in the text field.

tip

- When you create a new Date object in the manner shown in Step 3, the object is initialized with the current date and time.

Executing Code When a User Leaves a Page for Another

Just as it is possible to execute code when a page finishes loading, it is also possible to specify JavaScript code to execute when the page unloads. Page unloading occurs when the user enters a new URL to visit or clicks on a link to another page.

You specify this code using the onUnload event handler in the body tag of your document. The most common use of this event handler is perhaps the most pernicious one: pop-up ads that don't go away. Some sites will pop up an advertisement only when you leave the page and then will keep popping up a new ad for each window that you close.

Still, there are valid reasons why you might want to use the onUnload event handler:

- Keeping a user on a page of your application until he or she completes an important or required task

- Displaying a farewell message

- Performing some cleanup tasks, such as removing cookies that you want to eliminate the instant a user leaves your site

The following example uses onUnload to display a farewell message to the user in a simple dialog box:

1. Create your HTML document as you normally would. A simple HTML document might look like the following:

```
<html>
   <head>
      <title>Simple HTML</title>
   </head>
   <body>
      Hello World
   </body>
</html>
```

2. Add the onUnload attribute to the body tag:

```
<body onUnload="">
```

3. Enter **window.alert** followed by an open bracket and a single quote as the first part of the attribute's value:

```
<body onUnload="window.alert('">
```

note

- Pop-up ads have become such a problem on the Internet that some popular PC security packages will automatically prevent the pop-ups from occurring.

4. Enter your farewell message; in this case the message is "Goodbye World":

```
<body onUnload="window.alert('Goodbye World
```

5. Finish the function call with a single quote and a closing bracket:

```
<body onUnload="window.alert('Goodbye World')">
```

6. Open this page in your browser, and you see a page like Figure 226-1. Proceed to open another URL; the browser displays the Goodbye World message in a dialog box, as in Figure 226-2.

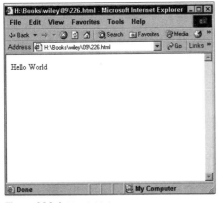

Figure 226-1: The initial page.

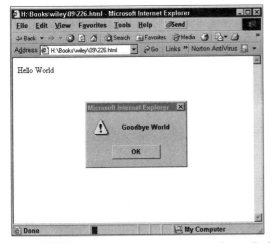

Figure 226-2: Using the `onUnload` event handler to display a farewell message.

tip

- The `window.alert` method takes a single argument: a string. It then displays that string as the content of a dialog box. The dialog box will contain a single button the user can use to close the dialog box (see Step 3).

cross-reference

- Refer to Task 25 for information on how to create an alert dialog box.

Taking Action When a User Makes a Selection in a Selection List

note

- In event handlers inside the form tag, the this keyword refers to the object associated with the form itself. The object for the selection list has a form property that refers to the form object for the form containing the selection list (see Step 8).

A common feature of many dynamic forms provided in Web applications today is for a user's selections in one selection list of a form to determine the values of other form fields or even to determine the available options in another selection list. To do this, you need to be able to invoke specific JavaScript code whenever the selected item in a list changes. This is done with the onChange event handler, which is specified in the select tag.

The following example creates a simple form in which the value of a user's selection in a selection list is displayed in a text field sitting next to the selection list:

1. Start your form with an appropriate form tag:

   ```
   <form method="post" action="http://my.url/">
   ```

2. Start your selection list with a select tag, and name the field myList:

   ```
   <select name="myList">
   ```

3. Provide entries for the list as a series of option tags; make sure the displayed text and the value of the entry are different:

   ```
   <option value="1">One</option>
   <option value="2">Two</option>
   <option value="3">Three</option>
   ```

4. Close the select list with a closing select tag; this produces a selection list like the one in Figure 227-1:

   ```
   </select>
   ```

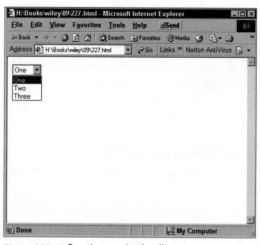

Figure 227-1: Creating a selection list.

5. Create an empty text field named `myText`:

   ```
   <input type="text" name="myText">
   ```

6. Close the form with a closing `form` tag so that the form looks like this:

   ```
   <form method="post" action="http://my.url/">
      <select name="myList">
         <option value="1">One</option>
         <option value="2">Two</option>
         <option value="3">Three</option>
      </select>
      <input type="text" name="myText">
   </form>
   ```

7. Add the `onChange` attribute to the `select` tag in the `form`:

   ```
   <select name="myList" onChange="">
   ```

8. Assign the following value to the `onChange` tag `this.form.myText.value = this.value` to assign the value of the selected item to the `myText` text field when a new item is selected:

   ```
   <select name="myList" onChange="this.form.myText.↩
   value = this.value">
   ```

9. Open the page in a browser, and select an item in the list; its value is displayed in the text field as in Figure 227-2.

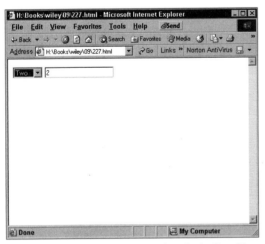

Figure 227-2: Responding to selections in the list with `onSelect`.

cross-reference

■ The techniques for working with selection lists in forms are outlined in Tasks 82 to 86.

Part 10: Bookmarklets

Task 228 Downloading and Installing Bookmarklets

Bookmarklets are short, single-line JavaScript scripts presented as URLs in the form `javascript:JavaScript code`. They can be added as a bookmark or favorite to your browser and then invoked by being selected from the bookmarks or favorites list of the browser.

There are numerous sources of bookmarklets on the Web. These sites present bookmarklets as links, and you can install them in your browser by right-clicking on the link and selecting Add to Favorites (Internet Explorer) or Bookmark This Link (Netscape) from the pop-up menu.

If you want to create your own bookmarklets, as is done throughout this part of the book, then you need to know how to easily install your own bookmarklets.

For Internet Explorer, you can use the following steps:

1. Create your bookmarklet in your preferred editor.
2. Copy the bookmarklet to the clipboard.
3. In your browser, select Favorites ⇨ Add to Favorites from the menu.
4. In the Add Favorite dialog box (Figure 228-1), give the favorite a name and click on the OK button.

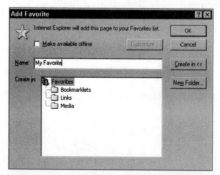

Figure 228-1: The Add Favorite dialog box.

5. In the Favorites menu, right-click on the new favorite you created, and select Properties from the context menu that appears.
6. In the Properties dialog box (Figure 228-2), paste the bookmarklet into the URL field and click on the OK button.

Figure 228-2: Properties for a favorite in Internet Explorer.

For Netscape 6 and above, use the following steps:

1. Create your bookmarklet in your preferred editor.

2. Copy the bookmarklet to the clipboard.

3. In your browser, select Bookmarks ⇨ Manage Bookmarks from the menu. Netscape displays the bookmarks management window.

4. Select File ⇨ New ⇨ Bookmark from the menu. Netscape displays the Add Bookmark dialog box, as illustrated in Figure 228-3.

Figure 228-3: The Add Bookmark dialog box.

Enter a name for the bookmark in the Name field, and then paste the bookmarklet in the Location field and click on the OK button.

tips

- There are plenty of Web sites that offer book-marklets for you to use. Check out the following three as good starting points: www.bookmarklets.com, www.squarefree.com/bookmarklets, and www.sam-i-am.com/work/bookmarklets/dev_debugging.html.

- There is another approach to installing your own book-marklets in Internet Explorer or Netscape. Just create an HTML file and create a link with the book-marklet code as a javasccript: URL in the link. Then you can open the HTML file, right-click on the link, and install the bookmarklet as a favorite or bookmark like you would for any other link.

- Bookmarklets can also work in other browsers than Internet Explorer and Netscape. Browsers that support JavaScript to a greater or lesser degree should be able to run some of the bookmarklets presented in this part. The methods for creating a bookmarklet will vary from browser to browser; if you use another browser, consult its documentation.

Checking Page Freshness with a Bookmarklet

note

- To make developing bookmarklets easy, it is best to start by editing the code in your regular code editor and then copy and paste the bookmarklet into your favorites or bookmarks list at the end.

Using a bookmarklet, you can check the date of last modification of a page based on information the server provided to the browser when the page was requested by the user. This task depends on the `document.lastModified` property, which indicates the date and time provided by the server as the last modification date of a document.

To illustrate this property, consider the following code, which outputs the modification date in an HTML document:

```
<body>
   Last Modified:
   <script language="JavaScript">
      document.write(document.lastModified);
   </script>
</body>
```

This results in output like Figure 229-1 in Internet Explorer and Figure 229-2 in Netscape.

Figure 229-1: Displaying the last modification date in a document in Internet Explorer.

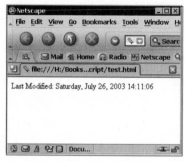

Figure 229-2: Displaying the last modification date in a document in Netscape.

The following steps create the bookmarklet:

1. Open the text editor you normally use for writing JavaScript.

2. Use the `window.alert` method to display the last modification date in a dialog box:

   ```
   window.alert(document.lastModified);
   ```

3. Add `javascript:` to the start of the command to create a single-line URL:

   ```
   javascript:window.alert(document.lastModified);
   ```

4. Create a bookmark or favorite using this code as the URL.

5. To test the bookmarklet, select the new bookmark or favorite you created, and a dialog box should be displayed containing the last modification date and time, as illustrated in Figure 229-3.

Figure 229-3: Displaying the last modification date in a dialog box.

Task 229

tip

- Notice how Internet Explorer displays the modification date using different formats.

cross-references

- Part 2 discusses the `document` object and the use of the `document.write` method for outputting to the browser window.

- Task 115 discusses how to use the `window.alert` method to display a dialog box.

Checking for E-mail Links with a Bookmarklet

notes

▪ Each link in the `document.links` array is an object and not a string. Using the `toString` method of the object returns the URL as a string.

▪ The `substring` method of the `String` object returns a portion of the string. The two arguments are the first character index and the last character index of the portion of the string to be returned by the `substring` method.

▪ The new-line character is one of several special characters that are written in JavaScript using what is known as "escaping." With escaping, the backslash character indicates that the character following the backslash should be interpreted and not just used normally. In this case, \n implies a new-line character instead of the letter n.

This task outlines how to search a page for e-mail links and then display those addresses in a dialog box—all with a bookmarklet. The principle of this is simple. The `document.links` array provides access to all links in a document. E-mail links will appear in this list and take the form `mailto:e-mail address`. Based on this, any check to e-mail links involves looping through the `document.links` array, checking the protocol of the link, and then, if necessary, outputting the address of the link if the protocol of the link is `mailto:`.

This task uses this logic to build a bookmarklet that collects all such addresses in a list and then displays the list in a dialog box.

1. Open the text editor you normally use for writing JavaScript.

2. Create an empty string variable named `emailList` that will hold a list of all addresses found by the end of the script:

   ```
   emailList = "";
   ```

3. Start a `for` loop. Loop from 0 up to the length of the `document.links` array:

   ```
   for (i = 0; i < document.links.length; i ++) {
   ```

4. Use an `if` statement to check if the current entry in the `document.links` array uses the `mailto:` protocol:

   ```
   if (document.links[i].protocol == "mailto:") {
   ```

5. If the link is an e-mail address, extract the link from the link and save it in a temporary variable called `thisEmail`:

   ```
   thisEmail = document.links[i].toString();
   ```

6. Remove the `mailto:` part of the string by using the substring method to remove the first 7 characters of the link, and store the result back into `thisEmail`:

   ```
   thisEmail = thisEmail.substring(7,thisEmail.length);
   ```

7. Append the e-mail address to the end of the `emailList` string, and add a new-line character after the e-mail address:

   ```
   emailList += thisEmail + "\n";
   ```

8. Close the `if` and `for` blocks, and then use the `window.alert` method to display the value of the `emailList` string so that the script looks like this:

```
emailList = "";
for (i = 0; i < document.links.length; i ++) {
    if (document.links[i].protocol == "mailto:") {
        thisEmail = document.links[i].toString();
        thisEmail = thisEmail.substring(7,thisEmail.length);
        emailList += thisEmail + "\n";
    }
}
window.alert(emailList);
```

9. Remove the line separations and blank spaces from the script, and add the `javascript:` protocol to the start of the script, so that the result is a one-line URL with all extraneous spaces removed:

```
javascript:emailList="";for(i=0;i<document.links.length;
i++){if(document.links[i].protocol=="mailto:"){this
Email=document.links[i].toString();thisEmail=thisEmail.
substring(7,thisEmail.length);emailList+=thisEmail+"\n";
}}window.alert(emailList);
```

10. Create a bookmark or favorite using this code as the URL. To test the bookmarklet, open a Web page in your browser. For instance, open the Yahoo! home page. Select the new bookmark or favorite you created, and a dialog box should be displayed containing the e-mail addresses from the page, as illustrated in Figure 230-1.

Figure 230-1: Displaying the e-mail addresses from the Yahoo! home page in a dialog box.

tip

- You can identify the protocol of a link in the `links` array with the `protocol` property of the link. For instance, the protocol of the first link in a document is `document.links[0].protocol`. A `mailto:` link will have a `protocol` value of `mailto`.

cross-reference

- Task 228 discusses how to create a bookmark or favorite for a JavaScript bookmarklet.

E-mailing Selected Text with a Bookmarklet in Internet Explorer

A common task performed by users on the Web is to e-mail part of a page to someone. The usual approach is to select the text, copy it, paste it into an e-mail, and send the e-mail.

Using JavaScript in Internet Explorer, you can build a bookmarklet that e-mails text the user sent in the page by invoking the user's default e-mail client and pre-populating the e-mail with the selected text.

This bookmarklet relies on the following:

- Internet Explorer provides the `document.selection` object to reflect the text currently selected in a Web page.

- The `createRange` method of the `document.selection` object returns a pointer to the selected range that has a `text` property containing the selected text.

- Using a `mailto:` link triggers an outgoing message with the user's default mail client. The body of the message can be set with a URL of the form `mailto:?BODY=body of the document`.

The following steps show how to create this bookmarklet:

1. Open the text editor you normally use for writing JavaScript.

2. Save the currently selected text in the variable `selectedText`:

   ```
   selectedText = document.selection.createRange().text;
   ```

3. Use the `escape` function to convert the selected text to URL-encoded format, and save the result back into `selectedText`:

   ```
   selectedText = escape(selectedText);
   ```

4. Set `location.href` to an appropriate `mailto:` URL, including the selected text as the body of the message, so that the final script looks like this:

   ```
   selectedText = document.selection.createRange().text;
   selectedText = escape(selectedText);
   location.href='mailto:?BODY=' + selectedText;
   ```

5. Enclose the last command in a `void` statement; otherwise, the browser will try to display the URL string after assigning it to the `location.href` property, and this will cause an empty page with the URL displayed to replace the current page:

   ```
   selectedText = document.selection.createRange().text;
   selectedText = escape(selectedText);
   void(location.href='mailto:?BODY=' + selectedText);
   ```

---

notes

- This bookmarklet only works in Internet Explorer.

- The `location.href` property reflects the URL of the current page. When a new URL is assigned to it, the new URL will be displayed by the browser.

6. Remove the line separations and blank spaces from the script, and add the `javascript:` protocol to the start of the script, so that the result is a one-line URL with all extraneous spaces removed:

```
javascript:selectedText=document.selection.createRange().↵
text;selectedText=escape(selectedText);void(location.↵
href='mailto:?BODY='+selectedText);
```

7. Create a favorite using this code as the URL. To test the book-marklet, open a Web page in your browser and select some text, as illustrated in Figure 231-1. Select the new favorite you created, and your e-mail client should open with the body of the message set to your selected text, as illustrated in Figure 231-2.

tip

▪ To make developing book-marklets easy, it is best to start by editing the code in your regular code editor and then copy and paste the bookmarklet into your favorites or bookmarks list at the end.

Figure 231-1: A Web page with text selected.

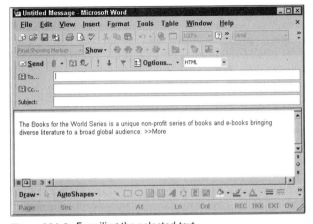

Figure 231-2: E-mailing the selected text.

E-mailing Selected Text with a Bookmarklet in Netscape

A common task performed by users on the Web is to e-mail part of a page to someone. The usual approach is to select the text, copy it, paste it into an e-mail, and send the e-mail.

Using JavaScript in Netscape, you can build a bookmarklet that e-mails text the user sent in the page by invoking the user's default e-mail client and prepopulating the e-mail with the selected text.

This bookmarklet relies on the following:

- Netscape provides the `document.getSelection` method, which returns the selected text.

- Using a `mailto:` link triggers an outgoing message with the user's default mail client. The body of the message can be set with a URL of the form `mailto:?BODY=body of the document`.

The following steps show how to create this bookmarklet:

1. Open the text editor you normally use for writing JavaScript.

2. Save the currently selected text in the variable `selectedText`:

   ```
   selectedText = document.getSelection();
   ```

3. Use the `escape` function to convert the selected text to URL-encoded format and save the result back into `selectedText`:

   ```
   selectedText = escape(selectedText);
   ```

4. Set `location.href` to an appropriate `mailto:` URL, including the selected text as the body of the message, so that the final script looks like this:

   ```
   selectedText = document.getSelection();
   selectedText = escape(selectedText);
   location.href='mailto:?BODY=' + selectedText;
   ```

5. Enclose the last command in a `void` statement; otherwise, the browser will try to display the URL string after assigning it to the `location.href` property, and this will cause an empty page with the URL displayed to replace the current page:

   ```
   selectedText = document.getSelection();
   selectedText = escape(selectedText);
   void(location.href='mailto:?BODY=' + selectedText);
   ```

notes

- This bookmarklet only works in Netscape.

- The `location.href` property reflects the URL of the current page. When a new URL is assigned to it, the new URL will be displayed by the browser.

6. Remove the line separations and blank spaces from the script, and add the `javascript:` protocol to the start of the script, so that the result is a one-line URL with all extraneous spaces removed:

```
javascript:selectedText=document.getSelection();↵
selectedText=escape(selectedText);void(location.href=↵
'mailto:?BODY='+selectedText);
```

7. Create a bookmark using this code as the URL. To test the bookmarklet, open a Web page in your browser and select some text, as illustrated in Figure 232-1. Select the new bookmark you created, and your e-mail client should open with the body of the message set to your selected text, as illustrated in Figure 232-2.

tip

▪ To make developing bookmarklets easy, it is best to start by editing the code in your regular code editor and then copy and paste the bookmarklet into your favorites or bookmarks list at the end.

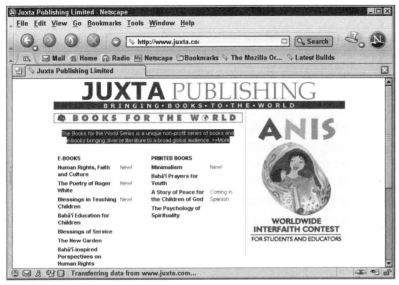

Figure 232-1: A Web page with text selected.

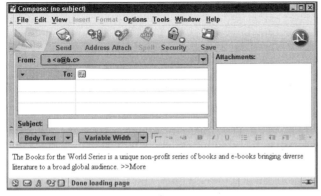

Figure 232-2: E-mailing the selected text.

Task 233

Displaying Images from a Page with a Bookmarklet

This task shows how to build a bookmarklet to display all images included in a Web page in the center of the browser window in a column. This is useful for testing and debugging when you are building Web pages yourself.

This task relies on the `document.images` array, which contains an `Image` object for each image in a page. These objects have a `src` property that points to the source of the image.

The following steps show how to build this bookmarklet:

1. Open the text editor you normally use for writing JavaScript.

2. Create a variable named `imageList`, and assign it the empty string:

   ```
   imageList = '';
   ```

3. Use a `for` loop to loop through the `document.images` array:

   ```
   for (i = 0; i < document.images.length; i ++) {
   ```

4. For each image, use the source of the image to build a new `img` tag, and add it to the `imageList` string:

   ```
   imageList += '<img src=' + document.images[i].src ⤵
   +'><br>';
   ```

5. Close the `for` loop:

   ```
   }
   ```

6. Use the `document.write` method to output the image list centered in the page:

   ```
   document.write('<center>' + imageList + '</center>');
   ```

7. Use the `document.close` method to close the document stream:

   ```
   document.close();
   ```

8. Wrap the last command in a `void` statement so that the final script looks like this:

   ```
   imageList = '';
   for (i = 0; i < document.images.length; i ++) {
   imageList += '<img src=' + document.images[i].src ⤵
   +'><br>';
   }
   document.write('<center>' + imageList + '</center>');
   void(document.close());
   ```

9. Remove the line separations and blank spaces from the script, and add the `javascript:` protocol to the start of the script, so that the result is a one-line URL with all extraneous spaces removed:

```
javascript:imageList='';for(i=0;i<document.images.length;
i++){imageList+='<img src='+document.images[i].src+'>
<br>';}document.write('<center>'+imageList+'</center>');
void(document.close
```

10. Create a bookmark or favorite using this code as the URL. To test the bookmarklet, open a Web page in your browser. For instance, Figure 233-1 shows the Juxta Publishing home page displayed in a browser. Select the new bookmark or favorite you created, and the images should be displayed as in Figure 233-2.

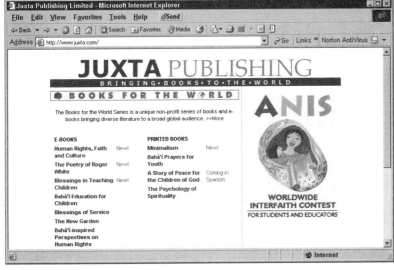

Figure 233-1: The Juxta Publishing home page.

Figure 233-2: The images from the Juxta Publishing home page.

tips

▪ To make developing bookmarklets easy, it is best to start by editing the code in your regular code editor and then copy and paste the bookmarklet into your favorites or bookmarks list at the end.

▪ The `void` function is used to prevent any value being returned by the code. In the case of your bookmarklets, any values returned by the last function or method call in the URL can cause unexpected behavior in the browser. You don't really care about the value returned by `document.close`, so you hide that value with the `void` function.

cross-references

▪ Part 3 of the book discusses how to work with images, including using the `document.images` array and image objects.

▪ Task 228 discusses how to create a bookmark or favorite for a JavaScript bookmarklet.

Changing Background Color with a Bookmarklet

notes

■ This bookmarklet only works with pages with no frames.

■ When entering colors, you should enter them as standard hexadecimal triplets. This is a six-digit hexadecimal number where the first two digits represent red, the next two represent green, and the final two represent blue. You can find examples of these triple codes at www.geocities.com/ Paris/2734/.

This task shows how to create a bookmarklet that allows users to replace any background color or image in a page with the background color of their choice. This is particularly useful when viewing pages where the author has made a poor choice of design and made the text of the page particularly hard to read.

The technique used in this bookmarklet relies on several principles:

- The `document.body.background` property indicates the image used for the background. When set to the empty string, any existing background image is removed from the page.

- The `document.bgColor` property indicates the background color of the page.

The following steps outline the creation of a bookmarklet to change the background color of a page:

1. Open the text editor you normally use for writing JavaScript.

2. Check to make sure that the document doesn't use frames by testing the length of the frames array; if the length is less than 1, then there are no frames:

```
if (frames.length < 1) {
```

3. If the page has no frames, remove any background images by setting `document.body.background` to an empty string:

```
document.body.background = '';
```

4. Use the `window.prompt` method to ask the user to enter a background color, and save the result returned in `document.bgColor`:

```
document.bgColor = window.prompt('Enter a background ⤵
color:');
```

5. Place the last line inside a `void` statement; otherwise, Netscape browsers will actually try to display the value entered by the user in the dialog box after applying it to the page, and this will cause the page in question to disappear:

```
void(document.bgColor = window.prompt('Enter a ⤵
background color:'));
```

6. Close the `if` block so that the script looks like this:

```
if (frames.length < 1) {
   document.body.background = '';
   document.bgColor = window.prompt('Enter a ⤵
background color:');
}
```

7. Remove the line separations and blank spaces from the script, and add the `javascript:` protocol to the start of the script, so that the result is a one-line URL with all extraneous spaces removed:

```
javascript:if(frames.length<1){document.body.background
='';void(document.bgColor=window.prompt('Enter a
background color:'));}
```

8. Create a bookmark or favorite using this code as the URL. To test the bookmarklet, open a Web page in your browser. For instance, you could open the Juxta Publishing home page at `www.juxta.com`. Select the new bookmark or favorite you created, and enter a background color in the dialog box, as shown in Figure 234-1. The page should be updated to use the new background color, as in Figure 234-2.

tip
▪ To make developing book-marklets easy, it is best to start by editing the code in your regular code editor and then copy and paste the bookmarklet into your favorites or bookmarks list at the end.

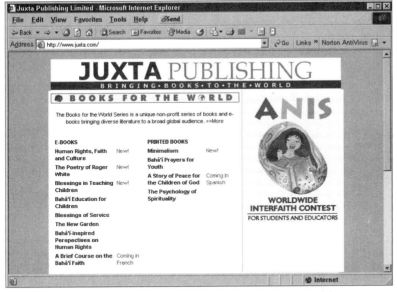

Figure 234-1: A dialog box for entering a color.

Figure 234-2: The home page with a new background color (in grayscale).

cross-reference
▪ Task 117 discusses how to use the `window.prompt` method to prompt the user for information in a dialog box.

Removing Background Images with a Bookmarklet

note

- When assigning a URL for a background image to the `background` property, you can use either an absolute or relative URL.

This task illustrates a simple technique for removing background images from the current document the user is viewing by using a bookmarklet. This is a useful function for times when a page author has placed text over a distracting background image, making the text hard to read.

The actual work is achieved by simply setting the `document.body.background` property to an empty string. This property indicates the background image of a page, and when set to the empty string, any existing background image is removed from the page. You should set the value of this property to the URL of an image as in the following examples:

```
document.body.background = "myImage.gif";
document.body.background = "../images/anotherImage.gif";
document.body.background = "http://some.domain/remoteImage";
```

The following steps show how to create this bookmarklet:

1. Open the text editor you normally use for writing JavaScript.

2. Assign an empty string to the `document.body.background` property:

    ```
    document.body.background = '';
    ```

3. Enclose the last command in a `void` statement; otherwise, the browser will try to display the empty string after assigning it to the `document.body.background` property, and this will cause an empty page to replace the current page:

    ```
    void(document.body.background = '');
    ```

4. Remove blank spaces from the script, and add the `javascript:` protocol to the start of the script, so that the result is a one-line URL with all extraneous spaces removed:

    ```
    javascript:void(document.body.background='');
    ```

5. Create a bookmark or favorite using this code as the URL. To test the bookmarklet, open a Web page containing a background image in your browser, as illustrated in Figure 235-1. Select the new bookmark or favorite you created and the background image disappears, as illustrated in Figure 235-2.

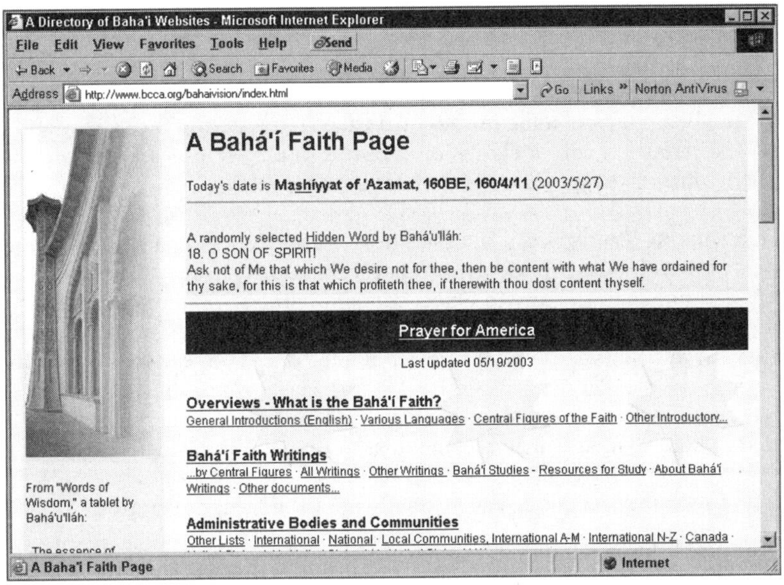

Figure 235-1: A home page with a background image.

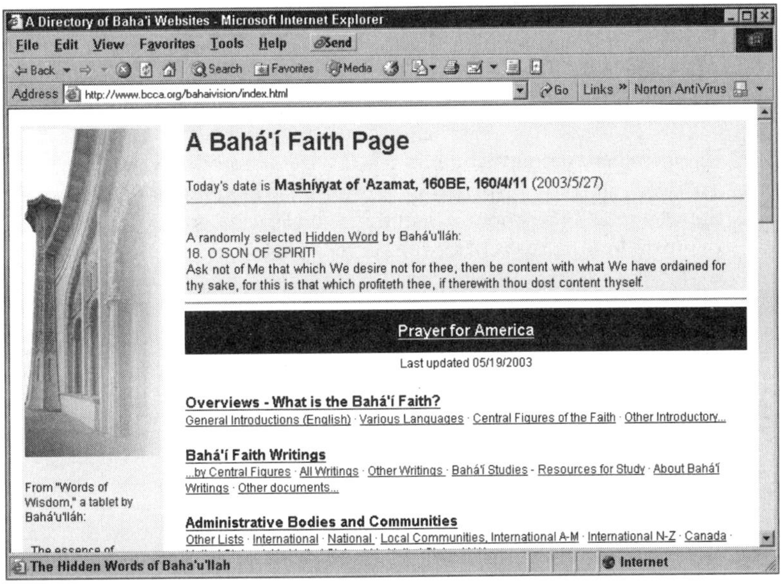

Figure 235-2: The page after the background image has been removed.

Task 235

tip

- To make developing bookmarklets easy, it is best to start by editing the code in your regular code editor and then copy and paste the bookmarklet into your favorites or bookmarks list at the end.

Hiding Images with a Bookmarklet

note

- A for loop allows you to count. That is, the code inside the loop is executed once for each iteration of the loop, and in each iteration of the loop, a counter variable's value is adjusted. In this case, the counter variable is i and is initially set to a value of zero. Each iteration through the loop i is increased by 1 until it reaches the same value as the total number of images in the document.

This task shows how you can hide images in a page using a bookmarklet. This can be useful when the images on a page are cluttering the display and you need to remove them for clarity, or in testing your own pages to see where exactly images are appearing and where they aren't.

This example leverages the fact that the document.image array contains an object for each image in the current page. Each Image object has a style property that points to the style object containing the style settings of that image. One the properties of this style object is the visibility property, which, when set to hidden, causes the object in question to be rendered as invisible.

The result is that a simple loop through the document.images array can be used to hide all images in a document, as in the following steps:

1. Open the text editor you normally use for writing JavaScript.

2. Use a for loop to loop from 0 to the length of the document.images array:

   ```
   for (i = 0; i < document.images.length; i ++) {
   ```

3. In the loop, assign 'hidden' to the visibility property of the style object for the given image:

   ```
   document.images[i].style.visibility = 'hidden';
   ```

4. Enclose the last command in a void statement; otherwise, the browser will try to display the 'hidden' string after assigning it to the visibility property, and this will cause an empty page with the text "hidden" to replace the current page:

   ```
   void(document.images[i].style.visibility = 'hidden');
   ```

5. Close the for loop so that the final script looks like this:

   ```
   for (i = 0; i < document.images.length; i ++) {
      void(document.images[i].style.visibility = 'hidden');
   }
   ```

6. Remove the line separations and blank spaces from the script, and add the javascript: protocol to the start of the script, so that the result is a one-line URL with all extraneous spaces removed:

   ```
   javacript:for(i=0;i<document.images.length;i++) ⮐
   {void(document.images[i].style.visibility='hidden's
   ```

7. Create a bookmark or favorite using this code as the URL. To test the bookmarklet, open a Web page containing images in your browser, as illustrated in Figure 236-1. Select the new bookmark or favorite you created and the images disappears, as illustrated in Figure 236-2.

Figure 236-1: A Web page with images.

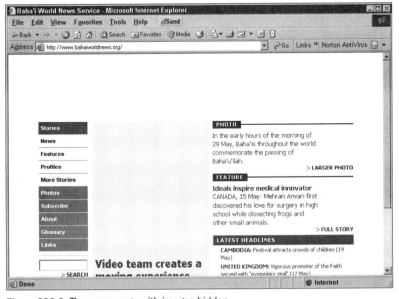

Figure 236-2: The same page with images hidden.

tip

- To make developing bookmarklets easy, it is best to start by editing the code in your regular code editor and then copy and paste the bookmarklet into your favorites or bookmarks list at the end.

cross-references

- Part 3 of the book discusses how to work with images, including using the `document.images` array and image objects

- Part 7 of the book discusses how to work with style sheets and the `style` object.

Hiding Banners with a Bookmarklet

This task is a variation of Task 236. Here, instead of hiding all images, only images likely to be banner advertisements will be hidden. This is a nice tool if you like to avoid banner images.

The principle behind this task is that banner advertisements usually are the same size: 468 by 60 pixels. This is because this is the size dictated by most major advertising networks and Web sites that sell banner advertisement placement.

This means the script developed in Task 236 needs to be extended to check the height and width of the image before proceeding to hide it. This is easy to do, because each `Image` object in the `document.images` array has height and width properties that can be checked to determine the size of an image.

The following steps show how to create a bookmarklet to hide banner advertisements:

1. Open the text editor you normally use for writing JavaScript.

2. Use a `for` loop to loop from 0 to the length of the `document.images` array:

   ```
   for (i = 0; i < document.images.length; i ++) {
   ```

3. In the loop, check each image's size to see if it is 468 by 60 pixels by using an `if` statement:

   ```
   if (document.images[i].width == 468 &&
   document.images[i].height == 60) {
   ```

4. If the image is 468 by 60 pixels, assign `'hidden'` to the `visibility` property of the `style` object for the given image:

   ```
   document.images[i].style.visibility = 'hidden';
   ```

5. Enclose the last command in a `void` statement; otherwise, the browser will try to display the `'hidden'` string after assigning it to the `visibility` property, and this will cause an empty page with the text "hidden" to replace the current page:

   ```
   void(document.images[i].style.visibility = 'hidden');
   ```

6. Close the `if` statement and `for` loop so that the final script looks like:

   ```
   for (i = 0; i < document.images.length; i ++) {
      if (document.images[i].width == 468 &&
   document.images[i].height == 60) {
         void(document.images[i].style.visibility =
   'hidden');
      }
   }
   ```

7. Remove the line separations and blank spaces from the script, and add the `javascript:` protocol to the start of the script, so that the result is a one-line URL with all extraneous spaces removed:

note

- This script isn't a foolproof way to remove banner advertisements for several reasons: Today, not all banner advertisements are images and not all adhere to the 468 by 60 pixel size. Some banners today are implemented in Flash and won't be accessible in the `document.images` array and other advertisements don't use the simple horizontal shape of traditional banners; for instance, many advertisements today are vertical rather than horizontal.

```
javascript:for(i=0;i<document.images.length;i++){if
(document.images[i].width==468&&document.images[i].height
==60){void(document.images[i].style.visibility='hidden'
```

8. Create a bookmark or favorite using this code as the URL. To test the bookmarklet, open a Web page containing banner advertisements in your browser, as illustrated in Figure 237-1. Select the new bookmark or favorite you created and the banners will disappear, as illustrated in Figure 237-2.

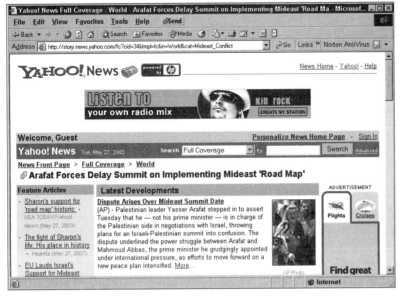

Figure 237-1: A Web page with banner advertisements.

Figure 237-2: The same page with banner advertisements hidden.

tip

- To make developing book-marklets easy, it is best to start by editing the code in your regular code editor and then copy and paste the bookmarklet into your favorites or bookmarks list at the end.

cross-reference

- Part 7 of the book dis-cusses how to work with style sheets and the `style` object. The visibility of objects is discussed specifically in Task 192

Task 238

Opening All Links in a New Window with a Bookmarklet

This task shows how to build a bookmarklet that adjusts the links in a page so that when you click on a link, every link opens in a new window. This is particularly useful when you are following links from a page but want to maintain access to the page. This allows you to freely click on links without having to right-click and select to open the link in a new window from the context menu for the link.

This task uses the fact that the `document.links` array provides an object for every link in a page and that each object has a target property that specifies, and can be used to set, the `target` window for a link. Setting the target to `_blank` causes the link to open in a new window.

The following steps show how to build this bookmarklet:

1. Open the text editor you normally use for writing JavaScript.

2. Use a `for` loop to loop through the `document.links` array:

   ```
   for (i = 0; i < document.links.length; i ++) {
   ```

3. For each link set the target to `_blank`:

   ```
   document.links[i].target = '_blank';
   ```

4. Enclose the last command in a `void` statement; otherwise, the browser will try to display `_blank` after assigning it to the `target` property, and this will cause a page containing just "_blank" to replace the current page:

   ```
   void(document.links[i].target = '_blank');
   ```

5. Close the `for` loop so that the script looks like this:

   ```
   for (i = 0; i < document.links.length; i ++) {
      void(document.links[i].target = '_blank');
   }
   ```

6. Remove line separations and blank spaces from the script, and add the `javascript:` protocol to the start of the script, so that the result is a one-line URL with all extraneous spaces removed:

   ```
   javascript:for(i=0;i<document.links.length;i ↵
   ++){void(document.links[i].target='_blank');}
   ```

7. Create a bookmark or favorite using this code as the URL. To test the bookmarklet, open a Web page in your browser, as illustrated in Figure 238-1, and then select the new bookmark or favorite you created. If you follow a link, it should open in a new window, as illustrated in Figure 238-2.

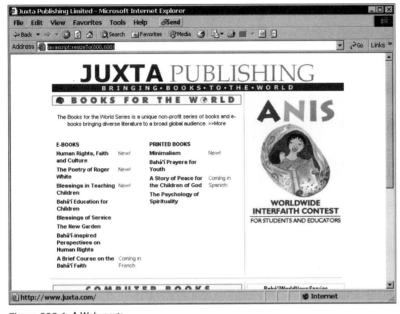

Figure 238-1: A Web page.

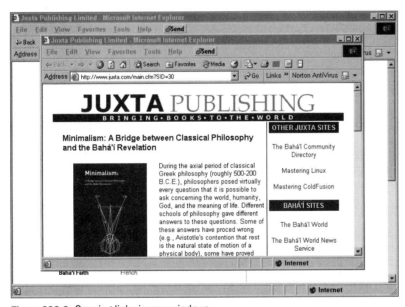

Figure 238-2: Opening links in new windows.

tips

- You can identify the target of a link in the `links` array with the `target` property of the link. For instance, the target of the first link in a document is `document.links[0].target`.

- To make developing bookmarklets easy, it is best to start by editing the code in your regular code editor and then copy and paste the bookmarklet into your favorites or bookmarks list at the end.

Changing Page Fonts with a Bookmarklet

S ometimes Web pages use hard-to-read fonts. At other times they specify fonts that are missing on your system and your system defaults to a poor alternative. For these cases, this task shows how to use a bookmarklet to set the default font style to your preferred font.

This task relies on the fact that the document body is represented in the `document.body` object. This object has a `style` property containing an object reflecting the style attributes for the body of the document. The `fontFamily` property of this object can be used to specify a new font by name.

For instance, to set the default body font of a document to Times, you would use the following:

```
document.body.style.fontFamily = "Times";
```

You can also specify a list of fonts just like in a style sheet. The browser will use the first font on the list that it has available:

```
document.body.style.fontFamily = "Garamond, Times, SERIF";
```

Several generic fonts names are available, including: SERIF (which indicates the default serif font in the browser), SANS-SERIF (which indicates the default sans serif font in the browser), and MONOSPACE (which indicates the default fixed-width font in the browser).

The following steps show how to build a bookmarklet to set the default font to Arial:

1. Open the text editor you normally use for writing JavaScript.

2. Assign `Arial` to the `document.body.style.fontFamily` property:

   ```
   document.body.style.fontFamily = 'Arial';
   ```

3. Enclose the last command in a `void` statement; otherwise, the browser will try to display the font name after assigning it to the `document.body.style.fontFamily` property, and this will cause a page containing just the name of the font to replace the current page:

   ```
   void(document.body.style.fontFamily = 'Arial');
   ```

4. Remove blank spaces from the script, and add the `javascript:` protocol to the start of the script, so that the result is a one-line URL with all extraneous spaces removed:

   ```
   javascript:void(document.body.style.fontFamily='Arial');
   ```

5. Create a bookmark or favorite using this code as the URL. To test the bookmarklet, open a Web page in your browser, as illustrated in Figure 239-1. Select the new bookmark or favorite you created, and the default font changes to Arial, as illustrated in Figure 239-2.

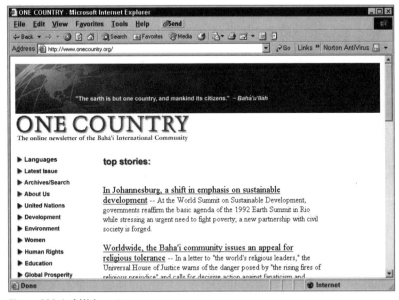

Figure 239-1: A Web page.

Figure 239-2: Changing the default body font of a Web page.

tip

- To make developing book-marklets easy, it is best to start by editing the code in your regular code editor and then copy and paste the bookmarklet into your favorites or bookmarks list at the end.

cross-reference

- Step 174 specifically dis-cusses how to set text for a page element (and the body tag is just one of the elements of a page).

Highlighting Page Links with a Bookmarklet

Sometimes Web page authors fail to ensure that the links in the page are evident to the user. This task shows how to create a bookmarklet to highlight all links in a page so that they are readily visible to the user.

This bookmarklet relies on the fact that all tags are represented in the `document.all` array in Internet Explorer.

In the `document.all` array, each object represents a tag. Each object has a property called `tagName` that can be used to test for A tags that represent links. Each object also has a `style` property containing an object representing all style attributes of the link. The `backgroundColor` property of this `style` object is used to specify a background color for the link. For instance, the following example sets the background color for the first tag in a document to yellow:

```
document.all[0].style.backgroundColor = 'yellow';
```

The following steps show how to build a bookmarklet to highlight all links in cyan:

1. Open the text editor you normally use for writing JavaScript.

2. Use a `for` loop to loop though the `document.all` array:

   ```
   for (i = 0; i < document.all.length; i ++) {
   ```

3. Inside the loop, test if the given tag is an A tag using an `if` statement:

   ```
   if (document.all[i].tagName == 'A') {
   ```

4. If the tag is an A tag, then assign cyan as the background color:

   ```
   document.all[i].style.backgroundColor = 'cyan';
   ```

5. Enclose the last command in a `void` statement; otherwise, the browser will try to display the `'cyan'` string after assigning it to the `backgroundColor` property, and this will cause an empty page with the text "cyan" to replace the current page:

   ```
   void(document.all[i].style.backgroundColor = 'cyan');
   ```

6. Close the `if` statement and `for` loop so that the final script looks like this:

   ```
   for (i = 0; i < document.all.length; i ++) {
      if (document.all[i].tagName == 'A') {
         void(document.all[i].style.backgroundColor = ⤶
   'cyan');
      }
   }
   ```

7. Remove the line separations and blank spaces from the script, and add the `javascript:` protocol to the start of the script, so that the result is a one-line URL with all extraneous spaces removed:

note

- The `document.all` array is not available in Netscape, so it will not work on that browser.

```
javascript:for(i=0;i<document.all.length;i++){if
(document.all[i].tagName=='A'){void(document.all[i].
style.backgroundColor='cyan');}}
```

8. Create a bookmark or favorite using this code as the URL. To test the bookmarklet, open a Web page in your browser, as illustrated in Figure 240-1. Select the new bookmark or favorite you created, and the links are highlighted, as illustrated in Figure 240-2.

tip

• To make developing book-marklets easy, it is best to start by editing the code in your regular code editor and then copy and paste the bookmarklet into your favorites or bookmarks list at the end.

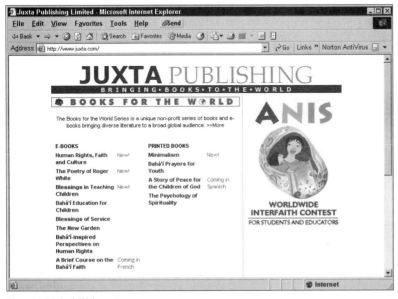

Figure 240-1: A Web page.

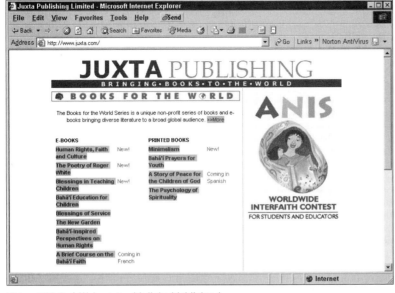

Figure 240-2: A Web page with links highlighted.

Task 241

Checking the Current Date and Time with a Bookmarklet

JavaScript's Date object provides an easy way to display the current date and time to the user. This can be used to create a bookmarklet to display the date and time in a dialog box.

The `toLocaleString` method of the Date object will output the Date object's current date and time in a format appropriate to the user's locale when using Internet Explorer. These locales differ in the formatting. For instance, in the United States, you typically see the following:

```
Wednesday, 23 July, 2003 22:38:15
```

At the same time, in the United Kingdom you should see the following:

```
23 July 2003 22:40:44
```

Locales also specify the language of the month and day names, as in the Czech Republic, which is illustrated in Figure 241-1, and Japan, which is illustrated in Figure 241-2.

Figure 241-1: Displaying the date in the Czech Republic's locale.

Figure 241-2: Displaying the date in Japan's locale.

By contast, in newer versions of Netscape, the date is always output in a standard default fashion based on the language of the browser and ignoring the operating system's specified locale settings.

The following steps create a bookmarklet for outputting the current date in a dialog box in the current locale (in Internet Explorer):

1. Open the text editor you normally use for writing JavaScript.

2. Create a new `Date` object and assign it to the variable `today`:

   ```
   today = new Date();
   ```

3. Use the `window.alert` method to display the date and time formatted for the user's locale; the final script will look like this:

   ```
   today = new Date();
   window.alert(today.toLocaleString());
   ```

4. Remove blank spaces from the script, and add the `javascript:` protocol to the start of the script, so that the result is a one-line URL with all extraneous spaces removed; notice that the space between `new` and `Date` is not extraneous and cannot be removed:

   ```
   javascript:today=new Date();window.alert↩
   (today.toLocaleString());
   ```

5. Create a bookmark or favorite using this code as the URL. To test the bookmarklet, select the new bookmark or favorite you created, and the date and time is displayed in a dialog box, as illustrated in Figure 241-3.

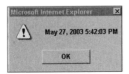

Figure 241-3: Displaying the date and time in a dialog box.

tips

- In Windows 2000, you set the locale for Windows in the Control Panel's Regional Option tool.

- To make developing bookmarklets easy, it is best to start by editing the code in your regular code editor and then copy and paste the bookmarklet into your favorites or bookmarks list at the end.

cross-reference

- Task 47 illustrates how to use the `Date` object to output the current date.

Checking Your IP Address with a Bookmarklet

note

■ This bookmarklet only works in Netscape and cannot be used in Internet Explorer.

This task shows how to use Netscape and Java to create a bookmarklet to display the user's computer's IP address in a dialog box. Doing so relies on the fact that through JavaScript in Netscape you can access the Java environment available in the browser. This Java environment provides the `java.net.InetAddress.getLocalHost().getHostAddress()` method to access the IP address.

`java.net` is the class that contains numerous objects, and associated methods and properties, for working with networks and their hosts. This class is a standard part of typical Java installations and should be available on any modern Netscape browser with Java support installed.

The `getLocalHost` method returns a `host` object containing information about the local, as well as methods for accessing that information. The `getHostAddress` of the `host` object returns the IP address of the host.

This method should only be called if the user has Java enabled. This can be tested by referring to the `navigator.javaEnabled` method, which returns `true` if Java is, in fact, enabled. The result is the following steps to create the bookmarklet:

1. Open the text editor you normally use for writing JavaScript.

2. Use an `if` statement to test if Java is enabled:

   ```
   if (navigator.javaEnabled()) {
   ```

3. If Java is enabled, display the current IP address in a dialog box by using the `window.alert` method:

   ```
   window.alert(java.net.InetAddress.getLocalHost().⤸
   getHostAddress());
   ```

4. Close the `if` statement so that the final script looks like this:

   ```
   if (navigator.javaEnabled()) {
      window.alert(java.net.InetAddress.getLocalHost().⤸
   getHostAddress());
   }
   ```

5. Remove line separations and blank spaces from the script, and add the `javascript:` protocol to the start of the script, so that the result is a one-line URL with all extraneous spaces removed:

```
javascript:if(navigator.javaEnabled()){window.alert⤴
(java.net.InetAddress.getLocalHost().getHostAddress());}
```

6. Create a bookmark using this code as the URL. To test the bookmarklet, select the new bookmark or favorite you created, and the computer's IP address is displayed in a dialog box, as illustrated in Figure 242-1. If you attempt to run the bookmarklet in Internet Explorer, you get an error, as illustrated in Figure 242-2.

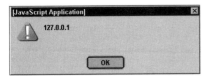

Figure 242-1: Displaying the IP address in a dialog box.

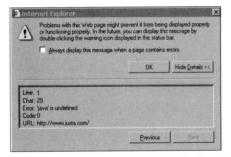

Figure 242-2: In Internet Explorer, the bookmarklet causes an error.

Searching Yahoo! with a Bookmarklet in Internet Explorer

A common task performed by users is to search a popular search engine such as Yahoo! for a word or phrase they find in a Web page. The usually approach is to select the word or phrase, copy it, open Yahoo!, and then paste the word or phrase into the search box.

Using JavaScript in Internet Explorer, you can build a bookmarklet so that the user can simply select the word or phrase and then select the bookmarklet to automatically trigger the appropriate search on Yahoo!.

This bookmarklet relies on the following:

- Internet Explorer provides the `document.selection` object to reflect the text currently selected in a Web page.

- The `createRange` method of the `document.selection` object returns a pointer to the selected range that has a `text` property containing the selected text.

- Yahoo! expects a search query in the URL in the form `http://search.yahoo.com/bin/search?p=search query here`.

The following steps show how to create this bookmarklet:

1. Open the text editor you normally use for writing JavaScript.

2. Save the currently selected text in the variable `searchQuery`:

   ```
   searchQuery = document.selection.createRange().text;
   ```

3. Use the `escape` function to convert the selected text to URL-encoded format and save the result back into `searchQuery`:

   ```
   searchQuery = escape(searchQuery);
   ```

4. Set `location.href` to the Yahoo! search URL, and append the value of `searchQuery` to the end of the URL; the final script will look like this:

   ```
   searchQuery = document.selection.createRange().text;
   searchQuery = escape(searchQuery);
   location.href = 'http://search.yahoo.com/bin/search?p=' ⮌
   + searchQuery;
   ```

5. Remove the line separations and blank spaces from the script, and add the `javascript:` protocol to the start of the script, so that the result is a one-line URL with all extraneous spaces removed:

   ```
   javascript:searchQuery=document.selection.createRange(). ⮌
   text;searchQuery=escape(searchQuery);location.href= ⮌
   'http://search.yahoo.com/bin/search?p='+searchQuery;
   ```

notes

- The `document.selection` object is only available in Internet Explorer. This task will not work in Netscape Navigator.

- The `location.href` property reflects the URL of the current page. When a new URL is assigned to it, the new URL will be displayed by the browser.

6. Create a favorite using this code as the URL. To test the book-marklet, open a Web page in your browser and select some text, as illustrated in Figure 243-1. Select the new favorite you created, and your browser is redirected to Yahoo!, where search results are displayed as illustrated in Figure 243-2.

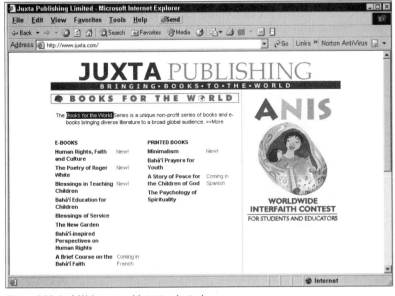

Figure 243-1: A Web page with text selected.

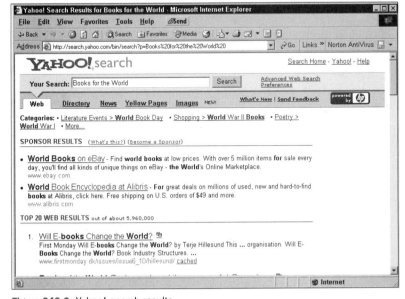

Figure 243-2: Yahoo! search results.

tip

- To make developing bookmarklets easy, it is best to start by editing the code in your regular code editor and then copy and paste the bookmarklet into your favorites or bookmarks list at the end.

Searching Yahoo! with a Bookmarklet in Netscape

notes

▪ The `document.get Selection` method is only available in Netscape. This task will not work in Internet Explorer.

▪ The `location.href` property reflects the URL of the current page. When a new URL is assigned to it, the new URL will be displayed by the browser.

A common task performed by users is to search a popular search engine such as Yahoo! for a word or phrase they find in a Web page. The usually approach to this is to select the word or phrase, copy it, open Yahoo!, and then paste the word or phrase into the search box.

Using JavaScript in Netscape, you can build a bookmarklet so that the user can simply select the word or phrase and then select the bookmarklet to automatically trigger the appropriate search on Yahoo!.

This bookmarklet relies on the following:

- Netscape provides the `document.getSelection` method to retrieve the currently selected text in a Web page.

- Yahoo! expects a search query in the URL in the form `http:// search.yahoo.com/bin/search?p=search query here`.

The following steps show how to create this bookmarklet:

1. Open the text editor you normally use for writing JavaScript.

2. Save the currently selected text in the variable `searchQuery`:

   ```
   searchQuery = document.getSelection();
   ```

3. Use the `escape` function to convert the selected text to URL-encoded format and save the result back into `searchQuery`:

   ```
   searchQuery = escape(searchQuery);
   ```

4. Set `location.href` to the Yahoo! search URL, and append the value of `searchQuery` to the end of the URL; the final script will look like this:

   ```
   searchQuery = document.getSelection();
   searchQuery = escape(searchQuery);
   location.href = 'http://search.yahoo.com/bin/search?p='
   + searchQuery;
   ```

5. Remove the line separations and blank spaces from the script, and add the `javascript:` protocol to the start of the script, so that the result is a one-line URL with all extraneous spaces removed:

   ```
   javascript:searchQuery=document.getSelection();search
   Query=escape(searchQuery);location.href='http://search.
   yahoo.com/bin/search?p='+searchQuery; @
   ```

6. Create a bookmark using this code as the URL. To test the book-marklet, open a Web page in your browser and select some text, as illustrated in Figure 244-1. Select the new favorite you created, and your browser is redirected to Yahoo!, where search results are displayed as illustrated in Figure 244-2.

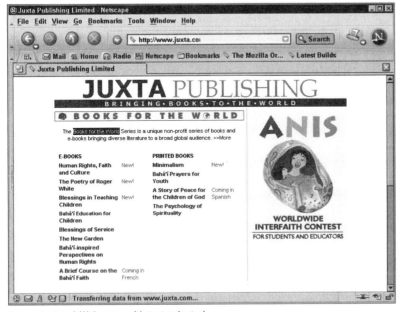

Figure 244-1: A Web page with text selected.

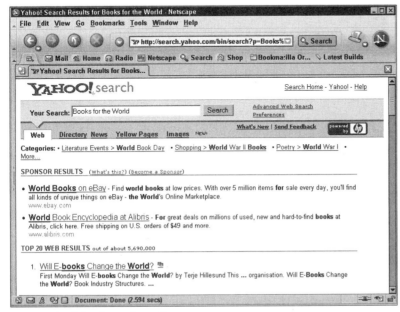

Figure 244-2: Yahoo! search results.

tip

- To make developing book-marklets easy, it is best to start by editing the code in your regular code editor and then copy and paste the bookmarklet into your favorites or bookmarks list at the end.

Part 11: Cross-Browser Compatibility and Issues

Task 245

Detecting the Browser Type

Using JavaScript you can determine the type of browser the user is running. This proves useful if you want to implement features in your applications that require different code in different browsers. By detecting the browser the user is using, you can account for that in the code that actually is run by the user.

The key to determining the browser the user is using is the `navigator` object. The `navigator` object provides several properties you can use to tell you the type of browser being used:

- `navigator.appName`: This property returns a string indicating the browser that is being used. For instance, this string might be "Microsoft Internet Explorer" or "Netscape".

- `navigator.appCodeName`: This property returns the browser name that the browser claims to be. For instance, in Internet Explorer 6, this will actually be "Mozilla," as it also will be in Netscape 7.

- `navigator.userAgent`: This property returns the entire user agent string. The user agent string is a string sent by the browser to the server identifying itself to the server. It is from the user agent string that the application name and the code name are derived. Following are examples of user agent strings:

  - Internet Explorer 6: `Mozilla/4.0 (compatible; MSIE 6.0; Windows NT 5.0; .NET CLR 1.0.3705)`

  - Netscape 7: `Mozilla/5.0 (Windows; U; Windows NT 5.0; en-US; rv:1.0.2) Gecko/20030208 Netscape/7.02`

The following task shows how to display the browser's application name, code name, and user agent to the user:

1. Create a new document in your preferred editor.

2. In the body of the document, create a script block with opening and closing `script` tags:

```
<body>

    <script language="JavaScript">

    </script>

</body>
```

3. Use the `document.write` method to output the application name:

```
        document.write("Browser Type: " + navigator.⊃
appName + "<br>");
```

notes

- There are many reasons why you might want to account for a user's browser version in your applications. For instance, some browsers have poor support for advanced features of cascading style sheets, and you want to avoid using those features on these browsers.

- Browsers will often make claims to being a different browser. For instance, both Internet Explorer and Netscape claim to be Mozilla in an attempt to ensure that sites send them the same versions of their code. This can be problematic, since Internet Explorer and Mozilla don't actually have identical JavaScript implementations.

4. Use the `document.write` method to output the code name:

```
document.write("Code Name: " + navigator.⤸
appCodeName + "<br>");
```

5. Use the `document.write` method to output the user agent string. The final page should look like Listing 245-1.

```
<body>

    <script language="JavaScript">

        document.write("Browser Type: " + navigator.appName ⤸
+ "<br>");
        document.write("Code Name: " + navigator.appCodeName ⤸
+ "<br>");
        document.write("User Agent: " + navigator.userAgent ⤸
+ "<br>");

    </script>

</body>
```

Listing 245-1: Displaying browser version information.

6. Save the file and close it.

7. Open the file in your browser. In Internet Explorer, the display should look similar to Figure 245-1.

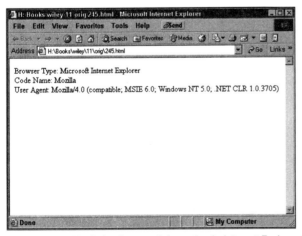

Figure 245-1: Displaying browser information in Internet Explorer 6.

cross-reference

- Task 9 discusses generating output to the browser from JavaScript using the `document.write` method. The method takes a single string argument. In this case, you are building a string by concatenating two strings.

Detecting the Browser Version

In Task 245 you saw how to detect the browser type by using the `navigator` object. In addition to this information, the `navigator` object can tell you which version of a particular browser is in use. This is important because there can be significant functionality differences between individual versions. For instance, the difference between the Netscape 4.7x and the Netscape 7 browsers is more significant than the differences between Netscape 7 and Internet Explorer 6.

To check the version of a particular browser, you need to use the `navigator.appVersion` property. In Internet Explorer 6, this would return the following:

```
4.0 (compatible; MSIE 6.0; Windows NT 5.0; .NET CLR 1.0.3705)
```

In Netscape 7, this returns the following:

```
5.0 (Windows; en-US)
```

These version strings provide you with information about the platform involved and the version.

The following task shows how to display the browser version and user agent string in the browser window:

1. Create a new document in your preferred editor.

2. In the body of the document, create a script block with opening and closing `script` tags:

   ```
   <body>

       <script language="JavaScript">

       </script>

   </body>
   ```

3. Use the `document.write` method to output the browser version:

   ```
       document.write("Browser Version: " + ⏎
   navigator.appVersion + "<br>");
   ```

4. Use the `document.write` method to output the user agent string. The final page looks like Listing 246-1.

5. Save the file and close it.

6. Open the file in your browser. In Internet Explorer, the display should look similar to Figure 246-1. In Mozilla, it should appear like Figure 246-2.

notes

- Notice that Internet Explorer purports to be version 4.0. This actually reflects the version of the browser represented in the code name. That is, Internet Explorer 6 claims to be the same as Mozilla 4.0. Insider the parentheses, Internet Explorer then provides an accurate representation of its real version.

- Netscape 6 and later is actually a true Mozilla-based browser. Therefore, Netscape 7 reports itself as Mozilla (as the code name and application name) and then provides a version to place itself in the Mozilla line. This version number does not reflect the release number of the Mozilla version used in the Netscape browser, but instead an internal number also reported if you check the browser version in an actual Mozilla browser.

- Notice that the browser version reported by `navigator.appVersion` contains some part of the user agent string that is in parentheses. In Internet Explorer, this could be the entire part of the user agent string that is in parentheses, while in Mozilla and Netscape, this is just a subset of that part of the user agent string.

Task 246

```
<body>

    <script language="JavaScript">

        document.write("Browser Version: " + ⤸
navigator.appVersion + "<br>");
        document.write("User Agent: " + navigator.userAgent ⤸
+ "<br>");

    </script>

</body>
```

Listing 246-1: Displaying a browser's user agent string.

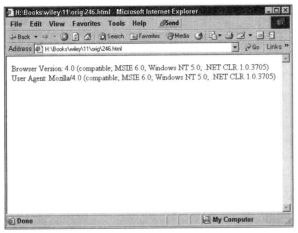

Figure 246-1: Displaying browser information in Internet Explorer 6.

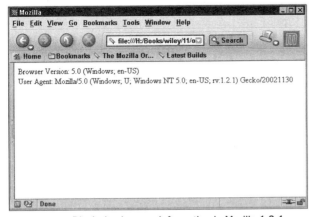

Figure 246-2: Displaying browser information in Mozilla 1.2.1.

Browser Detection Using Object Testing

I n the previous tasks, examples were given of how to determine what browser and version a user is using by examining properties of the `navigator` object. However, it is generally the case that using these properties in practical real-world applications is difficult at best.

Because of this, the technique of object testing has emerged as the preferred method for determining what browser is in use. This means you can simply determine browser versions by testing for the existence of these objects:

```
if (object name) { object exists }
```

The following lists key objects you can use in determining browser versions:

- `document.all`: IE4+

- `document.getElementById`: IE5+/NS6+

- `document.layers`: NS4

- `document.fireEvent`: IE5.5+

- `document.createComment`: IE6+

Using these, you can build conditions that test for various browser environments:

- NS4/IE4+: `(document.all || document.layers)`

- NS4+: `(!document.all)`

- IE4+: `(document.all)`

- NS4 only: `(document.layers && !document.getElementById)`

- IE 4 only: `(document.all && !document.getElementById)`

- NS6+/IE5+: `(document.getElementById)`

- NS6+: `(document.getElementById && !document.all)`

- IE5+: `(document.all && document.getElementById)`

- IE5.5+: `(document.all && document.fireEvent)`

- IE6 only: `(document.all && document.createComment)`

- IE5 only: `(document.all && document.getElementById && !document.fireEvent)`

- IE5.5 only: `(document.all && document.fireEvent && !document.createComment)`

notes

- The way that the user agents of different browsers represent themselves means you need to perform complex string analysis just to figure what browser the user really is running.

- There are other browsers as well, such as Opera, and some of these tests will be true with certain versions of these browsers. However, such an overwhelming majority of users either use Netscape or Internet Explorer that in some applications, accounting for these marginal browsers may be more effort than it's worth; you need to judge that for each application you build. This task provides examples for Internet Explorer and Netscape, but you can extend the concept to other browsers as well by looking at the JavaScript documentation for those browsers and identifying appropriate objects to use in your tests.

The following task builds a page that displays information about the current browser based on some of these object-testing conditions:

1. In the body of a new document, create a script block.

2. In the script, use an `if` statement to test for the existence of `document.all` to separate Internet Explorer browsers from Netscape browsers.

3. Based on the initial test, display the browser type and then test for, and display, the version of the browser, so that the final page looks like Listing 247-1.

```
<body>
    <script language="JavaScript">
        if (document.all) {
            document.write("Microsoft IE.<br>");
            if (!document.getElementById) {
                document.write("Version 4.");
            }
            if (document.getElementById && !document.⤸
fireEvent) {
                document.write("Version 5.");
            }
            if (document.fireEvent && !document.⤸
createComment) {
                document.write("Version 5.5.");
            }
            if (document.createComment) {
                document.write("Version 6.");
            }
        } else {
            document.write("Netscape.<br>");
            if (document.getElementById) {
                document.write("Version 6+.");
            } else {
                document.write("Version 4.");
            }
        }
    </script>
</body>
```

Listing 247-1: Using object testing to determine browser version.

4. Save the file and close it.

5. Open the file in a browser. You see a message about the type of browser you are using.

tip

- The premise of object testing is simple: Each browser has at least some objects that it implements that other browsers do not. You can test for the existence of an object easily by using the object as the condition of an `if` statement. For instance, you can test if `document.all` exists with `if (document.all)`.

Task 248

Creating Browser Detection Variables

In Task 247 you saw how object testing could be used to build conditions to determine which browser was in use. In practical terms, though, you typically will not want to be using these complex conditions in multiple places in your code to determine what browser is being used to view your pages.

Instead, a common practice is to build a list of variables at the start of your script. These variables would each represent a specific browser and version and would take a value of true or false. For instance, the variable `ie4` could be true or false to indicate if the user is using Internet Explorer 4. Then you could test if the user is using that browser in your code with the following:

```
if (ie4) {
    Code to execute if the user is using Internet Explorer 4
}
```

You can create these variables by assigning boolean expressions to them; these conditions were outlined in Task 247:

- NS4/IE4+: `(document.all || document.layers)`

- NS4+: `(!document.all)`

- IE4+: `(document.all)`

- NS4 only: `(document.layers && !document.getElementById)`

- IE 4 only: `(document.all && !document.getElementById)`

- NS6+/IE5+: `(document.getElementById)`

- NS6+: `(document.getElementById && !document.all)`

- IE5+: `(document.all && document.getElementById)`

- IE5.5+: `(document.all && document.fireEvent)`

- IE6 only: `(document.all && document.createComment)`

- IE5 only: `(document.all && document.getElementById && !document.fireEvent)`

- IE5.5 only: `(document.all && document.fireEvent && !document.createComment)`

The following task shows how to build JavaScript code to create these sorts of variables for each of the main versions of Internet Explorer and Netscape:

1. In the header of any document where you need to perform browser detection, create a script block.

note

- The variables created in this script are being assigned expressions. Each of these expressions evaluates to a boolean value (true or false), so `ie4` will be true on Internet Explorer 4 but will be false in Netscape 6, for instance.

2. In the script, create a variable named `ie4` to represent Internet Explorer 4, and assign the result of the Internet Explorer 4 test condition to the variable:

```
var ie4 = (document.all && !document.getElementById);
```

3. In the script, create a variable named `ie5` to represent Internet Explorer 5, and assign the result of the Internet Explorer 5 test condition to the variable:

```
var ie5 = (document.all && document.getElementById && ⮑
!document.fireEvent);
```

4. In the script, create a variable named `ie55` to represent Internet Explorer 5.5, and assign the result of the Internet Explorer 5.5 test condition to the variable:

```
var ie55 = (document.all && document.fireEvent && ⮑
!document.createComment);
```

5. In the script, create a variable named `ie6` to represent Internet Explorer 6, and assign the result of the Internet Explorer 6 test condition to the variable:

```
var ie6 = (document.all && document.createComment);
```

6. In the script, create a variable named `ns4` to represent Netscape 4, and assign the result of the Netscape 4 test condition to the variable:

```
var ns4 = (document.layers && !document.getElementById);
```

7. In the script, create a variable named `ns6` to represent Netscape 6 and higher, and assign the result of Netscape 6 and higher. The final set of variable assignments should look like Listing 248-1.

```
<script language="JavaScript">
    var ie4 = (document.all && !document.getElementById);
    var ie5 = (document.all && document.getElementById && ⮑
!document.fireEvent);
    var ie55 = (document.all && document.fireEvent && ⮑
!document.createComment);
    var ie6 = (document.all && document.createComment);
    var ns4 = (document.layers && !document.getElementById);
    var ns6 = document.getElementById && !document.all);
</script>
```

Listing 248-1: Creating browser detection variables.

Dealing with Differences in Object Placement in Newer Browsers

notes

- The span tag has three main purposes: to assign an ID to a page element, to assign a class to a page element, or to directly assign one or more style attributes to a page element. In a document, all IDs assigned to tags should be unique, but classes can be shared. Both IDs and tags can be associated with style definitions, which, in turn, are applied to matching page elements.

- It is important to note that the document. getElementById method is not available in Internet Explorer 4 or Netscape 4-series browsers; the solution here is for newer browsers.

When working directly with elements of your pages from within JavaScript, you need to be aware of some critical differences between Internet Explorer and Netscape browsers. Recall that it is possible to assign IDs to any object in your HTML with the id attribute. For instance, the following HTML creates a span of text with the ID myText:

```
<span id="myText">Some text goes here</span>
```

If you want to reference this span of text in JavaScript, you have to refer to it differently in the two browsers. Netscape refers to page elements by their IDs right under the document object. This means this text could be referenced with the following:

```
document.myText
```

By comparison, you reference page elements by their IDs in Internet Explorer under document.all:

```
document.all.myText
```

Luckily, you can account for this difference using the document.getElementById method: Given the ID string for a page element, this method returns a reference to the object associated with the method and is supported on Internet Explorer 5 or greater and Netscape 6 or greater.

To use this method to refer to the text span earlier, you would use the following:

```
document.getElementById("myText");
```

The following task illustrates the use of this method. The user is presented with a link; when he or she clicks the link, the text is replaced by new text:

1. Create a new document in your editor.

2. In the body of the document, create a new text span:

   ```
   <body>

       <span>

       </span>

   </body>
   ```

3. Specify an ID for the span using the id attribute of the span tag:

   ```
   <span id="mySpan">
   ```

4. In the text span, create a link for the user to click to change the text in the span:

```
<a href="">Change this text</a>
```

5. As the URL for the link, use a `javascript:` URL to change the text attribute of the object associated with the text span page element. The final page is shown in Listing 249-1.

```
<body>

    <span id="mySpan">

        <a ↵
href="javascript:document.getElementById('mySpan').text = ↵
'New Text';">Change this text</a>

    </span>

</body>
```

Listing 249-1: Accessing a page element.

6. Save the file and close it.

7. Open the file in a browser and you see a link.

8. Click on the link and the link disappears and is replaced with the new text, as illustrated in Figure 249-1.

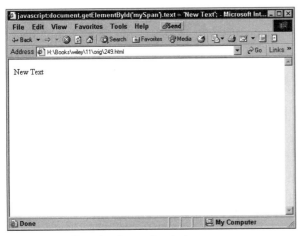

Figure 249-1: Changing the text in a text span.

cross-reference

▪ The span tag is discussed in Task 181.

Creating Layers with the `div` Tag

T he emergence of Dynamic HTML as a powerful combination of JavaScript and cascading style sheets has opened new doors for page development. At the core of these developments is the notion of a layer.

Layers are created with the `div` tag. Their initial placement and appearance are specified using style sheets: Either a style sheet class is defined in a document-wide style sheet and then associated with the layer using the `class` attribute of the `div` tag, or specific style attributes are specified for the layer in the `style` attribute of the `div` tag.

For instance, in the following example, a simple class is defined in a style sheet and then applied to a layer:

```
<head>
   <style type="text/css">
      .myStyle {
         background-color: lightgrey;
         width: 100px;
         height: 100px;
      }
   </style>
</head>

<body>
   <div class="myStyle">This is a layer</div>
</body>
```

The following sample illustrates the creation of two layers. The first layer actually sits on top of, and obscures part of, the second layer:

1. Create a new document in your preferred editor.

2. In the body of the document, create a new layer with opening and closing `div` tags:

   ```
   <body>
      <div>

      </div>
   </body>
   ```

3. Specify styles for the layer with the `style` attribute of the `div` tag:

   ```
   <div style="position:relative; font-size:50px; ⊃
   background-color: lightgrey; z-index:2;">
   ```

4. Specify text to appear in the layer:

   ```
   This is the top layer
   ```

notes

- Notice the use of the `z-index` style attribute. This attribute specifies how layers stack on top of each other. Layers with larger `z-index` values will appear on top of layers with lower values if the positioning of the layers overlaps. See Task 254 for more discussion of this attribute.

- In this task you use the `top` and `left` style attributes to adjust the placement of the layer relative to where it would normally be placed by the browser when rendering the page. When you use a negative value for the `top` attribute, the layer is moved up to overlap some of the place taken by the first layer. These style attributes are discussed further in Task 251.

5. Create a second layer with opening and closing `div` tags, and specify the styles for the layer with the `style` attribute of the `div` tag:

```
<div style="position:relative; top:-25; left:25; ⤶
color:blue; font-size:80px; background-color: yellow; ⤶
z-index:1;">
```

6. Specify text to appear in the layer, so that the final document looks like Listing 250-1.

```
<body>
    <div style="position:relative; font-size:50px; ⤶
background-color: lightgrey; z-index:2;">
        This is the top layer
    </div>
    <div style="position:relative; top:-25; left:25; ⤶
color:blue; font-size:80px; background-color: yellow; ⤶
z-index:1;">
        This is the bottom layer
    </div>
</body>
```

Listing 250-1: Creating two layers using `div` tags.

7. Save the file and close it.

8. Open the file in your browser. You should see the layers on top of each other, as in Figure 250-1.

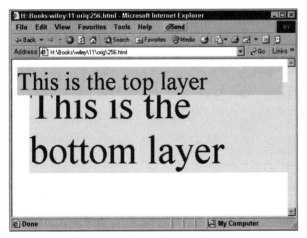

Figure 250-1: Creating two layers that overlap.

tip

- You can also specify styles directly using the `style` attribute of the `div` tag. In this particular example, you could dispense with the style sheet and simply use this `div` tag: `<div style="background-color: lightgrey; width: 100px; height: 100px`

cross-references

- A *layer* is an arbitrary block of HTML code that can be manipulated as a unit: It can be allocated a certain amount of space on the page, it can be placed precisely on the page, and all aspects of its appearance can then be manipulated in JavaScript. Layers are created with the `div` tag, which is introduced in Task 169.

- Notice the use of the `position` style attribute. This attribute is discussed further in Task 251.

Controlling Layer Placement in HTML

Using cascading style sheets, you can control the placement of layers. If you don't specify a position, the browser should just render the layers in the order they appear in the HTML file: vertically, with one on top of the other.

Consider the following three layers:

```
<div style="background-color: lightgrey;">Layer 1</div>
<div style="background-color: white;">Layer 2</div>
<div style="background-color: yellow;">Layer 3</div>
```

Using the following attributes, you can adjust the placement of these layers:

- `position`: This attribute takes one of two possible values: `relative` or `absolute`.

- `top`: This attribute specifies an offset, normally in pixels, for the top of the layer.

- `left`: This attribute specifies an offset, normally in pixels, for the left side of the layer.

The following task places two layers with absolute and relative positioning:

1. Create a new document in your preferred editor, and create a paragraph of opening text in the body of the document:

   ```
   <p>
       This is opening text. There is lots of it. This is ⊃
   opening text. There is lots of it. etc.
   </p>
   ```

2. Create a new layer after the paragraph using opening and closing `div` tags, and use the `style` attribute to specify relative positioning and to place the layer down 100 pixels and to the right by 100 pixels:

   ```
   <div style="position:relative; top: 100px; left: 100px; ⊃
   background-color: yellow;">
   ```

3. Place some text in the layer.

4. Create another layer using opening and closing `div` tags, and use the `style` attribute to specify absolute positioning and to place the layer down 100 pixels and to the right by 100 pixels:

   ```
   <div style="position: absolute; top: 100px; left: 100px; ⊃
   background-color: lightgrey;">
   ```

5. Place some text in the layer, so that the final page looks like Listing 251-1.

notes

- With relative positioning, any adjustments specified in the `top` and `left` attributes are relative to where the browser would normally have placed the layer based on the rest of the HTML in the file. With absolute positioning, any offsets in the `top` and `left` attributes are relative to the top left corner of the display area of the browser window regardless of the rest of the HTML in the file.

- With the `top` attribute, you can move a layer down by 100 pixels from its normal position (relative positioning) or from the top of the display area of the window (absolute positioning) by setting this attribute to `100px`.

- With the `left` attribute, you can move a layer to the right by 200 pixels from its normal position (relative positioning) or from the left of the display area of the window (absolute positioning) by setting this attribute to `200px`.

- Notice the difference between absolute and relative positioning: The absolutely positioned layer is much higher up and to the left of the relatively positioned layer. This is because the relatively positioned layer is placed relative to its normal position: just below the paragraph of text.

```
<body>
    <p>
        This is opening text. There is lots of it. This ⤶
is opening text. There is lots of it. etc.
    </p>
    <div style="position:relative; top: 100px; left: ⤶
100px; background-color: yellow;">
        (100,100) relative
    </div>
    <div style="position: absolute; top: 100px; left: ⤶
100px; background-color: lightgrey;">
        (100,100) absolute
    </div>
</body>
```

Listing 251-1: Using absolute and relative positioning.

6. Save the file and close it. Now open the file in your browser, and you should see the two layers placed as in Figure 251-1.

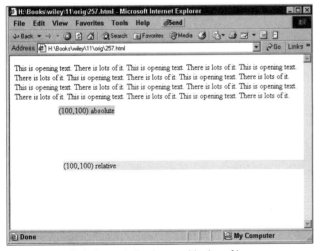

Figure 251-1: Relative and absolute positioning of layers.

cross-reference

▪ You can also control layer placement in JavaScript. Refer to Task 255 for details.

Controlling Layer Size in HTML

Using cascading style sheets, you can control the size of layers precisely. If you don't specify the size, the browser just renders the layers so that the height accommodates all the text and HTML placed in the layer and the width fills the normal width of the display area. Consider the following layer:

```
<div style="background-color: lightgrey;">
    Layer 1<br>
    with two lines of text
</div>
```

The results look like Figure 252-1.

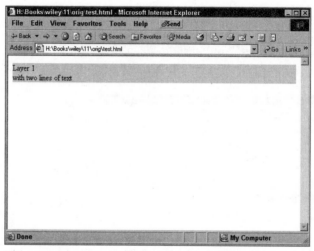

Figure 252-1: Layers auto-size if no size is specified.

Using the width and height style attributes, you can control the size of layers:

- **width:** This attribute specifies the width of a layer, normally in pixels. This overrides the default behavior to extend a layer across the width of the browser window.

- **height:** This attribute specifies the height of a layer, normally in pixels. This overrides the default behavior to make the height of the layer just enough to accommodate the text and HTML displayed in the layer.

The following task creates two layers with different sizes:

1. Create a new document in your preferred editor.

2. In the body of the document, create a new layer with opening and closing div tags, and specify the style attributes for the layer, making the layer 100 pixels by 100 pixels in size:

```
<div style="position:relative; background-color: ⊃
lightgrey; width: 100px; height: 100px;">
```

3. Place some text to display in the layer.

4. Create a second layer with opening and closing `div` tags, and specify the style attributes for the layer, making the layer 300 pixels by 300 pixels in size:

```
<div style="position:relative; color:blue; background-⊃
color: yellow; width: 300px; height: 300px;">
```

5. Place some text to display in the layer, so that the final page looks like Listing 252-1.

```
<body>
    <div style="position:relative; background-color: ⊃
lightgrey; width: 100px; height: 100px;">
        A small box
    </div>
    <div style="position:relative; color:blue; background-⊃
color: yellow; width: 300px; height: 300px;">
        A larger box
    </div>
</body>
```

Listing 252-1: Controlling the size of layers.

6. Save the file and close it.

7. Open the file in a browser and you should see two layers, as in Figure 252-2.

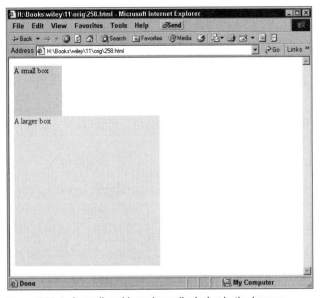

Figure 252-2: A small and large layer displaying in the browser.

cross-references

▪ A *layer* is an arbitrary block of HTML code that can be manipulated as a unit: It can be allocated a certain amount of space on the page, it can be placed precisely on the page, and all aspects of its appearance can then be manipulated in JavaScript. Layers are created with the `div` tag, which is introduced in Task 169.

▪ The use of the `position` attribute for relative positioning is discussed in Task 251.

Task 253

Controlling Layer Visibility in HTML

U sing cascading style sheets, you can control the visibility of layers. By default, all layers are displayed. Using the `visibility` style attribute, however, you can hide a layer so that it is not displayed. This attribute takes two possible values:

- `hidden`: The layer will not be visible.

- `visible`: The layer will be visible.

For instance, the following layer would not be displayed:

```
<div style="visibility: hidden;">
   You can't see this layer.
</div>
```

The following task creates two layers; the first is hidden and the second is visible:

1. Create a new document in your preferred editor.

2. In the body of the document, create a layer with opening and closing `div` tags:

   ```
   <body>
      <div>

      </div>
   </body>
   ```

3. Use the `style` attribute of the `div` tag to specify the appearance of the layer; make sure the layer is not visible:

   ```
   <div style="position:relative; background-color: ⤸
   lightgrey; width: 100px; height: 100px; visibility: ⤸
   hidden;">
   ```

4. Place text in the layer as desired:

   ```
   A small box
   ```

5. Create a second layer with opening and closing `div` tags:

   ```
   <div>

   </div>
   ```

6. Use the `style` attribute of the `div` tag to specify the appearance of the layer; make sure the layer is visible:

   ```
   <div style="position:relative; color:blue; background-⤸
   color: yellow; width: 300px; height: 300px; visibility: ⤸
   visible;">
   ```

7. Place text in the layer as desired, so that the final code looks like Listing 253-1.

```
<body>
    <div style="position:relative; background-color:
lightgrey; width: 100px; height: 100px; visibility:
hidden;">
        A small box
    </div>
    <div style="position:relative; color:blue; background-
color: yellow; width: 300px; height: 300px; visibility:
visible;">
        A larger box
    </div>
</body>
```

Listing 253-1: Controlling layer visibility.

8. Save the file and close it.

9. Open the file in your browser and you should see a page like Figure 253-1.

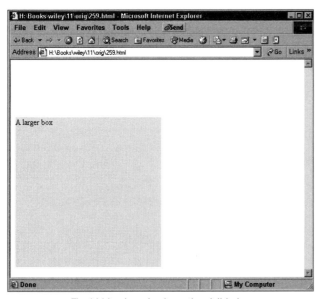

Figure 253-1: The hidden layer is above the visible layer.

cross-references

- You can control the visibility of a layer after it is created by using JavaScript as outlined in Task 256. For instance, a layer may initially be hidden, and then you can use JavaScript to display the layer when it is needed.

- Layers are created with the `div` tag, which is introduced in Task 169.

- The use of the `position` attribute for relative positioning is discussed in Task 251.

Task 254

Controlling Layer Ordering in HTML

Using cascading style sheets, you can control the relative stacking order of layers. The stacking order of layers determines which layers appear on top of other layers when they overlap with each other.

By default, layers stack on top of each other in the order in which they appear in the HTML file. Consider the following three layers:

```
<div style="position: absolute; left: 0px; top: 0px; width: 100px;
height: 100px; background-color: yellow;">Bottom Layer</div>
<div style="position: absolute; left: 50px; top: 50px; width:
100px; height: 100px; background-color: lightgrey;">Middle Layer</div>
<div style="position: absolute; left: 100px; top: 100px; width:
100px; height: 100px; background-color: cyan;">Top Layer</div>
```

By default, the last layer is the top of the stack and the first layer is the bottom. You can control this stacking order with the z-index style attribute. This attribute takes a numeric value, and the larger the value, the higher a layer is in the stack.

The following task creates three layers where the first layer specified is the top layer, the second is the bottom layer, and the third is the middle layer:

1. Create a new document in your preferred editor.

2. In the body of the document, create a new layer and set the z-index style attribute to 3:

```
<body>
   <div style="position:absolute; top: 0px; left:
0px;font-size:50px; background-color: lightgrey;
z-index:3;">
      This is the top layer
   </div>
</body>
```

3. Create another layer and set the z-index style attribute to 1 so it appears below the previous layer:

```
<body>
   <div style="position:absolute; top: 0px; left:
0px;font-size:50px; background-color: lightgrey;
z-index:3;">
      This is the top layer
   </div>
   <div style="position:absolute; top:40; left:40;
color:blue; font-size:80px; background-color: yellow;
z-index:1;">
      This is the bottom layer
   </div>
</body>
```

note

• A *layer* is an arbitrary block of HTML code that can be manipulated as a unit: It can be allocated a certain amount of space on the page, it can be placed precisely on the page, and all aspects of its appearance can then be manipulated in JavaScript. Layers are created with the div tag, which is introduced in Task 169.

4. Create a third layer and set the `z-index` style attribute to 2 so it appears between the previous two layers; place the layer so that it should overlap both of the previous layers:

```
<body>
    <div style="position:absolute; top: 0px; left: ⤴
0px;font-size:50px; background-color: lightgrey; ⤴
z-index:3;">
        This is the top layer
    </div>
    <div style="position:absolute; top:40; left:40; ⤴
color:blue; font-size:80px; background-color: yellow; ⤴
z-index:1;">
        This is the bottom layer
    </div>
    <div style="position:absolute; top:20; left:20; ⤴
color:red; font-size:70px; background-color: cyan; ⤴
z-index:2;">
        This is the middle layer
    </div>
</body>
```

5. Save the file and close it.

6. Open the file in a browser and you should see three overlapping layers, as shown in Figure 254-1.

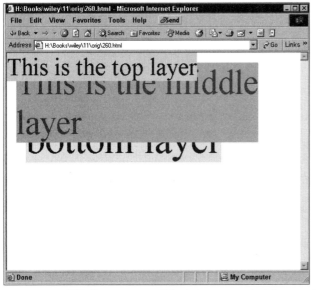

Figure 254-1: With the `z-index` attribute, layers can stack in any order regardless of the order of appearance in the HTML file.

cross-references

- You can control layer stacking order in JavaScript. This is outlined in Task 257.

- The use of the `position` attribute for absolute positioning is discussed in Task 251.

Changing Layer Placement and Size in JavaScript

ask 251 showed how to place layers using style attributes, and 252 showed how to control the size of layers using style attributes. However, once a page is rendered, these style attributes cannot be adjusted unless you use JavaScript.

As an example, consider the following layer:

```
<div id="mylayer" style="height: 100px;">This layer is 100 pixels ⤸
high</div>
```

You could change the height of the layer to 200 pixels with this:

```
document.getElementByID("myLayer").style.height = 200;
```

The following task creates two layers; the first has a link that causes the layer to move. The second has a link that causes the layer to resize:

1. In a script block in the header of a new document, create a new function named moveLayer that takes no arguments:

   ```
   function moveLayer()
   ```

2. In the function, reset the left style attribute of the layer with the ID firstLayer to 300 pixels:

   ```
   document.getElementById("firstLayer").style.left = 300;
   ```

3. In the script block, create a second function named resizeLayer that takes no arguments:

   ```
   function resizeLayer()
   ```

4. In the function, reset the width and height style attributes of the layer with the ID secondLayer to 300 pixels and 400 pixels:

   ```
   document.getElementById("secondLayer").style.width = 300;
   document.getElementById("secondLayer").style.height = 400;
   ```

5. In the body of the document, create a layer with the ID firstLayer:

   ```
   <div id="firstLayer" style="position: relative; ⤸
   background-color: lightgrey; width: 100px; height: ⤸
   100px;">
   ```

6. In the layer, create a link that calls the moveLayer function when the user clicks on the link:

   ```
   <p><a href="javascript:moveLayer()">Move layer</a></p>
   ```

7. Create another layer with the ID secondLayer:

```
<div id="secondLayer" style="background-color: ⏎
yellow; width: 100px; height: 100px;">
```

8. In the layer, create a link that calls the resizeLayer function when the user clicks on the link, so that the final page looks like Listing 255-1:

```
<head>
    <script language="JavaScript">
        function moveLayer() {
            document.getElementById("firstLayer").style.⏎
left = 300;
        }
        function resizeLayer() {
            document.getElementById("secondLayer").style.⏎
width = 300;
            document.getElementById("secondLayer").style.⏎
height = 400;
        }
    </script>
</head>
<body>
    <div id="firstLayer" style="position: relative; ⏎
background-color: lightgrey; width: 100px; height: 100px;">
        <p><a href="javascript:moveLayer()">Move layer</a></p>
    </div>
    <div id="secondLayer" style="background-color: yellow; ⏎
width: 100px; height: 100px;">
        <p><a href="javascript:resizeLayer()">Resize ⏎
layer</a></p>
    </div>
</body>
```

Listing 255-1: Resizing and moving layers in JavaScript.

9. Save the file and close it. Open the file in a browser, and you should see the two initial layers. Click on the Move Layer link, and the top layer should jump to the right. Click on the Resize Layer link, and the bottom layer should grow.

Changing Layer Visibility in JavaScript

Task 253 showed how to control the visibility of layers using style attributes. However, once a page is rendered, these style attributes cannot be adjusted unless you use JavaScript. As an example, consider the following layer:

```
<div id="mylayer" style="visibility: visible;">This layer is ⊃
visible</div>
```

You could hide the layer with this:

```
document.getElementByID("myLayer").style.visibility = "hidden";
```

The following task creates a layer and then provides two links to allow the user to hide or show the layer:

1. Create a new function named `hideLayer` that takes no arguments:

   ```
   function hideLayer()
   ```

2. In the function, reset the `visibility` style attribute of the layer with the ID `firstLayer` to `hidden`:

   ```
   document.getElementById("firstLayer").style.visibility = ⊃
   "hidden";
   ```

3. In the script block, create a second function named `showLayer` that takes no arguments:

   ```
   function showLayer()
   ```

4. In the function, reset the `visibility` style attribute of the layer with the ID `firstLayer` to `visible`, so that the final script looks like this:

   ```
   document.getElementById("firstLayer").style.visibility = ⊃
   "visible";
   ```

5. In the body of the document create a layer with the ID `firstLayer`:

   ```
   <div id="firstLayer" style="background-color: lightgrey; ⊃
   width: 100px; height: 100px;">
   ```

6. After the layer, create a link that calls the `hideLayer` function when the user clicks on the link:

   ```
   <a href="javascript:hideLayer()">Hide layer</a>
   ```

7. Create another link that calls the `showLayer` function when the user clicks on the link. The final page should look like Listing 256-1.

note
- The `document.getElementById` property is available in newer versions of Internet Explorer and Netscape. However, earlier browsers, such as Netscape 4, lacked this method. In addition, there was no style property associated with the layer object. Instead, you would need to access the style properties with `document.layerID.styleProperty`. Of course, Netscape 4 series browsers also supported far less of the cascading style sheet specification, which made it harder to achieve many of the effects described in this part of the book.

```
<head>
    <script language="JavaScript">
        function hideLayer(target) {
            document.getElementById("firstLayer").style.⤸
visibility = "hidden";
        }
        function showLayer(target) {
            document.getElementById("firstLayer")⤸
.style.visibility = "visible";
        }
    </script>
</head>
<body>
    <div id="firstLayer" style="background-color: ⤸
lightgrey; width: 100px; height: 100px;">
        The layer
    </div>
    <p><a href="javascript:hideLayer()">Hide layer</a></p>
    <p><a href="javascript:showLayer()">Show layer</a></p>
</body>
```

Listing 256-1: Hiding and showing layers from JavaScript.

8. Save the file and close it.

9. Open the file in a browser and you see the layer and two links, as illustrated in Figure 256-1.

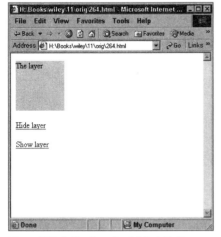

Figure 256-1: The layer is visible initially.

cross-reference

- The creation of your own functions is discussed in Task 27.

10. Click on the Hide Layer link and the layer disappears. Click on the Show Layer link and the layer reappears.

Changing Layer Ordering in JavaScript

Task 254 showed how to control the stacking order of layers using style attributes. However, once a page is rendered, these style attributes cannot be adjusted unless you use JavaScript.

As an example, consider the following layer:

```
<div id="mylayer" style="z-index: 1;">This layer has a
stacking order of 1</div>
```

You could change the z-index value to 2 with this:

```
document.getElementByID("myLayer").style.zIndex = 2;
```

The following task creates two overlapping layers; each layer has a link that brings the layer to the top of the stack:

1. In a script in the header of a new document, create a function named swapLayer that takes two arguments names topTarget and bottomTarget (for the IDs of the layers to move to the top and bottom):

   ```
   function swapLayer(topTarget,bottomTarget) {
   ```

2. In the function, set the stacking order for the desired top layer to 2:

   ```
   document.getElementById(topTarget).style.zIndex = 2;
   ```

3. Set the stacking order for the desired bottom layer to 1:

   ```
   document.getElementById(bottomTarget).style.zIndex = 1;
   ```

4. In the body of the document, create a layer named firstLayer with a stacking order of 1:

   ```
   <div id="firstLayer" style="position: absolute; left:
   10px; top: 10px; width: 100px; height: 100px; background-
   color: yellow; z-index: 1;">
   ```

5. In the layer, create a link to call swapLayer designed to move the layer to the top of the stack; specify 'firstLayer' as the first argument and 'secondLayer' as the second argument:

   ```
   <p><a
   href="javascript:swapLayer('firstLayer','secondLayer')">
   Move to top</a></P>
   ```

6. Create a second layer named secondLayer with a stacking order of 2:

   ```
   <div id="secondLayer" style="position: absolute; left:
   60px; top: 60px; width: 100px; height: 100px; background-
   color: lightgrey; z-index: 2;">
   ```

note

- Simply resetting one layer's stacking order doesn't alter other page element's stacking order. To cause the layers to flip positions in the stack as in this example, you need to change both layers' stacking order positions.

7. In the layer, create a link to call `swapLayer` design to move the layer to the top of the stack; specify `'secondLayer'` as the first argument and `'firstLayer'` as the second argument. The final page should look like Listing 257-1.

```
<head>
    <script language="JavaScript">
        function swapLayer(topTarget,bottomTarget) ⏎
{
            document.getElementById(topTarget).style.⏎
zIndex = 2;
            document.getElementById(bottomTarget).style.⏎
zIndex = 1;
        }
    </script>
</head>
<body>
    <div id="firstLayer" style="position: absolute; left: ⏎
10px; top: 10px; width: 100px; height: 100px; background-⏎
color: yellow; z-index: 1;">
        <p><a href="javascript:swapLayer('firstLayer','⏎
secondLayer')">Move to top</a></P>
    </div>
    <div id="secondLayer" style="position: absolute; left: ⏎
60px; top: 60px; width: 100px; height: 100px; background-⏎
color: lightgrey; z-index: 2;">
        <p><a href="javascript:swapLayer('secondLayer','⏎
firstLayer')">Move to top</a></P>
    </div>
</body>
```

Listing 257-1: Changing stacking order with JavaScript.

8. Save the file and close it. Open the file in a browser, and you see two overlapping layers.

9. Click on the Move to Top link in the bottom layer, and it comes to the top of the stack. Click on the Move to Top link in the other layer, and you should return to the original state of the page.

Fading Objects

In the newer versions of Internet Explorer and Netscape, style sheet extensions are available to control the opacity of objects on the page. Unfortunately, you control opacity differently in Internet Explorer and Netscape. You control the opacity with the following filter in your style definitions for Internet Explorer:

```
filter:alpha(opacity=opacity value);
```

By contrast, in Netscape you control the opacity as follows:

```
-moz-opacity: opacity value;
```

Since each browser will ignore attributes it doesn't understand in your style definitions, you can actually combine these two style attributes in your styles. The following task creates two layers. A form is provided to allow the user to adjust the opacity of the top layer.

1. In a script block in the header of a new document, create a new function named `setOpacity` that takes two arguments (the ID of a layer and an opacity as a percentage):

    ```
    function setOpacity(target,percentage) {
    ```

2. In the function, test for the existence of `document.all`, and use it to set the value of the layer object's appropriate property:

    ```
    if (document.all) {
       document.all(target).filters.alpha.opacity = ⏎
    percentage;
    } else if (document.getElementById) {
       document.getElementById(target).style.MozOpacity = ⏎
    percentage/100;
    }
    ```

3. In the body of the document, create the bottom layer:

    ```
    <div id="backLayer" style="position: absolute; ⏎
    font-size: 60pt; left: 10px; top: 10px;">
    ```

4. Create the top layer, which overlaps the bottom and obscures it:

    ```
    <div id="topLayer" style="position: absolute; left: ⏎
    200px; top: 10px; width: 100px; height: 100px; ⏎
    background-color: yellow; filter:alpha(opacity=100); ⏎
    -moz-opacity:1;">
    ```

5. Create a form with the ID `buttonForm`, and position the form below the previous two layers:

    ```
    <form id="buttonForm" style="position: absolute; left: ⏎
    200px; top: 200px;">
    ```

6. In the form, create two form elements; the first is a text field named `opacity` where the user can enter a percentage value for the opacity of the top layer, and the second is a button that, when clicked, calls the `setOpacity`. The final page should look like Listing 258-1.

```
<head>
    <script language="JavaScript">
        function setOpacity(target,percentage) {
            if (document.all) {
                document.all(target).filters.alpha.opacity =
percentage;
            } else if (document.getElementById) {
                document.getElementById(target).style.
MozOpacity = percentage/100;
            }
        }
    </script>
</head>
<body>
    <div id="backLayer" style="position: absolute;
font-size: 60pt; left: 10px; top: 10px;">
        This Text is in the Background
    </div>
    <div id="topLayer" style="position: absolute;  left:
200px; top: 10px; width: 100px; height: 100px; background-
color: yellow; filter:alpha(opacity=100); -moz-opacity:1;">
        This Layer is on Top
    </div>
    <form id="buttonForm" style="position: absolute; left:
200px; top: 200px;">
        Opacity: <input type="text" name="opacity">%<br>
        <input type="button" value="Set Opacity"
onClick="setOpacity('topLayer',this.form.opacity.value)">
    </form>
</body>
```

Listing 258-1: Controlling layer opacity.

tips

- In Internet Explorer, the opacity value can range from 0 to 100, where 100 means the layer is completely opaque and you cannot see anything hidden behind the layer. At 0, the layer is completely transparent and you cannot see the layer itself.

- In Netscape, the opacity is a value from 0 to 1, where 1 is completely opaque and 0 is completely transparent.

7. Save the file and open it in a browser. Initially, the top layer completely obscures part of the bottom layer.

8. Enter an opacity value in the form field, and click on the Set Opacity button. The top layer fades to the opacity you specified.

Creating a Page Transition in Internet Explorer

Since version 4, Internet Explorer has offered a feature that allows you to specify special effect page transitions to control how one page appears to replace another. You control the page transition effects through meta tags placed in the header of your HTML documents. The tags are used to set Page-Enter or Page-Exit HTTP headers to specify transitions for entering and leaving a page. As the value for these HTTP headers, you specify the following:

```
RevealTrans(Duration: number of seconds, Transition: type of ⤸
transition)
```

The duration indicates how many seconds it should take to complete the transition, while the transition type is a numeric value specifying one of two dozen available effects. These include the following:

- 0: Box in
- 1: Box out
- 2: Circle in
- 3: Circle out
- 4: Wipe up
- 5: Wipe down
- 6: Wipe right
- 7: Wipe left
- 8: Vertical blinds
- 9: Horizontal blinds
- 10: Checkerboard across
- 11: Checkerboard down

The following task illustrates page transitions by creating a page with exit and enter page effects:

1. In the header of a new document, create a meta tag for specifying a transition for when the user enters the page. The transition effect specified is for a checkerboard effect across the page:

   ```
   <meta http-equiv="Page-Enter" content="RevealTrans ⤸
   (Duration=3, Transition=10)">
   ```

notes

- As an example, when a user clicks a link, the new page might slide in from the right to replace the browser, or an effect similar to the rotating of vertical window blinds might cause one page to replace another in the browser window.

- These page transition effects are not available in any version of Netscape. The techniques described here do not apply to Netscape.

- meta tags allow you to specify extra information to be sent in the header of the response from the server to the browser. Internet Explorer will pay attention to the Page-Enter and Page-Exit headers if they exist, but other browsers will simply ignore HTTP headers that they don't understand.

2. Specify a second `meta` tag for the page exit. and use the vertical-blinds transition effect:

```
<meta http-equiv="Page-Exit" content="RevealTrans
(Duration=2, Transition=1)">
```

3. Specify any body text that you want displayed in the page, so that the final page looks like Listing 259-1.

```
<head>
    <meta http-equiv="Page-Enter" content="RevealTrans
(Duration=3, Transition=10)">
    <meta http-equiv="Page-Exit" content="RevealTrans
(Duration=2, Transition=11)">
</head>
<body>
    This is the new page.
</body>
```

Listing 259-1: Specifying page transitions.

4. Save the file and close it. Open your favorite Web site in your browser.

5. In the same browser window, open the file you just created. You should see the page transition to the new one using the checkerboard-across effect, as in Figure 259-1. In the same browser window, open some other Web page and you should see the exit transition with the vertical-blinds effect.

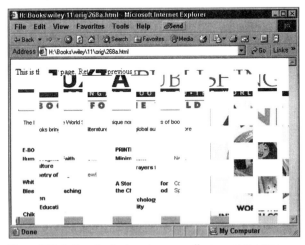

Figure 259-1: The checkerboard-across effect on page entry.

Installing the X Cross-Browser Compatibility Library

notes

- Make sure the path to x.js is correct in the script tag. If x.js is not in the same directory as the HTML file, then specify the relative path to the file.

- The x.js file is the only file needed to use the X cross-browser function library.

As most of this part illustrates, the task of building cross-browser-compatible code is difficult, especially if you plan to manipulate page elements such as layers from within JavaScript. Luckily, many individuals have produced freely available cross-browser Dynamic HTML libraries you can use to simplify this process.

With these libraries, you generally call functions from the library to manipulate objects, rather than use the direct JavaScript methods you normally would. Sometimes you will even create all your page elements by calling functions in the libraries.

These libraries include the following:

- CBE: www.cross-browser.com

- X: www.cross-browser.com

- DynAPI: http://dynapi.sourceforge.net/dynapi/

- Glimmer: www.inkless.com/glimmer

- DHTML Library: www.dhtmlcentral.com/projects/lib

The X library's Web site is illustrated in Figure 260-1.

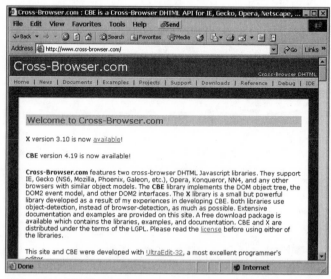

Figure 260-1: The X cross-browser compatibility library's Web site.

For the purposes of this part of the book and the tasks that follow, you will use the X library. Unlike some of the libraries listed here that are large, fully featured libraries that manage the entire process of object creation through manipulation, X is simply a series of functions that encapsulate manipulation tasks on existing page elements in a browser-compatible way.

This task shows how to install the library into any application you are building:

1. Download the most recent version of the X library from www.cross-browser.com. The most recent version as of the publication of this book was in a file named x38.zip.

2. Extract the contents of the ZIP archive file to the directory where you want to store the library files for future reference.

3. Copy the x.js file to the directory where you are building the files for your JavaScript application.

4. In each page that will need to perform cross-browser page element manipulation, include the following line in the header of the HTML file:

```
<script language="JavaScript" src="x.js"></script>
```

5. Make calls in these pages to any of the X library methods as shown in the remaining tasks in this part of the book.

tip

- If you want to build pages and sites that make even moderate use of Dynamic HTML and you want those pages to function reasonably well for most users, you should seriously consider the use of a library rather than coding the Dynamic HTML yourself. It will make it easier to focus on the functionality of your page rather than the code you will need to generate to make the functionality possible in each browser.

Task 261

Showing and Hiding Elements with X

The X cross-browser function library, introduced in Task 260, simplifies the process of showing and hiding page elements such as layers. Showing or hiding a layer with the X library requires two steps:

1. Include the x.js script library file in the header of your document.

2. Use the xShow and xHide functions to show and hide page elements:

```
xShow("element ID");
xHide("element ID");
```

The following task illustrates how to use these functions to display a layer and then provide links to the user to show and hide the layer:

1. Create a new document in your preferred editor.

2. In the header of the document, include the x.js script library file:

```
<script language="JavaScript" src="x.js"></script>
```

3. In the body of the document, create a layer with the ID myLayer:

```
<div id="myLayer" style="width: 100px; height: 100px; ⊃
background-color: lightgrey;">
    This is a layer
</div>
```

4. Create a link for showing the layer; the link should call xShow when the user clicks on it:

```
<a href="javascript:xShow('myLayer');">Show Layer</a>
```

5. Create a link for hiding the layer; the link should call xHide when the user clicks on it. The final page should look like Listing 261-1.

```
<head>
    <script language="JavaScript" src="x.js"></script>
</head>
<body>

background-color: lightgrey;">
        This is a layer
    </div>
    <a href="javascript:xShow('myLayer');">Show Layer</a>
    <br>
    <a href="javascript:xHide('myLayer');">Hide Layer</a>
</body>
```

Listing 261-1: Using xShow and xHide.

caution

- While cross-browser libraries provide the benefit of making it easy to develop Dynamic HTML applications for multiple browsers, they can affect the size and download time of your pages. Remember, the library is included in every page. As a general-purpose tool, a library necessarily has more code than if you handled the cross-browser compatibility code yourself and made it specific to your needs.

6. Save the file and close it.

7. Open the file in your browser. You should see the layer followed by the two links, as in Figure 261-1.

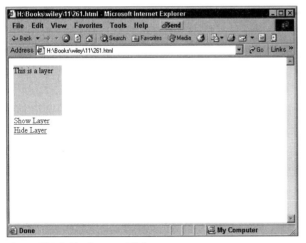

Figure 261-1: The layer and links.

8. Click on the Hide Layer link and the layer should disappear, as illustrated in Figure 261-2. Click on the Show Layer link to return to the original state.

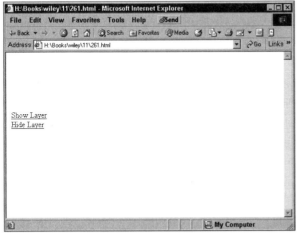

Figure 261-2: Hiding the layer.

cross-reference

- Refer to Task 260 to learn how to properly include the X library in your pages.

Task 262

Controlling Stacking Order with X

The X cross-browser function library, introduced in Task 260, simplifies the process of controlling the stacking order of page elements such as layers. Changing the stacking order of an element with the X library requires two steps:

1. Include the `x.js` script library file in the header of your document.

2. Use the `xZIndex` function to specify a new stacking order value:

```
xZIndex("element ID", stacking order value);
```

note

- The stacking order should be an integer numeric value; lower values are stacked below elements with higher values.

The following task illustrates how to use this function to display two overlapping layers and then to provide links that the user selects to choose which layer to display at the top of the stack:

1. Create a new document in your preferred editor.

2. In the header of the document, include the `x.js` script library file:

```
<script language="JavaScript" src="x.js"></script>
```

3. In the body of the document, create a layer with the ID `firstLayer`. The layer should contain a link that calls `xZIndex` twice to set the appropriate stacking order for the two layers:

```
<div id="firstLayer" style="position: absolute; width:
100px; height: 100px; left: 10px; top: 10px; background-
color: lightgrey; z-index: 1;">
   <a href="#" onClick="xZIndex('firstLayer',2);xZIndex
('secondLayer',1); return false;">Move to Top</a>
</div>
```

4. Create another layer that overlaps the first layer with the ID `secondLayer`. The layer should contain a link that calls `xZIndex` twice to set the appropriate stacking order for the two layers. The final page should look like Listing 262-1.

5. Save the file and close it.

6. Open the file in your browser. You should see the two layers containing links, as in Figure 262-1.

7. Click on the Move to Top link, and the bottom layer and the layer should move to the top.

```
<head>
   <script language="JavaScript" src="x.js"></script>
</head>
<body>
   <div id="firstLayer" style="position: absolute; width:
100px; height: 100px; left: 10px; top: 10px; background-
color: lightgrey; z-index: 1;">
      <a href="#"
onClick="xZIndex('firstLayer',2);xZIndex('secondLayer',1);
return false;">Move to Top</a>
   </div>
   <div id="secondLayer" style="position: absolute; width:
100px; height: 100px; left: 60px; top: 60px; background-
color: yellow; z-index: 2;">
      <a href="#"onClick="xZIndex('secondLayer',2);xZIndex
('firstLayer',1); return false;">Move to Top</a>
   </div>
</body>
```

Listing 262-1: Using xZIndex.

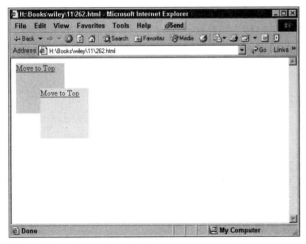

Figure 262-1: Two overlapping layers.

Changing Text Color with X

The X cross-browser function library, introduced in Task 260, simplifies the process of changing the text color of page elements such as layers. Changing the text color of a layer with the X library requires two steps:

1. Include the `x.js` script library file in the header of your document.

2. Use the `xColor` function to change the color of page elements:

   ```
   xColor("element ID","Color");
   ```

The following task illustrates how to use these functions to display a layer and then provide a form the user can use to change the text color in the layer:

1. Create a new document in your preferred editor.

2. In the header of the document, include the `x.js` script library file:

   ```
   <script language="JavaScript" src="x.js"></script>
   ```

3. In the body of the document, create a layer with the ID `myLayer`:

   ```
   <div id="myLayer" style="font-size: 40pt; color: blue;">
      This is my text
   </div>
   ```

4. Create a form following the layer. The form should have a text field named `textColor` and a button that is used to call the `xColor` method to set the layer's text color to the color specified in the text field. The final page should look like Listing 263-1.

```
<head>

   <script language="JavaScript" src="x.js"></script>

</head>

<body>

   <div id="myLayer" style="font-size: 40pt; color: blue;">
      This is my text
   </div>

   <form>
      Color: <input type="text" name="textColor">
      <input type="button" ⊃
onClick="xColor('myLayer',this.form.textColor.value);" ⊃
value="Set Color">
   </form>

</body>
```

Listing 263-1: Using `xColor`.

note

- You can see the second argument passed in calling the function is `this.form.textColor.value`. The `this` keyword refers to the object associated with the button itself. For each `form` element, the associated object has a property called `form` that references the object of the form in which the element is contained. From here you can reference other form fields by their names and values.

5. Save the file and close it.

6. Open the file in your browser. You should see the layer followed by the form, as in Figure 263-1.

Figure 263-1: The layer and form.

7. Enter a color in the form and click the Set Color button. The text color in the layer changes as shown in Figure 263-2.

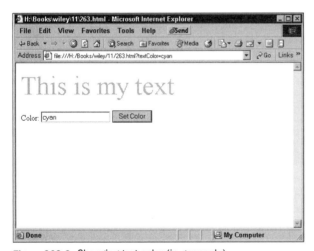

Figure 263-2: Changing text color (in grayscale).

Task **263**

Setting a Background Color with X

The X cross-browser function library, introduced in Task 260, simplifies the process of changing the background color of page elements such as layers. Changing the background color of a layer with the X library requires two steps:

1. Include the `x.js` script library file in the header of your document.

2. Use the `xBackground` function to change the background color of page elements:

```
xColor("element ID","Color");
```

The following task illustrates how to use these functions to display a layer and then provide a form the user can use to change the background color in the layer:

1. Create a new document in your preferred editor.

2. In the header of the document, include the `x.js` script library file:

```
<script language="JavaScript" src="x.js"></script>
```

3. In the body of the document, create a layer with the ID `myLayer`:

```
<div id="myLayer" style="font-size: 40pt; color: blue; ⮑
background-color: lightgrey;">
   This is my text
</div>
```

4. Create a form following the layer. The form should have a text field named `backgroundColor` and a button that is used to call the `xBackground` method to set the layer's background color to the color specified in the text field. The final page should look like Listing 264-1.

```
<head>
   <script language="JavaScript" src="x.js"></script>
</head>
<body>
   <div id="myLayer" style="font-size: 40pt; color: blue; ⮑
background-color: lightgrey;">
      This is my text
   </div>
   <form>
      Color for background: <input type="text" ⮑
name="backgroundColor">
      <input type="button" onClick="xBackground('myLayer',⮑
this.form.textColor.value);" value="Set Color">
   </form>
</body>
```

Listing 264-1: Using `xBackground`.

note

- You can see the second argument passed in calling the function is `this. form.backgroundColo r.value`. The `this` keyword refers to the object associated with the button itself. For each `form` element, the associated object has a property called `form` that references the object of the form in which the element is contained. From here you can reference other form fields by their names and values.

5. Save the file and close it.

6. Open the file in your browser. You should see the layer followed by the form, as in Figure 264-1.

Figure 264-1: The layer and form.

7. Enter a color in the form and click the Set Color button. The background color in the layer changes as shown in Figure 264-2.

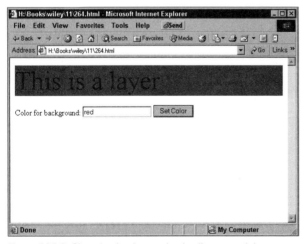

Figure 264-2: Changing background color (in grayscale).

Setting a Background Image with X

The X cross-browser function library, introduced in Task 260, simplifies the process of applying a background image to page elements such as layers. Applying a background image to a page element with the X library requires two steps:

1. Include the `x.js` script library file in the header of your document.

2. Use the `XBackground` function to set the background image for page elements:

   ```
   xBackground("element ID","color","image path or URL");
   ```

The following task illustrates how to use these functions to display a layer and then provide a link to apply a background image to the layer:

1. Create a new document in your preferred editor.

2. In the header of the document, include the `x.js` script library file:

   ```
   <script language="JavaScript" src="x.js"></script>
   ```

3. In the body of the document, create a layer with the ID `myLayer`:

   ```
   <div id="myLayer" style="font-size: 40pt; color: blue; ⏎
   background-color: lightgrey; width: 300px; height: ⏎
   300px;">
      This is a layer
   </div>
   ```

4. Create a link for applying the background image; the link should call `xBackground` when the user clicks on it. The final page should look like Listing 265-1.

```
<head>
   <script language="JavaScript" src="x.js"></script>
</head>
<body>
   <div id="myLayer" style="font-size: 40pt; color: blue; ⏎
background-color: lightgrey; width: 300px; height: 300px;">
      This is a layer
   </div>
   <a href="#" ⏎
onClick="xBackground('mylayer','lightgrey','ethan.jpg');">⏎
Set background image for layer</a>
</body>
```

Listing 265-1: Using `xBackground`.

notes

▪ Notice that the background color is being set as well; this is because the image must be the third argument to the function; the image will override the background color.

▪ If an image is smaller than a layer, it is normally tiled in the layer as shown here.

5. Save the file and close it.

6. Open the file in your browser. You should see the layer followed by the link, as in Figure 265-1.

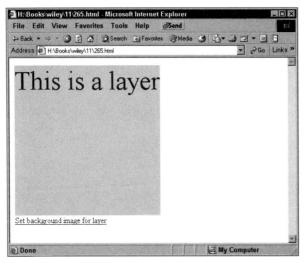

Figure 265-1: The layer and link.

7. Click on the link and the layer should take on a background image, as illustrated in Figure 265-2.

Figure 265-2: Setting the background image for a layer.

Task **266**

Repositioning an Element with X

The X cross-browser function library, introduced in Task 260, simplifies the process of repositioning page elements such as layers. Changing the position of a page element with the X library requires two steps:

1. Include the x.js script library file in the header of your document.

2. Use the xMoveTo function to change the position of page elements:

```
xMoveTo("element ID", x position, y position);
```

The following task illustrates how to use these functions to display a layer and then provide a form the user can use to change the position of the layer:

1. Create a new document in your preferred editor.

2. In the header of the document, include the x.js script library file:

```
<script language="JavaScript" src="x.js"></script>
```

3. In the body of the document, create a layer with the ID myLayer:

```
<div id="myLayer" style="position: absolute; width: ⊃
100px; height: 100px; left: 10px; top: 10px; background-⊃
color: lightgrey;">
   This is a layer
</div>
```

4. Create a form following the layer. The form should have two text fields named x and y and a button that is used to call the xMoveTo function to set the layer's position as specified in the text fields. The final page should look like Listing 266-1.

```
<head>
   <script language="JavaScript" src="x.js"></script>
</head>
<body>
   <div id="myLayer" style="position: absolute; width: ⊃
100px; height: 100px; left: 10px; top: 10px; background-⊃
color: lightgrey;">
      This is a layer
   </div>
   <form style="position: absolute; left: 10px; top: ⊃
120px;">
      X: <input type="text" name="x"><br>
      Y: <input type="text" name="y"><br>
      <input type="button" value="Reset Position" ⊃
onClick="xMoveTo('myLayer',this.form.x.value,this.form.y.⊃
value);">
   </form>
</body>
```

Listing 266-1: Using xMoveTo.

note

- You can see the second argument passed in calling the function is this.form.x.value. The this keyword refers to the objet associated with the button itself. For each form element, the associated object has a property called form that references the object of the form in which the element is contained. From here you can reference other form fields by their names and values, as is done in the third argument as well.

5. Save the file and close it.

6. Open the file in your browser. You should see the layer followed by the form, as in Figure 266-1.

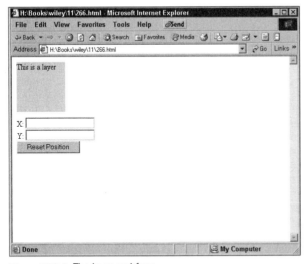

Figure 266-1: The layer and form.

7. Enter a new position in the form and click the Reset Position button. The position of the layer changes as shown in Figure 266-2.

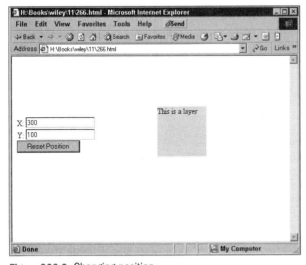

Figure 266-2: Changing position.

Sliding an Element with X

The X cross-browser function library, introduced in Task 260, simplifies the process of repositioning page elements such as layers. Changing the position of a page element by sliding it with the X library requires two steps:

1. Include the `x.js` script library file in the header of your document.

2. Use the `xSlideTo` function to slide page elements to new positions:

```
xSlideTo("element ID", x position, y position, duration);
```

The following task illustrates how to use these functions to display a layer and then provide a form the user can use to change the position of the layer by sliding the layer:

1. Create a new document in your preferred editor.

2. In the header of the document, include the `x.js` script library file:

```
<script language="JavaScript" src="x.js"></script>
```

3. In the body of the document, create a layer with the ID `myLayer`:

```
<div id="myLayer" style="position: absolute; width:
100px; height: 100px; left: 10px; top: 10px; background-
color: lightgrey;">
   This is a layer
</div>
```

4. Create a form following the layer. The form should have two text fields named `x` and `y` and a button that is used to call the `xSlideTo` function to set the layer's position as specified in the text fields. The final page should look like Listing 267-1.

```
<head>
   <script language="JavaScript" src="x.js"></script>
</head>
<body>
   <div id="myLayer" style="position: absolute; width:
100px; height: 100px; left: 10px; top: 10px; background-
color: lightgrey;">
       This is a layer
   </div>
   <form style="position: absolute; left: 10px; top:
120px;">
       X: <input type="text" name="x"><br>
       Y: <input type="text" name="y"><br>
       <input type="button" value="Reset Position"
onClick="xSlideTo('myLayer',this.form.x.value,this.form.y.
value);">
   </form>
</body>
```

Listing 267-1: Using `xSlideTo`.

note

- You can see the second argument passed in calling the function is `this.form.x.value`. The `this` keyword refers to the object associated with the button itself. For each `form` element, the associated object has a property called `form` that references the object of the form in which the element is contained. From here you can reference other form fields by their names and values, as is done in the third argument as well.

5. Save the file and close it.

6. Open the file in your browser. You should see the layer followed by the form, as in Figure 267-1.

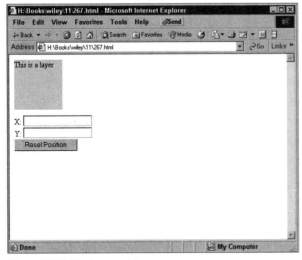

Figure 267-1: The layer and form.

tip

▪ The duration is specified in milliseconds and indicates how long it should take to slide the element from its original location to the new location.

7. Enter a new position in the form and click the Reset Position button. The layer slides to the new position, as shown in Figure 267-2.

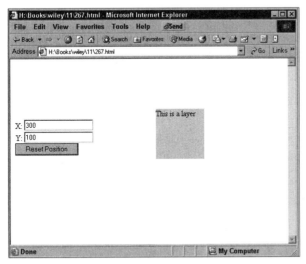

Figure 267-2: Changing position with sliding.

Changing Layer Sizes with X

The X cross-browser function library, introduced in Task 260, simplifies the process of resizing page elements such as layers. Changing the size of a page element with the X library requires two steps:

note

- You can see the second argument passed in calling the function is `this.form.width.value`. The `this` keyword refers to the object associated with the button itself. For each `form` element, the associated object has a property called `form` that references the object of the form in which the element is contained. From here you can reference other form fields by their names and values, as is done in the third argument as well.

1. Include the `x.js` script library file in the header of your document.

2. Use the `xResizeTo` function to change the size of page elements:

```
xResizeTo("element ID", width, height);
```

The following task illustrates how to use these functions to display a layer and then provide a form the user can use to change the size of the layer:

1. Create a new document in your preferred editor.

2. In the header of the document, include the `x.js` script library file:

```
<script language="JavaScript" src="x.js"></script>
```

3. In the body of the document, create a layer with the ID `myLayer`:

```
<div id="myLayer" style="position: absolute; width:
100px; height: 100px; left: 10px; top: 120px; background-
color: lightgrey;">
   This is a layer
</div>
```

4. Create a form following the layer. The form should have two text fields named `width` and `height` and a button that is used to call the `xResizeTo` function to set the layer's size as specified in the text fields. The final page should look like Listing 268-1.

```
<head>
    <script language="JavaScript" src="x.js"></script>
</head>
<body>
    <div id="myLayer" style="position: absolute; width:
100px; height: 100px; left: 10px; top: 120px; background-
color: lightgrey;">
        This is a layer
    </div>
    <form style="position: absolute; left: 10px; top: 10px;">
        Width: <input type="text" name="x"><br>
        Height: <input type="text" name="y"><br>
        <input type="button" value="Reset Size"
onClick="xResizeTo('myLayer',this.form.x.value,this.
form.y.value);">
    </form>
</body>
```

Listing 268-1: Using `xResizeTo`.

5. Save the file and close it.

6. Open the file in your browser. You should see the layer followed by the form, as in Figure 268-1.

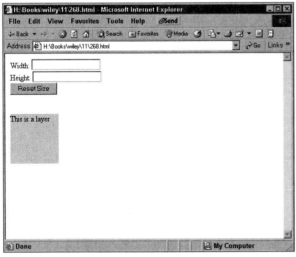

Figure 268-1: The layer and form.

7. Enter a new size in the form and click the Reset Size button. The size of the layer changes as shown in Figure 268-2.

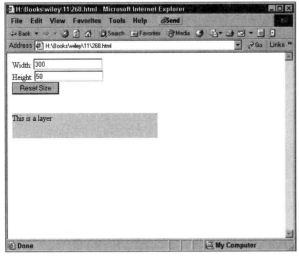

Figure 268-2: Changing size.

Appendix A
JavaScript Quick Reference

The following reference outlines the properties and methods associated with JavaScript objects and indicates the browser support for each using a series of icons:

Icon	Browser
N₃	Netscape 3
N₄	Netscape 4
N₆	Netscape 6
N₇	Netscape 7 and above
e4	Microsoft Internet Explorer 4
e5	Microsoft Internet Explorer 5
e5.5	Microsoft Internet Explorer 5.5
e6	Microsoft Internet Explorer 6

In the reference listings for each object, the following colors indicate if an item is a property or method:

Text Color Coding	Description
▬	Property in black
▬	Method in blue

By no means is this a comprehensive reference but instead provides a quick reference to the objects that are most commonly used in JavaScript. Obscure, older, or rarely used objects may not be included.

Anchor Object e4 e5 e5.5 e6 N₄ N₆ N₇

name	e4 e5 e5.5 e6 N₄ N₆ N₇
text	N₄ N₆ N₇
x	N₄ N₆ N₇
y	N₄ N₆ N₇

Applet Object e4 e5 e5.5 e6 N₆ N₇

| align | e4 e5 e5.5 e6 N₆ N₇ |

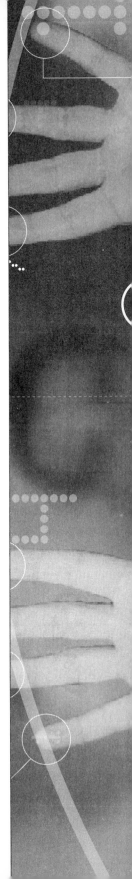

Property	IE4	IE5	IE5.5	IE6	N4	N6	N7
code	●	●	●	●	●	●	
codeBase	●	●	●	●	●	●	
height	●	●	●	●	●	●	
hspace	●	●	●	●	●	●	
name	●	●	●	●	●	●	
vspace	●	●	●	●	●	●	
width	●	●	●	●	●	●	
blur	●	●	●	●	●	●	
focus	●	●	●	●	●	●	

Area Object

Property	IE4	IE5	IE5.5	IE6	N4	N6	N7
(Area Object)	●	●	●	●	●	●	●
alt	●	●	●	●	●	●	
coords	●	●	●	●	●	●	
hash	●	●	●	●	●	●	●
host	●	●	●	●	●	●	●
hostname	●	●	●	●	●	●	●
href	●	●	●	●	●	●	●
noHref	●	●	●	●	●	●	
pathname	●	●	●	●	●	●	●
port	●	●	●	●	●	●	●
protocol	●	●	●	●	●	●	●
search	●	●	●	●	●	●	●
shape	●	●	●	●	●	●	
target	●	●	●	●	●	●	●
x	●	●	●	●	●	●	●
y	●	●	●	●	●	●	●

Array Object

Property	IE4	IE5	IE5.5	IE6	N4	N6	N7
(Array Object)	●	●	●	●	●	●	●
constructor	●	●	●	●	●	●	●
index					●	●	●
input					●	●	●
length	●	●	●	●	●	●	●
prototype	●	●	●	●	●	●	●

	e4	e5	e5.5	e6	N4	N6	N7
concat	e4	e5	e5.5	e6	N4	N6	N7
join	e4	e5	e5.5	e6	N4	N6	N7
pop	e5.5	e6	N4	N6	N7		
push	e5.5	e6	N4	N6	N7		
reverse	e4	e5	e5.5	e6	N4	N6	N7
shift	e5.5	e6	N4	N6	N7		
slice	e4	e5	e5.5	e6	N4	N6	N7
sort	e4	e5	e5.5	e6	N4	N6	N7
slice	e4	e5	e5.5	e6	N4	N6	N7
toLocaleString		e4	e5	e5.5	e6		
toSource		N4	N6	N7			
toString	e4	e5	e5.5	e6	N4	N6	N7
unshift	e5.5	e6	N4	N6	N7		
valueOf	e4	e5	e5.5	e6	N4	N6	N7

Boolean Object e4 e5 e5.5 e6 N4 N6 N7

	e4	e5	e5.5	e6	N4	N6	N7
constructor		e4	e5	e5.5	e6	N4	N6	N7
prototype		e4	e5	e5.5	e6	N4	N6	N7
toSource		N4	N6	N7			
toString	e4	e5	e5.5	e6	N4	N6	N7
valueOf	e4	e5	e5.5	e6	N4	N6	N7

Button Object e4 e5 e5.5 e6 N4 N6 N7

	e4	e5	e5.5	e6	N4	N6	N7
form	e4	e5	e5.5	e6	N4	N6	N7
name	e4	e5	e5.5	e6	N4	N6	N7
type	e4	e5	e5.5	e6	N4	N6	N7
value	e4	e5	e5.5	e6	N4	N6	N7
blur	e4	e5	e5.5	e6	N4	N6	N7
click	e4	e5	e5.5	e6	N4	N6	N7
focus	e4	e5	e5.5	e6	N4	N6	N7
handleEvent		N4					

Checkbox Object e⁴ e⁵ e⁵·⁵ e⁶ N₄ N₆ N₇

	e4	e5	e5.5	e6	N4	N6	N7
checked	e4	e5	e5.5	e6	N4	N6	N7
defaultChecked	e4	e5	e5.5	e6	N4	N6	N7
form	e4	e5	e5.5	e6	N4	N6	N7
name	e4	e5	e5.5	e6	N4	N6	N7
type	e4	e5	e5.5	e6	N4	N6	N7
value	e4	e5	e5.5	e6	N4	N6	N7
blur	e4	e5	e5.5	e6	N4	N6	N7
click	e4	e5	e5.5	e6	N4	N6	N7
focus	e4	e5	e5.5	e6	N4	N6	N7
handleEvent					N4		

cssRule Object N₆ N₇

	N6	N7
cssText	N6	N7
parentStyleSheet	N6	N7
selectorText	N6	N7
style	N6	N7

Debug Object e⁴ e⁵ e⁵·⁵ e⁶

	e5	e5.5	e6
write	e5	e5.5	e6
writeln	e5	e5.5	e6

Date Object e⁴ e⁵ e⁵·⁵ e⁶ N₄ N₆ N₇

	e4	e5	e5.5	e6	N4	N6	N7
constructor	e4	e5	e5.5	e6	N4	N6	N7
prototype	e4	e5	e5.5	e6	N4	N6	N7
getDate	e4	e5	e5.5	e6	N4	N6	N7
getDay	e4	e5	e5.5	e6	N4	N6	N7
getFullYear	e4	e5	e5.5	e6	N4	N6	N7
getHours	e4	e5	e5.5	e6	N4	N6	N7
getMilliseconds	e4	e5	e5.5	e6	N4	N6	N7
getMinutes	e4	e5	e5.5	e6	N4	N6	N7
getMonth	e4	e5	e5.5	e6	N4	N6	N7
getSeconds	e4	e5	e5.5	e6	N4	N6	N7

	IE4	IE5	IE5.5	IE6	N4	N6	N7
getTime	e4	e5	e5.5	e6	N4	N6	N7
getTimezoneOffset	e4	e5	e5.5	e6	N4	N6	N7
getUTCDate	e4	e5	e5.5	e6	N4	N6	N7
getUTCDay	e4	e5	e5.5	e6	N4	N6	N7
getUTCFullYear	e4	e5	e5.5	e6	N4	N6	N7
getUTCHours	e4	e5	e5.5	e6	N4	N6	N7
getUTCMilliseconds	e4	e5	e5.5	e6	N4	N6	N7
getUTCMinutes	e4	e5	e5.5	e6	N4	N6	N7
getUTCMonth	e4	e5	e5.5	e6	N4	N6	N7
getUTCSeconds	e4	e5	e5.5	e6	N4	N6	N7
getVarDate	e4	e5	e5.5	e6			
getYear	e4	e5	e5.5	e6	N4	N6	N7
parse	e4	e5	e5.5	e6	N4	N6	N7
setDate	e4	e5	e5.5	e6	N4	N6	N7
setFullYear	e4	e5	e5.5	e6	N4	N6	N7
setHours	e4	e5	e5.5	e6	N4	N6	N7
setMilliseconds	e4	e5	e5.5	e6	N4	N6	N7
setMinutes	e4	e5	e5.5	e6	N4	N6	N7
setMonth	e4	e5	e5.5	e6	N4	N6	N7
setSeconds	e4	e5	e5.5	e6	N4	N6	N7
setTime	e4	e5	e5.5	e6	N4	N6	N7
setUTCDate	e4	e5	e5.5	e6	N4	N6	N7
setUTCFullYear	e4	e5	e5.5	e6	N4	N6	N7
setUTCHours	e4	e5	e5.5	e6	N4	N6	N7
setUTCMilliseconds	e4	e5	e5.5	e6	N4	N6	N7
setUTCMinutes	e4	e5	e5.5	e6	N4	N6	N7
setUTCMonth	e4	e5	e5.5	e6	N4	N6	N7
setUTCSeconds	e4	e5	e5.5	e6	N4	N6	N7
setYear	e4	e5	e5.5	e6	N4	N6	N7
toDateString			e5.5	e6			
toGMTString	e4	e5	e5.5	e6	N4	N6	N7
toLocaleDateString	e4	e5	e5.5	e6	N4	N7	

Property / Method	Browser support
toLocaleString	e4, e5, e5.5, e6, N4, N6, N7
toLocaleTimeString	e4, e5, e5.5, e6, N4, N6
toSource	N4, N6, N7
toString	e4, e5, e5.5, e6, N4, N6, N7
toTimeString	e5.5, e6
toUTCString	e4, e5, e5.5, e6, N4, N6, N7
UTC	e4, e5, e5.5, e6, N4, N6, N7
valueOf	e4, e5, e5.5, e6, N4, N6, N7

document Object   e4, e5, e5.5, e6, N4, N6, N7

Property	Browser support
activeElement	e4, e5, e5.5, e6
attributes	e5, e5.5, e6, N6, N7
alinkColor	e4, e5, e5.5, e6, N4, N6, N7
all	e4, e5, e5.5, e6
anchors	e4, e5, e5.5, e6, N4, N6, N7
applets	e4, e5, e5.5, e6, N4, N6, N7
areas	e4, e5, e5.5, e6
bgColor	e4, e5, e5.5, e6, N4, N6, N7
body	e4, e5, e5.5, e6, N6, N7
charset	e4, e5, e5.5, e6
characterSet	N6, N7
childNodes	e5, e5.5, e6, N6, N7
children	e4, e5, e5.5, e6
compatMode	N6, N7
classes	N4
cookie	e4, e5, e5.5, e6, N4, N6, N7
contentWindow	N6, N7
defaultCharset	e4, e5, e5.5, e6
documentElement	e5, e5.5, e6, N6, N7
doctype	N6, N7
domain	e4, e5, e5.5, e6, N4, N6, N7
embeds	e4, e5, e5.5, e6, N4, N6, N7

Property	Supported browsers
expando	e4 e5 e5.5 e6
fgColor	e4 e5 e5.5 e6 N4 N6 N7
firstChild	e5 e5.5 e6 N6 N7
forms	e4 e5 e5.5 e6 N4 N6 N7
height	N4 N6 N7
ids	N4
images	e4 e5 e5.5 e6 N4 N6 N7
implementation	N6 N7
lastChild	e5 e5.5 e6 N6 N7
lastModified	e4 e5 e5.5 e6 N4 N6 N7
layers	N4
linkColor	e4 e5 e5.5 e6 N4 N6 N7
links	e4 e5 e5.5 e6 N4 N6 N7
location	e4 e5 e5.5 e6 N4 N6 N7
namespaceURI	e5 e5.5 e6 N6 N7
nextSibling	e5 e5.5 e6 N6 N7
nodeName	e5 e5.5 e6 N6 N7
nodeType	e5 e5.5 e6 N6 N7
nodeValue	N6 N7
ownerDocument	N6 N7
parentNode	e5 e5.5 e6 N6 N7
plugins	e4 e5 e5.5 e6 N4 N6 N7
previousSibling	e5 e5.5 e6 N6 N7
referrer	e4 e5 e5.5 e6 N4 N6 N7
scripts	e4 e5 e5.5 e6
stylesheets	e4 e5 e5.5 e6 N6 N7
tags	N4
title	e4 e5 e5.5 e6 N4 N6 N7
URL	e4 e5 e5.5 e6 N4 N6 N7
vlinkColor	e4 e5 e5.5 e6 N4 N6 N7
width	e4 e5 e5.5 e6 N4 N6 N7
clear	e4 e5 e5.5 e6 N4 N6 N7

	IE4	IE5	IE5.5	IE6	N4	N6	N7
close	e4	e5	e5.5	e6	N4	N6	N7
createAttribute	N6	N7					
createDocumentFragment	N6	N7					
createElement	e4	e5	e5.5	e6	N6	N7	
createStylesheet	e4	e5	e5.5	e6			
createTextNode		e5	e5.5	e6	N6	N7	
captureEvents	N4						
contextual	N4						
elementFromPoint	e4	e5	e5.5	e6			
focus	e4	e5	e5.5	e6	N6	N7	
getElementById		e5	e5.5	e6	N6	N7	
getElementsByName		e5	e5.5	e6	N6	N7	
getElementsByTagName		e5	e5.5	e6	N6	N7	
getSelection	N4						
handleEvent	N4						
open	e4	e5	e5.5	e6	N4	N6	N7
releaseEvents	N4						
routeEvent	N4						
write	e4	e5	e5.5	e6	N4	N6	N7
writeln	e4	e5	e5.5	e6	N4	N6	N7

Enumerator Object e4 e5 e5.5 e6

attends e4 e5 e5.5 e6

item e4 e5 e5.5 e6

moveFirst e4 e5 e5.5 e6

moveNext e4 e5 e5.5 e6

Error Object e5 e5.5 e6

description e5 e5.5 e6

message e5 e5.5 e6

name e5.5 e6

number e5 e5.5 e6

event Object N. N. N.

Property			
altKey	**N.**	**N.**	
bubbles	**N.**	**N.**	
cancelBubble		**N.**	**N.**
cancelable		**N.**	**N.**
charCode		**N.**	**N.**
clientX	**N.**	**N.**	
clientY	**N.**	**N.**	
ctrlKey	**N.**	**N.**	
currentTarget		**N.**	**N.**
data	**N.**		
detail	**N.**	**N.**	
eventPhase		**N.**	**N.**
height	**N.**		
isChar	**N.**	**N.**	
keyCode		**N.**	**N.**
layerX	**N.**	**N.**	**N.**
layerY	**N.**	**N.**	**N.**
metaKey		**N.**	**N.**
modifiers		**N.**	
pageX	**N.**	**N.**	**N.**
pageY	**N.**	**N.**	**N.**
relatedTarget		**N.**	**N.**
screenX	**N.**	**N.**	**N.**
screenY	**N.**	**N.**	**N.**
shiftKey		**N.**	**N.**
target	**N.**	**N.**	**N.**
timeStamp		**N.**	**N.**
type	**N.**	**N.**	**N.**
view	**N.**	**N.**	
width	**N.**		
which	**N.**		

x   **N.**

y   **N.**

initEvent   **N.** **N.**

initMouseEvent **N.** **N.**

initUIEvent   **N.** **N.**

preventDefault **N.** **N.**

stopPropagation **N.** **N.**

FileUpload Object e⁴ e⁵ e⁵·⁵ e⁶ N. N. N.

	e⁴	e⁵	e⁵·⁵	e⁶	N.	N.	N.
form	e⁴	e⁵	e⁵·⁵	e⁶	N.	N.	N.
name	e⁴	e⁵	e⁵·⁵	e⁶	N.	N.	N.
type	e⁴	e⁵	e⁵·⁵	e⁶	N.	N.	N.
value	e⁴	e⁵	e⁵·⁵	e⁶	N.	N.	N.
blur	e⁴	e⁵	e⁵·⁵	e⁶	N.	N.	N.
focus	e⁴	e⁵	e⁵·⁵	e⁶	N.	N.	N.
handleEvent	N.						
select	e⁴	e⁵	e⁵·⁵	e⁶	N.	N.	N.

Form Object e⁴ e⁵ e⁵·⁵ e⁶ N. N. N.

	e⁴	e⁵	e⁵·⁵	e⁶	N.	N.	N.
action	e⁴	e⁵	e⁵·⁵	e⁶	N.	N.	N.
acceptCharset					N.	N.	
elements		e⁴	e⁵	e⁵·⁵	e⁶	N.	N.	N.
encoding		e⁴	e⁵	e⁵·⁵	e⁶	N.	N.	N.
enctype	e⁴	e⁵	e⁵·⁵	e⁶	N.	N.	
length	e⁴	e⁵	e⁵·⁵	e⁶	N.	N.	N.
method	e⁴	e⁵	e⁵·⁵	e⁶	N.	N.	N.
name	e⁴	e⁵	e⁵·⁵	e⁶	N.	N.	N.
target	e⁴	e⁵	e⁵·⁵	e⁶	N.	N.	N.
handleEvent	N.						
reset	e⁴	e⁵	e⁵·⁵	e⁶	N.	N.	N.
submit	e⁴	e⁵	e⁵·⁵	e⁶	N.	N.	N.

FrameSet Object N6 N7

cols N6 N7

rows N6 N7

Frame Object N6 N7

contentDocument N6 N7

contentWindow N6 N7

frameBorder N6 N7

longDesc N6 N7

marginHeight N6 N7

marginWidth N6 N7

name N4 N6 N7

noResize N6 N7

scrolling N6 N7

src N6 N7

Function Object e4 e5 e5.5 e6 N4 N6 N7

arguments e4 e5 e5.5 e6 N4 N6 N7

arguments.callee N4 N6 N7

arguments.caller N4 N6 N7

arguments.length N4 N6 N7

callee e5.5 e6

caller e4 e5 e5.5 e6

arity N4 N6 N7

constructor e4 e5 e5.5 e6 N4 N6 N7

length e4 e5 e5.5 e6 N4 N6 N7

prototype e4 e5 e5.5 e6 N4 N6 N7

apply e5.5 e6 N4 N6 N7

call e5.5 e6 N4 N6 N7

toSource N4 N6 N7

toString e4 e5 e5.5 e6 N4 N6 N7

valueOf e4 e5 e5.5 e6 N4 N6 N7

Global Object e⁵ e⁵·⁵ e⁶

	e⁵	e⁵·⁵	e⁶
Infinity	e⁵	e⁵·⁵	e⁶
NaN	e⁵	e⁵·⁵	e⁶
undefined		e⁵·⁵	e⁶
decodeURI		e⁵·⁵	e⁶
decodeURIComponent		e⁵·⁵	e⁶
encodeURI		e⁵·⁵	e⁶
encodeURIComponent		e⁵·⁵	e⁶
escape	e⁵	e⁵·⁵	e⁶
eval	e⁵	e⁵·⁵	e⁶
isFinite	e⁵	e⁵·⁵	e⁶
isNaN	e⁵	e⁵·⁵	e⁶
parseFloat	e⁵	e⁵·⁵	e⁶
parseInt	e⁵	e⁵·⁵	e⁶
unescape	e⁵	e⁵·⁵	e⁶

Hidden Object e⁴ e⁵·⁵ e⁶ N₄ N₆ N₇

	e⁴	e⁵	e⁵·⁵	e⁶	N₄	N₆	N₇
form	e⁴	e⁵	e⁵·⁵	e⁶	N₄	N₆	N₇
maxLength		e⁵	e⁵·⁵	e⁶		N₆	N₇
name	e⁴	e⁵	e⁵·⁵	e⁶	N₄	N₆	N₇
readOnly		e⁵	e⁵·⁵	e⁶		N₆	N₇
size		e⁵	e⁵·⁵	e⁶	N₄	N₆	
type	e⁴	e⁵	e⁵·⁵	e⁶	N₄	N₆	N₇
value	e⁴	e⁵	e⁵·⁵	e⁶	N₄	N₆	N₇

History Object e⁴ e⁵ e⁵·⁵ e⁶ N₄ N₆ N₇

	e⁴	e⁵	e⁵·⁵	e⁶	N₄	N₆	N₇
current					N₄		
length	e⁴	e⁵	e⁵·⁵	e⁶	N₄	N₆	N₇
next					N₄		
previous				N₄			
back	e⁴	e⁵	e⁵·⁵	e⁶	N₄	N₆	N₇
forward	e⁴	e⁵	e⁵·⁵	e⁶	N₄	N₆	N₇

	IE4	IE5	IE5.5	IE6	NN4	NN6	NN7
go	●	●	●	●	●	●	●

Iframe Object   NN6 NN7

Property	NN4	NN6	NN7
align		●	●
contentDocument		●	●
contentWindow		●	●
frameBorder		●	●
longDesc		●	●
marginHeight		●	●
marginWidth		●	●
name	●	●	●
noResize		●	●
scrolling		●	●
src		●	●

Image Object   IE4 IE5 IE5.5 IE6 NN4 NN6 NN7

Property	IE4	IE5	IE5.5	IE6	NN4	NN6	NN7
align	●	●	●	●	●	●	
alt	●	●	●	●	●	●	
border	●	●	●	●	●	●	●
complete	●	●	●	●	●	●	●
height	●	●	●	●	●	●	●
href	●	●	●	●	●		●
hspace	●	●	●	●	●	●	●
isMap	●	●	●	●	●		●
lowsrc	●	●	●	●	●	●	●
name	●	●	●	●	●	●	●
src	●	●	●	●	●	●	●
useMap	●	●	●	●	●		●
vpsace	●	●	●	●	●	●	●
width	●	●	●	●	●	●	●
x					●		
y					●		
handleEvent					●		

Layer Object N.

above   N.

background   N.

bgColor   N.

below   N.

clip.bottom   N.

clip.height   N.

clip.left   N.

clip.right   N.

clip.top   N.

clip.width   N.

document   N.

left   N.

name   N.

pageX   N.

pageY   N.

parentLayer   N.

siblingAbove   N.

siblingBelow   N.

src   N.

top   N.

visibility   N.

window   N.

x   N.

y   N.

zIndex   N.

captureEvents   N.

handleEvent   N.

load   N.

moveAbove   N.

moveBelow   N.

moveBy   N.

	N4
moveTo	N4
moveToAbsolute	N4
releaseEvents	N4
resizeBy	N4
resizeTo	N4
routeEvent	N4

Link Object e4 e5 e5.5 e6 N4 N6 N7

	e4	e5	e5.5	e6	N4	N6	N7
hash	e4	e5	e5.5	e6	N4	N6	N7
host	e4	e5	e5.5	e6	N4	N6	N7
hostname	e4	e5	e5.5	e6	N4	N6	N7
href	e4	e5	e5.5	e6	N4	N6	N7
name	e4	e5	e5.5	e6	N4		N7
pathname	e4	e5	e5.5	e6	N4	N6	N7
port	e4	e5	e5.5	e6	N4	N6	N7
protocol	e4	e5	e5.5	e6	N4	N6	N7
rel	e4	e5	e5.5	e6	N4		N7
rev	e4	e5	e5.5	e6		N6	N7
search	e4	e5	e5.5	e6	N4	N6	N7
target	e4	e5	e5.5	e6	N4	N6	N7
text					N4		
x					N4		
y					N4		
handleEvent					N4		

Location Object e4 e5 e5.5 e6 N4 N6 N7

	e4	e5	e5.5	e6	N4	N6	N7
hash	e4	e5	e5.5	e6	N4	N6	N7
host	e4	e5	e5.5	e6	N4	N6	N7
hostname	e4	e5	e5.5	e6	N4	N6	N7
href	e4	e5	e5.5	e6	N4	N6	N7
pathname	e4	e5	e5.5	e6	N4	N6	N7
port	e4	e5	e5.5	e6	N4	N6	N7
protocol	e4	e5	e5.5	e6	N4	N6	N7

	e4	e5	e5.5	e6	N4	N6	N7
search	e4	e5	e5.5	e6	N4	N6	N7
reload	e4	e5	e5.5	e6	N4	N6	N7
replace	e4	e5	e5.5	e6	N4	N6	N7

Math Object e4 e5 e5.5 e6 N4 N6 N7

	e4	e5	e5.5	e6	N4	N6	N7
E	e4	e5	e5.5	e6	N4	N6	N7
LN2	e4	e5	e5.5	e6	N4	N6	N7
LN10	e4	e5	e5.5	e6	N4	N6	N7
LOG2E		e4	e5	e5.5	e6	N4	N6	N7
LOG10E		e4	e5	e5.5	e6	N4	N6	N7
PI	e4	e5	e5.5	e6	N4	N6	N7
SQRT1_2		e4	e5	e5.5	e6	N4	N6	N7
SQRT2	e4	e5	e5.5	e6	N4	N6	N7
abs	e4	e5	e5.5	e6	N4	N6	N7
acos	e4	e5	e5.5	e6	N4	N6	N7
asin	e4	e5	e5.5	e6	N4	N6	N7
atan	e4	e5	e5.5	e6	N4	N6	N7
atan2	e4	e5	e5.5	e6	N4	N6	N7
ceil	e4	e5	e5.5	e6	N4	N6	N7
cos	e4	e5	e5.5	e6	N4	N6	N7
exp	e4	e5	e5.5	e6	N4	N6	N7
floor	e4	e5	e5.5	e6	N4	N6	N7
log	e4	e5	e5.5	e6	N4	N6	N7
max	e4	e5	e5.5	e6	N4	N6	N7
min	e4	e5	e5.5	e6	N4	N6	N7
pow	e4	e5	e5.5	e6	N4	N6	N7
random	e4	e5	e5.5	e6	N4	N6	N7
round	e4	e5	e5.5	e6	N4	N6	N7
sin	e4	e5	e5.5	e6	N4	N6	N7
sqrt	e4	e5	e5.5	e6	N4	N6	N7
tan	e4	e5	e5.5	e6	N4	N6	N7

MimeType Object

Property	IE4	IE5	IE5.5	IE6	NN4	NN6	NN7
MimeType Object	✓	✓	✓	✓	✓	✓	✓
description	✓	✓	✓	✓	✓	✓	✓
enabledPlugin	✓	✓	✓	✓	✓	✓	✓
suffixes	✓	✓	✓	✓	✓	✓	✓
type	✓	✓	✓	✓	✓	✓	✓

navigator Object

Property	IE4	IE5	IE5.5	IE6	NN4	NN6	NN7
navigator Object	✓	✓	✓	✓	✓	✓	✓
appCodeName	✓	✓	✓	✓	✓	✓	✓
appMinorVersion	✓	✓	✓	✓			
appName	✓	✓	✓	✓	✓	✓	✓
appVersion	✓	✓	✓	✓	✓	✓	✓
browserLanguage	✓	✓	✓	✓			
cookieEnabled	✓	✓	✓	✓	✓	✓	
cpuClass	✓	✓	✓	✓			
language					✓	✓	✓
mimeTypes	✓	✓	✓	✓	✓	✓	✓
online	✓	✓	✓	✓			
oscpu						✓	✓
platform	✓	✓	✓	✓	✓	✓	✓
plugins	✓	✓	✓	✓	✓	✓	✓
product						✓	✓
productSub						✓	✓
systemLanguage	✓	✓	✓	✓			
userAgent	✓	✓	✓	✓	✓	✓	✓
userLanguage	✓	✓	✓	✓			
userProfile	✓	✓	✓	✓			
vendor						✓	✓
vendorSub						✓	✓
javaEnabled	✓	✓	✓	✓	✓	✓	✓
plugins.refresh					✓		
preference					✓		
savePreferences					✓		

	e4	e5	e5.5	e6	N4	N6	N7
taintEnabled	●	●	●	●	●	●	●
Number Object	●	●	●	●	●	●	●
MAX_VALUE	●	●	●	●	●	●	●
MIN_VALUE	●	●	●	●	●	●	●
NaN	●	●	●	●	●	●	●
NEGATIVE_INFINITY	●	●	●	●	●	●	●
POSITIVE_INFINITY	●	●	●	●	●	●	●
constructor	●	●	●	●	●	●	●
prototype	●	●	●	●	●	●	●
toExponential			●	●		●	●
toFixed			●	●		●	●
toLocaleString	●	●	●	●			
toPrecision			●	●		●	●
toSource					●	●	●
toString	●	●	●	●	●	●	●
valueOf	●	●	●	●	●	●	●
Object Object	●	●	●	●		●	●
prototype	●	●	●	●	●	●	●
constructor	●	●	●	●	●	●	●
propertyIsEnumerable			●	●			
eval					●	●	●
isPrototypeOf			●	●			
hasOwnProperty			●	●			
toLocaleString	●	●	●	●			
toSource					●	●	●
toString	●	●	●	●	●	●	●
unwatch					●	●	●
valueOf	●	●	●	●	●	●	●
watch					●	●	●
Option Object	●	●	●	●	●	●	●
defaultSelected	●	●	●	●	●	●	●

	IE4	IE5	IE5.5	IE6	N4	N6	N7
index	e4	e5	e5.5	e6	N4	N6	N7
form	e4	e5	e5.5	e6	N4	N6	
length					N4		
selected	e4	e5	e5.5	e6	N4	N6	N7
text	e4	e5	e5.5	e6	N4	N6	N7
value	e4	e5	e5.5	e6	N4	N6	N7
remove		e5	e5.5	e6	N6	N7	

Password Object e4 e5 e5.5 e6 N4 N6 N7

	IE4	IE5	IE5.5	IE6	N4	N6	N7
defaultValue		e4	e5	e5.5	e6	N4	N6 N7
form	e4	e5	e5.5	e6	N4	N6	N7
maxLength		e4	e5	e5.5	e6	N6	N7
name	e4	e5	e5.5	e6	N4	N6	N7
readOnly		e4	e5	e5.5	e6	N6	N7
size	e4	e5	e5.5	e6	N4	N7	
type	e4	e5	e5.5	e6	N4	N6	N7
value	e4	e5	e5.5	e6	N4	N6	N7
blur	e4	e5	e5.5	e6	N4	N6	N7
focus	e4	e5	e5.5	e6	N4	N6	N7
handleEvent					N4		
select	e4	e5	e5.5	e6	N4	N6	N7

Plugin Object e4 e5 e5.5 e6 N4 N6 N7

	IE4	IE5	IE5.5	IE6	N4	N6	N7
description		e4	e5	e5.5	e6	N4	N6 N7
filename		e4	e5	e5.5	e6	N4	N6 N7
length	e4	e5	e5.5	e6	N4	N6	N7
name	e4	e5	e5.5	e6	N4	N6	N7
refresh	e4	e5	e5.5	e6	N4	N6	N7

Radio Object e4 e5 e5.5 e6 N4 N6 N7

	IE4	IE5	IE5.5	IE6	N4	N6	N7
checked	e4	e5	e5.5	e6	N4	N6	N7
defaultChecked	e4	e5	e5.5	e6	N4	N6	N7
form	e4	e5	e5.5	e6	N4	N6	N7

name	e⁴	e⁵	e⁵·⁵	e⁶	N₄	N₆	N₇
type	e⁴	e⁵	e⁵·⁵	e⁶	N₄	N₆	N₇
value	e⁴	e⁵	e⁵·⁵	e⁶	N₄	N₆	N₇
blur	e⁴	e⁵	e⁵·⁵	e⁶	N₄	N₆	N₇
click	e⁴	e⁵	e⁵·⁵	e⁶	N₄	N₆	N₇
focus	e⁴	e⁵	e⁵·⁵	e⁶	N₄	N₆	N₇
handleEvent	N₄						

Range Object N₆ N₇

collapsed	N₆	N₇
commonAncestorContainer	N₆	N₇
endContainer	N₆	N₇
endOffset	N₆	N₇
startContainer	N₆	N₇
startOffset	N₆	N₇
createRange	N₆	N₇
setStart	N₆	N₇
setEnd	N₆	N₇
setStartBefore	N₆	N₇
setStartAfter	N₆	N₇
setEndBefore	N₆	N₇
setEndAfter	N₆	N₇
selectNode	N₆	N₇
selectNodeContents	N₆	N₇
collapse	N₆	N₇
cloneContents	N₆	N₇
deleteContents	N₆	N₇
extractContents	N₆	N₇
insertNode	N₆	N₇
surroundContents	N₆	N₇
compareBoundaryPoints	N₆	N₇
cloneRange	N₆	N₇

detach   N.   N.

toString   N.   N.

RegExp Object   e⁴   e⁵   e⁵·⁵   e⁶   N.   N.   N.

constructor   N.   N.   N.

global   N.   N.   N.

ignoreCase   N.   N.   N.

index   e⁴   e⁵   e⁵·⁵   e⁶

input   e⁴   e⁵   e⁵·⁵   e⁶   N.

lastIndex   e⁴   e⁵   e⁵·⁵   e⁶   N.   N.   N.

lastMatch   e⁵·⁵   e⁶   N.

lastParen   e⁵·⁵   e⁶   N.

leftContext   e⁵·⁵   e⁶   N.

multiline   N.   N.   N.

prototype   N.   N.   N.

rightContext   e⁵·⁵   e⁶   N.

source   N.   N.   N.

compile   N.

exec   N.   N.   N.

test   N.   N.   N.

toSource   N.   N.   N.

toString   N.   N.   N.

valueOf   N.

Regular Expression Object   e⁴   e⁵   e⁵·⁵   e⁶

global   e⁵·⁵   e⁶

ignoreCase   e⁵·⁵   e⁶

multiline   e⁵·⁵   e⁶

source   e⁴   e⁵   e⁵·⁵   e⁶

compile   e⁴   e⁵   e⁵·⁵   e⁶

exec   e⁴   e⁵   e⁵·⁵   e⁶

test   e⁴   e⁵   e⁵·⁵   e⁶

Reset Object e4 e5 e5.5 e6 N4 N6 N7

	e4	e5	e5.5	e6	N4	N6	N7
form	e4	e5	e5.5	e6	N4	N6	N7
name	e4	e5	e5.5	e6	N4	N6	N7
type	e4	e5	e5.5	e6	N4	N6	N7
value	e4	e5	e5.5	e6	N4	N6	N7
blur	e4	e5	e5.5	e6	N4	N6	N7
click	e4	e5	e5.5	e6	N4	N6	N7
focus	e4	e5	e5.5	e6	N4	N6	N7
handleEvent					N4		

screen Object e4 e5 e5.5 e6 N4 N6 N7

	e4	e5	e5.5	e6	N4	N6	N7
availHeight	e4	e5	e5.5	e6	N4	N6	N7
availLeft					N4	N6	N7
availTop					N4	N6	N7
availWidth	e4	e5	e5.5	e6	N4	N6	N7
bufferDepth	e4	e5	e5.5	e6			
colorDepth	e4	e5	e5.5	e6	N4	N6	N7
fontSmoothingEnabled	e4	e5	e5.5	e6			
height	e4	e5	e5.5	e6	N4	N6	N7
left						N6	N7
pixelDepth	e4	e5	e5.5	e6	N4	N6	N7
top						N6	N7
updateInterval	e4	e5	e5.5	e6			
width	e4	e5	e5.5	e6	N4	N6	N7

Script Object e4 e5 e5.5 e6 N6 N7

	e4	e5	e5.5	e6	N6	N7
defer	e4	e5	e5.5	e6	N6	N7
event	e4	e5	e5.5	e6	N6	N7
htmlFor	e4	e5	e5.5	e6	N6	N7
language	e4	e5	e5.5	e6	N6	N7
src	e4	e5	e5.5	e6	N6	N7

	IE4	IE5	IE5.5	IE6	NN4	NN6	NN7
text	e4	e5	e5.5	e6	N4	N6	
type	e4	e5	e5.5	e6	N4	N6	

Select Object · e4 e5 e5.5 e6 N4 N6 N7

	IE4	IE5	IE5.5	IE6	NN4	NN6	NN7
form	e4	e5	e5.5	e6	N4	N6	N7
length	e4	e5	e5.5	e6	N4	N6	N7
multiple	e4	e5	e5.5	e6		N6	N7
name	e4	e5	e5.5	e6	N4	N6	N7
options	e4	e5	e5.5	e6	N4	N6	N7
selectedIndex	e4	e5	e5.5	e6	N4	N6	N7
size	e4	e5	e5.5	e6	N4	N6	
type	e4	e5	e5.5	e6	N4	N6	N7
value	e4	e5	e5.5	e6	N4	N6	
blur	e4	e5	e5.5	e6	N4	N6	N7
focus	e4	e5	e5.5	e6	N4	N6	N7
handleEvent					N4		

String Object · e4 e5 e5.5 e6 N4 N6 N7

	IE4	IE5	IE5.5	IE6	NN4	NN6	NN7
constructor	e4	e5	e5.5	e6	N4	N6	N7
length	e4	e5	e5.5	e6	N4	N6	N7
prototype	e4	e5	e5.5	e6	N4	N6	N7
anchor	e4	e5	e5.5	e6	N4	N6	N7
big	e4	e5	e5.5	e6	N4	N6	N7
blink	e4	e5	e5.5	e6	N4	N6	N7
bold	e4	e5	e5.5	e6	N4	N6	N7
charAt	e4	e5	e5.5	e6	N4	N6	N7
charCodeAt			e5.5	e6	N4	N6	N7
concat	e4	e5	e5.5	e6	N4	N6	N7
fixed	e4	e5	e5.5	e6	N4	N6	N7
fontcolor	e4	e5	e5.5	e6	N4	N6	N7
fontsize	e4	e5	e5.5	e6	N4	N6	N7
fromCharCode	e4	e5	e5.5	e6	N4	N6	N7

indexOf	e4	e5	e5.5	e6	N4	N6	N7
italics	e4	e5	e5.5	e6	N4	N6	N7
lastIndexOf	e4	e5	e5.5	e6	N4	N6	N7
link	e4	e5	e5.5	e6	N4	N6	N7
localeCompare	e5.5	e6	N6	N7			
match	e4	e5	e5.5	e6	N4	N6	N7
replace	e4	e5	e5.5	e6	N4	N6	N7
search	e4	e5	e5.5	e6	N4	N6	N7
slice	e4	e5	e5.5	e6	N4	N6	N7
small	e4	e5	e5.5	e6	N4	N6	N7
split	e4	e5	e5.5	e6	N4	N6	N7
strike	e4	e5	e5.5	e6	N4	N6	N7
sub	e4	e5	e5.5	e6	N4	N6	N7
substr	e4	e5	e5.5	e6	N4	N6	N7
substring	e4	e5	e5.5	e6	N4	N6	N7
sup	e4	e5	e5.5	e6	N4	N6	N7
toLocaleLowerCase	e5.5	e6					
toLocaleUpperCase	e5.5	e6					
toLowerCase	e4	e5	e5.5	e6	N4	N6	N7
toUpperCase	e4	e5	e5.5	e6	N4	N6	N7
toSource	N4	N6	N7				
toString	e4	e5	e5.5	e6	N4	N6	N7
valueOf	e4	e5	e5.5	e6	N4	N6	N7

Style Object   e4   e5   e5.5   e6   N6   N7

accelerator			N6	N7		
azimuth			N6	N7		
align						
background			e4	e5	e5.5	e6	N6	N7
backgroundAttachment			e4	e5	e5.5	e6	N6	N7
backgroundColor			e4	e5	e5.5	e6	N6	N7

	e4	e5	e5.5	e6	N6	N7
backgroundImage	e4	e5	e5.5	e6	N6	N7
backgroundPosition	e4	e5	e5.5	e6	N6	N7
backgroundPositionX	e4	e5	e5.5	e6		
backgroundPositionY	e4	e5	e5.5	e6		
backgroundRepeat	e4	e5	e5.5	e6	N6	N7
border	e4	e5	e5.5	e6	N6	N7
borderBottom	e4	e5	e5.5	e6	N6	N7
borderBottomColor	e4	e5	e5.5	e6	N6	N7
borderBottomStyle	e4	e5	e5.5	e6	N6	N7
borderBottomWidth	e4	e5	e5.5	e6	N6	N7
borderCollapse					N6	N7
borderColor	e4	e5	e5.5	e6	N6	N7
borderLeft	e4	e5	e5.5	e6	N6	N7
borderLeftColor	e4	e5	e5.5	e6	N6	N7
borderLeftStyle	e4	e5	e5.5	e6	N6	N7
borderLeftWidth	e4	e5	e5.5	e6	N6	N7
borderRight	e4	e5	e5.5	e6	N6	N7
borderRightColor	e4	e5	e5.5	e6	N6	N7
borderRightStyle	e4	e5	e5.5	e6	N6	N7
borderRightWidth	e4	e5	e5.5	e6	N6	N7
borderSpacing					N6	N7
borderStyle	e4	e5	e5.5	e6	N6	N7
borderTop	e4	e5	e5.5	e6	N6	N7
borderTopColor	e4	e5	e5.5	e6	N6	N7
borderTopStyle	e4	e5	e5.5	e6	N6	N7
borderTopWidth	e4	e5	e5.5	e6	N6	N7
borderWidth	e4	e5	e5.5	e6	N6	N7
bottom		e5	e5.5	e6	N6	N7
captionSide					N6	N7
clear	e4	e5	e5.5	e6	N6	N7
clip	e4	e5	e5.5	e6	N6	N7
color	e4	e5	e5.5	e6	N6	N7

Property						
content	N	N				
counterIncrement	N	N				
counterReset	N	N				
cssFloat	N	N				
cssText	e4	e5	e5.5	e6	N	N
cue	N	N				
cueAfter	N	N				
cueBefore	N	N				
cursor	e4	e5	e5.5	e6	N	N
direction	e5	e5.5	e6	N	N	
display	e4	e5	e5.5	e6	N	N
elevation	N	N				
emptyCells	N	N				
font	e4	e5	e5.5	e6	N	N
fontFamily	e4	e5	e5.5	e6	N	N
fontSize	e4	e5	e5.5	e6	N	N
fontSizeAdjust	N	N				
fontStretch	N	N				
fontStyle	e4	e5	e5.5	e6	N	N
fontVariant	e4	e5	e5.5	e6	N	N
fontWeight	e4	e5	e5.5	e6	N	N
height	e4	e5	e5.5	e6	N	N
left	e4	e5	e5.5	e6	N	N
length	N	N				
letterSpacing	N	N				
lineHeight	e4	e5	e5.5	e6	N	N
listStyle	e4	e5	e5.5	e6	N	N
listStyleImage	e4	e5	e5.5	e6	N	N
listStylePosition	e4	e5	e5.5	e6	N	N
listStyleType	e4	e5	e5.5	e6	N	N
margin	e4	e5	e5.5	e6	N	N
marginBottom	e4	e5	e5.5	e6	N	N

	e4	e5	e5.5	e6	N6	N7
marginLeft	e4	e5	e5.5	e6	N6	N7
marginRight	e4	e5	e5.5	e6	N6	N7
marginTop	e4	e5	e5.5	e6	N6	N7
markerOffset					N6	N7
marks					N6	N7
maxHeight					N6	N7
maxWidth					N6	N7
media					N6	N7
minHeight					N6	N7
minWidth					N6	N7
MozBinding					N6	N7
MozOpacity					N6	N7
orphans					N6	N7
outline					N6	N7
outlineColor					N6	N7
outlineStyle					N6	N7
outlineWidth					N6	N7
overflow	e4	e5	e5.5	e6	N6	N7
padding	e4	e5	e5.5	e6	N6	N7
paddingBottom	e4	e5	e5.5	e6	N6	N7
paddingLeft	e4	e5	e5.5	e6	N6	N7
paddingRight	e4	e5	e5.5	e6	N6	N7
paddingTop	e4	e5	e5.5	e6	N6	N7
page					N6	N7
pageBreakAfter	e4	e5	e5.5	e6	N6	N7
pageBreakBefore	e4	e5	e5.5	e6	N6	N7
pageBreakInside					N6	N7
parentRule					N6	N7
pause					N6	N7
pauseAfter					N6	N7
pauseBefore					N6	N7
pitch					N6	N7

Property	IE4	IE5	IE5.5	IE6	NN6	NN7
pitchRange					N6	N7
playDuring					N6	N7
pixelHeight	e4	e5	e5.5	e6		
pixelLeft	e4	e5	e5.5	e6		
pixelTop	e4	e5	e5.5	e6		
pixelWidth	e4	e5	e5.5	e6		
posHeight	e4	e5	e5.5	e6		
position	e4	e5	e5.5	e6	N6	N7
posLeft	e4	e5	e5.5	e6		
posTop	e4	e5	e5.5	e6		
posWidth	e4	e5	e5.5	e6		
quotes					N6	N7
richness					N6	N7
right		e5	e5.5	e6	N6	N7
size					N6	N7
speak					N6	N7
speakHeader					N6	N7
speakNumeral					N6	N7
speakPunctuation					N6	N7
speechRate					N6	N7
stress					N6	N7
styleFloat	e4	e5	e5.5	e6		
tableLayout		e5	e5.5	e6	N6	N7
textAlign	e4	e5	e5.5	e6	N6	N7
textDecoration	e4	e5	e5.5	e6	N6	N7
textDecorationBlink	e4	e5	e5.5	e6		
textDecorationLineThrough	e4	e5	e5.5	e6		
textDecorationNone	e4	e5	e5.5	e6		
textDecorationOverline	e4	e5	e5.5	e6		
textDecorationUnderline	e4	e5	e5.5	e6		
textIndent	e4	e5	e5.5	e6	N6	N7
textShadow					N6	N7

	e4	e5	e5.5	e6	N.	N.
textTransform	e4	e5	e5.5	e6	N.	N.
top	e4	e5	e5.5	e6	N.	N.
type					N.	N.
unicodeBidi		e5	e5.5	e6	N.	N.
verticalAlign	e4	e5	e5.5	e6	N.	N.
visibility	e4	e5	e5.5	e6	N.	N.
voiceFamily					N.	N.
volume					N.	N.
whiteSpace	e4	e5	e5.5	e6	N.	N.
widows					N.	N.
width	e4	e5	e5.5	e6	N.	N.
wordSpacing	e4	e5	e5.5	e6	N.	N.
zIndex	e4	e5	e5.5	e6	N.	N.

styleSheet Object e4 e5 e5.5 e6 N. N.

	e4	e5	e5.5	e6	N.	N.
cssRules		e5	e5.5	e6	N.	N.
disabled	e4	e5	e5.5	e6	N.	N.
href	e4	e5	e5.5	e6	N.	N.
id	e4	e5	e5.5	e6		
imports	e4	e5	e5.5	e6		
media	e4	e5	e5.5	e6	N.	N.
owningElement	e4	e5	e5.5	e6		
ownerNode					N.	N.
ownerRule					N.	N.
parentStyleSheet	e4	e5	e5.5	e6	N.	N.
readOnly	e4	e5	e5.5	e6		
rules	e4	e5	e5.5	e6		
title	e4	e5	e5.5	e6	N.	N.
type	e4	e5	e5.5	e6	N.	N.
addImport	e4	e5	e5.5	e6	N.	N.
addRule	e4	e5	e5.5	e6	N.	N.

	e4	e5	e5.5	e6	N4	N6	N7
removeRule	e4	e5	e5.5	e6		N6	N7
deleteRule						N6	N7
insertRule						N6	N7

Submit Object   e4   e5   e5.5   e6   N4   N6   N7

	e4	e5	e5.5	e6	N4	N6	N7
form	e4	e5	e5.5	e6	N4	N6	N7
name	e4	e5	e5.5	e6	N4	N6	N7
type	e4	e5	e5.5	e6	N4	N6	N7
value	e4	e5	e5.5	e6	N4	N6	N7
blur	e4	e5	e5.5	e6	N4	N6	N7
click	e4	e5	e5.5	e6	N4	N6	N7
focus	e4	e5	e5.5	e6	N4	N6	N7
handleEvent					N4		

Text Object   e4   e5   e5.5   e6   N4   N6   N7

	e4	e5	e5.5	e6	N4	N6	N7
defaultValue		e4	e5	e5.5	e6	N4	N6	N7
form	e4	e5	e5.5	e6	N4	N6	N7
maxLength		e4	e5	e5.5	e6	N4	N7
name	e4	e5	e5.5	e6	N4	N6	N7
readOnly		e4	e5	e5.5	e6	N6	N7
size	e4	e5	e5.5	e6	N4	N7
type	e4	e5	e5.5	e6	N4	N6	N7
value	e4	e5	e5.5	e6	N4	N6	N7
blur	e4	e5	e5.5	e6	N4	N6	N7
click	e4	e5	e5.5	e6	N4	N6	N7
focus	e4	e5	e5.5	e6	N4	N6	N7
handleEvent					N4		
select	e4	e5	e5.5	e6	N4	N6	N7

Textarea Object   e4   e5   e5.5   e6   N4   N6   N7

	e4	e5	e5.5	e6	N4	N6	N7
cols	e4	e5	e5.5	e6	N4	N7
defaultValue		e4	e5	e5.5	e6	N4	N6	N7
form	e4	e5	e5.5	e6	N4	N6	N7

	IE4	IE5	IE5.5	IE6	N4	N6	N7
name	e4	e5	e5.5	e6	N4	N6	N7
readOnly		e4	e5	e5.5	e6	N6	N7
rows	e4	e5	e5.5	e6	N4	N6	
type	e4	e5	e5.5	e6	N4	N6	N7
value	e4	e5	e5.5	e6	N4	N6	N7
wrap	e4	e5	e5.5	e6	N4	N6	
blur	e4	e5	e5.5	e6	N4	N6	N7
click	e4	e5	e5.5	e6	N4	N6	N7
createTextRange	e4	e5	e5.5	e6			
focus	e4	e5	e5.5	e6	N4	N6	N7
handleEvent					N4		
select	e4	e5	e5.5	e6	N4	N6	N7

window Object e4 e5 e5.5 e6 N4 N6 N7

	IE4	IE5	IE5.5	IE6	N4	N6	N7
clientInformation	e4	e5	e5.5	e6			
closed	e4	e5	e5.5	e6	N4	N6	N7
content						N6	N7
Components						N6	N7
controllers						N6	N7
crypto					N4	N6	N7
defaultStatus	e4	e5	e5.5	e6	N4	N6	N7
dialogArguments	e4	e5	e5.5	e6			
dialogHeight	e4	e5	e5.5	e6			
dialogLeft	e4	e5	e5.5	e6			
dialogTop	e4	e5	e5.5	e6			
dialogWidth	e4	e5	e5.5	e6			
directories						N6	N7
document	e4	e5	e5.5	e6	N4	N6	N7
event	e4	e5	e5.5	e6			
external	e4	e5	e5.5	e6			
frames	e4	e5	e5.5	e6	N4	N6	N7
history	e4	e5	e5.5	e6	N4	N6	N7

Property	Browser Support
innerHeight	N4 N6 N7
innerWidth	N4 N6 N7
length	e4 e5 e5.5 e6 N6 N7
location	e4 e5 e5.5 e6 N4 N6 N7
locationbar	N4 N6 N7
menubar	N4 N6 N7
name	e4 e5 e5.5 e6 N4 N6 N7
navigator	e4 e5 e5.5 e6 N6 N7
offscreenBuffering	e4 e5 e5.5 e6
opener	e4 e5 e5.5 e6 N4 N6 N7
outerHeight	N4 N6 N7
outerWidth	N4 N6 N7
pageXOffset	N4 N6 N7
pageYOffset	N4 N6 N7
parent	e4 e5 e5.5 e6 N4 N6 N7
personalbar	N4 N6 N7
pkcs11	N6 N7
prompter	N6 N7
screen	e4 e5 e5.5 e6 N6 N7
screenX	N4 N6 N7
screenY	N4 N6 N7
scrollbars	N4 N6 N7
scrollX	N6 N7
scrollY	N6 N7
self	e4 e5 e5.5 e6 N4 N6 N7
sidebar	N6 N7
status	e4 e5 e5.5 e6 N4 N6 N7
statusbar	N4 N6 N7
toolbar	N4 N6 N7
top	e4 e5 e5.5 e6 N4 N6 N7
alert	e4 e5 e5.5 e6 N4 N6 N7
atob	N4

back	N4	N6	N7				
blur	e4	e5	e5.5	e6	N4	N6	N7
btoa	N4						
captureEvents	N4	N6	N7				
clearInterval	e4	e5	e5.5	e6	N4	N6	N7
clearTimeout	e4	e5	e5.5	e6	N4	N6	N7
close	e4	e5	e5.5	e6	N4	N6	N7
confirm	e4	e5	e5.5	e6	N4	N6	N7
dump	N6	N7					
crypto.random	N4						
crypto.signText	N4						
disableExternalCapture	N4						
dump	N6	N7					
enableExternalCapture	N4						
escape	N6	N7					
find	N4						
focus	e4	e5	e5.5	e6	N4	N6	N7
forward	N4	N6	N7				
GetAttention	N6	N7					
getSelection	N6	N7					
handleEvent	N4						
home	N4	N6	N7				
moveBy	e4	e5	e5.5	e6	N4	N6	N7
moveTo	e4	e5	e5.5	e6	N4	N6	N7
navigate	e4	e5	e5.5	e6			
open	e4	e5	e5.5	e6	N4	N6	N7
print	e4	e5	e5.5	e6	N4	N6	N7
prompt	e4	e5	e5.5	e6	N4	N6	N7
releaseEvents	N4	N6	N7				
resizeBy	e4	e5	e5.5	e6	N4	N6	N7
resizeTo	e4	e5	e5.5	e6	N4	N6	N7
routeEvent	N4						

scroll	e4	e5	e5.5	e6	N4	N6	N7
scrollBy	e4	e5	e5.5	e6	N4	N6	N7
scrollByLines	N6	N7					
scrollByPages	N6	N7					
scrollTo	e4	e5	e5.5	e6	N4	N6	N7
setCursor	N6	N7					
setHotKeys	N4						
setInterval	e4	e5	e5.5	e6	N4	N6	N7
setResizable	N4						
setTimeout	e4	e5	e5.5	e6	N4	N6	N7
sizeToContent	N6	N7					
setZOptions	N4						
stop	N4	N6	N7				
unescape	N6	N7					
updateCommands	N6	N7					

Appendix B
CSS Quick Reference

The following reference outlines the properties and pseudo-classes and elements in the cascading style sheets level. The following icons are used to indicate browser compatibility:

Icon	Browser
N₃	Netscape 3
N₄	Netscape 4
N₆	Netscape 6
N₇	Netscape 7 and above
e4	Microsoft Internet Explorer 4
e5	Microsoft Internet Explorer 5
e5.5	Microsoft Internet Explorer 5.5
e6	Microsoft Internet Explorer 6

By no means is this a comprehensive reference but instead provides a quick reference to the properties that are most commonly used in CSS. It is possible that browser support is only partial if a property is listed as supported by a particular browser. Also, these compatibility listings are based on the Windows version of browsers; slight inconsistencies may exist between versions of the same browser on different operating systems.

background property e4 e5 e5.5 e6 N₄ N₆ N₇

background-attachment property e4 e5 e5.5 e6 N₆ N₇

scroll   e4 e5 e5.5 e6 N₆ N₇

fixed   e4 e5 e5.5 e6 N₆ N₇

background-color property e4 e5 e5.5 e6 N₆ N₇

transparent   e4 e5 e5.5 e6 N₆ N₇

background-image property e4 e5 e5.5 e6 N₄ N₆ N₇

none   e4 e5 e5.5 e6 N₄ N₆ N₇

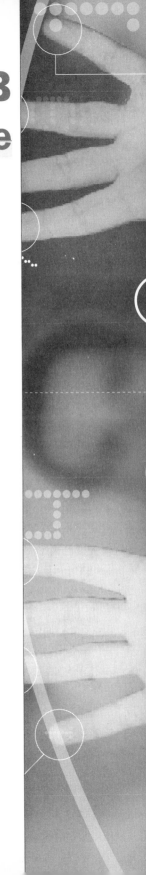

background-position property e4 e5 e5.5 e6 N6 N7

	e4	e5	e5.5	e6	N4	N6	N7
bottom	e4	e5	e5.5	e6		N6	N7
center	e4	e5	e5.5	e6		N6	N7
left	e4	e5	e5.5	e6		N6	N7
right	e4	e5	e5.5	e6		N6	N7
top	e4	e5	e5.5	e6		N6	N7

background-repeat property e4 e5 e5.5 e6 N4 N6 N7

	e4	e5	e5.5	e6	N4	N6	N7
repeat		e5	e5.5	e6	N4	N6	N7
repeat-x		e5	e5.5	e6	N4	N6	N7
repeat-y		e5	e5.5	e6	N4	N6	N7
no-repeat	e4	e5	e5.5	e6	N4	N6	N7

border property e4 e5 e5.5 e6 N4 N6 N7

border-bottom property e4 e5 e5.5 e6 N6 N7

border-bottom-width property e4 e5 e5.5 e6 N6 N7

	e4	e5	e5.5	e6	N4	N6	N7
medium	e4	e5	e5.5	e6		N6	N7
thick	e4	e5	e5.5	e6		N6	N7
thin	e4	e5	e5.5	e6		N6	N7

border-color property e4 e5 e5.5 e6 N4 N6 N7

border-left property e4 e5 e5.5 e6 N6 N7

border-left-width property e4 e5 e5.5 e6 N4 N6 N7

	e4	e5	e5.5	e6	N4	N6	N7
medium	e4	e5	e5.5	e6	N4	N6	N7
thick	e4	e5	e5.5	e6	N4	N6	N7
thin	e4	e5	e5.5	e6	N4	N6	N7

border-right property e4 e5 e5.5 e6 N6 N7

border-right-width property e4 e5 e5.5 e6 N4 N6 N7

	e4	e5	e5.5	e6	N4	N6	N7
medium	e4	e5	e5.5	e6	N4	N6	N7
thick	e4	e5	e5.5	e6	N4	N6	N7
thin	e4	e5	e5.5	e6	N4	N6	N7

border-style property e4 e5 e5.5 e6 N4 N6 N7

dashed	e5.5	e6	N6	N7
dotted	e5.5	e6	N6	N7
double	e4	e5	e5.5	e6	N4	N6	N7
groove	e4	e5	e5.5	e6	N4	N6	N7
inset	e4	e5	e5.5	e6	N4	N6	N7
none	e4	e5	e5.5	e6	N4	N6	N7
outset	e4	e5	e5.5	e6	N4	N6	N7
ridge	e4	e5	e5.5	e6	N4	N6	N7
solid	e4	e5	e5.5	e6	N4	N6	N7

border-top property e4 e5 e5.5 e6 N6 N7

border-top-width property e4 e5 e5.5 e6 N4 N6 N7

medium	e4	e5	e5.5	e6	N4	N6	N7
thick	e4	e5	e5.5	e6	N4	N6	N7
thin	e4	e5	e5.5	e6	N4	N6	N7

border-width property e4 e5 e5.5 e6 N4 N6 N7

medium	e4	e5	e5.5	e6	N4	N6	N7
thick	e4	e5	e5.5	e6	N4	N6	N7
thin	e4	e5	e5.5	e6	N4	N6	N7

clear property e4 e5 e5.5 e6 N4 N6 N7

both	e4	e5	e5.5	e6	N4	N6	N7
left	e5.5	e6	N6	N7
none	e4	e5	e5.5	e6	N4	N6	N7
right	e5.5	e6	N6	N7

color property e4 e5 e5.5 e6 N4 N6 N7

display property e4 e5 e5.5 e6 N4 N6 N7

block	e5.5	e6	N6	N7
inline	e5.5	e6	N6	N7
list-item	e6	N6	N7

none   **e**⁴ **e**⁵ **e**⁵·⁵ **e**⁶ **N**₄ **N**₆ **N**₇

float property e₄ e₅ e₅.₅ e₆ N₄ N₆ N₇

left   **e**⁵·⁵ **e**⁶ **N**₆ **N**₇

none   **e**⁴ **e**⁵ **e**⁵·⁵ **e**⁶ **N**₄ **N**₆ **N**₇

right   **e**⁵·⁵ **e**⁶ **N**₆ **N**₇

font property e₄ e₅ e₅.₅ e₆ N₄ N₆ N₇

font-family property e₄ e₅ e₅.₅ e₆ N₄ N₆ N₇

cursive   **e**⁴ **e**⁵ **e**⁵·⁵ **e**⁶ **N**₆ **N**₇

fantasy   **e**⁴ **e**⁵ **e**⁵·⁵ **e**⁶ **N**₆ **N**₇

monospace   **e**⁴ **e**⁵ **e**⁵·⁵ **e**⁶ **N**₆ **N**₇

sans-serif **e**⁴ **e**⁵ **e**⁵·⁵ **e**⁶ **N**₄ **N**₆ **N**₇

serif   **e**⁴ **e**⁵ **e**⁵·⁵ **e**⁶ **N**₄ **N**₆ **N**₇

font-size property e₄ e₅ e₅.₅ e₆ N₄ N₆ N₇

medium   **e**⁴ **e**⁵ **e**⁵·⁵ **e**⁶ **N**₄ **N**₆ **N**₇

large   **e**⁴ **e**⁵ **e**⁵·⁵ **e**⁶ **N**₄ **N**₆ **N**₇

larger   **e**⁴ **e**⁵ **e**⁶ **N**₄ **N**₆ **N**₇

small   **e**⁴ **e**⁵ **e**⁵·⁵ **e**⁶ **N**₄ **N**₆ **N**₇

smaller **e**⁴ **e**⁵ **e**⁶ **N**₄ **N**₆ **N**₇

x-large **e**⁴ **e**⁵ **e**⁵·⁵ **e**⁶ **N**₄ **N**₆ **N**₇

x-small **e**⁴ **e**⁵ **e**⁵·⁵ **e**⁶ **N**₄ **N**₆ **N**₇

xx-large **e**⁴ **e**⁵ **e**⁵·⁵ **e**⁶ **N**₄ **N**₆ **N**₇

xx-small **e**⁴ **e**⁵ **e**⁵·⁵ **e**⁶ **N**₄ **N**₆ **N**₇

font-style property e₄ e₅ e₅.₅ e₆ N₄ N₆ N₇

italic   **e**⁴ **e**⁵ **e**⁵·⁵ **e**⁶ **N**₄ **N**₆ **N**₇

normal   **e**⁴ **e**⁵ **e**⁵·⁵ **e**⁶ **N**₄ **N**₆ **N**₇

oblique **e**⁴ **e**⁵ **e**⁵·⁵ **e**⁶ **N**₆ **N**₇

font-variant property e₄ e₅ e₅.₅ e₆ N₆ N₇

normal   **e**⁴ **e**⁵ **e**⁵·⁵ **e**⁶ **N**₆ **N**₇

small-caps **e**⁴ **e**⁵ **e**⁵·⁵ **e**⁶ **N**₆ **N**₇

font-weight property e4 e5 e5.5 e6 N4 N6 N7

bold   e4 e5 e5.5 e6 N4 N6 N7

bolder   e4 e5 e5.5 e6 N4 N6 N7

lighter   e4 e5 e5.5 e6 N4 N6

normal   e4 e5 e5.5 e6 N4 N6 N7

height property e4 e5 e5.5 e6 N4 N6

auto   e4 e5 e5.5 e6 N4 N6

letter-spacing property e4 e5 e5.5 e6 N4 N7

normal   e4 e5 e5.5 e6 N4 N7

line-height property e4 e5 e5.5 e6 N4 N6 N7

normal   e4 e5 e5.5 e6 N4 N6 N7

list-style property e4 e5 e5.5 e6 N4 N6 N7

list-style-image property e4 e5 e5.5 e6 N4 N7

none   e4 e5 e5.5 e6 N4 N7

list-style-position property e4 e5 e5.5 e6 N4 N7

inside   e4 e5 e5.5 e6 N4 N7

outside   e4 e5 e5.5 e6 N4 N7

list-style-type property e4 e5 e5.5 e6 N4 N6 N7

circle   e4 e5 e5.5 e6 N4 N6 N7

decimal   e4 e5 e5.5 e6 N4 N6 N7

disc   e4 e5 e5.5 e6 N4 N6 N7

lower-alpha   e4 e5 e5.5 e6 N4 N6 N7

lower-roman   e4 e5 e5.5 e6 N4 N6 N7

none   e4 e5 e5.5 e6 N4 N6 N7

square   e4 e5 e5.5 e6 N4 N6 N7

upper-alpha   e4 e5 e5.5 e6 N4 N6 N7

upper-roman   e4 e5 e5.5 e6 N4 N6 N7

margin property e4 e5 e5.5 e6 N4 N7

auto   e4 e5 e5.5 e6 N4 N7

margin-bottom property e4 e5 e5.5 e6 N4 N7

auto e4 e5 e5.5 e6 N4 N7

margin-left property e4 e5 e5.5 e6 N4 N7

auto e5.5 e6 N4 N7

margin-right property e4 e5 e5.5 e6 N4 N7

auto e5.5 e6 N4 N7

margin-top property e4 e5 e5.5 e6 N4 N6 N7

auto e4 e5 e5.5 e6 N4 N6 N7

padding property e4 e5 e5.5 e6 N4 N7

padding-bottom property e4 e5 e5.5 e6 N4 N7

padding-left property e4 e5 e5.5 e6 N4 N7

padding-right property e4 e5 e5.5 e6 N4 N7

padding-top property e4 e5 e5.5 e6 N4 N7

text-align property e4 e5 e5.5 e6 N4 N6 N7

center e4 e5 e5.5 e6 N4 N6 N7

left e4 e5 e5.5 e6 N4 N6 N7

justify e4 e5 e5.5 e6 N4 N7

right e4 e5 e5.5 e6 N4 N6 N7

text-decoration property e4 e5 e5.5 e6 N4 N6 N7

blink N4 N6 N7

line-through e4 e5 e5.5 e6 N4 N6 N7

none e4 e5 e5.5 e6 N4 N6 N7

overline e4 e5 e5.5 e6 N4 N7

underline e4 e5 e5.5 e6 N4 N6 N7

text-indent property e4 e5 e5.5 e6 N4 N5 N7

text-transform property e4 e5 e5.5 e6 N4 N5 N7

capitalize	e4	e5	e5.5	e6	N4	N5	N7
lowercase	e4	e5	e5.5	e6	N4	N5	N7
none	e4	e5	e5.5	e6	N4	N5	N7
uppercase	e4	e5	e5.5	e6	N4	N5	N7

vertical-align property e4 e5 e5.5 e6 N4 N7

baseline	e4	e5	e5.5	e6	N4	N7
bottom			e5.5	e6	N4	N7
middle			e5.5	e6	N4	N7
sub	e4	e5	e5.5	e6	N4	N7
super	e4	e5	e5.5	e6	N4	N7
text-bottom			e5.5	e6	N4	N7
text-top			e5.5	e6	N4	N7
top			e5.5	e6	N4	N7

white-space property e5.5 e6 N4 N5 N7

normal		e5.5	e6	N4	N5	N7
nowrap		e5.5	e6	N4	N7
pre				N4	N5	N7

width property e4 e5 e5.5 e6 N4 N5 N7

auto	e4	e5	e5.5	e6	N4	N5	N7

word-spacing property e6 N4

normal	e6	N4

Pseudo-classes and Pseudo-elements

active	e4	e5	e5.5	e6	N4	N7
first-line			e5.5	e6	N4	N7
first-letter			e5.5	e6	N4	N7
link	e4	e5	e5.5	e6	N4	N5	N7
visited	e4	e5	e5.5	e6	N4	N7

Index